FROM MUMMERS TO MADNESS

A SOCIAL HISTORY OF POPULAR MUSIC IN ENGLAND, c.1770s to c.1970s

DAVID TAYLOR

Published by University of Huddersfield Press

University of Huddersfield Press
The University of Huddersfield
Queensgate
Huddersfield HD1 3DH

Email enquiries university.press@hud.ac.uk

Text © David Taylor 2021

This work is licensed under a Creative Commons Attribution 4.0 International License

Images © as attributed

Every effort has been made to locate copyright holders of materials included and to obtain permission for their publication.

The publisher is not responsible for the continued existence and accuracy of websites referenced in the text.

A CIP catalogue record for this book is available from the British Library.

ISBN: 978-1-86218-192-2

Designed by Dawn Cockcroft

Front cover Madness photograph © Virginia Turbett

Dedication

To Frankie and Ruby
and all the musicians, the instrumentalists, singers and dancers,
in the family, past and present.

Preface

THIS BOOK IS in many ways the sound-track to my life. It is the product of two important strands that have shaped me. The first, the professional, is my academic career as a social historian with an interest, not just in policing, but in leisure in general and popular music in particular, which stretches over 50 years. The second, the amateur, is my participation in various forms of music-making, of varying degrees of mediocrity on my part, and largely within a family setting, which stretches over my lifetime.

My considerable debt to other scholars working in this field is abundantly clear from a perusal of the footnotes. Any errors or misrepresentations of their views are entirely my responsibility. I am grateful to my university colleagues, especially Rupert Till and Keith Laybourn, for their constructive comments and encouragement at times when my confidence in the project wavered. I am also grateful to Dawn Cockcroft of the University Press for her assistance and forbearance. My gratitude also goes to Becky Taylor, the Yorkshire piper, who kindly transcribed the tunes in the appendix. Finally, I must thank my students over many years, but particularly those from the Huddersfield University of the Third Age in 2017/18 and 2018/19, without whose enthusiasm and perceptive comments this book would never have been started

My greater debt to the family is less immediately obvious but no less important. My paternal great grandmother, a regular attender at the music halls of north London in the late-nineteenth century, had an encyclopaedic knowledge of songs from music hall and minstrelsy, which she handed down to her grandson, my father, whose infectious style of piano-playing ensured many evenings of enthusiastic, multi-generational singing and playing that was greatly enjoyable for the participants, if not for the neighbours. My mother brought a love of country dancing and, through her father, a range of Irish songs, from 'Bold Robert Emmett' to 'McNamara's Band,' a particular favourite for a family from Tottenham. It has been my good fortune to have a family who have taken seriously their responsibility to broaden my musical knowledge. In particular, my wife, Thelma, as well as weeding out the clumsier expressions and more long-winded sentences through her proof-reading, has been an invaluable source of information. My heart-felt thanks to you all.

Contents

Chapter 1   Introduction: How can I keep from singing … and dancing?   1

PART 1: POPULAR MUSIC IN ENGLAND IN THE ACOUSTIC AGE, C. 1770S TO C. 1900S

Section 1: Nymphs and Shepherds? Popular music c.1770s – c.1840s

Chapter 2   'Aive down your prong and stamp along': Festivals, feasts, and fairs   17

Chapter 3   'Between the jigs and the reels': Popular dance and dancing   33

Chapter 4   'I'll sing you a song and a very pretty one': Broadsides, ballads and more   53

Chapter 5   'Come all you bold heroes, give ear to my Song': Sport, drink and sex   69

Chapter 6   'In Maidstone gaol, I am lamenting': Crime, punishment and socio-political comment   85

Section 2: Music-hall and its rivals, c.1840s – c.1900s

Chapter 7   'Sing, sing! Why shouldn't we sing?' Popular music in the age of the music hall   105

Chapter 8   'Dancing to the organ (in the Mile End Road)': Dance and Dancing Saloons   125

Chapter 9	*'Champagne Charlie is my name'*: The swell, the Irish and the cockney	141
Chapter 10	*'A little of what you fancy'*: Love, marriage and other social problems	163
Chapter 11	*'The Boers have got my daddy'*: Politics domestic and foreign	183
Chapter 12	*'The Minstrels Parade'*: Blackface minstrelsy and the music hall	197

PART 2: ENGLISH POPULAR MUSIC IN THE AGE OF TECHNOLOGY, C.1900S TO C.1970S

Section 3: Variety and its rivals, c.1890s – c.1950s

Chapter 13	*'Fings ain't what they used to be'*: The strange and lingering death of variety theatre	215
Chapter 14	*'I wish I could shimmy like my sister Kate'*: Dance halls and dancing between the wars	233
Chapter 15	*'Let's have a song upon the gramophone'*: Manufactured music - records, radio and the cinema	249
Chapter 16	*'I like bananas'*: Popular songs of the 1920s and 1930s	269
Chapter 17	*'Music while you work' … and play: Popular music c.1940-1955*	285

Section 4: The empires strike back, c.1950s – c.1970s

Chapter 18	*'Don't You Rock Me, Daddy-O'*: Skiffle and rock 'n' roll	305
Chapter 19	*'Twist and shout'*: Illusion and disillusion in the 1960s and 1970s	321
Chapter 20	*'Woke Up This Morning:'* How we got the (rhythm and) blues – and found some soul	341

Chapter 21	'Islands in the Sun': Calypso to reggae	359
Chapter 22	Conclusion: Mummers to Madness- the broader picture	385
Appendix		
	Late-eighteenth/early-nineteenthcentury tunes	395
	General Index	411
	Song and Tune Index	425

CHAPTER 1

Introduction: How can I keep from singing ... and dancing?

>Enjoy yourself it's later than you think
>Enjoy yourself while you're still in the pink.
>The years go by as quickly as a wink
>Enjoy yourself, enjoy yourself
>It's later than you think.
>
>Madness, 'Enjoy Yourself
>(It's Later Than You Think)'

FOR MANY YEARS popular music was looked down upon in academia, though few matched Hugo Reimann's dismissive comment that it embodied 'the lowest musical instincts of the masses addicted to arsehole art.'[1] From the 1960s onwards this changed dramatically as academics from various disciplines – history, musicology, sociology and others – started to pay serious attention to popular culture in general and popular music in particular.[2] As a consequence, there has been a growing number of books, articles and PhDs devoted to various aspects of popular music. However, it remains the case that few attempts have been made to provide a broader overview. This is disappointing, as Dave Russell's outstanding pioneering study, *Popular music in England, 1840-1914* was first published over thirty years ago.[3] Given the sheer volume of material, primary and secondary, not to mention conceptual complexities, it is not entirely surprising. Ignoring Johnny Mercer's observation – 'fools rush in where wise men never go' – *From Mummers to Madness* is a social history of popular music in England from the late-eighteenth century to the late-twentieth, which explores the popular songs and dances, from Georgian to Elizabethan England, and the meanings they had at the time.

The importance of music is difficult to overstate. As historian R W Malcolmson noted, it was the most accessible and democratic of the creative arts, with the ability to give expression to a range of fundamental emotions.[4] From a different perspective, musicologist, Philip Tagg emphasised how music and dance are 'particularly suited to expressing the *affective and corporeal identity* of individuals and communities in relationship to themselves and each other, and to their social, as well as their physical surroundings,' and stressed the need to understand music in its specific socio-cultural environment.[5] Almost everyone could sing or dance – albeit with varying degrees of skill – and many people were competent performers on fiddles and flutes, cornets and concertinas. The extent of informal singing and dancing can never be measured with accuracy, but a wide range of anecdotal evidence bears witness to the continuing popularity of singing round the piano at home or a 'knees up' in the local ale house, pub or club. Further, a growing number of people could experience music at various venues, from travelling shows to impromptu penny gaffs, from music halls and variety theatres. as well as in dancing booths, dancing saloons and later dance halls. In the twentieth century the growth of the record industry, the boom in film (especially musicals) and the advent of radio and television extended the availability of popular music in increasingly accessible forms. Individually, singing, dancing or playing, provided a means of expressing a range of often profound emotions, of voicing aspirations or fears, of commenting on and coping with the vicissitudes of everyday life, and of developing creative skills and the sense of satisfaction and identity that followed therefrom. Above all, music and music-making were sources of enjoyment – a fact that over-serious historians too easily ignore. Collectively, these activities could create a sense of identity and give meaning to an otherwise hostile or bewildering world through a range of celebrations – familial and communal – which, through affirmation or condemnation, could either consolidate the bonds that held together local communities or help to bring about change. The 'roles' of music were many and varied, its 'purposes' equally diverse, and, as often as not, subject to dispute. What cannot be denied is the ubiquity of popular music and music-making and its far-reaching significance in day-to-day life.

From Mummers to Madness: the chronological framework

If the purpose of *From Mummers to Madness* is simply stated, three important sets of questions remain. The first set relates to the time frame. There is a fuzziness about the terminal dates of the period covered because there is no obvious starting point, no obvious conclusion. In large measure this stems from the nature of the subject matter. Popular music, in its many forms, constantly evolved and defied simple chronological compartmentalising. Nonetheless, the book is organised chronologically, with three thematic strands running through the different time periods. This framework encompasses 'the three 'moments' of radical situational change,' identified by Richard Middleton.[6] – the bourgeois revolution of the years from the late-eighteenth century to the 1840s, the mass culture of the years from the late-nineteenth century to the 1930s and the pop culture of the post-World War II years – but with a modified periodisation. Broadly, the book falls into two parts, with the turn of the twentieth century as the dividing point, reflecting the changing technological basis of both music-making and music-consumption. Each part is further sub-divided. In light of Tagg's observation, and to avoid repetition later, a brief outline of the key characteristics of each section will be given to indicate the framework in which popular music developed: responding to, commenting on but also helping to shape attitudes and events.

Section 1 covers the 'pre-music hall' period from c.1770s to c.1840s, commonly associated with the first 'Industrial Revolution,' but better understood in terms of urbanization and commercialization. Urbanization, that steady long-term shift of population from hamlet and village to town and city, had a profound effect in terms of the scale and location of music making and consumption. Commercialization, was a wide-ranging phenomenon, encompassing agriculture, industry and services, including leisure provision, and was linked to improvements in transportation and communication, furthering integration in economic but also) in cultural terms. Equally important, though still a contentious issue, was a slow, often irregular improvement in working-class real earnings, which, combined with a willingness to devote some income to non-essential expenditure, turned the potential demand of a growing population into effective demand for, amongst other things, leisure.

Closely related were changes in the structure and values of society, as the old socio-economic and political order, with its emphasis on hierarchy, paternalism and (vertical) interests, was steadily replaced by a society organised more horizontally(into classes) and in which the 'moral economy,' with its notion of the 'just price,' was being replaced by ideas of the market.[7] Equally important, was the ongoing redefinition of gender roles. Initially, this ideological struggle was directed more against an aristocratic 'libertine' lifestyle and code of behaviour. Increasingly, and coinciding with the concentration of working-class men and women in distinct areas of the rapidly growing towns and cities, expectations of 'being a man' were refashioned to guide the working man, as opposed to the gentleman of leisure. Acceptable codes of femininity were similarly refined to take into account the differing experiences of working and middle-class women. Finally, this period also saw a prolonged period of conflict with France in which questions of national identity and national pride loomed large.

The changes identified here were incomplete and ongoing. There were also important elements of continuity, often reflecting the strength and tenacity of popular attitudes, but there was a perceptible contrast between the England of the 1840s and the England of the 1800s, let alone that of the 1770s.

Section 2 covers the hey-day of the music-hall, from c.1840s to c.1900s and largely coincides with Victoria's reign. The process of urbanization, and indeed sub-urbanization, proceeded apace, to such an extent that by the early twentieth century 80 per cent of the population of England was classified as urban. The 'flight from the countryside' was a reality of the last quarter of the nineteenth century, even though it was often a short-distance move – from 'Lark Rise' to 'Candleford' – and gave rise in some quarters to a romanticising of rural life inconceivable in contemporary France or Germany. Similarly, further developments in transportation and communication facilitated geographical mobility and increased awareness of regional differences as well as contributing to a sense of national, rather than local identity. Continuing economic growth and development led, not simply to a second Industrial Revolution based on chemicals and electricity, but also to the emergence of a mass consumer market in goods and services, with new means of production and modes of distribution. The organisation of capitalism also changed, though the extent of 'monopoly capitalism' is easily overstated.

After a period of apparent social equilibrium in the third quarter of the nineteenth century, there was a growing awareness of social problems, a (re)discovery of poverty, poor housing and disease. These were years of social and political tensions. Strikes and demonstrations by the unemployed in the 1880s and the early twentieth century spoke of class divisions. So too, the demand for political reform. Arguments for working-class male enfranchisement posed difficulties for those who believed in the property basis of politics, though they could be resolved in terms of responsibility and education. Demands for female enfranchisement were far more problematic for a patriarchal society, under attack, not least by vilified 'new women' and 'bluestockings,' demanding access to higher education and the professions. Gender problems were not confined to women. The late-nineteenth century appeared to witness saw a male flight from domesticity, and a series of high-profile homosexual scandals raised fears about the threats to dominant (heterosexual) masculinity.

Finally, the international context became increasingly problematic. No longer the only industrialised nation, there was an increasing awareness of growing competition, notably from Germany and the United States of America, which in turn raised questions about the virility of the nation and its inhabitants. Rivalry with other 'Great Powers' was also a feature of these years. The size of the British Empire grew spectacularly but the years of high imperialism were also years of tension with France and Russia, even Germany. Worse, conflict in South Africa, cast doubts on national status and the physical condition of the urban working classes. The fear of degeneration lurked behind Imperial bravado.

Section 3 covers the years from c.1900s to c.1950s, a period of decline for variety theatres and diversity in terms of the dance hall, recordings, radio, film and television. In economic terms these were difficult years. The pre-1914 years had seen a stagnation in real wages and a rise in industrial militancy. The early 1920s depression was one of the severest the country had experienced and the recovery that followed was sluggish, certainly in comparison to America, though, as a consequence, the Great Depression of 1929-32, was less severe than in other countries. Nonetheless, its impact in areas of traditional, export-based industries was severe. The recovery was more dynamic but the emergence of new industries, in which there were greater opportunities for women, further highlighted regional disparities. Industrial tensions, notably the General Strike, revealed a divided nation, as did another (re)discovery of poverty in the 1930s. The second world war brought an end to mass unemployment but necessitated rationing that continued into the 1950s. Post-war austerity, again, underlined the economic costs of war and reconstruction.

Both world wars were associated with social dislocation. The mobilization of women into industry, the easing of social constraints, the absence of male role models and hasty but unstable marriages created considerable short-term anxieties. The wars accelerated longer-term changes. Growing demands for women's rights, coupled with a greater awareness of the harshness of life, especially for working-class women, led to a reassessment of gender roles and the nature of marriage, which challenged the assumptions of Victorian patriarchy. Being a man was less clear cut in the light of wartime carnage, but there were fears that the feminization of society would undermine familial and societal stability. Tensions between advocates of change and defenders of the status quo played out in different spheres, including the cultural. The seemingly irresponsible 'flapper,' dancing the Charleston in the 1920s, or the teddy boy-cum-juvenile offender, jiving in the 1950s, was seen as living manifestations of wider social problems.

Nor was the international context any brighter. The unresolved international tensions after the Treaty of Versailles were a continued source of anxiety, compounded by the emerging challenges to empire, notably in Ireland and India. Finally, as America emerged as the dominant world economic and financial power, clearly the case after the second world war, it was also seen as a cultural threat. Mass democracy, mass education and mass culture posed challenges to the (self-appointed) guardians of cultural values. The new forms of communication – radio, later television, films and records – became important sites of change and conflict.

Section 4 covers the years from the mid-1950s to the late-1970s/early 1980s. Many of the earlier technological changes were further refined with the appearance of portable radios and record players, tape-recorders, cassettes and compact discs. In economic terms the third quarter of the twentieth century was associated with growing economic prosperity, full employment and the growth of mass consumerism, especially associated with teenagers, but the economic consensus ('Butskellism') crumbled under the pressure of the dramatic short-term rise in oil prices from 1973 onwards, and more general concerns with 'stagflation.' In social terms the absence of fathers during the war, the sharp increase in divorces immediately after the war and a rise in juvenile delinquency created interlocking anxieties about marriage and the family, which were increasingly associated with the perceived threats of youth sub-cultures, from teddy boys and mods, to skinheads and punks. In turn, they fed into fears about the threat posed by the 'Americanization' of popular culture.

Finally, these years saw considerable anxiety surrounding the loss of empire and the growing numbers (exaggerated in the popular imagination) of new commonwealth immigration. The African-Caribbean community was never homogenous. Class and gender divisions were important. So too were generational differences. Those born in the Caribbean and emigrating to Britain in the late-1940s and 1950s were very conscious of the economic problems besetting the islands and came with a particular view of Britain shaped by their education. Despite considerable, often overt, prejudice, there was a greater willingness to tolerate discrimination than found among their daughters and sons. The first British-born generation were more conscious of their distinct 'black British' identity, expressed, by some, in Rasta culture and politics. Generational differences were also found in the 'white' population. The post-war generation grew up in an overwhelmingly white society, whereas their children did so in a clearly visible multi-ethnic society. For both generations, the meaning of being British (or English) could not be taken for granted and had to be negotiated in socio-political and cultural terms. Although it is oversimplistic and misleading to discuss immigration in terms of problems and conflict, racial prejudice and periodic conflict, from the Notting Hill riots of 1958 to the inner-city riots of 1981, had a profound effect on society, and specifically on the development of popular music.

Running through all four sections are three major themes, or clusters of issues. The first relates to the alleged problematic nature of working-class leisure. While precise details varied over time, there were recurring panics about the threat posed to the economic productivity, moral well-being, and even political stability, of the country if certain forms of popular music (and indeed other forms of leisure) were not contained and civilised. From Stamford bull-runners in the late eighteenth century to mods and rockers in the mid-twentieth century the authorities (moral as much as political) complained about and tried to suppress popular cultural activities. The focus on working-class leisure obscures concerns that the 'virtuous and respectable' middle-classes might also succumb to seductive but corrupting new forms of music. Closely related to this is the recurring concern with the alleged threat to English culture posed by a variety of external, alien and uncivilised cultural forces and exacerbated by commercialization. Time and again references were made to an 'authentic' popular English culture. In fact, there was never an authentic, non-commercial indigenous popular music. Fusion – of commercial and non-commercial music as much as of different musical cultures – was a central feature of the evolution of popular music in England.

This relates to the second theme: popular music and identity. Popular music was intimately intertwined with notions of identity, be they parochial or national. The importance of the village or parish was not confined to eighteenth-century mummers or morris dancers but was to be seen in many of the songs of the Kinks and some of the early songs of the Beatles. Notions of Englishness were particularly important at certain times, from the Napoleonic war years, through the era of high imperialism, to the war years of the twentieth century. And there were other times when English culture was seen to be threatened by vulgar American invaders. Finally, music and identity were central for members of various sub-cultures, most obviously, teddy boys in the 1950s, mods and rockers in the 1960s, and skinheads and punks in the 1970s but also for different generations of immigrant communities.

The third theme centres on internationalization and cultural fusion. Notwithstanding the strength of a popular mythology that celebrates the sturdy, island independence of the English, the country had always been part of a wider world, cultural and otherwise. The fortunes of the English were closely intertwined, firstly with their immediate neighbours in Scotland, Ireland and Wales (the original English empire), and secondly with members of their first and second formal empires, as part of that 'intercultural and transnational formation … the black Atlantic,' which had such far-reaching social and cultural effects.[8] Despite recurring complaints about 'alien' music, songs and dances travelled across the Atlantic as much as across the United Kingdom, and were adopted, adapted and incorporated into a dynamic popular culture, which renewed and reinvigorated itself over the decades.

From Mummers to Madness: the geographical context

The second set of questions relate to the geographical focus of this study. If applying temporal boundaries to popular music is arbitrary (to the point of meaninglessness), so too is applying geographical boundaries. There was a long-standing, shared popular musical culture that transcended the boundary between England and Scotland. Similarly, the music-hall and variety-theatre circuits of the nineteenth and twentieth centuries did not stop at national borders but stretched to Aberdeen in the north of Scotland and to Cork in the south of Ireland. Equally, population movements were also cultural movements. The Welsh families travelling to the nineteenth-century iron and steel works of Cleveland brought their poetry and their music and were instrumental in establishing eisteddfau in Middlesbrough. The Irish, as much in the 1950s and 1960s as in the 1840s and 1850s, brought their songs and dance music to many parts of mainland Britain, maintaining a link with places and family left behind, creating a sense of identity in the new and often alien environment. but also fusing with and modifying the existing popular music.[9] So too did immigrants from the Caribbean. There were local variations, to be sure, that reflected the strength of local tradition in all parts of the United Kingdom but, more importantly, there were constant and complex cultural flows that made a nonsense of geographical borders. The focus on England is, therefore, partly a convenience, partly a reflection of authorial preference – particularly in the choice of detailed evidence from London, the north-east of England and the West Riding of Yorkshire – and partly a pragmatic decision reflecting the balance of historical research and popular writing and the limitations of space.[10] But if at times there is more than England on offer, there are others when there is less. There are only limited references to Devon and Cornwall, and Cumberland and Westmorland.

From Mummers to Madness: what is popular music?

The third, and most intractable, problem is one of definition. What is 'popular music'? The ongoing debate bears witness to the problematic nature of the term and the continuing absence of a widely-accepted definition, reflected in Cole's reference to 'the deadlocks of definition' and Parker's observation on 'the elusive, perhaps delusive' attempt to find a precise definition.[11] It is tempting to reject the attempts at theorising and fall back on a 'common-sense' empiricism, but this would be a mistake that effectively turns a blind eye to complex but important issues.[12] The arguments in this book are based on two sets of propositions.

First, popular music is not a single, coherent category but embraces a range of musical forms that vary over time and cannot be understood neither in terms of class ownership nor of a high art/low art dichotomy. Like any popular cultural form, it is unstable (in the sense of being subject to constant change, both internal and external) and lacking in coherence to the point of being contradictory at certain times. Further, it is negotiated, rather than pre-determined, and is the product of complex interactions influenced by class, gender, race and age within a broad socio-economic and political framework and in specific time periods.

Second, because it is negotiated, popular music can only be understood in its historical contexts. Popular music, like any popular cultural form, is not simply a product of underlying socio-economic forces, or part of a superstructure, but can be both cause and effect of change. Further, because it is the product of complex struggles regarding its form and content, popular music is neither necessarily confrontational nor conformist. The 'meaning' of popular music is complex and multi-layered, dependent partly on performer/producer intent and partly upon audience response.

Such an approach may be criticised (with some justification) for its 'conceptual messiness' but, perhaps, as Tagg observed in an earlier discussion, this may be 'one of its most useful characteristics.'[13]

Considerations of space necessitate decisions on content. Classical concerts, operas and operettas have been excluded, except in so far as extracts (overtures or 'hit songs') found their way onto the stage.[14] Sacred music has also been excluded, even though Victorian choral societies attracted considerable numbers of performers and audience members from across the social spectrum. Similarly, limited references are made to brass bands, despite their importance in regions such as Yorkshire, and to concertina bands, handbell ringers, let alone Jiggerum Juggerum bands. The two folk revivals, jazz and ragtime, will not be covered in detail, even though both can be seen as popular and important musical forms. More specifically, and particularly in part 4, certain aspects of popular music, Heavy Metal, Glam Rock and Prog Rockare not discussed; and this is the only mention of ABBA! Perhaps the most significant omission is a detailed consideration of bhangra and other forms of south-Asian popular music. Such omissions will disappoint some and anger others, but hopefully they will provoke debate.

Some problems of evidence

It is important to recognise the limitations of the available sources. The first set of problems relate to the range of popular songs and dances. The breadth of research and the extent of digitalisation means that there is more (and more accessible) primary material than ever before. The sheer volume of, for example, music-hall songs is both exhilarating and overwhelming; so too, the detail to be found in the pages of the local and trade press. However, there is a danger of assuming that these treasure-troves provide us with a clear and accurate guide to music-making and music consumption in the past. In fact, and clearly more so as one goes back in time, we have an incomplete guide. Much material was ephemeral and simply did not survive, or if it did, owed much to chance. In some cases, only the title of a song or tune has survived and, even when there are words and music, we do not know how widely a song was sung or a tune played, particularly in times when copyright protection was weak and music was easily and frequently pirated. Looking at the early nineteenth, let alone the late eighteenth-century, when there was a stronger oral/aural tradition and printed material more ephemeral, the gaps in our basic knowledge are considerable. But even the seemingly information-rich twentieth century has its problems. For example, the 'charts', especially in their early years, were based on very limited returns; and even when the coverage was improved, independent retailers went below the radar. Again, it is very difficult to establish the frequency with which pieces were played in the various 'palaises,' let alone in the town and village halls or pubs and clubs.

Nor was performance straightforward. Songs are more than the tune and the lyrics, dance tunes more than notes. With songs, in particular, the combination of words and music is crucial. Stirring calls to arms ('A Nation Once Again') can be enhanced; comic lyrics heightened ('If It Wasn't for the 'Ouses in Between'); and even banal lyrics can be transformed by a simple but evocative tune ('Danny Boy'). All too often, we have little or no idea how the music was performed, notwithstanding comments in the local press. We do not know how the early music-hall stars, such as Sam Cowell or Clement Scott sounded.[15] Similarly, the sound of the much-vaunted Wombwell menagerie band must remain a mystery. Nor are these problems 'solved' with the advent of recording and filming. The technical limitations of early recordings are well known, perhaps less well known are the restrictions imposed by early filming with a single, fixed camera.[16] Additionally, there is the issue of deliberate censorship of image – notably the decision to restrict coverage of the early Elvis to his upper body.

A further complication is performer intent. Several historians have analysed the lyrics of eighteenth-century ballads, nineteenth-century music-hall songs and twentieth-century protest songs (among others) to uncover meaning. In certain cases – for example, social-commentary industrial ballads, such as 'The Cotton Lords of Preston' – interpretation is relatively straightforward, but in others, for example 'Wait Till the Work Comes Round,' less so. And then there is the question of innuendo, be it political or sexual. As the regular complaints of Victorian music-hall proprietors make clear, there was often a significant difference between the lyrics submitted by an artist and the actual performance. If half of the anecdotes relating to Marie Lloyd or Max Miller are to be believed – and they probably shouldn't – a nod or a wink, not to mention a minor textual adjustment, could render a seemingly respectable song risqué, even indecent.[17]

Lastly, there are issues relating to audience response for which evidence is both scant and difficult to interpret. Does applause for a song indicate approval of the overall performance including the sentiments contained in the lyrics? The applause for the Great MacDermott probably reflected sympathy for his political and patriotic songs but could the same be said of that Hyde Park audience, applauding the Rolling Stones? Was it approving the misogyny of some of the lyrics? Or simply responding to the showmanship of Mick Jagger? In fact, did audiences (themselves not homogenous) take any 'message' intended by the songwriter and/or the performer? Two-Tone bands intended to provide music to dance to and lyrics to ponder: their audiences generally did the former, but did they do the latter? After all, much of the attraction of rock 'n' roll or northern soul, was that it was music to dance to and enjoy, rather than lyrics to be listened to and analysed. These problems should not be minimized but, as in any form of history, the evidence, carefully assessed still allows for meaningful, if tentative, conclusions to be drawn.

There is a further problem which relates to the overt and offensive sexist, homophobic and racist language to be found in certain song lyrics and so forth. Such language if uttered or endorsed today would be unacceptable. Some would argue that simply repeating the sexism or racism of the past is equally unacceptable and should not happen. The approach in this book, to include the language of the day, has been adopted for two reasons. Firstly, a full appreciation of popular culture, at any point in time, can only be achieved by recognising the range of values and attitudes that existed and the language that was used at the time. To excise certain words or phrases would be to distort the past *with no benefit to the present*; because, secondly, only by appreciating the extent and tenacity of support for sexist, homophobic and racist ideas in the past can one hope to understand the persistence of such attitudes today. To understand is not to endorse or condone but, crucially, is an avenue to change.

Finally, and without minimizing its multi-faceted importance, it remains the case that popular music has always been, for the vast majority of men and women, irrespective of class, creed and ethnicity, about enjoyment and escape from humdrum realities, the drudgery and tedium of quotidian life. Popular music was (and is) fun – and a history of popular music should be the same. In the words of Madness: 'Enjoy yourself! It's later than you think.'[18]

Endnotes

1   Cited in P Tagg, *Music's Meanings: a modern musicology for non-musos*, New York & Huddersfield, Mass Media Music Scholars' Press, 2013, p.99
2   For example, the Centre for Contemporary Cultural Studies was set up in 1964, Popular Music and Society first appeared in 1971 and the Social History Society was founded in 1976. The commercialization of leisure in the eighteenth century was associated with the growth of a middle-class with cultural as well as political aspirations. The classic statement is J H Plumb, *The Commercialization of Leisure in Eighteenth Century England*, University of Reading, 1973 but, more generally, see also P Earle, *The Making of the English Middle Class*, London, 1989 and L Davidoff & C Hall, *Family Fortunes: Men and women of the English middle class, 1780-1850*, London, Hutchinson, 1987. Early general histories of leisure include R W Malcolmson, *Popular Recreation in English Society, 1700-1850*, Cambridge University Press, 1973, H Cunningham, *Leisure in the Industrial Revolution*, London, Croom Helm, 1980, S G Jones, *Workers at Play: a social and economic history of leisure, 1918-1939*, London, Routledge & Kegan Paul, 1986 and J Walvin, *Leisure and Society, 1750-1950*, London, Longmans, 1987
3   D Russell, *Popular music in England, 1840-1914. A social history*, Manchester University Press, 1987. See also L Bristow-Smith, *A History of Music in the British Isles, volume 2: Empire and Aftermath*, London, Letterworth Press, 2017,

which covers the nineteenth and twentieth centuries but attempts a survey of all forms of music. There is a considerable amount of information, but the approach is essentially descriptive, and such is the author's ambitious intent that in-depth coverage of individuals and movements is necessarily limited.

4 R W Malcolmson, *Life and Labour in England*, London, Hutchinson, 1981, p.99.

5 Tagg, *Music's Meanings,* pp.45-6. He elaborates on the ability of music to express a range of emotions, and even contradictory emotions at the same time. Given the complex reaction of the brain, he sees music as a holistic form of musical expression.

6 See also R Middleton, 'Continuity and change: Articulating musical meaning/re-constructing musical history/locating the 'popular', *Popular Music*, 5, 1, 1985, pp.6-43 at p.10ff. This is not to say that such an approach is an endorsement of Middleton's analysis with its debt to Mandel's model of the growth of industrial capitalism. See R. Middleton, *Studying Popular Music*, Milton Keynes, Open University Press, 1995, pp. 11-16, especially p.15.

7 The response to such changes can also be seen in some of the poetry of John Clare and certain melodramas.

8 P Gilroy, *The Black Atlantic: Modernity and Double Consciousness*, London, Verso, 1999, p. ix

9 Additionally, as they returned 'home' they also brought a new music to Ireland.

10 There are parts of the United Kingdom, notably north Wales and, to a lesser extent, the Scottish Highlands that have not been as extensively covered in recent research. In contrast, such is the volume of material relating to popular music in Ireland that it would merit a volume in its own right.

11 H N Parker, 'Towards a Definition of Popular Culture,' *History and Theory*, 50 (May 2011), pp.147-70 and R Cole, 'Notes on troubling 'the popular',' *Popular Music*, vol.37/3, 2018, pp.392-414. Many of the questions posed by the editor in the first volume of *Popular Music* remain unanswered today. Editor's Introduction, *Popular Music*, vol.1, 1981, pp.3-7. It is almost compulsory to make reference to Adorno, so see T W Adorno, 'On popular music' in *Essays on Music*, ed., R Leppert, Berkeley, University of California Press, 2002, pp.437-69 but for a critique see Tagg, *Music's Meanings*, especially pp.139-43. Among several problems with a quantitative/descriptive approach – popular is that which is liked by many people – is flawed in several ways. What is the cut-off point above which something is popular? Are all things that fall below this cut-off point necessarily not popular? And, on a more practical level, how can popularity be measured, particularly further back in time? Similarly, a qualitative/judgmental approach that defines popular culture in terms of what is left over from high culture is equally problematic. Definitions of popular culture that link it to either an ill-defined notion of 'the people' or to an equally ill-defined mass culture are unsatisfactory.

12 The questions raised in the conclusion of the editorial introduction of the very first volume of *Popular Music* remain pertinent. Is it possible to subsume the wide range of musical experiences within a single category of 'popular music'? And is it possible to identify suitable methods of study for this multiplicity of musical forms? The optimistically implied answers in 1981

were 'yes'; the experience of forty years' study might appear to point to 'no.' *Popular Music*, vol.1, 1981, at p.6
13   Quoted in Cole 'Notes' p. 393
14   They were also to be found in brass band repertoires.
15   Though many agreed that Scott's repertoire was one of 'unadulterated indecency and filth.'
16   Gus Elen is a good example. A meticulous artist, he kept notes of the choreography of each song. When he was filmed in the early 1930s, not only was his voice well past its best, but his stage performance was literally restricted by the need to remain in view of the camera. Nonetheless, to see a stage performance of 'Great Big Shame' puts a seemingly harmless comic song in a different light as Elen uses his hammer to hit the nagging wife who hen-pecked his mate!
17   Lloyd fell foul of the licensing authorities on several occasions. Having been reprimanded for including in the chorus of a song the line 'She sits among the cabbages and peas' she allegedly substituted 'leaks' for 'peas'. Likewise, she is alleged to have rendered indecent the hitherto impeccable 'Come Into the Garden Maud'.
18   The song, which dates from 1949, has been recorded by artists as varied as Prince Buster. The Specials, Jools Holland and His Rhythm and Blues Orchestra, The Supremes, Bing Crosby and Doris Day.

CHAPTER 2 17

'Aive down your prong and stamp along': Festivals, feasts, and fairs

> Here's one, two, three jolly lads, all of one mind,
> We have come a pace-egging and we hope you'll prove kind.
> We hope you'll prove kind with your eggs and strong beer,
> For we'll come no more nigh you until the next year.
>
> Pace-egging song (aka Heysham Peace-egging song)

SUCH IS THE hold on the popular imagination of the term 'the Industrial Revolution,' that it is commonplace to see England in the third quarter of the eighteenth century as an essentially rural-based customary society and economy. From the mid-nineteenth century onwards, critics from both the left and right of the political spectrum created a myth of a pre-lapsarian, untainted people with a culture characterised by custom rather than commercialization. There undoubtedly, was a traditional, customary calendar, celebrated with music and dancing, which was an important part of local identity, but it co-existed with more commercialised music-making. There were tensions and, particularly in the second quarter of the nineteenth century, certain customs were either abandoned or suppressed, but many survived into the mid-nineteenth century.

The customary calendar

When mummers, pace-eggers, plough-bullocks and wassailers, not to mention catterners and clemmers, made their way through the streets and lanes, their music and song brought both colour and meaning to the lives of the inhabitants of England's villages and towns in the late-eighteenth and early nineteenth centuries.[1] Pace-egging groups around Blackburn, for example, were 'dressed in various fantastic garbs, and wearing masks – some of the groups accompanied by a player or two on the violin – [who] go from house to house singing, dancing, and capering.'[2] Elsewhere, morris dancers, including 'Old Toss Pot,' performed a St. George and the Turk play, which also managed to praise both Lord Nelson and Lord Collingwood. And everywhere 'the extent and exertion of the dance!'[3] These were among several collective, often processional, celebrations that reinforced parochial identity. Many of the rituals and accompanying songs were concerned with alms-giving in money or kind.[4] Soulers sang for 'an apple, a pear, a plum or a cherry,' while pace-eggers hoped to be rewarded with 'eggs and strong beer,' with the emphasis on the responsibilities of the wealthy, the legitimacy of the request for a dole and a reminder of penalties that might follow from failing to comply.[5]

Mummers were to be seen on many occasions, especially at Christmas and Easter, but also on dole days and at local feasts and wakes. The plots of their plays were simple (combat, cure, and a request for alms!) but the spectacle was enhanced by highly decorative, often outlandish, costumes and the highly stylized performances. Many villages had itinerant troupes of dancers whose performances were part of parochial rivalries.[6] Much has been made of the different styles of morris dancing – and no-one would confuse north-western clogdancers with Cotswold morris men, while the Abbotts Bromley horn dancers were unique – but many morris tunes, perhaps with minor local variation, were to be found in different parts of the country. 'Greensleeves' was ubiquitous and both 'Shepherd's Hey'* and 'Old Woman Tossed Up' were widely played.

There was a nation-wide culture, as musicians and their tunes travelled across the four countries that were to comprise the United Kingdom.[7] Titles may have been changed to give greater topicality and the notes may have been tweaked (or simply misheard, misremembered or mis-transcribed) but

---

*   See Appendix for a version of this tune.

the underlying tune remained essentially the same[8]. Customs varied in time and form, not least because of differences in the local economy. Sheep-shearing was celebrated in the Cotswolds and on the South Downs; harvest-home in the arable districts of Dorset and Wiltshire and Norfolk and Lincolnshire. Occupational identity was also important. The feast of St. Blaise (3 February) was celebrated by woollen combers in town and country. Likewise, St. Crispin's day (25 October) by shoemakers and St. Clement's day (23 November) by blacksmiths.[9] Celebrations of the harvest or sheep-shearing were more than a recognition of the economic significance of the event. They were an opportunity to stress communal interdependence, common interest, and social cohesion. 'Here there is no distinction of person but masters and servants sit at the same table … and spend … the night in dancing, singing, etc' wrote John Brand of harvest-home in 1813.[10] However, there is a danger of romanticizing harsh realities in an ever-more commercial world of capitalist agriculture. The 'jolly boys' who went 'together with our masters to shear the lambs and yowes' in one of the Copper family's sheep-shearing songs, praised 'our master [who] will bring us beer whenever we do lack' but also recognized that they worked 'hard … until our backs do break.'[11] On the surface, songs celebrating harvest and sheep-shearing were full of praise for the farmer and his wife, but there was something calculative about the sentiments: 'our master's very kind … and our mistress is always as good as good,' in the words of one North Wiltshire harvest song, but one would hardly expect other in a communal song.[12] But, as writers as varied as John Clare, Thomas Hardy and Flora Thompson noted, social cohesion was weakening, if not broken.[13] Other customs were coming under pressure. Pace-eggers and plough-bullocks were viewed with growing concern, especially by church and chapel and the 'respectable' local press, from the 1820s onwards.[14] The last Bishop Blaise Fair in Bradford, combining masters and workers in marching, feasting and drinking was held in 1825.[15]

The old ways were changing in other ways. There were commercial opportunities. As early as the 1740s, 'the famous Bath Morris-Dancers' appeared at St. Bartholomew's fair.[16] By the late eighteenth century morris dancers were appearing at fairs and even in the new indoor venues in London, such as the

Pantheon in Oxford Street, where 'a set of Morrice Dancers from the North, gave an excellent display of the Cumberland Sword dance.'[17] For many performers, custom and commerce were complementary. For others custom was unequivocally commercial. 'Whistling Billy,' interviewed by Mayhew, in the mid-nineteenth century, is a case in point. An itinerant dancer and tin-whistle player, his best times were during the three or four weeks of harvest-time, with the opportunity to play for coppers while harvesters were working in the field, and, more important, at the harvest suppers. There was good money to be made: 'the farmer himself would give me 4s 6d or 5s the night, beside my quart of ale. Then I'd pick up 6s or 7s in the ha'pence among the men.'[18] Moving from farm to farm, he played 'two harvest suppers a week for three weeks or a month.'[19]

Fairs, travelling theatres and menageries

By the mid to late-eighteenth century, popular music was increasingly itinerant and commercialized. Fairs, many dating back centuries, played an important role in this process. While still retaining a range of important economic functions – hiring, wholesaling and retailing – they were becoming more leisure-oriented.[20] This in itself aroused fears, at a time when the boundaries of acceptable behaviour were being redefined. A number of fairs disappeared. Much attention was focussed on London, where the highest profile loss was Southwark fair, which succumbed in 1762 Others – Bow, Stepney and Tothill – eventually disappeared in the 1820s, after many years campaigning; but some, notably Greenwich survived, while new fairs appeared at Battersea, Deptford, and King's Cross. In the country at large, several smaller, rural fairs were abandoned but others, notably Oxford's St. Giles' Fair, Nottingham Goose Fair and the Pack Monday Fair at Sherborne, recreated themselves.[21]

At a time when, outside the cities and large (or very fashionable) towns, there was insufficient demand to justify investment in permanent buildings, the fair and its associated panoply of itinerant performers, was an important source of popular leisure, of which music was a central component. At St. Bartholomew's fair about 40 per cent of licensed stalls were devoted to music booths, theatres, menageries, and 'circus' acts, all of which had important musical elements.[22] The component parts of Victorian music hall were already in evidence and making money for the new entrepreneurs of leisure in late-Georgian England. The fair, which generated its own cautionary ballads, such as 'The Countryman's Visit to Bartholomew's Fair' (c.1810), provided an opportunity for the aspiring (or indigent) local musician and ballad-singer. Nightingale, the ballad-singer, immortalized in Johnson's *Bartholomew's Fair* was not a figment of the author's imagination.[23] William Hone, writing about Greenwich fair, was appalled by the 'never to be forgotten orgy of noise, swings, dancing booths, oil lamps, fried fish, fat women, giants, dwarfs, gingerbread nuts, unappreciated actors, jugglers and acrobats, mud, dirt, drink, gin, beer and skittles.'[24] A more sympathetic opinion was given by Charles Dickens, who saw the fair as no more than 'a spring rash, a three days' fever' after which 'the old habits of plodding industry' were resumed.[25] Among the many amusements, 'the grandest and most numerously-frequented booth' was "The Crown and Anchor," a large, temporary ball-room and a scene of boisterousness that 'beggars description. The noise of the various instruments, the orchestra, the shouting, the "scratchers" and the dancing is bewildering.'[26]

Nor were large-scale celebrations confined to the capital. By the mid-nineteenth century leisure had become the major function of the Nottingham Goose Fair. Local civic dignitaries took part in the opening ceremony and each year 'all kind of strollers, beggars, gypsies, singers, dancers, players on harps, Indian jugglers, Punch and Judy exhibitors, and similar wandering artists and professors' made their way there.[27] On a smaller scale, Huddersfield Fair saw 'the usual scene of bustle and gaiety' especially in certain parts of town, such as 'King-street and the bottom end of Ramsden-street [which] were literally crammed with stools, booths and caravans and the usual attendants at a fair ground.'[28] Furthermore, in the smaller villages nearby – Honley and Holmfirth in particular – the annual feasts were similarly well attended as hospitality for returning family as well as visitors, combined with conviviality. Local landlords 'hired singers, fiddlers, piano-players etc and during the day-light music, song singing, fiddling and even dancing was indulged in.'[29] Similarly, in Lancashire the wakes were important events. Bamford describes the Middleton rush carts with their 'banners and garlands, and silver ornaments and morrice bells, and other music, quite joyous and delightful.'[30] As in other villages, 'musicians are also secured … a fiddler for the chamber dancing always, and never less than two fifers and a drummer to play before the [rush] cart.' Further, funds permitting, 'a set of morrice dancers … some score or two of young men, with hats trimmed and decked out [who] precede the [cart] drawers, dancing in couples …[and even] a band of instrumentalists,' though, as Bamford conceded, they were 'often a sorry affair certainly, but still a "band" to swear to.'[31] Wakes remained popular in north west and central England and resisted efforts to civilize them until the mid-nineteenth century when the celebrations were rationalised in terms of their timing and nature.[32] Until then, as arch-reformer, Josiah Wedgewood was forced to admit: 'Our men have been to play 4 days this week, it being Burslem Wakes. I have rough'd and smoothed them over, & promised them a long Xmass, but I know it is all in vain, for Wakes must be observed though the World was to end with them.'[33]

Although variety was of the essence in fairground entertainment, the dancing booth was one of the central attractions. As one observer noted in 1844, 'the grand feature of [Greenwich] fair was, as usual, Algar's Crown and Anchor, an enormous dancing booth;' another declaring it 'the most splendid thing in its way in Europe.'[34] Booths in other parts of the country were praised for their size and brightness.[35] Nor were they restricted to fairs or feasts. Algar provided a booth in Hyde Park as part of Queen Victoria's wedding celebrations, another was to be found at the Royal Agricultural Society's show at Southampton. Other events, notably at various race meetings across the country, boasted a dancing booth. Some of the earliest entrepreneurs sought to attract a respectable, genteel clientele. William Darby's 'dining and dancing booth' at Bury fair offered 'admittance free to all respectable Persons until Dancing commences' and, even when it did, gentlemen paid 2s and ladies 1s, at least on Wednesdays and Saturdays – on other days gentlemen merely paid 1s.[36] Respectability did not guarantee profitability; and by the mid-century its doors had been thrown open more widely, so that, as the *Leeds Times* observed, 'the company, *as might be expected*, was "quite promiscuous."[37] The men or women behind these enterprises are largely unknown – Algar and his daughter are exceptions. There are several references to gypsy families, but most commonly local publicans were the driving force. The profitability of the ventures is impossible to establish, but there were considerable hazards. Poor weather could reduce attendances and thus income; worse, storm could destroy both tent and fittings. A widely-reported "whirlwind" in August 1848 in Brighton wreaked havoc on a number of entertainment booths while, five years earlier, Hart's dancing-booth (as well as Wild's theatre) was unroofed and destroyed at the annual October fair in Hull.[38] In addition, dancing-booths were seen to be a particularly problematic aspect of a wider problem of criminality and immorality. Thefts and assaults were commonplace, the illegal sale of beer and spirits not infrequent and very occasionally there was a manslaughter case that arose out of a dancing-booth brawl. Local ruling elites were often extremely critical, though, in most instances, not enough to stop income-generating activities.[39] But there were exceptions. In Portsmouth, it was alleged that 'in 1820 the introduction of a drinking and dancing booth called "Crown and Anchor" led to others of a like character, thus converting a mercantile fair into a saturnalia of vice and profligacy.'[40] For a decade from the mid-1830s a campaign was mounted to abolish the fair, only for reformers to fall foul of ancient statute. Finally, having agreed to abandon these ancient rights, reformers triumphed when the local Improvement Act included a clause that made possible the abolition of the fair. Equally long running, and more personalized, was a dispute in Bury St Edmunds. Between 1835 and 1843 there was an ongoing clash between members of the town corporation, who opposed the erection of 'a dancing, singing and drinking booth' on Angel Field at the annual fair by a local publican, Mr. King. The critics condemned 'the perfect nuisances [and] immorality occasioned by such places.' King repeatedly ignored the corporation, which retaliated by ordering the booth to be pulled down and he successfully sued for damages; and, as matters came to a head in the early 1840s, he prosecuted the mayor for trespass. The corporation claimed that it had the right in law to ban King's dancing booth. The case was eventually argued before the full Court of Queen's

Bench in 1843. To the dismay of reformers, the court decided that the byelaw in question could not be sustained. King appears to have disappeared from the scene but the following year the corporation was still attempting – and still failing – to prevent Ellwood's dancing-booth appearing at the annual town fair.[41] Entrepreneurial determination and popular support sustained the dance-booth in Bury, but such was the growing confidence in the local police that within a matter of years, councillors had no qualms in licensing dance-booths.[42]

Travelling theatre companies and menageries also had a strong musical component. Among the earliest and most famous was Richardson's, whose large, garishly-lit booth offered 'a melodrama (with three murders and a ghost), a pantomime, a comic song, an overture, and some incidental music, all done in twenty-five minutes.'[43] Captured in paint by Rowlandson, Richardson's was closely associated with St Bartholomew's Fair, but this was part of a much wider circuit in the south of England. In 1826 the company appeared at sixty-six fairs. Many were in or around London, but others were as far south as Dover, Bristol, and Portsmouth and as far north as Cambridge, Ipswich, and Bury St Edmunds. There were other less well-known travelling showmen and their companies. In the north-east of England and southern Scotland, Billy Purvis was the outstanding figure. Starting as a 'drummer extraordinaire' in Newcastle, he developed a range of theatrical skills, including dancing, gymnastics, and dialect renditions of Shakespeare. In the early 1830s, as an itinerant musician (he was adept on the Northumbrian pipes) and comic, he played in a variety of locations – fairs and pubs for the most part – before achieving a breakthrough at Newcastle races in 1834. Two years later he opened the timber-built Victoria theatre but he still toured with his company, offering music and melodrama into old age until he died 'broken in body, spirit, and fortune' in 1853.[44] Further south, James Wild, commonly referred to as 'Old Wild' was known as 'the Yorkshire Richardson's.' The company started in the late-eighteenth century and continued, under Wild's son, until the mid-nineteenth. Music – 'the dancing and the singing, and the downright rollicking fun' – was integral to their entertainment. Wild senior was 'passionately fond of music and an excellent player on the clarionet. [sic]' In his teens he joined Cleckheaton Old Band, quickly becoming its leader, before joining Kite and Morris's Circus Band as its conductor. The band, with four members as its core – two Kent bugles, a trumpet and a trombone – promenaded the streets of the cities, towns and villages of the West Riding and south Lancashire to drum up trade. Their number was augmented by 'amateur musicians who lived locally [and] came after their daily labours were over' and even, occasionally 'Germans – those delightful discoursers of music, who, during the day, go out "busking" in the villages.' Such was the younger Wild's commitment to 'a good band' that in 1856 he 'engaged as leader Mr. John Hope, formerly bandmaster of Her Majesty's 98th Regiment of Foot, India.'[45]

Travelling menageries, a great novelty of the early and mid-nineteenth century, also added to musical life. The most famous, Wombwell's, started modestly in 1804.[46] By 1810 he had taken to the road with a fifteen-wagon travelling menagerie and, more pertinently, a brass band. Wombwell's was famed for its 'fine band of musicians in their beef-eater costumes.'[47] '[N]ot the least attraction was the band which accompanied the menagerie, the gentlemen of which performed some favourite pieces in a very excellent manner.'[48] There was an interesting flow into and out of the band. For aspiring young musicians, joining the menagerie band could be the first step in a performing career; conversely, enticing an experienced band member to give up life on the road could be a big fillip to a local town band.

Pleasure gardens

Pleasure gardens provided another venue for dancing and other delights. Entrepreneurs like Jonathan Tyer and music directors such as James Hook, Louis Emanuel and William Moncrieff were pioneers of mass entertainment – and mass catering – but initially, and particularly in London, there was an emphasis on social exclusivity. Entry charges, not least season tickets, were intended to exclude. Further, the music itself was more elite than popular. However, their social exclusivity was lost in the nineteenth century and, as their clientele changed, the entertainment became more popular. Vauxhall, Ranelagh and the Cremorne attracted considerable attention but among the sixty or so pleasure gardens in London there were smaller gardens, such as Cuper's or the 'Dog and Duck' St. George's Field that offered leisure opportunities for the middle- and working-classes. Similarly, across the country, pleasure gardens, such as the various Vauxhall gardens in towns like Boston and Great Yarmouth, attracted a diverse audience. Music, including popular song, was an increasingly central component in the entertainment 'packages' of the day. The gardens provided a venue for a two-way transmission of songs with 'hit' songs from the latest operas being sung, and popular ballads incorporated into 'high' art. The popularity of ballad operas in the middle decades of the eighteenth century contributed significantly to this musical melange. *The Beggar's Opera* was the greatest success – in no small measure due to the audacious dancing of Nancy Dawson – but Coffey's lesser known *The Devil to Pay* or *The Wives Metamorphos'd* (1731) came close to rivalling it. The opera contained sixteen songs set to well-known airs. 'Come Jolly Bacchus, God of Wine' was set to the air 'King Charles of Sweden'* and 'O Charming, Cunning Man' to 'Within a Furlong.'

Similarly, John O'Keefe's *The Poor Soldier* (1783), a comic opera centring on the return of British soldiers from the American War of Independence, utilized several popular tunes, notably 'Pease Upon a Trencher'† and 'The Little House Under the Hill,' as well as some O'Carolan tunes, such as 'Planxty John O'Connor.' ‡ In addition, the emergent popular musical culture provided considerable commercial opportunities for the printers and publishers of songsters such as *The Songs, Trios, Glees, etc, etc as sung by Mr Dignum, Master Welsh, Mr Denman, Mrs Franklin, and Mrs Fountain, This Season at Vauxhall, 1797*, which will be explored later.

Some concluding observations

The years between the 1770s and 1840s saw profound socio-economic and cultural changes in England but the resilience and adaptability of 'traditional' musical culture was striking. There was coexistence with and, more importantly, cross-fertilization between the customary and the commercial. Undoubtedly there were tensions and conflicts between old and new, but they

---

*   See Appendix for this tune.
†   See Appendix for this tune.
‡   See Appendix for this tune.

are easily overstated. Agriculture was in *relative* decline, but it grew in absolute terms until the mid-nineteenth century and many customs retained meaning and popularity. Urbanization could strengthen, rather than weaken, the appeal of village feasts, while improvements in transportation made it easier for 'friends and families' to return for the annual celebrations. The commercialization of leisure gave new life to old tunes and provided new opportunities for 'traditional' performers. Morris dancers like the men from Bath who appeared at St. Bartholomew's Fair in the 1740s showed that there was no clear-cut distinction between custom and commerce. John Clare was no admirer of enclosure and its consequences, but his collection of tunes showed that he was already part of the same modern world. Even the growing moral concern with 'uncivilized' recreations had less impact than contemporary reformers and some later historians have suggested.

There was much that was 'new' in the popular music of the mid-eighteenth century and much that was 'old' about the mid-nineteenth century. In particular, the old tunes that were printed in (and in some cases predated) Playford were still being played and old customs were still being celebrated. Popular culture was more than a reflection of developments taking place elsewhere, but was part of that wider, contested process of adaptation and change. However, the balance was shifting in favour of the new. In the mid-eighteenth century there was a (relatively) high propensity to consume and entrepreneurs willing to respond to this demand for (among other things) leisure. This intensified as the economy grew, and the expanding population became more urban. There was now less need to bring entertainment to its audience. The more concentrated populations of the burgeoning towns and cities presented opportunities for the development of various forms of fixed-site entertainment. Music-hall might be set to become the dominant culture, but its day had yet to come in the early years of Victoria's reign.

Endnotes

1. Commonly associated with labourers, there is evidence to suggest the involvement of the 'middling sort' of people. See J Wooders, '"With Snail Shells instead of Bells": Music, Morris Dancing and the 'Middling Sort' of People in Eighteenth-Century Berkshire,' *Folk Music Journal*, 10 (5), 2015, pp.550-74
2. J Harland & T T Wilkinson, *Lancashire Folk-Lore*, London, Frederick Warne & Co., 1867, pp.229 at www.gutenberg.org/files/41148/41148-h/41148-h.htm
3. Harland & Wilkinson, *Lancashire Folk-Lore*, p.231 and p.236. Dancing was 'to a fiddle, playing a jig in double-quick time.' The songs and tunes are not named. There is an editorial reference to J Harland, *Ballads and Songs of Lancashire*, London, George Routledge & Sons, 1875 for song details. This extensive collection includes a wide range of lyrics, both old and new, but does not specify when and where they were sung.
4. Dole days were concentrated in the winter months and included All Souls' Day (2 November) and especially St. Thomas's Day (21 December).
5. Plough-bullocks, young men of the village, were known to plough up the dunghills of the miserly, while on Shrove Tuesdays Lent crockers expressed their disapproval of miserliness by throwing broken crockery at the doors of those who failed to meet their demands and fulfil their responsibilities. There were also 'lawless' days, such as Pack Monday at Sherborne and Furry Day at Helston. when the social order was inverted.
6. This was clearly seen in Oldham around the turn of the nineteenth century when rush carts and attendant morris dancers from different parts of the town and outlying villages came together – often violently, much to the disgust of 'respectable' citizens. See R Poole, 'Oldham Wakes' in J Walton & J Walvin, eds., *Leisure in Britain, 1780-1939*, Manchester University Press, 1983, pp.72-98.
7. This is discussed in detail in chapter 3.
8. There is a further complication of 'crooked' playing, including the addition of an extra beat to a bar to fit the dance for which the tune was being played.
9. For more detail see Bob Bushway, *By Rite. Custom, Ceremony and Community in England, 1780-1880*, London, Junction Books, 1982 and Steve Roud, *The English Year*, London, Penguin, 2008. Plough Monday was the Monday following Epiphany Sunday; catterners and clemmers went out of the dole days associated with St. Clement (23 November) and St. Catherine (25 November); pace-eggers went out at Easter and wassailers at Christmas.
10. John Brand, *Observations on Popular Antiquities*, London, Reeves & Turner, 1813, vol.1, p.439 at www.archive.org/details/cu31924027937949/
11. Bob Copper, *A Song for Every Season*, St. Albans, Granada, 1971, p.257
12. A Williams, *Folk Songs of the Upper Thames*, London, Duckworth, 1923, p.56 and cited in Bushway, *By Rite*, p.125. Other Wiltshire songs collected by Williams clearly reflect a sense of injustice among labourers. For example, 'The Wiltshire Labourers,' Vaughan Williams Memorial Library, Alfred Williams Collection Bundle 4: Wiltshire Songs, AW/4/128 at www.vwml.org/archives-catalogue/AW

13 John Clare, *The Parish*, published posthumously, was a biting critique of the new generation of farmers in and around Northamptonshire, who 'view old customs with disdainful eyes.' (Line 154) Hardy, in *Far From the Madding Crowd*, set in the 1840s, is more gentle in his critique of Bathsheba Everdene's social distancing (chapter 36), while the generally sympathetic Flora Thompson condemned the local farmers who paid starvation wages throughout the year but provided one good meal at harvest time.

14 Plough-bullock traditions in the Nottingham district survived into the third quarter of the nineteenth century and even experience a revival in the 1880s and 1890s. P Millington, ''Plough Bullocks' and related Plough Monday Customs in the Nottingham Area, 1800-1930', *Transactions of the Thoroton Society of Nottinghamshire*, 2005, pp.127-37 at www.eprints.whiterose.ac.uk/1204/1/MillingtonThoroton2005.pdf . See also R Greig, 'The Plough Play in Lincolnshire,' Tradition Today, 3, December 2013, www. centre-for-english-traditional-heritage.org/traditiontodayal.html. The tradition was strongest in the midlands and eastern counties of England and survived in attenuated form into the early twentieth century. In Bedfordshire in the 1920s local agricultural labourers, men and boys, still walked the streets in disguise 'singing and shaking tins and saying – "Give the poor ploughboy a halfpenny or a penny." They knock on doors, and on being admitted, sing and sometimes dance, and expect money and beer or wine.' Taken from *Folklore*, 1926.

15 The next celebration never occurred, suppressed by the employers who feared it because of the tensions and animosity of the times.

16 *Daily Advertiser*, 22 August and 10 September 1743. Cited in M Heaney, 'Folk Dance and Theatrical Performance in the Eighteenth Century,' *Folk Music Journal*, 11 (2), pp.6-16 at p.8

17 Heaney, 'Folk Dance and Theatrical Performance' p.12. The report in the *Morning Chronicle and London Advertiser*, 2 February 1788, refers to a team of 14, including Bessey, Fiddler, Songster and Interpreter. Among other examples see Surrey Zoological Gardens anniversary celebrations, which featured morris dancers among other entertainments. *The Age*, 22 June 1834. The troupe would then dance its way home, performing to raise money on the way.

18 'The Whistling and Dancing Boy,' *Mayhew's Characters*, edited P Quennell, London, Spring Books, 1951, p.280

19 'The Whistling and Dancing Boy,' *Mayhew's Characters*, p.280

20 There were also links with travelling circuses and, from the late-eighteenth century onwards, menageries. For brief introductions see J Walvin, *Leisure and Society, 1830-1950*, London, Longman, 1978, pp.114-5, H Cunningham, *Leisure in the Industrial Revolution*, London, Croom Helm, 1980, pp.33-7 and J M Golby & A W Purdue, *The Civilization of the Crowd: Popular Culture in England, 1750-1900*, London, Batsford, 1984, pp.38-40 and 68-9. For more detailed information see L Smith, *The Greatest Shows on Earth: A History of the Circus*, London, Reaktion Books, 2014, C Grigson, *Menagerie: A History of Exotic Animals in England, 110-1837*, Oxford University Press, 2016, and H Cowie, 'Elephants, education and entertainment: travelling menageries in nineteenth-century Britain,' *Journal of the History of Collections*, 2013, 15(1), pp.138-54. See also K Marius, 'Astley's Amphitheatre and the early circus in

England, 1768-1830,' unpublished D.Phil., University of Oxford, 1995 and C J S Plumb, 'Exotic animals in eighteenth-century Britain,' unpublished Ph.D., University of Manchester, 2010. The University of Sheffield National Fairground and Circus Archive has much valuable information including a Brief History of Circus at www.sheffield.ac.uk/nfca/researchandarticles/circus history and www.sheffield.ac.uk/nfca/projectsmenaginerieshistory

21 M Judd, '"The oddest combination of town and country." Popular culture and the London fairs,' in Walton & Walvin, *Leisure in Britain*, pp. 12-30. R W Malcolmson, *Popular Recreations in English Society, 1700-1850*, Cambridge University Press, 1979, H Cunningham, *Leisure in the Industrial Revolution*, London, Croom Helm, 1980 and Bushway, *By Rite*.
22 Gingerbread-sellers accounted for about a third of all licensed stallholders, while toy (that is, trinket) sellers accounted for a further quarter.
23 His repertoire included 'The Ferret and the Coney,' 'St. George that O! did break the dragon's heart,' 'A Caveat for Cutpurses,' and 'The Windmill blown down by the Witch's Fart.'
24 W Hone, *Every-day Book*, London, T Tegg, 23 May at http://honearchive.org/etexts/edb/day-pages/143-may23.htm
25 C Dickens, 'Greenwich Fair,' *Sketches by Boz*, London, Walter Scott, 1884, pp.82-8, at p.88
26 Dickens, 'Greenwich Fair,' p.88. For similar sentiments see, for example, *Standard*, 24 May 1836, *Northampton Mercury*, 28 May 1836 and *London Dispatch*, 21 May 1837
27 W Howett, *Rural Life of England*, 1844, reprinted Shannon, Irish University Press, 1971, p.498
28 *Leeds Times*, 21 May 1836 and *Leeds Intelligencer*, 17 May 1851
29 *Huddersfield Chronicle*, 26 September 1868
30 S Bamford, *Passages in the Life of A Radical*, 1st published 1848/9, chapter 4 at https://minorvictorianwriters.org.uk/bamford/c_radical_(1).htm
31 Bamford, *Passages* as above
32 See Poole, 'Oldham Wakes'
33 Cited in Cunningham, *Leisure in the Industrial Revolution*, p.45. See also B Dolan, *Josiah Wedgwood: Entrepreneur to the Enlightenment*, London, HarperCollins, 2005.
34 *Standard*, 9 April 1844 and *London Dispatch*, 21 May 1837
35 See for example *Jackson's Oxford Journal*, 10 September 1836 (St. Gile's fair), *Leeds Times*, 12 November 1842, *Salisbury and Winchester Journal*, 22 April 1843 (Stepney fair) and *Morning Post*, 4 September 1845 (Hoxton). Actual dimensions are rarely given but a dancing booth at Bury St Edmunds was 96 feet long by 22 feet wide (*Bury and Norwich Post*, 5 August 1835) while one sold at Portsmouth was 82 feet long by 32 feet wide with 60 feet of dancing boards. (*Hampshire Telegraph* 8 April 1848). The sale advert also referred to two gross of lamps.
36 *Bury and Norwich Post*, 4 October 1826. The following year he decided to introduce comic singing between the dances though 'none but persons of respectability will be admitted.' *Bury and Norwich Post*, 12 September 1827.
37 *Leeds Times*, 12 November 1842. Italics added.
38 The original article in the *Brighton Herald* was reproduced in numerous

provincial papers including the *Liverpool Mercury*, 11 August 1848. The Hull fair disaster was reported in *Hull Packet*, 13 October 1823. Fire was also a problem. The Stepney-field conflagration that saw the destruction of several booths including Jerrold's dancing-booth and Turner's dancing-booth. *Northampton Mercury*, 22 May 1847

39 Typical was Northampton town council, where it was proposed to set rates of three guineas per day for theatrical, wrestling or conjuring booths but five guineas per day for drinking and dancing booths. *Northampton Mercury*, 7 October 1848.

40 *Hampshire Advertiser*, 17 July 1847

41 *Ipswich Journal*, 1 August 1835 and 15 November 1845, *Bury and Norwich Post*, 5 August 1835, 18 October and 20 December 1843, 3 January 1844, 3 July 1844 and *Norfolk Chronicle*, 15 June 1844

42 *Bury and Norwich Post*, 6 February 1866

43 Cited in Cunningham, *Civilization of the Crowd*, pp.30-3

44 J P Robson, *The Life of Billy Purvis, the extraordinary, witty and comical showman*, 1875 edition reprinted by Frank Graham, Newcastle, 1981

45 *The original, complete and only authentic story of "Old Wild's"*, edited by "Trim", London, G Vickers, 1888, reprinted by The Society for Theatrical Research, 1989

46 Wombwell spent £75 on two boa constrictors, which he exhibited with surprising success in the taverns of London.

47 Howett, *Rural Life*, p.499

48 *Huddersfield Chronicle*, 18 May 1850, describing Honley fair, referred to their 'first-rate band, who perform some of the best selections of music during the afternoons and evenings of each day.' *Huddersfield Chronicle*, 8 February 1851.

CHAPTER 3

'Between the jigs and the reels': Popular dance and dancing

> You lasses and lads, take leave of your dads, And
>   away to the maypole hie,
> For every he has gotten a she, And the fiddlers
>   standing by;
> For Jockey has gotten his Jenny, And Johnny has got
>   his Joan.
> And there they do jugget and jugget, And jugget up
>   and down.
>   'Lasses and Lads,' traditional[1]

SOCIAL DANCING, WHETHER at the local fair or in the local inn, was a central, but poorly recorded, part of popular leisure. There are occasional glimpses, for example, in the poetry of John Clare or the recollections of Samuel Bamford, but much remains unknown and unknowable. The printed collections of country dance tunes that appeared with increasing frequency, especially from the 1780s onwards, as well as the private manuscripts of local musicians provide various insights. Popular dance tunes were, for the most part, relatively simple. Their range rarely strayed beyond two octaves. These were tunes that could be played with relative ease on unkeyed flutes, seven-keyed (Northumbrian) smallpipes, or on fiddles, without going beyond first position.[2] A limited number of keys were used – C, G and D major and A and E minor being among the most common.[3] The tunes were relatively straightforward, with little metrical complexity, for the most part. They were, first and foremost, tunes for dancing.

While claims were made for several regional cultures, notably in the north-east of England, the evidence points as much to an emerging national 'tune book,' as musicians, and their music, traversed the country. Further, it contained long-standing traditional tunes, alongside recently composed, commercial pieces, and it adapted pieces from 'high art' and incorporated tunes from abroad.

Playford's Dancing Master and other collections of country dances

For many years it was widely claimed that country dances had been taken up from the village greens and barns into the ballrooms of 'society' via compilations such as Playford's *Dancing Master*.[4] In fact, the opposite appears to have been the case: dance tunes for elite society filtered down into popular culture. Either way, any discussion must start with Playford's *Dancing Master*, which, was the basis of social dancing in stately homes and assembly rooms since its first publication in 1651, and a rich source for later compilers. Running to several editions, various dances were included: longways and rounds for four, six or eight couples or 'as many as will', square dances for eight couples and so forth.[5] In all, it contained just over 1000 distinct dance tunes. Some were drawn from earlier English sources, others from outside England. Some were well-known, others written specifically for the collection. Among the most popular (then and later) was 'the finishing song ... Sir Roger de Coverley.'[6]* And there were others that retained their popularity through into the nineteenth century, such as 'Packington's Pound,' which probably dated back to the late sixteenth century, and 'Sellenger's Round.'[7]† These tunes were sufficiently well known to be incorporated into popular songs, notably 'Come Lasses and Lads,' in which, at the start of the maypole dancing, 'Moll and Jess' want to begin with 'Packington's Pound' but 'Bess' favours 'Sellenger's Round.'[8]

Playford was not the only publisher of country dance tunes. Robert Bremner published several collections of *Scotch Reels or Country Dances* in the 1760s. C & S Thompson's two-volume, *Compleat Collection of 200 Favourite Country Dances* was

---

*   See Appendix for this tune.
†   See Appendix for this tune.

published in 1765 but one of the most important was J Aird's six-part *Collection of Scotch, English and Foreign Airs* published in the 1780s and 1790s.[9] Aird brought together old tunes that would have been familiar to Playford, such as 'Greensleeves,' 'Pease upon a Trencher,' and 'Dainty Davie,' with more recent pieces, such as 'Soldier's Joy'* and 'Nancy Dawson,'† dating from the 1760s, as well as Burn's songs, albeit using older tunes, such as 'De'il Awa with the Excisemen' and 'John Anderson, My Jo.' But there were also a wide range of regimental quick marches and quick steps, fashionable cotillions, recently introduced from France, other French songs, tunes from 'West India' and even Handel's 'See the Conquering Hero Comes.'[10] Precisely how and when these tunes migrated from the ballroom to the barroom is unclear but there is little doubt that the process of popularisation was taking place in the late-eighteenth century, and probably before. Professional musicians may well have bought these collections, but the tunes spread in other ways. John Clare was unusual in recording that he copied tunes from printed collections, but he was unlikely to have been unique among village fiddlers.

Manuscript collections

In addition, there are a smaller but growing number of manuscript collections. One of the earliest was the Henry Atkinson manuscript. Atkinson probably came from the north-east of England – the collection includes tunes such as 'The Keel Row,' 'Bobby Shaftoe', 'Wylam Away' and 'The Flower of Yarrow,' better known, when later modified and renamed, as 'Sir John Fenwick's the Flower Amang Them A'.' Atkinson was an accomplished violinist, quite possibly an itinerant teacher.[11] The importance of the collection lies in its heterogeneity. It included Playford tunes, Scottish tunes, songs from D'Urfey's *Pills to Purge Melancholy*[12] and the *Beggar's Opera*, military pieces and relatively recent popular tunes such as 'Over the Hills and Far Away.' A similar picture emerges from the late-eighteenth century Vicker's manuscript, dated 1770, which contains just under 600 tunes.[13] This was more than a collection of

---

*   See Appendix for this tune.
†   See Appendix for this tune.

traditional music.¹⁴ It also contained cotillions, Scottish tunes such as 'Flowers of Edenborough,' [sic] 'The Real [sic] of Tullack,' 'Lady Mackintosh's Real' (first published in 1757 in Robert Bremner's collection, *Knit the Pocky*); tunes, such as 'Admiral Rodney's Delight' and 'Butter'd Pease' from the well-known Thompson collection, *200 Favourite Country Dances*, 1765; a variant of the Irish tune 'Highway to Dublin,' which appeared under the title of 'Cow's courant, or Gallop and shite,' the border pipe tune, 'Lasses pisses brandy' as well as several hornpipes, including the well-known 'College Hornpipe.'

Another important late-eighteenth century collection came from north Yorkshire. Joshua Jackson was a corn-miller and fiddler from Burton Leonard, who probably played at a variety of locations, from the house of the Earl of Harewood, to local musical societies and inns. His manuscript contains around 500 tunes.¹⁵ Again, diversity is the dominant feature. Well-established favourites, such as 'Brighton Camp',¹⁶ 'Flowers of Edinburgh,'* and 'Nancy Dawson'† sit alongside more modern tunes, composed to reflect current issues, such as ''Lunardies trip in the Air Balloon,' 'Down with the French' and 'The Battle of the Nile.' The diffusion of tunes from high culture can be seen with the inclusion of 'Tho' Prudence may press me,' which had appeared in Charles Dibdin's 1773 opera *The Deserter*. There is a goodly smattering of martial music – 'The 22ⁿᵈ Regiment's Quick-step' and 'Captn Reeds or 2d of Gards March' [sic] as well as 'Rule Britannia' – and also classical 'hits,' taken from their original setting to become part of a more popular repertoire: Arne's 'Water Parted From The Sea' and three tunes taken from Handel: 'See The Conquering Hero,' 'Water Piece' and 'Clarenet.' A similar picture emerges from an analysis of the tune-book of William Calvert of Wensleydale, which also dates from the early nineteenth century.¹⁷ The 52 tunes (excluding fifteen psalms and hymns), which he 'pricked down' included a large number of relatively recent tunes, some of which were copied, others written from memory (including misheard titles, such as 'The Dutch Slipper' rather than 'The Duchess's Slipper' and 'The Chapter of Things' rather than

---

*   See Appendix for this tune.
†   See Appendix for this tune.

'The Chapter of Kings'). Recent 'pop' tunes included 'The Heaving of the Lead,' composed in 1792 by William Shields for the operatic farce, 'Hartford Bridge,' and 'Life Let Us Cherish,' which was an anglicised version of the Swiss song 'Freut Euch des Lebens.'

It is not surprising to find martial music in the repertoire of jobbing musicians like Jackson as there was (and had been for many years) a two-way interchange of tunes. Traditional airs were taken up by the army as marches, quick marches and retreats. John Buttrey joined the 34th Regiment as a fifer in Lincoln in 1797 and served, mainly in South Africa and India, until his discharge in 1814. The manuscript which carries his name was, in all probability, the regimental tune-book to which he added a number of tunes.[18] Many of the tunes were taken from Aird's *Collection of ... Airs*, but also included the much-published 'Orange' tune, 'Croppies Lie Down' and the 1808 adaptation of Robert Tannahill's 'Jessie the Flower of Dunblane.' Among the tunes used for retreats were 'The Cock and Hen' (a.k.a. 'The Peacock Followed the Hen') and 'Roger Decovley' [sic]; and among the various march tunes were 'Saton's Island' ('Staten Island'), 'The Irish Washerwoman' and 'Rakes of Mallow.'*

These manuscript sources are important. They were compiled by professional or semi-professional musicians, who needed to be aware of the preferences of their audiences.[19] As such the collections give an insight into changing popular tastes in certain sections of society. The fact that each played for a distinct audience (or audiences) makes generalization hazardous but it is striking to find certain tunes – 'The Gabio,' 'Off She Goes,'† 'Saxona's Hornpipe, 'Speed the Plough'‡ and 'Tink a Tink' – appearing in early-nineteenth century manuscript collections from Westmorland in the north to Dorset in the south, Lincolnshire in the east to Shropshire in the west.[20]

The village fiddler: John Clare and William Winter

Much less is known of the more ordinary village fiddlers

---

*   See Appendix for this tune.
†   See Appendix for this tune.
‡   See Appendix for this tune.

and their repertoire. Although not necessarily typical, two collections will be considered in detail.[21] The first was compiled in the 1820s by the Helpston labourer, John Clare, best-known as a poet, but also a fiddler and a collector of songs and tunes. His poetry, most notably *The Village Minstrel* and *The Shepherd's Calendar*, clearly reveals the importance of music in his world and that of the community he describes and the archival record reveals the extent of his collection of songs and tunes.[22] How he learnt to play is unclear, though he makes reference to learning tunes by ear from a well-known local gypsy family; and how he built up his repertoire is similarly obscure, though he mentions copying tunes from printed collections in a Stamford bookshop. Clare was more than an unaffected rustic musician. He was concerned with the disappearance of an old way of life, eroded by the steady encroachment of modern agriculture and modern society, and, as such, he was not an accurate recorder but 'a selector from and mediator of the village tradition of pre-enclosure and childhood.'[23] But Clare was not simply part of a threatened 'oral/aural' folk culture, as the diversity of his collection makes clear.

Clare's collection comprises 263 tunes, of which thirty-eight are duplicates/variations, and the majority were probably copied from a range of printed collections. Four out of five tunes were in the fiddle-friendly keys of D (46 per cent) and G (34 per cent).[24] 41 per cent were written in common time, comprising reels, hornpipes and marches, and a further 18 per cent in 2/4 time, including tunes identified as quick steps and gavottes. 30 per cent were mainly jigs (36 per cent if slip-jigs are included) but also a few marked as marches or polkas.[25] Of the remaining tunes, twenty-one were waltzes, mainly in 3/4 time.[26] The precise sources are impossible to identify but, for example, there are striking similarities between Preston's *Twenty-four Country Dances for the Year 1793* and *Twenty-four Country Dances for the Year 1800* and the transcriptions in the Clare manuscript.[27] Some of his tunes – for example 'Bobbing Joan' (59), 'Dusty Miller' (84) or 'Brighton Camp'(105) – appeared in eighteenth-century collections, but can be traced back to the late-sixteenth or early-seventeenth centuries.[28] Others were

Playford tunes: 'The Irish Washerwoman' (160)* was included in his *Dancing Master* while 'The White Cockade' (27 and 102)† appeared in his *Apollo's Banquet*, 1687, entitled a 'Scots tune.' But other tunes hardly dated from 'time immemorial.' 'Black Ey'd Susan' (192 and 215) had been written by John Gay, 'The Lass of Richmond Hill,' (10) music by James Hook, dated from 1789, while 'Speed the Plough' (76) was composed by the Covent Garden violinist, John Moorehead in 1799. An even more striking example of downward transmission is 'Off She Goes' (262). The tune appears in a dance manual by the prolific Thomas Wilson, dancing master to the King's Theatre, London, entitled *The Treasure of Terpsichore, or the Companion to the Ballroom*, (1808). and was enthusiastically reviewed in the *Stamford Mercury*.[29] More interesting, is the inclusion of patriotic songs and tunes, such as the anti-American 'Yankee Doodle (201) and the anti-French 'The Downfall of Paris' (149)‡, both highly-popular early nineteenth-century tunes played as marches by various regimental bands.[30]

In addition, his collection included. Dibdin's 'Sailor's Journal,' (165) one of eleven such songs (including the better-known 'Tom Tackle'), which was published in 1800, alongside 'Hearts of Oak' (39), 'Roast Beef of Old England' (127) and 'Rule Britannia' (45). In a different vein, he also included some classically derived tunes, such as 'Mozart Waltz' (183), 'March in Scipio' (60), 'Lord Cathcart (Haydn) (94) and 'Handels Gavot' (239 and 256).[31] Three tunes pieces merit particular mention. 'The Battle of Prague' (8) and 'Turks March' (179) were taken from a more elaborate descriptive piece, 'The Battle of Prague' composed for piano, violin, cello and drums, by the Bohemian-born František Koczwara, (Dublin, 1788) but transposed to the key of D.[32] The third tune, 'La Dansomanic' (206), appears to be an inaccurate copying of 'La Dansomanie,' the French comedy ballet of 1800.

The second collection, comprising some 400 dance tunes, was compiled by William Winter, a shoemaker and fiddler, living in the Quantocks, Somerset.[33] Although dated 1848-51, the tunes were probably collected over several decades. Almost

---

*   See Appendix for this tune.
†   See Appendix for this tune.
‡   See Appendix for this tune.

40 per cent were written in 6/8 time, mainly jigs, and a similar number in 4/4 or 2/4 time, comprising reels, hornpipes and marches. There are only a small number of waltzes. Once again, the sources of the collection are unclear. Certain runs of tunes appear to have been copied in order from various editions of Thompson's collection of country dances, others taken – complete with dance steps – from Thomas Tegg, *Analysis of the London Ballroom*, 1825; and some may have been copied from the magazine, *Musical Bijou*.[34] There were tunes that would have been familiar to Clare – 'Brighton Camp.' Haste to the Wedding,'* 'Speed the Plough' and 'White Cockade' for example – others, notably those from Thompson, not so. The Winter collection, like many others, drew on a wide variety of sources. The presence of twenty-seven marches, such as 'The Duke of York's Troops' again bears witness to the important of military music in the early nineteenth century. Some tunes had a theatrical origin – 'La Belle Jeanette,' 'La Fille Sauvage' and 'The Duke of Reichstadt's Waltz – others, such as 'Jim Crow' and 'Oh' – drew on the recent popularity of blackface minstrelsy. The collection also contains several song tunes, which again reveal a diversity of sources. The words to 'Believe Me If All Those Endearing Young Charms' appeared in Thomas Moore's *A Selection of Irish Melodies*, 1808, though the tune ('My Lodging Is In the Cold, Cold Ground') was older. 'Away With Melancholy' originated in Mozart's *Magic Flute*; 'Mary Blane' was known as an Ethiopian song. 'Sweet Jessie' was a Scottish song/tune; and 'Poor Mary Ann' ('All Through The Night') was Welsh. Also included are the tunes for more recently written, commercial songs include 'Darby Kelly,' 'Hearts of Oak,' 'Woodman Spare That Tree;' and for reasons that are not immediately apparent, 'The Last Melody of Pestal,' which was published in 1845 and celebrated the death of the Polish martyr in the 1825 Decembrist uprising against the tsar of Russia!

Although both collections contain long-known tunes, it is striking that they also include recent commercially produced music, including adaptations from 'high-brow' music. As with the country dance compilations, eclecticism is the order of the

---

*   See Appendix for this tune.

day, reflecting, in no small measure, changing popular tastes and the need to maintain a varied and up-to-date repertoire.

Dances, old and new

Tune collections provided important insights, but much remains unknown about popular dancing. There are tantalising references to 'old' dances (as opposed to the new country dances of Playford and others), and the slow transition to the new. The rate of change varied considerably across the country. In the Yorkshire dales, for example, the old jigs, reels and hornpipes continued to be danced well into the mid-nineteenth century, while elsewhere in the county were to be found newer quadrilles, waltzes and polkas.[35] Drawing on his knowledge of dancing around the turn of the nineteenth century, Thomas Hardy, a knowledgeable and sympathetic observer, told the English Dance Society that the 'work folk,' as he described them, had 'their own dances, which were reels of all sorts, jigs, a long dance called the "horse race"; another called "thread the needle".'[36] Country dances were introduced into village life around 1800, he claims, but were not met with great enthusiasm' The work folk 'would lapse back again to their own dances at their own unmixed merrymakings.'[37] In this older dance world, 'reels were resorted to hereabouts by the more robust spirits, for the reduction of superfluous energy' and the devilish 'Mop' Ollamoor, the fiddler of the reels, 'a fiddle player in a show at Greenhill Fair, [played] the old dance tunes … country jigs, reels and 'Favourite Quick Steps' of the last century.' It is also the mid-nineteenth century world of young Margery in 'The Romantic Adventures of a Milkmaid,' who dances 'reels and jigs and country dances like the New-Rigged Ship, Follow-My-Lover and Haste to the Wedding and the College Hornpipe, and the Favourite Quickstep, and Captain White's Dance,' but has to be taught the polka – the latest craze about which 'young people … are ecstatic'—before she goes to the Yeomanry Ball.[38] Dancing was characterised by exuberance rather than elegance. At the Tranters' party, in *Under the Greenwood Tree*, proceedings open with the relatively sedate 'Follow My Lover,' but Dick and Fancy 'dance more wildly' in a 'six-hands-round' to an unnamed reel.[39] The work folk's 'own dances' were equally, if not more, energetic, being 'danced with hops, leg-crossings, and rather boisterous movements.'[40]

A similar lack of decorum was to be seen at Dicken's Greenwich Fair, and at the costermongers 'two-penny hops,' as recounted to Mayhew, where, across an evening that started about 8 p.m. and ended as late as 2 a.m., there was a mixture of 'clog-hornpipes' and 'flash jigs' but also 'polkas and country dances.' Only waltzes were absent.[41] Elsewhere in London new-fangled, one-time 'society' dances were becoming more widely heard. Street performers had to adapt. A disgruntled performer on drum and pipes, whose love was for 'the old tunes' told Mayhew that 'new tunes come up every day.' Consequently, he was forced to 'play waltzes and polkas now chiefly.' Interestingly, his 'old tunes' included not only 'Off She Goes' and 'The White Cockade' but also tunes, such as 'The Downfall of Paris' and 'Bonaparte's March,' which had been new 50 years before.[42]

This intermingling of old dance tunes, newer country dances, hornpipes, jigs and reels and later waltzes, polkas and mazurkas came about in a variety of ways. In some cases, society 'fashions' – notably, polkas and mazurkas – became more popular dances as dancing masters (and other music teachers) found it necessary to extend their clientele.[43] Tunes were also disseminated via the activities of working-class dancing masters. Little is known about them, but scattered evidence points to their importance. The showman Billy Purvis supplemented his income as an itinerant dancing master in and around Newcastle. Robert Whinham, the Morpeth-born fiddler, travelled the district, making a living from performances in local farms and inns, composing songs for local people and teaching dancing. He was not alone. H M Neville, reflecting on life in the third quarter of the nineteenth century in Northumberland, was one of many 'who recall the travelling dancing masters ... men of the working class ... fond of dancing and good fiddlers.' They would stay in the village for maybe a month or more, during the winter, giving lessons in a hired room or loft, before giving a public performance to showcase their success before moving on.[44] Other itinerant musicians, of varying degrees of ability, contributed to the dissemination of tunes. One of Mayhew's interviewees, 'The Whistling Man' spent much of his time in London, where he had a 'pitch' in New-street, Covent Garden as well as performing outside hotels, in public houses, taverns and even club houses.[45] He also played outside London, in towns and villages, from Hounslow to Maidenhead. His roaming pales into insignificance compared with that of 'The Whistling and Dancing Boy,' who played at regattas in Brighton and Dover, inside and outside of public houses (and occasionally in concert rooms) as he wandered across southern England as far as Devon and Cornwall.[46] Hornpipes and jigs predominated, the latter more popular among Irish labourers. 'The Whistling Man' had a repertoire that included 'The Barley Stack' and 'The Little House Under the Hill,' popular among 'country chaps' who paid a penny a dance each. Similarly, the 'Whistling and Dancing Boy' built up a repertoire from six to fifty tunes. These include well-established favourites, such as 'The Girl I Left Behind Me' (aka 'Brighton Camp'), 'Rory O'More,' 'St Patrick's Day,' and two hornpipes (Fisher's and the Sailor's), but also new songs, such as 'The Shells of the Ocean.' This was a common pattern. In the Yorkshire dales, 'minstrels,' each with their own 'walk,' played and sang at feasts and festivals, weddings and informal dances around the turn of the nineteenth century.[47] William Wrigley, 'the Leyburn Minstrel,' an agricultural labourer, played for both religious and secular celebrations, as well as being a fiddle teacher. William Cliffe, a professional fiddler at country fairs, doubled as a 'flying stationer,' hawking broadsheets and books, while William (Billy) Bolton, 'the Dales Minstrel,' was a tinker, mending pots and pans or sharpening knives and razors when not playing the fiddle or union pipes. So too, the 'strolling companies,' perhaps with their own tent, or simply playing in any venue that they could hire, and gypsies, from whom John Clare, for one, learned several tunes. By such means, old tunes were perpetuated, and new tunes propagated within and across regions and between generations.

In the mid-nineteenth century it was commonplace to distinguish between different types of dance tunes: reels were in common time (4/4), hornpipes also in 4/4, jigs commonly in 6/8 and waltzes in 3/4. There was also a (misleading) association between different dances and different countries – reels with Scotland, jigs with Ireland and hornpipes with England. This had not always been the case. Until the early nineteenth century, 'the terms jig, hornpipe and reel were often used interchangeably, as none of them was a distinct form in either style or rhythm,'[48] Playford's 1651 edition of *The English Dancing Master* contains three tunes explicitly termed 'jegges' and all are in common time.[49] In general terms, a jig was simply a dance that involved skipping and leaping without being tied to a specific time or a specific set of steps. In many cases, particularly on stage, it was a solo dance. Crucial in the process of evolution and differentiation were the dancing schools and dancing masters of the late-eighteenth and early-nineteenth centuries. A further complication came with the increasing popularity of the joak ('The Black Joak,' 'The White Joak,' 'The Nut Brown Joak,' etc), which, though in 6/8 time, was categorized separately, for example, in Walsh's *Collection of Lancashire Jiggs, Hornpipes, Joaks, etc*, c.1730.[50] However, by the nineteenth century, jigs (single or double in 6/8 and slip jigs in 9/8) were recognisably distinctive.

Reels were not unique to Scotland but from the 1730s onwards publishers actively promoted 'distinctive' Scottish dances, most importantly in Walsh's series of *Caledonian Country Dances* (1733-40).[51] This trend drew strength from the works of the outstanding Scottish fiddle composers such as Neil and Nathaniel Gow (father and son), Robert Mackintosh and William Marshall, whose compositions were a major part of Fraser's monumental *Airs and Melodies Peculiar to the Highlands of Scotland*, 1815.[52] However, there was no pure regional or national music. There was an interaction and fusion between different strands – aristocratic and plebeian, Scottish and English. Thus, the emblematic 'Scottish' reel, 'Dashing White Sergeant,' first published in 1826, was written by an Englishman, H R Bishop.[53] While the 'threesome reel,' seen as the predecessor of the equally emblematic 'Eightsome Reel,' had its roots in part in the French quadrille and was little more than a reel in name.[54] There was a popular reel – characterized by its distinct combination of travelling and stepping – danced not just in Scotland and noted by dancing masters from Aberdeen to London. The popularity of the reel in England is reflected in the manuscript collections from the late eighteenth and early nineteenth centuries, notably those of Clare and Thomas Hardy's father.[55] Unlike the jig with its variable time, reels appear to have been played consistently in either 2/2 or 4/4 time, though there were still variations

– notably the slower strathspey, which dates from the mid-eighteenth century, and the livelier rant, often found in the north-east of England.

For many Victorian writers the hornpipe was not simply 'the sailor's dance' but also (and fittingly, in their eyes) Britain's 'national dance *par excellence*.'[56] In fact, the association between sailors and hornpipes only dated back to the 1740s whereas the dance had a much longer history. It is not entirely clear that the hornpipe was a distinctly English dance, but there are several sixteenth-century references to the hornpipe in Lancashire and Cheshire, some describing dancing in a circle, others 'longways for as many as will.' Further, for much of the eighteenth-century hornpipes were written/played in triple time such as 'John of the Greeny Cheshire Way,' (3/2) and 'The Cheshire Rolling Hornpipe' (in both 6/4 and 9/4).* Only in the late eighteenth century did 2/4 and 4/4 become common – the latter becoming the dominant form by the mid-nineteenth century. Furthermore, even in common time, hornpipes could be either even rhythmed, such as 'Soldier's Joy'† or dotted, such as the 'Trumpet Hornpipe'. The latter, commonly, though not exclusively, was associated with clog-dancing especially in the midland and north-western counties of England.‡

The process of evolution, transmission and dissemination was complex. The hornpipe was one of a range of steps taught by eighteenth-century dancing masters and several hornpipes were included in later editions of the *Dancing Master*. The 1740s saw the first appearances on stage of 'a hornpipe in the character of a Jack Tar' at Drury Lane and Covent Garden and it was further popularized by the raunchy dancing of Nancy Dawson in the 1759 revival of the *Beggar's Opera*. Such was its popularity that C & S Thompson brought out three collections of 'Favourite Hornpipes' in the 1760s. There was a further fillip in the early nineteenth century, following the success of Douglas Jerrold's nautical melodrama, *Black Eyed Susan*, starring T P Cooke and featuring a sailor's hornpipe. Indeed, 'the Sailor's hornpipe' became a popular exhibition dance.[57] There were other stage performers who gave their

---

* See Appendix for this tune.
† See Appendix for this tune.
‡ See Appendix for this tune.

names to specific tunes – 'Durang's Hornpipe' or 'Miss Baker's Hornpipe' – but more important was the wider attention given to the hornpipe. Gallini, commenting in 1770 on the popularity of the hornpipe in respectable circles claimed that 'the lower class of people [also] used hornpipe steps.'[58] Whether these were one and the same is a moot point.

There was also an earlier, popular step-dancing tradition which continued in part through the clog-dancing that developed rapidly in the north-west of England from the early nineteenth century. Although popularly linked with industrial Lancashire, clog-dancing was found in Cheshire, Cumberland and Westmoreland and also in parts of the midlands, East Anglia and Devon. Dancing was often competitive and was incorporated into the expanding world of popular leisure as itinerant troupes of clogdancers began to appear in rented rooms or in their own booths. Professionalism led to the development of better footwear and, in turn, a different style of dancing, characterized by high stepping on toes.[59] The hornpipe, and especially clog-dancing, was yet another bridge to the new forms of urban entertainment, which regularly featured clog-dancing. Many dancers were minor figures, largely unknown to later history, but two major figures started their careers in this way. Dan Leno, first came to attention at Sherwood's 'Free and Easy' in Wakefield, where the highlight of the evening was a clog-dancing contest. From these inauspicious beginnings there developed a career that saw Leno crowned 'Champion Clog Dancer of the World' at Princess's Palace, Leeds. This was the start of an illustrious career. Similarly, early in his stage career, Charlie Chaplin was a member of the Eight Lancashire Lads, Characteristic and Champion Clog Dancers.[60]

Some concluding observations

Standing back from the detail of specific collections of dance tunes, a number of general points stand out. Without denying the existence of an oral and aural tradition of playing (and singing), collections of dance music, comprising printed material and hand-written manuscripts, were an important part of popular music culture, from the mid to late seventeenth century onwards, and increasingly so from the third quarter of the eighteenth century. These collections were an intermixture of old and new, which evolved over time, reflecting the dynamic nature of popular music. Furthermore, these collections of dance tunes were part of a wider commercialization of popular leisure. The selections that were made reflected varying demand across the country and changing preferences over time. There was a degree of continuity. Some tunes were regularly reprinted over centuries, but there was no static canon of tunes. Old one fell out of favour and were replaced by new. As Mayhew's drum and pipe player had found to his cost, the hits of 1800 were no longer popular in the 1850s His survival depended on adapting to popular demand for polkas and waltzes.

Further, despite the existence of strong regional identities, not just in the north-east of England, and of contemporary fads, particularly for 'Scotch' reels, there was an emerging common culture that transcended regional boundaries. The precise means whereby tunes were distributed across the country is unclear, but the network of fairs and feasts and the growing number of itinerant musicians were important elements in the process. Tunes such as 'The Friendly Visit' or 'Tripping Upstairs'* crop up in collections from across the UK, despite often being claimed as a traditional 'regional' tune.[61]† And others simply changed names. But did the popular jig transmute from 'The Rollicking Irishman' to 'Yorkshire Lasses' as it travelled west to east? Or did the name change come as the tune moved in the opposite direction?

Although some titles were altered, minor changes made in notation and different playing style developed, there was a common stock of tunes to be drawn from, which came from across Ireland, Scotland, and to a lesser extent Wales, as well as from different parts of England.[62] The pre-occupation with 'English' hornpipes, 'Scottish' reels and 'Irish' jigs misrepresents a more complex reality. Further, long-established tunes sat alongside recent commercially produced compositions, including minstrelsy songs, and even highlights taken from 'high' art.

---

*   See Appendix for this tune.
†   See Appendix for these tunes.

Endnotes

1. There are numerous versions of this song with varying combinations of Dicks, Willys and Johnnys as well as Janes, Joans and Jills, all tripping it or jigging it up and down.
2. This oversimplifies the situation in which alternative, 'cross tunings' (such as ADAE, AEAE and AEAC#) were used. P E W Roberts, 'English Fiddling 1650-1850: reconstructing a lost idiom' in I Russell & M A Alburger, eds., *Play It Like It Is: Fiddle and Dance Studies from around the North Atlantic*, University of Aberdeen, 2006, pp.22-32 at p.23
3. The Northumbrian small pipes are particularly good example. Prior to the 1820s they were unkeyed, with a range of an octave, but the introduction of a seven-keyed chanter, though not fully chromatic, permitted the playing of an octave (notionally G – G) with a low D and a high B. Also as Roberts suggests, 'harder' keys such as C, F, B♭, E, C minor & G minor were used. Roberts, 'English fiddling,' p.26. Tunes would also be transcribed into different keys to suit the particular instrument being played.
4. Frank Kidson's contribution to the first edition of *Grove's Dictionary of Music and Musicians* was highly influential. C Marsh, *Music and Society in Early Modern England*, Cambridge University Press, 2010, p.384 & 339. Kidson was not the first to suggest this. Miss Mitford, writing in the mid-late 1820s praised 'an honest English country dance – (there had been some danger of waltzing and quadrilling) – with ladies and gentlemen at the top and country lads and lasses at the bottom.' M R Mitford, 'Our Maying' in *Our Village*, 1824-32, reprinted Oxford University Press, 1984, p.169
5. The first volume was reprinted eighteen times, the second four times and the third twice. S W J Campbell, 'Reconsidering and Contextualising the Vernacular Tradition: Popular Music and British Manuscript Compilation (1650-2000),' unpublished D.Phil., University of York, 2012 p.136. popularity of longways dances for 'as many as will' can be seen in the Jackson manuscript, which contains instructions for several dances.
6. See Thomas Wilson, *Complete System of English Country Dancing*, London, Sherwood, Neeley & Jones, 1820, pp.100-105 at https://www.strathspey.org/history/wilson-system.pdf
7. Playford *Dancing Master*, 1st edition facsimile at www.pbm.com/~lindahl/playford_1651 Not all dances are explained in detail but various figures (the hey or chain, threading the needle and strip the willow) are described.
8. The song first appeared in print in the *Westminster Drollery* 1672 before being included in *Pills to Purge Melancholy* (1719). It was still popular when William Chappell reproduced it, in slightly modified form as 'Come, lasses and lads,' in the second volume of *Popular Music of the Olden Time* (1859).
9. The number of published collections of dance tunes was beginning to fall away in the late eighteenth century. C Pendlebury, 'Jigs, Reels and Hornpipes: A History of 'Traditional' Dance Tunes of Britain and Ireland,' unpublished M.Phil., University of Sheffield, 2015,' figure at p.91
10. J Aird, *Collection of Scotch, English and Foreign Airs*, Glasgow, J McFadyen, and at https://archive.org/details/airdsselectionof00ingl

11 Campbell, 'Reconsidering and Contextualizing,' p.141. The manuscript does not contain dance steps but does have detailed bowing instructions for certain tunes. The inclusion of performance pieces such as 'Tollett's Ground' and 'Farinell's Ground' reinforce this view. The manuscript is available on the FARNE (Folk Archive Resource North East) website http://www.farnearchive.com/
12 This is discussed in more detail in chapter four.
13 This is also available via the FARNE website at http://www.farnearchive.com/
14 The claim is made in M Settle, ed., *The Great Northern Tunebook: William Vickers' Collection of Dance Tunes, AD 1770*, London English Folk Dance and Song Society, 2008.
http://www.farnearchive.com/
15 A selection can be found in G Bowen, et.al., *Tunes, Songs and Dances from the 1798 Manuscript of Joshua Jackson*, Ilkley, Yorkshire Dales Workshops, 1998. Tunes from the Jackson and Kilvington manuscripts can also be found in D Ashton, *The Yorkshire Lad*, 2014   *Mr Joshua Jackson Book 1798*, West Yorkshire, R & R Shepherd, 2011.
16 In 6/8 rather than the usual 2/4
17 Bob Ellis, *There was None of the Lazy Dancing! Folk Tunes and Dances from the Yorkshire Dales*, Hawes, Yorkshire Dales Folk Dance and Tune Project, 2020. I am indebted to the Yorkshire piper, Becky Taylor, for making me aware of this and the Buttrey collection.
18 https://buttreymilitarysocialtunes1800.wordpress.com
19 To take another example, the Winder family from Wrysedale, near Lancaster are responsible four extensive tune collections, dating from the late-eighteenth century to the mid-nineteenth century. However, John Winder was almost certainly a dancing master in the 1790s and, later, the family were the mainstay of the village band. www.village-music-project.org.uk/?page_id=84 for details of this and other manuscripts.
20 See for example, the Browne family, (c.1825), Troutbeck, and the Rev. R Harrison, (c.1810), Temple Sowerby, both in Westmorland; Thomas Dixon (1798), Market Rasen and Thomas Sands (c.1810) Grainsby, both in Lincolnshire; R Hughes (1823), Whitchurch, and J Blockshaw (1837), Ashfield both Shropshire; W Giles (1839) Bampton, Oxfordshire and T Hardy (early 19C) Higher Brockhampton, Dorset. Roughly a quarter of Calvert's tunes were also to be found in two or more other collections – a proto-Top Ten of early nineteenth century tunes.
21 A similar picture also appears from Gammon's study of the tune books of the Sussex fiddler, Michael Turner, compiled in the mid-nineteenth century. https://www.sussextraditions.org/record/michael-turner-a-19th-century-sussex-fiddler-by-vic-gammon/
22 G Deacon, *John Clare and the folk tradition*, London, Sinclair Browne, 1983 is the most detailed account but see the review by Vic Gammon, 'Review: John Clare and the Folk Tradition by George Deacon,' *Folk Music Journal*, 4 (5), 1984, pp.543-6.
23 Gammon, 'Review,' p.544

24 The analysis is based on the tunes as reproduced by Deacon, *John Clare*. In a small number of cases, amendments have been made by Deacon, for example a tune obviously in A but written with only one sharp. Three further amendments were made by the author: one tune in A but written with two sharps and finishing on D and two tunes clearly in G but written in the key of C. The keys of C and B♭ each accounted for 6%, 4% were written in A and a mere 2% in F and E minor. One tune was written in E♭ and one in E (four sharps).

25 A number of 6/8 tunes may well be marches but this is not clear as no tempo is given. There may be more 6/8 marches but in the absence of any indication of tempo the number is uncertain.

26 Fifteen were in 3/4 time, six in 3/8 time and six in 6/4 time Again there are errors in the text. One tune written in 5/4 time had four beats in every bar!

27 www.vwml.org/topics/historic-dance-and-tune-books/Prestons 1793 and 1800

28 The numbers in parentheses are those used by Deacon, *John Clare*, pp.307-80. The Clare manuscript also contains song, such as 'A Frog He Would A-wooing Go' that similarly dated back centuries.

29 *Stamford Mercury*, 30 December 1808.

30 Allegedly, Wellington banned the playing of this tune as his army marched into Paris after the battle of Waterloo. Not to be thwarted the band struck up 'Croppies Lie Down' – or so the story runs.

31 'The Fowler,' (178) appears to be taken from *The Magic Flute*

32 The original can be accessed at https://imslp.org/wiki/The_Battle_of_Prague%2C_Op.23

33 The following analysis draws heavily on G Woolfe, 'William Winter: Somerset village musician' https://www.mustrad.org.uk/articles/winter.htm

34 www.archive.org/details/musicalbijoualbu))burn/

35 B Ellis, *There was None of this Lazy Dancing: Folk Tunes and Dances from the Yorkshire Dales*, Ellis, Hawes, 2020, p.8

36 J C Brown, *Hardy's People: Figures in a Wessex Landscape*, London, Alison & Busby, 1991, p.245

37 Published in *English Folk Dance Journal*, 1927, pp.52-6 and quoted in Brown, *Hardy's People: Figures in a Wessex Landscape*, p.245

38 'The Fiddler of the Reels,' set at the time of the Great Exhibition, was first published in 1893 and was included in the 1894 collection of short stories, *Life's Little Ironies*. https://ebooks.adelaide.edu.au/h/hardy/thomas/fiddler/ 'The Romantic Adventures of a Milkmaid,' set in the 1840s was published in 1883. https://gutenberg.org/files/2996/2996-h/2996-h.htm. Hardy also references several dance tunes in his major novels e.g. "Miss McLeod of Ayr" in *The Mayor of Casterbridge* and "Soldier's Joy" in *Far From the Madding Crowd*. See also Ellis, *None of this Lazy dancing*, for a similar chronology of change in parts of Yorkshire.

39 T Hardy, *Under the Greenwood Tree*, New Wessex Edition, London, Macmillan, 1974, chapters 7 & 8, esp. pp.71 & 75-6.

40 Brown, *Hardy's People: Figures in a Wessex Landscape*, p.245. The view that jigs were 'full of leaping' can be traced back to the sixteenth century. See

Margaret Dean-Smith, 'Jig' in *Grove's Music Online*, https://doi-org.libaccess.hud.ac.uk/10.1093/gmo/9781561592630.article.14307

41 H Mayhew, *London Labour and London Poor*, reprinted London, Penguin, 1985, p.20. Such 'hops' attracted up to a hundred or more people, ranging in age from the early teens to the mid-40s. Village dances in the Yorkshire dales were similarly noted for their exuberance - there was no 'lazy dancing.' Ellis, *None of this Lazy dancing*, p.11

42 'Performer on Drum and Pipes' in *Mayhew's London*, ed. P Quennell, London, Spring Books, 1951, pp.532-3. He also mentioned the recent popularity of brass bands but lamented the fact that German musicians would play for 2s a day at a fair while 'Englishmen would expect 6s.'.

43 See Pendlebury 'Jigs, Reels and Hornpipes' p.116

44 G Dixon, *Remember Me. The Fiddle Music of Robert Whinham*, Pathead, Midlothian, Wallace Music, 1995, p.6. Similarly, Tommy Moore of Ingleton played for a peripatetic dancing teacher in the Yorkshire dales.

45 'The Whistling Man,' in *Mayhew's Characters*, ed. P Quennell, London, Spring Books, 1951, p.270

46 'The Whistling and Dancing Boy' *Mayhew's Characters*, pp.282-3

47 Ellis, *None of this Lazy Dancing*, pp.86-99

48 Margaret Dean-Smith, 'Jig' in *Grove's Music Online*, https://doi-org.libaccess.hud.ac.uk/10.1093/gmo/9781561592630.article.14307

49 The tunes are Millisons Jegge, Kemps Jegge and Lord Carnarvons Jegg [*sic*]. Variations are also to be found in the earlier Fitzwilliam Virginal Book. Volume 2 of the Dover edition contains five gigges – two in common time, two in 6/4 and one in 12/4.

50 'Joak' or 'Joke' was a well-known bawdy term that referred to female genitalia. See two articles by E V Roberts, 'An Unrecorded Meaning of 'Joke (Or 'Joak') in England,' *American Speech*, 37 (2), 1962, pp.137-40' and 'More About Joke,' *American Speech*, 38(2), 1963, pp.151-3

51 John Playford included a 'Scotch Dance' in his *English Dancing Master* and his son, Henry published *A Collection of Original Scotch Tunes (Full of Highland Humours)* in 1700.

52 J Hunter, *The Fiddle Music of Scotland*, Edinburgh, T & A Constable, 1979.

53 The lyrics are attributed to General John Burgoyne. The steps derived from Swedish circle dancing which was popular in early Victorian England. Bishop also wrote the melody to 'Home, Sweet Home.' The better-known 'Gay Gordons' was the product of the early twentieth century English ballrooms.

54 R Coupe, 'The Evolution of the 'Eightsome Reel',' *Folk Music Journal*, 2010, 10(5), pp.693-722. The eightsome reel of the late-nineteenth century was essentially aristocratic but was caught up in the cultural nationalism of the day.

55 The Lock-Hardy manuscript which contains tunes transcribed by Hardy's father includes a number of well-known reels (Mis Macleod of Eyer,[*sic*] Major Malley's Reel, The Triumph and Soldier's Joy and Row Dow Dow) but also jigs (Haste to the Wedding, Off She Goes, The New Rigged Ship and Garry Owen), hornpipes (Ashley's. Dorsetshire and Lord Nelson) as well as polkas (Jenny Lind and Redowa), waltzes (Mrs George Derring's and The Silver Lake of Varsoviane) and quadrilles (The Lancers and Off to Charlestown)

56 Mrs Lilly Grove, *Dancing*, London, Green & Co., 1895, chap. 5 'English Dances' quote at pp.124-5. Grove was convinced that the performance of the hornpipe reflected national character, notably the solemn face and the absence of gesticulation.
57 See, for example, James Scott Skinner, *The Ball Room Guide, or Dancing Taught without a Master*, Aberdeen, J Daniels & Sons, 1879
58 Giovanni Andrea Gallini was a distinguished dancer and dance director (at Covent Garden and the King's Theatre, Haymarket) and the author of *A Treatise on the Art of Dancing* (1762) and *Critical Observations on the Art of Dancing* (1770) See https://danceinhistory.com/tag/giovanni-andrea-gallini
59 Initially, dancing in everyday clogs had resulted in a flat-footed, heel and toe style. Better-fitting clogs opened up possibilities for more elaborate steps.
60 B Anthony, *The King's Jester. The Life of Dan Leno, Victorian Comic Genius*, London, I B Tauris, 2010, chapter 5, 'Monarch in Wooden Shoes' and (by the same author) *Chaplin's Music Hall. The Chaplins and their Circle in the Limelight*, London, I B Tauris, chapter 9, 'The Eight Lancashire Lads – Characteristic and Champion Clog Dancers.'
61 There are numerous other examples. 'Saddle the Pony,' a jig-tune used in many a feis and tune no.18 in the bible of Irish tunes, *O'Neill's' The Dance Music of Ireland. 1001 Gems,* appears in the first *Northumbrian Pipers' Tune Book*, which was published at a time (1970) when the society was highly suspicious of Irish influences subverting the tradition. Similarly, their second tune book (1981) contains 'Dingle Regatta' (perhaps a clue in the title?) while the third collection (1991), supposedly 'largely Northumbrian' contains those well-known north-eastern tunes 'Willafjord' and 'Stockholmslåten.' The NPS tune books provide most useful compilations for the amateur musician but the recent reference to 'a living tradition … that needs to remain acutely conscious of its unique roots' (Introduction, *Northumbrian Pipers' Fourth Tune Book*, 2019), sits a little strangely with a collection of tunes, many of which are very obviously to be found in all parts of the UK – and beyond!
62 See particularly Pendlebury, 'Jigs, Reels and Hornpipes' chapter 2.

CHAPTER 4

'I'll sing you a song and a very pretty one': Broadsides, ballads and more

> Here are catches, songs and glees/Some are twenty for a penny.
> You shall have whatever you please/Take your choice for here are many.
> Here is 'Nan of Glo'ster-Green'/Here's 'Lily of the Valley'
> Here is 'Kate of Aberdeen'/Here is 'Sally in Our Alley'
> Here is 'Mary's Dream' 'Poor Jack'/Here's 'The Tinker and the Tailor'
> Here's 'Bow Wow' and 'Paddy Whack'/'Tally Ho' 'The Hardy Sailor'
> Here's 'Dick Dook' 'The Heart Blade'/'Captain Wattle' and 'The Grinder'
> And I've got 'The Country Maid'/Confound me though, if I can find her.
> And 'Here's A Health to All Good Lasses'/Here's 'Come, Let Me Dance and Sing'
> And what's better far than any finer/Here's 'God Save Great George Our King',
> 'Hearts of Oak' and 'Rule Britannia.'
>
> 'The Ballad Singer' Fairburn's *Universal Songster, 1825*

ANY ATTEMPT TO describe and analyse popular song from the period c.1770s to 1840s faces a range of problems, from the conceptual (which songs should be considered popular?) to the evidential (how 'typical' are the songs that have survived?) and the interpretative (what meaning(s) did these songs have?), all of which make generalization a hazardous venture.¹ Further, while there are various glimpses into the world of popular song, much, particularly performance and audience response, remains unknown, which makes all the more important the 'hard leap of historical understanding [required] to think our way out of modern notions of the place of song in society into a very different situation.'² The purpose of this chapter is to consider the range of material, from ballads and broadsides, to chapbook and songsters, as background to the following two chapters which will consider the content of different types of songs and the insights they provide.

Although the precise contours are often unclear, singing was a common-place part of daily life. People sang at work, at the plough tail and at the loom, and there were even work songs. People sang at leisure. They sang privately, maybe solitarily, and they sang collectively. They sang in informal settings, not least the local inn or beerhouse, but they also sang in formal settings, some secular, others sacred; and in doing so, they drew from a variety of sources and traditions. But what did they sing? The question can be answered with some confidence in the case of the chapel choir or the choral society but much less so when talking about the ale-house sing-song. Little is known about the repertoires of ordinary men and women. John Clare's father, Parker Clare, allegedly knew more than a hundred songs, which he sang or recited.³ It is impossible to say how unusual he was, assuming the claim to be correct. Exceptionally, the Copper family of Rottingdean had a repertoire of songs passed down the generations, but more typically, Isaac Bawcombe, a young shepherd at the turn of the nineteenth century, sang 'old songs and ballads he had learnt in his young years – 'Down in the Village,' 'The Days of Queen Elizabeth,' 'The Blacksmith', 'The Gown of Green,' 'The Dawning of the Day' and many others.'⁴ It is likely that many people had a small range of songs, including one or two 'party pieces' to be sung at special occasions as well as other, well-known pieces to be sung collectively and informally.⁵ But how many people were like Clare's friend, Gregory? He was 'fond of amusement and a singer tho his notes was not more varied than that of the cuckoo as he had but 2 Songs one called 'the milking pail' and the other 'Jack with his broom.'"⁶

There were a small number of known local musicians of sufficient skill to be called upon to sing and play at various events; and a smaller number, who were semi-professional or professional, making their living in the streets of towns and cities, at fairs and feasts, often tramping the country in search of an opportunity to make money. Mayhew captured the variety and insecurity of such a lifestyle. When 'the fairs are frequent and the river steamers with their bands of music run off and regularly and outdoor music may be played until late, the calling of the street musician is 'at its best.'' But during wintertime he was 'frequently starving, especially if he be what is called 'a chance hand' and have not the privilege of playing in public-houses when the weather renders it impossible to collect a street audience.'[7] His respondents also provide an insight into the mix of music from which they made a living. Sensationalism was a prominent feature. 'There's nothing beats stunning murder, after all,' one running patterer boasted. 'There was Rush – I lived off him for a month or more.'[8] But more run-of-the-mill murders made for good copy, such as the 'Horrid and Inhuman Murder, Committed by T. Drory on the Body of Jael Denny at Donninghurst, a Village in Essex.' Using extracts lifted from a newspaper 'we worked it every way … We had half sheets, and copies of werses. A werry tidy book' he said with evident pride.[9] Another, female interviewee started as a glee singer with two others, performing in streets and squares and occasionally in tap-rooms.[10] 'We used to sing "Red Cross Knight," "Hail Smiling Morn," and harmonize "The Wolf."'[11] Popular songs of the day – 'Alice Gray,' 'The Tartar Drum' and 'The Mistletoe Bough' – were taken from the local concert-rooms and sung on the streets. However, 'the very best sentimental song that ever I had in my life, and which lasted me off and on for two years, was Bayley's "Isle of Beauty." I could get a meal quicker with that than any other.'

Ballads and the 'oral tradition'

The English are prone to mythologizing the countryside and its inhabitants. Reassuring visual images of an ordered landscape with a contented workforce are reinforced by a written arcadian imagery in which milkmaids and shepherdesses sing happily at work while the 'merry plough-boy … whistle[s] o'er the lea.'[12] Within this rural myth exists a more specific but equally misleading notion – that of a distinct popular oral tradition, rooted in the (often indeterminate) middle ages, which was corrupted and destroyed by the new commercial print culture, which culminated in the song-writing industry of the Victorian music hall. This view can be traced back through the folksong collectors of the late-nineteenth century, to Sir Walter Scott and Thomas Percy, whose *Reliques of Ancient English Poetry* (first published in 1765) referred to 'old ballads' as the 'select remains of our ancient English bards and minstrels.'[13] Nowhere was this aesthetic judgement clearer than in the work of the highly influential ballad scholar, Francis Child, for whom orally-transmitted ballads, 'the true popular ballads, the spontaneous products of nature,' were far superior to the 'vulgar' printed ballads.[14] The clash between oral and print ballads was thus confirmed as a cultural conflict. Printed ballads, in Child's view, 'are products of a low kind of art … thoroughly despicable and worthless.'[15] However, this idea of a distinct oral tradition was flawed from the outset. Child was not alone in being dependent on printed texts to complete certain ballads.[16] In contrast, in present thinking the old distinctions between oral and printed are less contentious, with the emphasis on 'cross-fertilization' and 'hybrid products,' which highlight the complex but productive interaction between printed, commercial songs and the older, oral tradition.[17]

There was a corpus of songs, which could be traced back through the centuries. Certain songs, such as 'Barbara Allen,' 'John Barleycorn' and even 'Three Blind Mice' had a long pedigree, though few (if any) can be confidently dated back beyond the sixteenth century. There were also long-standing 'heroic' ballads, most notably the celebration of the battle of Otterburn, 'Chevy Chase,' and other folkloric stories, such as 'The False Bride,' 'The Cruel Mother' and 'Broomfield Hill,' though they were relatively few in number.[18] Nor was there any obvious pattern to these songs. 'Give Us Once a Drink' was a straight-forward drinking song (better known later as 'The Barley Mow') and 'Martin Said to his Man' celebrated drink-induced nonsense; 'Noble Fox Hunting' was a sporting song, 'Come Write Me Down' a celebration of love and 'Don't Let Me Die an Old Maid' a self-explanatory lament. The resilience of these songs is striking and contradict claims of a 'mass extinction of old ballads' from the late-eighteenth century onwards.[19] Undoubtedly, some ballads, such as 'The Suffolk Miracle,' disappeared and others, such as 'The Knight and the Shepherd's Daughter' declined in popularity, but this was not the whole story. The time-honoured 'Chevy Chase,' according to Joseph Addison, 'the favourite ballad of the common people of England' in the early eighteenth century, evolved over time.[20] Later versions, such as that printed in Percy's *Reliques*, were significantly tidied-up versions of earlier 'minstrel' versions, highlighting how such songs were themselves part of a wider, commercially oriented, popular song market.[21] Similarly, tunes, such as 'Off She Goes' or 'We Won't Go Home Till Morning,' were recycled with new words. Some fifty songs, including execution ballads and other moralising songs, have been directly linked to the tune 'Aim Not Too Low' (or 'Fortune My Foe') while the better-known, 'Lillibulero' was similarly much used.[22] The very familiarity of the tune contributed – or so it was hoped – to the success of the song in a market that extended beyond the educated elite. The Diceys, William and Cluer, printed 'ancient ballads' in chapbooks and broadsides for a popular market.[23] John Clare's song collection included variants of Dicey broadside texts, even though by the second quarter of the nineteenth century such "old ballads" were beginning to sound distinctly dated.[24]

Collections and chapbooks

As with dance tunes, there was an intermingling of popular and elite culture. Thomas D'Urfy's *Wit and Mirth, or Pills to Purge Melancholy*, which ran to six volumes and over a thousand songs by the early eighteenth century, was an important source of popular songs and tunes.[25] D'Urfey moved in court circles, working with composers such as Henry Purcell and John Blow, which was partly reflected in his collection. Other songs, such as 'A Shepherd Kept Sheep On A Hill So High' he composed, but he also brought together material from a wide range of sources, including theatre songs, many of which already existed in broadside form, drolleries, such as *Sportive Wit* (1656) and *Merry Drollery* (1661) and folio song-books, such as *Banquet of Music* (1688-92) and *Thesaurus Musicus* (1693-6).[26] At times his debt to others was considerable. Thirty-three of the fifty-seven songs in volume five were taken from *Choice Ayres & Songs* (1684). Other songs were established favourites – 'Joan's Ale' and 'Yonder Comes a Courteous Knight;' others celebrated triumphs of the day – 'Sing Mighty Marlborough's Story;' and others were bawdy – 'There Was an Old Woman Liv'd under a Hill' and especially 'As Oyster Nan Stood by Her Tub' which appeared in a section entitled *Pleasant and Divertive*.[27] D'Urfey's volumes were not intended for a mass market. The first two volumes sold at 1s 6d (7.5p but the equivalent of £11 at present prices), while volume three could be purchased in three 6d instalments, or as a bound copy for 2s (10p or the equivalent of £14.50).* But, if few people purchased *Pills to Purge Melancholy*, it provided a valuable resource for professional and semi-professional singers, whose performances helped to disseminate these songs to a wider (and originally unintended) audience.

Technological improvements in papermaking and printing facilitated production on a larger scale and at cheaper prices. Chapbooks, small booklets of folded paper without binding or covers, became more common from the late eighteenth century onwards. Many were titled simply 'Garlands' and were little more than a collection of unrelated songs popular at the time, which sold for 6d. (2.5p or about £3 at current prices). Value for money was not guaranteed as the content could vary considerable in both quantitative and qualitative terms. Songs were often plundered from other sources and co-existed with broadside versions. Nonetheless, they were a welcome addition. The publisher William Tinsley recalled the popularity of the visits of the chapbook sellers to South Mimms (Hertfordshire) in the late 1830s and 1840s and their sales to the unschooled farm labourers of the village.[28]

London was an important centre of production but so too were certain provincial cities, notably Newcastle.[29] Chapbook production started here around the 1770s and continued until the 1860s, peaking in the first three decades of the nineteenth

---

* The weekly wage of an agricultural labourer in the late eighteenth century could be as low as 6s a week, making the bound version of volume three the equivalent of a quarter of the weekly wage. Looked at another way, at 2018 prices the same volume would cost c.£12.50. See measuringworth.com for a discussion of the methodology involved.

century. The trade was in the hand of ten or a dozen printers, including two family firms, Angus and Fordyce and the prolific John Marshall. Between the mid-1770s and the mid-1860s, the city's chapbook printers produced just under 400 chapbooks, containing 1860 songs, as well as a further 1000 broadside songs.[30] 'Barbara Allan' and 'Froggie Went A-Courtin'' where to be found alongside 'The Lass of Richmond Hill' and 'The Last Rose of Summer.' There were also a significant number of local songs, such as 'The Toon Improvement Bill' and 'The Quayside Shaver.' Once again, diversity was the order of the day. Other songs included 'John Anderson, My Jo,' 'Auld Lang Syne,' 'The Greenwich Pensioner' (written by Charles Dibdin), Henry Carey's sentimental 'Sally in our Alley' and, reflecting a craze of the day, 'Jim Crow from Kentucky' and 'Jim Crow's Visit to Newcastle.' As the chapbook trade started to decline, broadsides and songsters became more important and not just in the north-east. In the longer run, the chapbook was to disappear, squeezed out by the songsters of the mid-nineteenth century, but for half a century or more such song collections provided a conduit between the theatres and pleasure gardens and a wider audience.

Broadside ballads and songsters

Far more common and influential was the broadside ballad, which existed in a complex nation-wide system of production and distribution. Much discussion of publication has focussed on the 70 or so London-based printing firms – of whom James Pitt and James Catnach are the best known – but there were printers to be found across the country, notably in Newcastle and Birmingham, but also in smaller towns, such as the Merry family in Bedford, Thomas Porter in Highworth, near Swindon, and Robert Walker in Norwich, and in more rural settings in Hampshire and Wiltshire, as well as (occasionally) in remoter counties such as Devon and Cornwall.[31]

In the early nineteenth century a single broadside song cost ½d, (c.25p in current prices) a broadside containing two or three songs 1d. Broadside ballads reached a wider audience that went well beyond simple sales figures. They were pasted on cottages walls, as well as in beer houses and inns; pinned on looms, as well as being passed from hand to hand, deliberately or by accident; and their words learned by heart from the patterers, who sang them in the streets, at the fairs and wherever there was an audience. John Clare had little time for 'the ballad singers [who] rant and rave' but recognized their success in persuading 'hodge [the farm labourer] whose pockets wont stand treats more high' to part with his penny and wistfully noted that the 'ballad in the ploughman's pocket [brought] a greater fame than poets ever knew.'[32]

Broadside ballads were ephemeral, surviving haphazardly through a combination of chance and the whims of later antiquarian collectors. Again, they contained songs from an older, oral tradition alongside newer, theatre songs as well as songs from largely unknown street authors, broadside hacks, among whom only John Morgan and George Brown have entered the historical record.[33] Eighteenth-century broadside ballads generally contained only the words of the song, though it was common practice to suggest a tune. The fortunes of the broadside ballad fluctuated over time. For much of the eighteenth century they were rude in health (and often rude in content), but they came under attack in the 1790s and 1800s as the result of longer-term changes in morality and manners and short-term panics created by the war with France. Those, like magistrate and police reform advocate, Patrick Colquhoun, afeared of the French and dangerous radical ideas, demanded 'loyal' songs. Those, like Hannah More, affronted by ribaldry and fearful of immorality looked to uplifting literature. The success of such campaigns from above were limited. More's *Cheap Repository Tracts* were intended to provide a more uplifting form of balladry. Thousands of improving tracts were produced and freely disseminated but the very fact of their continued re-issue bore witness, not to their popularity, but to their limited impact. On the other hand, 'loyal' songs, particularly those written by Charles Dibdin, were better received, though this owed as much to the stirring tunes as to their sentiments.

Broadside ballads proved remarkably resilient and there may even have been a resurgence in their popularity in the early nineteenth century, but there were important changes in content, size and tone. By the 1820s ballads were more topical and novelty-oriented, shorter and even more respectable but, as an anonymous contributor to *National Review* noted as late as 1861, they were 'adapted to and meet the wants and views' of the poor.' Further, as 'they are almost all written by persons of the class to whom they are addressed,' they provided 'one of those windows through which we may get a glimpse at the very large body of our fellow-citizens of whom we know so little.'[34] Particularly outside the great towns and cities, they retained a central position in popular cultural life. As late as the 1840s, the 'chief circulation of the broad-sheet is in the country where the conservative instinct is strong,' and even twenty years later, 'the ballad-singer would pass slowly along the roadway by the front of the houses [in the village of Harpenden, Hertfordshire], singing some harrowing verses made up specially for the occasion.'[35] By then in town, 'the street ballad-singer is disappearing from amongst us,' and yet the street business was 'still enormous.'[36]

During the second quarter of the nineteenth newer forms for disseminating songs emerged. In particular, the songster – basically a pocket-sized anthology of popular song lyrics – came to play a more important role. Its origins are to be found in the eighteenth century and was a development of the more coherent chapbooks and other printed compilations of songs. Although part of the commercialization of leisure for the middle classes, the various Vauxhall Gardens songbooks illustrate the point well. Between 1745 to 1848 there were at least 240 printed collections of songs, some containing as few as three or four songs, others more than 200.[37] The mid-century publications were clearly aimed at a wealthy clientele. *Lyric Harmony*, a 31-page collection of eighteen 'entire new Ballads' written by Thomas Arne, was published in 1745 and sold for 6s. (£45 at current prices). *The Wreath*, published in 1755 was more ambitious, being 'a curious collection of above two hundred new songs, including those of the bottle, hunting, mirth, and jollity, with all those sung by the most eminent performers at Vauxhall, Ranlegh, Mary-bon, Cuypers-Garden, and all publick places of diversion.'[38] This formula continued to prove popular. *The British Songster for 1834* ran to 434 pages and 'comprised a selection of the most admired plaintive and comic songs' but also contained 'all the new pieces which have been received with approbation and applause at the Theatre,

Vauxhall Gardens, and other public places of amusement during the past season.' Other publications in similar vein included Jacob Beuler's *Comic Songs to Popular Tunes*, c.1820 and John Fairburn, junior, *The Everlasting Songster: Being an extensive collection of One Thousand Naval, Love, Comic, Hunting, Bacchanalian, Sentimental, Scotch and Irish Songs*, a compendium of about 1000 songs published in 1823.

The Fairburn family was one of the most important printers of songsters. John Fairburn senior was producing songsters round the turn of the nineteenth century.[39] In the mid-1820s his magnum opus appeared: the compendious *Universal Songster, or Museum of Mirth*. Initially published in eighty-four parts, each of 16 pages, and later as three 448-page volumes, it contained approximately 5000 songs. There were various categories of song – bacchanalian, sentimental, hunting, masonic and novelty as well as Irish, Scotch, Yorkshire and Provincial. The largest categories were comic songs (1111), amatory (909), sentimental (597) and bacchanalian (358).[40] In the introduction Fairburn made clear his intention 'to chronicle songs from the earliest period to the present day' based on his judgement of 'the pulse of public approbation.' The collection is something of a rag-bag. Volume 1, for example, contains 'God Save the King' and 'Rule Britannia' alongside songs from Shakespeare ('Who is Sylvia?'), Burns ('Macpherson's Lament'), and the Dibdins (Charles and Thomas) as well as 'Opossum Up a Gum Tree' and 'The Negro Drinking Song.' One wonders about the popularity of John Wilmot's 'My Jealous Heart Would Break, Should We Have One Day Asunder' or (allegedly) Richard Coeur de Lion's 'No Wretched Captive of His Prison Speaks Unless With Pain,' albeit translated from the French. And it was expensive. In the introduction to volume 3, Fairburn refers to 'rapid and extensive sale,' but this was not a cheap purchase. The first volume could be purchased in monthly parts for 1s (c.£4 at current prices), or weekly for 3d each. in the 1820s. The outlay for all eighty-four parts (or three volumes) would have been exorbitant, though by the 1840s some retailers advertised the three volumes for 14s, a mere £60 at present prices.[41]

By the mid-nineteenth century smaller, often unbound, songsters sold for as little as 1d., bringing them, potentially at least, into the range of a large swathe of people. The impact of such printed music is difficult to determine with any precision. It would also be naïve to assume that printed music, still relatively expensive, provides an accurate guide to popular preference.[42] Nonetheless, these were commercially produced works for which there was a market. More to the point, by increasing the available stock of songs, they enabled street singers and itinerant chanteurs to extend their repertoire with new, fashionable pieces and bring them to a wider audience. It is impossible to say how many of these songs were taken up, how quickly this happened and for how long they remained popular, but they had an impact well in excess of the number of songsters sold at the time.

Some concluding observations

Surveying the period from c.1770s to 1840s, the most striking feature is the wide range of sources for songs, the dynamic inter-relationship between oral and printed traditions and the transmission of material from 'elite' culture to 'popular.' Equally important, was the growing topicality of broadsides in particular, which, combined with the sheer size and geographical spread of the trade, points to a popular culture that was not easily controlled, if at all, from above. This has important implications for the meanings of these songs, but what did people sing about? It is time to turn to consider the main topics and their treatment.

Endnotes

1. Steve Roud argues it is 'a prime example of a field in which investigation at the micro level is still necessary before medium and higher-level theories will become feasible.' Introduction to D Atkinson & S Roud, eds., *Street Ballads in Nineteenth-century Britain, Ireland and North America*, London, Routledge, 2016, p.2. Undoubtedly, in view of the flurry of recent and ongoing research, any generalizations need to be tentative.
2. V Gammon, *Desire, Drink and Death in English Folk and Vernacular Song, 1600-1900*, Aldershot, Ashgate, 2008, p.10
3. According to Clare 'I have heard him make a boast of it over his horn of ale, with his merry companions at the Blue bell public house … that he could sing or recite above a hundred [ballads]; he had a tollerable [sic] good voice, & was often calld upon to sing at those convivial bacchanalian merry makings.' Quoted in G Deacon, *John Clare and the Folk Tradition*, London, Sinclair Brown, 1983, p.22
4. W H Hudson, *A Shepherd's Life*, 1910, reprinted, London, Macdonald Futura, 1981, p.53
5. In *Far from the Madding Crowd*, Hardy, a knowledgeable observer of rural life, describes a shearing supper at which several songs are sung, including 'a poor plain ballet' [i.e. ballad] by the nerve-wracked Joseph Poorgrass (Chapter 23) and the singing and dancing at the harvest supper and wedding feast. (Chapter 36)
6. E. Robson ed., J Clare, *Autobiographical Writings*, Oxford University Press, 1986, p.55
7. P Quennell, ed., *Mayhew's London*, London, Spring Books, 1951, p.195
8. The Rush case was shocking, involving the double murder of father and son, the former being the Recorder of Norwich. The sensational evidence of Emily Sandford, Rush's mistress, determined the outcome of the case. Several thousand people, many coming by train to Norwich, saw Rush executed at Norwich Castle on 21 April 1849.
9. P Quennell, ed., *London's Characters*, London, Spring Books, 1951, p.30
10. Quennell, *Mayhew's London*, p.537. Unfortunately, the woman does not identify the streets in which she sang.
11. The first, based on Spencer's *Faerie Queen*, was a glee written in 1797; the second a song written by R Spofforth, c.1810 but I have been unable to identify with confidence the last song.
12. For poetry, J Barrell and John Bull, eds., *English Pastoral Verse*, Harmondsworth, Penguin, provides a good introduction. Landscape paintings of the eighteenth and nineteenth centuries are discussed in J Barrell, *The Dark Side of the Landscape: the rural poor in English painting, 1730-1840*, Cambridge University Press, 1983, A Bermingham, *Landscape and Ideology: the English Rustic Tradition, 1740-1860*, London, Thames & Hudson, 1986, C. Payne, *Toil and Plenty: Images of the Agricultural Landscape in England, 1780-1890*, New Haven, Yale University Press, 1993 and C Wood, *Paradise Lost: Paintings of English Country Life and Landscape, 1850-1914*, London, Barrie & Jenkins, 1988.

13. Preface cited by P McDowell, 'The Manufacture and Lingua-facture of Ballad-Making: Broadside Ballads in Long Eighteenth-Century Ballad Discourse,' *The Eighteenth Century*, 47(2), 2006, pp.151-78 at p.164
14. F J Child, 'Preface,' *The English and Scottish Ballads* and quoted in McDowell 'Manufacture and Lingua-facture,' p.170
15. F J Child, 'Ballad Poetry' *Johnson's Universal Cyclopaedia*, 1, reprinted in *Journal of Folklore Research*, 31 (1994), pp.214-22 and cited by McDowell, 'Manufacture and Lingua-facture' p.171.
16. Worse, late-Victorian 'peasant' singers regaled the likes of the Reverend Sabine Baring Gould and Cecil Sharp with musical-hall ditties alongside time-honoured ballads.
17. See particularly, Atkinson & Roud, *Street Ballads* but see also S Roud, *Folk Song in England*, London, Faber & Faber, 2017.
18. Roud, *Folk Song in England*, discusses a dozen or so songs probably dating from before 1700 and a further 42 from the seventeenth century, half of which date from the latter part of the century. *Folk Song*, pp.242 & 271.
19. W St Clair, *The Reading Nation in the Romantic Period*, Cambridge University Press, 2004 and D Atkinson, 'Was there really a 'Mass Extinction of Old Ballads?' in Atkinson & Roud, *Street Ballads*. St Clair emphasises the monopoly effect of the Stationers' Company and the 1715 Copyright Act, which ended in a crucial ruling in 1774. This ended perpetual copyright, unfroze the 'popular canon' and, according to St Clair, broadened the range of reading material, thereby reducing the demand for the 'ancient canon' of ballads.
20. Roud, *Folk Song*, pp. 235-8, the reference to Addison is at p.237. The *Oxford Companion to English Literature* refers to an early version dating from the fifteenth century https://www-oxfordreference-com.libaccess.hud.ac.uk/view/10.1093/acref/9780192806871.001.0001/acref-9780192806871-e-1505
21. See the extract from a 1558 text associated with Richard Sheale 'minstrel' cited in Roud *Folk Song*, p.238.
22. The English Broadside Ballad Archive, University of California lists 53 songs to the tune 'Aim Not Too High' https://ebba.english.ucsb.edu/search_combined/?ft=fish&numkw=52&p=10 Among the various songs were 'Sad news from Salisbury. Dreadful Frost and Snow,' 'The bloody-minded Husband,' 'A Caveat for Young Men,' 'A Looking-Glass for a Christian Family' and 'The Young Man's Repentance.' See also S Williams, 'To the Tune of Witchcraft: Witchcraft, Popular Song and the Seventeenth-Century English Broadside Ballad, '*Journal of Seventeenth-Century Music*, 19 (1), 2013 published 2017 at https://sscm-jscm.org/jscm-issues/volume-19-no-1/to-the-tune-of-witchcraft/#Ch3 'Lillibulero' was strongly associated with anti-Catholic sentiments – it 'sung a king out of three kingdom' according to Thomas Wharton and quoted approvingly by Lord Macaulay – but was also used for such songs as 'The City Cheat Discovered' and 'Faint Heart never won fair Lady; or, Good Advice to Batchelors How to Court and Obtain a Young Lass'
23. D Dugaw, 'The Popular Marketing of "Old Ballads": The Ballad Revival and Eighteenth-Century Antiquarianism Reconsidered.' *Eighteenth-Century Studies*, 21 (1), 1987, pp.71-90

24 Exceptionally, collections of old ballads were still being printed in the late-1830s. Dugaw, 'Popular Marketing' p.89
25 *Pills to Purge Melancholy* is available at www.https://digital.nls.uk/special-collections-of-printed-music/archive/91519824
26 C L Day, 'Pills to Purge Melancholy', *Review of English Studies*, 8 (30), 1932, pp.77-84. www.jstor.org/stables/508831
27 From volume 5 of *Pills to Purge*. See National Library of Scotland, Glen Collection of printed music https://digital.nls.uk/special-collections-of-printed-music/archive/87909275
28 W Tinsley, *Random Recollections*, 1905 cited in L Shepard, *The History of Street Literature*, Newton Abbot, David & Charles, 1973, p.99
29 Approximately 20 per cent of chapbooks in the bibliography of chapbooks housed at the Victoria & Albert museum were printed in Newcastle. Thanks to Robert White, a nineteenth-century collector, there is substantial archive of local chapbooks. Wood, 'Newcastle Song Chapbooks' p.62
30 Wood, 'Newcastle Song Chapbooks' p.62. The figures in the table do not match statements elsewhere in the article. Wood later refers to 'more than 3,000 songs' (including repeats) of which he has identified '1,912 different songs' p.66
31 R. Palmer, 'Birmingham Broadsides and Oral Tradition' and Wood, 'Newcastle Song Chapbooks' in Atkinson & Roud, *Street Ballads*. There are several articles, some more antiquarian than others, in the Musical Tradition Internet Magazine www.mustrad.org.uk of which the following are of particular interest: R Palmer, 'Birmingham Ballad Printers,' P Wood, 'Tyneside Song' and a series of pieces by R. Brown, 'Hurd of Shaftesbury,' Robert Walker of Norwich,' 'Porter – a Cotswold Printer,' Norfolk printings of murder and execution,' Besley of Exeter,' 'Some Printers in Cornwall,' 'Some Devon Printers' and 'More Merry Ballad-making.'
32 Quoted in G Deacon, *John Clare and the Folk Tradition*, pp.49-50. He also noted how 'the ballad from his pocket lost forlorn' was claimed as his own by 'the rude bird boy in the field alone.'
33 Among major digitalised collections, see the English Broadside Ballad Archive, University of California, Santa Barbara http://ebba.english.ucsb.edu/ and the Full English Digital Archive and the Roud Folk Song Index and Broadside Index at the Vaughan Williams Memorial Library at https://www.vwml.org/
34 Anon, 'Street Ballads,' *National Review*, xiii, 1861, pp.397-419 at pp.399-400. Changes in tone are most clearly seen in bawdy songs and transgressive scaffold ballads, discussed later. There may have been changes in their collection rather than production A Bennett, 'Sources of popular song in early nineteenth-century Britain: problems and methods of research,' *Popular Music*, 2, 1982, pp.69-89.
35 E Grey, *Cottage Life in a Hertfordshire Village*, St. Albans, Fisher, Knight, 1935 cited in Palmer, *The Sound of History*, p.133
36 Anon, 'Street Ballads,' at pp. 399 and 400. See particularly Vic Gammons 'Introduction' to *Desire, Drink and Death* and Bates 'Morality for the Masses' especially chapter 7. Older chapbooks, such as 'Old Mother Shipton' that looked to preserve old customs and wisdom, while more modern ballads

focussed on contemporary issues. See V E Neuburg, 'The Literature of the Streets' in H J Dyos & M Wolff, eds., *The Victorian City*, Volume 1, London, Routledge & Kegan Paul, 1976, pp. 191-209 at pp.206-7.

37 D Coke, Vauxhall Gardens 1661-1859 at www.vauxhallgardens.com which complements D Coke & A Borg, *Vauxhall Gardens: A History*, Yale University Press, 2015

38 http://www.vauxhallgardens.com/vauxhall_gardens_songbooks_page.html

39 C.1810 he produced a six-volume *Songster's Multum in Parvo*, which sold in weekly parts at 2d., and during the 1810s a number of 6d numbers including a *Naval Songster*, containing 31 songs, and variously a *Whimsical Songster*, a *Quizzical Songster*, a *Tickling Songster* and a *Larking Songster*.

40 https://archive.org/details/universalsongst00unkngoog/ Most of the Irish, Yorkshire and Provincial songs were comic songs, many exploiting the 'yokel-up-in-town' motif. 'Zekiel Homespun's Trip to Town' is hardly a flattering picture of a Yorkshireman in London but 'Zedekiah the Jew' is positively hostile 'My customers – meet 'em/Mit pretty words – treat 'em/ Vat vhile I vas, cheat 'em/Is always my vay' etc., etc.

41 For example, *Newcastle Courant*, 25 December 1824 and *Leeds Mercury*, 14 March 1826. *Manchester Courant*, 14 October 1846. The bargain offer of 14s for the three volumes compared with the published price of £1-4s.

42 In contrast, the ease with which unsuccessful broadsides could be abandoned, suggests that repeat printings are an indicator of popularity.

CHAPTER 5

'Come all you bold heroes, give ear to my Song': Sport, drink and sex

> Come one and all, both great and small/With voices loud and clear,
> And let us sing bless Billy the King/Who bated the tax on beer.
> 'A Drop of Good Beer' c.1830 from J Ashton, *Modern Street Ballads*, 1888

Some preliminary comments

ENGLAND WAS A singing nation, but for many years, popular song, particularly the broadside ballad, was treated with a combination of condescension and contempt. Lyrics were dismissed as either luridly sensational (especially when dealing with crime and punishment) or banal and formulaic (especially when dealing with romance); tunes were seen as basic and performers untutored. With few exceptions, it was not until the emergence of social history as a distinctive area of academic study that popular songs were taken seriously as 'the voice of the poor.' The sheer scale of their production, and their lasting popularity, highlights their importance to an understanding of popular mentalities and socio-political relationships. Popular songs fulfilled a variety of purposes: entertainment; emotional expression; education, via the transmitting attitudes and values; and evaluation, through social and political commentary. In this and the following chapter the focus will be on song as observation; but there were also nonsense songs and tongue-twisters simply meant to entertain and others that gave voice to a range and mix of emotions. This chapter will focus on two areas. First, sport and drinking; second, those dealing with love, courtship, marriage and betrayal. The following chapter will be devoted to a further two categories: crime and punishment and social and political commentary.

The complexities of interpreting song are considerable. While there is much surviving evidence relating to words and tunes, there is virtually none relating to performance; and yet performance could enhance or subvert 'authorial' intent. Likewise, the intended messages of writer and performer were not necessarily the same as the responses of their various audiences, since 'meanings ... are never set, they are always dependent on cultural context and interpretation.'[1] Audiences – more accurately members of an audience –brought values and assumptions, some unspoken, which themselves varied over time and place.

Leisure and pleasure

Many songs, predominantly from a male perspective, celebrated a range of popular leisure activities, and the physical attributes of the participants. Further, these songs often equated personal qualities of courage and determination with national characteristics. Yet this was a time when plebeian leisure activities were being condemned and, as in the case of cockfighting, criminalised, and in which concerns with 'order and decorum,' embodied in the 'new police,' led to a range of pressures on working-class behaviour. The continuing popularity of these songs, and the distinctive physical masculinity celebrated in them, highlight the limits of the new 'respectable' masculinity, with its emphasis on man as the protector of the weak, including women, children and animals, and the rejection of violence. Old leisure activities, including blood sports, were stubbornly defended well into the nineteenth century.[2]

Sporting songs

The range of sporting activities celebrated in popular song was wide – cricket, rowing, wrestling, even bull-running – but hunting and boxing featured large. Tributes were paid to 'noble foxhunting' and 'hunting the hare' as well as cockfighting.[3] Such songs were still being printed in the third quarter of the nineteenth century. The poet and local historian, Ammon Wrigley of Saddleworth, noted in his 'Old Songs of the Inns,' men's preferences for hunting and poaching songs with 'the chorus singing … like a pack of hounds in full cry.'[4] Although there is a distinction to be made between songs about gentlemanly hunts (on horseback) and plebeian hunting (on foot), which was to be found particularly in northern England, particularly Cumberland, Westmorland and the West Riding of Yorkshire, there are a number of common themes. The participants were regularly described as 'brave boys' or 'bonny lads,' even though women were to be found at hunt. The hunt itself was almost invariably exhilarating. As 'The Morning Is Fair' made clear, 'the best of all pleasure is hunting the hare.' Equally praiseworthy were the hounds. Their canniness and tenacity were praised in 'Noble Foxhunting' (sometimes known as 'Dido, Bendigo'), a song to be found from Cumberland to Cornwall. More locally, 'Old Snowball' paid tribute to a beagle of the Holme Valley hunt.[5] Even the victims were celebrated. Cocks were lauded for their fighting spirit, foxes and hares for their ingenuity and elusiveness.

Such songs spoke to an older, Corinthian masculinity that was increasingly criticised from the late eighteenth century onwards. Its clearest celebration came in the songs about prize-fighting, appealing to 'you lovers of the manly art, wherever you may be.' Strength, endurance and fortitude were the 'virtues' praised in ballads such as 'The Newcastle Champion.'[6] The heroic individual, commonly eulogised as a lion, was presented as the embodiment of true Englishness. 'Lines on the Great Fight between Tom Sayers, Champion of England, and Bob Brettle of Birmingham' referred to Sayers as 'the noble champion [whose] manly determination [made him] champion of proud England, and the conqueror of all.' His defeated opponent, Brettle, was 'a man of courage bold [noted for] mighty deeds of manly art,' denied victory only by 'an accidental fall'. Likewise, in "Sayers' and Heenan's great fight,' the protagonists (again) fought like lions and with 'pluck and courage stout, each proved himself a man.' There was more at stake in this fight. John Carmel Heenan was an Irish-American and the bout was billed as a clash between the USA and Britain. One ballad, 'Sayers and Heenan's Struggle For the Championship and £400' was blatantly set to the tune 'Come All You Gallant Britons Bold.'[7] Another, 'The Death of Sayers,' claimed 'Tom was a gallant hero/No-one could him subdue,' conveniently glossing over the fact that the fight was declared a draw after 42 rounds, with many claiming that Heenan had been cheated of a victory. However, the balladeer was keen to praise Sayers' courage 'like a Briton bold and true.'[8] Even more brazen was the praise heaped on Tom Cribb after a controversial fight in 1811. The fight had added frisson as the American challenger was a former slave. Ballads, such as 'Crib [sic] and Molineaux', delighted in the Briton's triumph without mentioning that his victory owed much to a crowd invasion in which Molineaux was injured.

Drinking songs

The most celebrated leisure activity was drinking. The social significance for men of experience of the ale house (and later beer house) has long been recognized. Singing, particularly collective, convivial singing, was a key element. Some songs were tied to specific work events, notably harvest ('The Barley Mow'), sheep-shearing ('Black Ram'), or key dates in the calendar, notably Easter and Christmas, but others were a more general celebration of conviviality. The centrality of entertainment is most clearly seen in songs like 'Come Landlord Fill the Flowing Bowl,' with its rousing chorus of 'For tonight we'll merry, merry be ... tomorrow we'll be sober,' or in the many variants of 'Jones' Ale'.[9] It is no coincidence that the participants, varying in number and trade, in these songs are 'jovial' and 'good fellows.'[10] Furthermore, 'jolly good ale' (and even porter) is praised, not least for its healthy properties – 'Banish draught, pills and potions, they'll nothing avail/No draught so effectual as Roddam's good ale.'[11] In 'Bring Us In Good Ale,' a wassail song dating back in printed form to the fifteenth century, singers reject beef, bacon, mutton, capons and more, demanding 'For our Blessed Lady's sake, bring us in good ale.'[12] In other songs, beer becomes a good friend, not least in 'Good Ale' in which it is 'my darling ... my joy both night and morning.'[13]

A smaller number of ballads offered a less celebratory view of drink. Drinking becomes a coping mechanism in the face of the harshness of life and the inevitability of death. 'For the cares of this life are but grief and vexation/To death we must all be confined' says the drinker in 'With My Jug in One Hand.' Drink and be merry for tomorrow we die is a recurring theme. But as well as consolation there was also a sense of defiance of death and damnation. The much-travelled, heavy-drinking 'Roisin the Beau' views his final journey with equanimity. 'When I'm dead and laid out on the table/A voice you will hear from below/Saying "Send down a hogshead of Whisky"/ To drink with Old Roisin the Beau.' Death is imminent. 'I feel that great tyrant approaching,/That cruel remorseless old foe,' but, game to the end, 'I lift up my glass in his honour,/Take a drink with Old Roisin the Beau.'

The dangers of alcohol are explicitly stated in the relatively small number of temperance ballads, such as those produced by John Harkness, the Preston printer and temperance advocate. 'In the Days I Went Drinking a Long Time Ago' is a predictable catalogue of poverty, loss of employment, eviction and an unhappy wife and family, which is only reversed when the one-time drunkard finally gives up his dissolute lifestyle. 'Wholesome Advice to Drunkards' highlighted the exploitation of the drinking man. The 'blooming landlady, so saucy and fat' cajoled money from the poor for the benefit of her sons and daughters with their 'gold watches, rings, so dandified, they to boarding school must go.' Similarly, in 'A Warning to Drunkards,' landlords were seen as rapacious, taking every last penny before kicking out the drunken wretch,' while their wives 'drest in silk and bombazine [have] boas, rings and handsome pins/just like some foreign Princess or Queen.' The content of such ballads is unsurprising. More interesting, and perhaps more influential, were those non-temperance ballads which pointed up the dark side of drinking. To what extent singers and audiences identified with the sentiments expressed in these songs is unknowable but difficult issues were raised. There is a modern ring to those songs in which the sole purpose appears to be drinking to excess, drowning sorrows and care and escaping, albeit temporarily, the burden of everyday life. At times, as in 'The Drunkard Reformed' or 'The

Drunkard's Dream' there is a sense of remorse at the negative impact on the individual, family and friends, which leads to a positive resolution; but not always. 'The Alewives Invitation to Married-men and Bachelors' paints a grim picture of the fate awaiting those who delighted in 'drinking and ranting.' 'But now all is consumed wasted and gone/He may look o'er the bare walls and make his last moan.' Similarly, in 'Good Ale,' it is you [good ale] that makes my friend and foes/It is you that makes me wear old clothes.' It led to marital problems – 'And if my wife should me despise/How soon I'd give her two black eyes' – but exercised an unbreakable hold. The final verse runs: 'You have caused me debts and I've often swore/I never would drink strong ale anymore. /But you, for all that, I'll forgive/ And I'll drink strong ale as long as I live.'

The impact of drink on marital relationships is treated in a variety of ways. The most positive, such as 'Little Brown Jug,' paint a picture of good-natured harmony. Husband and wife live in 'a neat little cottage we call our own [and where] we have lots of fun.'[14] More often than not, drink is a source of discord and conflict.[15] The 'perils' of a drunken wife are recounted in 'A Married Man's Advice to the Batchelor' and 'The Drunken Wife' but the drunken, violent husband was a more common figure. The opening lines of the chorus of 'The Wife's Lamentation' are unambiguous. 'Drunk, drunk from morn to night, in a public house is he, /Smoking, drinking, then comes home at night and wallops me.' As well as causing domestic violence, Gammon has argued that drink was seen as a means of resolving conflict, either between partners, as in 'Bang Her Well Peter' and 'Poor Joe the Miller' or between neighbours.as in 'John Appleby.'[16] On closer examination, it is not obvious that this is the case. In 'Bang Her Well Peter,' the central issue is who wears the trousers. Peter accuses his wife of adultery (on two occasions) and the couple come to blows. Dorothy asks for mercy and suggests 'fetch up some beer and let us agree.' Having promised 'no more will I cuckold or strike you my dear,' she asks, 'come give me a kiss and a glass of good beer.' The ballad concludes with the following lines: 'Now bang her well Peter, /Now Peter has won, the breeches he'll wear' – more a triumph of patriarchal authority than of domestic harmony. Similarly, the resolution of conflict between 'Poor

Joe' and his wife raises more questions than it answers. Having been railed at by his wife for spending 'his bob' on 'good ale,' Peter brings home 'pots of ales' with which he 'made his wife well fuddled,' after which 'they kissed and hugged, she did not rail/But went to bed and cuddled.' Thereafter, 'they then would both together sup/together they would be muddle/Drunk as sows they'd have their sup/And reel to bed and cuddle.' Nor does 'John Appleby' simply end 'when all the neighbours are invited in for a merry, home-brewed-ale-drinking party.' In the final verse the neighbours run in to end the quarrel between John and his wife but, instead join in the drinking, leaving 'ne'er a drop' as they 'banged the barrel about, pulled out the spigot too.' The ballad ends on a bleak note: 'We'll all get drunk to night for what have we else to do.' A triumph for drunken oblivion. Occasionally, as in 'The Drunken Husband,' the wife is able to exact some revenge, initially by pawning his clothes, later by literally beating him at his own game. 'She blacked his eyes and broke his nose,/You villain, she cried, no more of your airs,/Then slap she bundled him over the stairs.' More often, wives lamented their married state, wishing to be single again, or that their husbands were dead.

Songs about sex, love and marriage

Many songs referred to matters sexual. Some were ribald, some were cautionary, some celebrated courtship and true love, some did not. Although many songs reflected a male perspective, a greater female voice was to be heard than with sporting songs. Further, in these songs one can detect changing attitudes and values. Old songs that were once acceptable fell out of common usage or were excluded from the mainstream; new songs treated matters in a different, more acceptable manner. Nowhere is this more clearly seen than in the decline of the bawdy song.

Bawdy and betrayal

If Francis Place is to be believed, 'Such [bawdy] songs as even 35 years ago produced applause would now [1819] cause the singer to be rolled in the mud.'[17] Bawdy songs, relying on euphemism and innuendo, as well as explicit and 'vulgar' language, and treating sexual encounters humorously, had a long tradition. Both 'Tom Tinker' and 'The Travelling Tinker,' in *Pills to Purge Melancholy*. were explicit in describing the delights of sex, for men and women and also young and old.[18] Among the songs included in Place's collection, 'A Pretty Maid She to the Miller Would Go' and 'Gee-ho Dobbin' were examples of occupational songs related to sex, relying upon references to grinding corn, the click-clack of stones and 'driving being my trade,' while 'A Hole to Put Poor Robin In' and 'Morgan Rattler' were more explicit.[19]

Bawdy songs operated in a variety of ways. There was the vicarious thrill of entering an underworld with its cant and flash language but also the sensationalism surrounding sexual scandal, especially in high places. 'The Naughty Lord & the Gay Young Lady, Damages, £10,000.' was included in Charles Hindley's *Curiosities of Street Literature*, as late as 1871. There was also the celebration of sexuality, commonly emphasising male conquest and pleasure, with sex likened to the hunt, most clearly seen in 'The Keeper.' The eponymous figure carries, under his arm, a bow 'all for to shoot a merry little doe.' In fact, depending upon the variant, he chances his arm with five, even seven such creatures.[20] The song, learned by generations of schoolchildren after its bowdlerization by Cecil Sharp, grew out of the eighteenth-century song 'The Frolicksome Farmer' (with its all-purpose line ('Tis of a brisk young farmer, in ---shire did dwell') whose actions were unambiguously predatory and sexual. Female sexual pleasure was also to be found, notably 'Oyster Nan [who] sighed for copulation'.

In an age when men and women across the social spectrum were well aware of puns and double meanings, there was considerable scope for combining a celebration of sexuality with humour in a variety of euphemistic descriptions; but an acceptable euphemism for one, might be offensive to another. The offended became more vocal from the late-eighteenth century onwards, bringing condemnation and prosecution. According to Richard Hayward, an associate of Place, 'obscene ballads and songs in praise of thieving were the only ones sung about the streets' in the 1780s but they generated a moral panic with the *Daily Universal Register* condemning 'obscene ballads sung about the streets by a set of wretches, so very low as to be incapable of feeling anything but the stroke of a whip' and called for action in 1785.[21] Moral entrepreneurs like Patrick Colquhoun likewise demanded a legal clamp-down on street singers and reformers like Hannah More produced wholesome alternatives on a massive scale. The question arises: why did attitudes change at this time? For much of the eighteenth century there was little concern with songs, which were thinly disguised descriptions of men and women enjoying sex. Many a 'fine fiddle' was played, not to mention equally phallic flutes and 'merry bagpipes'; ploughmen ploughed literal and metaphorical furrows, while milkmaids similarly plied their skills; many a nightingale sang sweetly for women whose amorous romping had left them with grass-stained 'green gowns.' Popular songs reflected and reinforced prevailing views of sexuality. In the third quarter of the eighteenth century (and before), there were cultural stereotypes – the ploughman and the milkmaid - of a healthy and fertile peasantry, which were not at odds with medical treatises, which contrasted a sexually healthy countryside with enfeebled, if not impotent, aristocrats and urban dwellers. From the late-eighteenth century onwards, there was a problematic and pessimistic view of an immoral and overpopulated country.[22] Reformers like Place spoke of 'the song … and lewd plays and interludes [which were] all calculated to produce mischief' by which he meant 'want of chastity in girls.'[23] Immorality and criminality were often explained in terms of the corrupting influence of popular culture. However, the problematizing of popular culture by moral entrepreneurs and improving radicals did not necessarily mean, *pace* Place, that bawdy songs had disappeared or were suppressed. Rather they were only driven from public spaces. Perhaps the most striking aspect of Place's recollections of life in and around his father's public house was that songs like 'Sandman Joe' were sung, particularly on Saturday nights, 'in an open space at the back of St. Clements in the Strand at the front of an alehouse door call'd the Crooked Billet by two women … amidst roars of Laughter.'[24] And even when singing took place indoors, 'the parlour doors [were] thrown wide open [so] that whoever was in the bar and the tap room might hear every word.'[25] Further, these songs were performed, without shame, by 'respectable tradesmen' and their performances were met with clapping of hands and rapping of tables. In similar vein, was the popularity of 'The Black Joke,' a well-known song (and tune[26]) widely known for its bawdy connotations, and used in theatrical entr'actes, featuring comic and vulgar peasant dances, in London and Dublin. In addition, it appeared in numerous eighteenth-century collections, many of which were aimed at a 'middling sort' market.[27]

By the 1820s and 1830s bawdy songs were less common on the streets – and some may have lost their bawdy connotations – but they were still to be heard in song-and-supper clubs and similar venues, and also in the penny gaffs, so hated by Mayhew. Shocked by the songs, he was appalled by 'one scene yet to come, that was perfect in its wickedness.' Although the tune is not named, the description of 'a ballet began between a man dressed up as a woman, and a country clown … [in which] the most disgusting attitudes were struck, the most immoral acts represented, without one dissenting voice' is consistent with other accounts of the 'Black Joke.'[28]

Such is the frequency of sexual encounters that it would be easy to suggest that popular songs, not simply celebrated but also reflected a world of sexual liberation; but this would be misleading. While many songs spoke of pleasure, there were words of warning, albeit delivered light-heartedly at times. Having 'tossed and tumbled' all night with 'a fair maid,' the eponymous 'gentleman soldier' makes clear that 'a wife I have already and children I have three.' Furthermore, nine months later, 'the poor girl she brought shame. She had a little militia boy but didn't know its name.' In another song, 'the brave grenadier' 'plays such merry tunes on [his] long fiddle' as he and his fair maid sat down 'to hear the nightingale sing' that his fair maid asks, 'play me one tune more.' However, on being asked to marry, the soldier (again) confesses to having 'a wife at home in my own country/And she is the fairest maid that you ever did see.' Generously, should he return, 'it will be in the spring and we'll both sit down together to hear the nightingale sing.' Soldiers may have been particularly unreliable but seducers (and deserters) are to be found across the social spectrum as well as across the range of occupations. These songs serve a warning. As John Clare bluntly observed, 'the common ballad teaches men betray.'[29] One solution offered in these songs of seduction and abandonment was to take care – 'Keep Your Hand Upon Your Little Ball of Yarn.' Another was to get married.

Marriage

Popular songs did not fall into discrete categories. Drinking songs dealt with marriage and showed that it was not a guaranteed route to happiness, particularly for women, but even sober husbands could be a disappointment. 'The Sandgate Lassie's Lament' is one of the best-known and eloquent laments – 'He's an ugly body, a bubbly body/An ill-faced hideous loon; / I have married a keelman/And my good days are done.' – but it was one of several 'wish I were single again' songs.[30] Equally problematic were marriages to inadequate, often old men. Having described failed stratagems – 'Each night when to bed he goes/I throw one leg right over him, / And my hand I clap between his thighs/But I can't put any courage in him.' – the long suffering wife in 'O Dear O,' advises 'fair maids 'where're you be, /Don't have a man before you try him.' There was also a sense of justified revenge for bad behaviour. The woman in 'The Silly Old Man' has no doubt her husband is a 'clown' but, in making him 'wear horns as long as a stag,' she and her lover will 'cuckold the miser and steal his gold bag.' Not surprisingly, there is a strong sense of male fear and dishonour found in the various 'cuckold' songs. There are also several songs in which philandering husbands are outwitted, usually by wives disguising themselves as servant girls. In their different ways, these negative depictions of marriage are another form of song-as-warning. The dangers of a hasty, mismatched marriage, or of unthinking and selfish behaviour, are real, and the consequences severe, and to be avoided. The implicit moral is that men and women should not have irresponsible dalliances that resulted in illegitimate children, husbands should be faithful and thoughtful, and wives dutiful. In this regard, such ballads were as much part of the maintenance of morality as the better known communal activities, such as 'rough music' and 'riding the stang,' which survived in certain parts of the country well into the nineteenth century.

However, there were songs – easily derided as romanticized and unrealistic – which paint a positive picture of love, courtship and marriage. More songs extolled the benefits of married life from a male (rather than female) perspective, as in 'The Charms of a Good Little Wife' or 'A Woman's the Pride of the Land,' though the paired ballads 'Worth of a Husband' and 'Worth of a Woman' see benefits for both parties. Some songs, such as 'Matrimonial Bliss,' combined an awareness of the trials of married life with its rewards, concluding 'Say what you will there's no joy in this life/Like that of a man who can boast a good wife.' Others, like the oft-printed 'John Anderson, My Jo,' celebrated (however sentimentally) the joys of a life-long partnership.

Some concluding observations

Ultimately popular songs, understood in context, provide a partial if tantalising insight into the thinking and feeling of generations of men and women for whom little direct evidence exists. Given the range of songs relating to sport, drink and sex, the different ways in which themes were treated and shifts in values over time, there are no simple conclusions to be drawn. However, several points deserve emphasis. Many of these songs were conservative in outlook. Sporting songs, celebrating hunting and boxing and praising physical attributes, perpetuated an older masculinity well into the nineteenth century that was increasingly at odds with the respectable model of the sensitive, caring and protective new man of late-Georgian and early Victorian England. Drinking songs, likewise, often celebrated a male conviviality more akin to eighteenth century aristocratic masculinity. Although some were less celebratory, they still praised stoicism, especially in the face of death. But some songs recognised the negative impact of drinking on interpersonal relationships. There was also a continuing moral conservatism about many of the songs about sex, with men and women warned against irresponsible sex and hasty marriage. However, the decline (or relocation) of the bawdy ballad points to a change in popular attitudes more in keeping with the new 'respectable' morality.

Endnotes

1. V Gammon, *Desire, Drink and Death in English Folk and Vernacular Song, 1600-1900*, Aldershot, Ashgate, 2008, p.4
2. See for example, C Hindley, *Curiosities of Street Literature*, London, Reeves & Turner, 1871. For a more general discussion of the persistence of blood sports see D Taylor, *Beerhouses, Brothels and Bobbies*, University of Huddersfield Press, 2016, esp. pp.247-56 and G Woolnough, 'Blood Sports in Victorian Cumbria,' *Journal of Victorian Culture*, 19(3), 2016, pp.278-94
3. Among many hunting songs, 'Dido, Bendigo' was known from Cumberland to Cornwall, and was probably part of a longer 'Fox Chase' which was printed c.1650 and is in the Roxburgh collection and appeared as a ballad printed by Pitts in the second quarter of the nineteenth century. 'The Hare Hunting Song' (or 'The Morning Looks Charming') can be traced back to 'A Hunting Song' that was first published in 1747. Volume III of the *Universal Songster*, published in 1834, contained several hunting songs, including 'Let's Over the Hills, My Brave Boys, to the Chase,' 'Up, Up! My Brave Boys to the Chase' and 'Away, ye brave foxhunting race.' The latter first appeared as 'A Song in my New Comedy of the Bath' in volume II of D'Urfey's *Pills to Purge Melancholy*. 'The Cockfight' or 'The Bonny Grey' celebrated the fight between a 'charcoal black' and a 'bonny grey' but the fight is located variously in Holbeck, Liverpool, Oldham etc.!
4. A Wrigley, *Rakings Up*, 1949 quoted in S Roud, *Folk Song in England*, London, Faber & Faber, 2017, p.325
5. The Holme Valley Beagles hunted hares on foot. C Ford & C B Woodcock, *Hunting in the Holme Valley: An Illustrated History of the Working Man's Hunt*, 1986, Mirfield, published by the authors. Their song book (the first of which appeared in the late nineteenth century, includes obvious hunting songs, not least 'The Morning Is Charming' and 'Old Snowball' (in praise of one of the dogs) but also 'Highland Lassie' and 'Pace Egging Song' and, unsurprisingly, 'Pratty Flowers' aka 'The Holmfirth Anthem.'
6. The ballad celebrated the 1824 fight between Wallace and Dunn, both of whom fought 'like lions.'
7. Balladeers on the other side of the Atlantic responded in kind. See 'Ballad in answer to Sayers, England's pride.'
8. Sayers' bravery cannot be doubted. He was significantly shorter and lighter than his opponent.
9. The song, variously titled 'When Joan's ale was new' and 'When Jones' ale was new' can be traced back to 1594. It appeared in D'Urfey's *Pills to Purge Melancholy* and appeared as a printed ballad as late as the 1850s. The song is closely linked to 'Six Jovial Tradesmen' and 'The Three Merry Travellers,' which also appeared in varying forms, particularly regarding the tradesmen who appeared in the song. *Pills to Purge Melancholy* contains numerous celebratory drinking songs, such as 'A Toping Song,' 'The Good Fellows,' 'The Praise of Hull Ale,' which does not confine itself to Hull, nor ale, and 'The Presbyter's Gill,' a cumulative songs more familiar in the form of 'The Barley Mow.' 'Come Landlord Fill the Flowing Bowl' was a later song, probably dating from the 1820s.

10 Women do make occasional appearances. The landlord's daughter gets kissed 'twixt nose and chin' while the landlord's wife appears as 'a buxom lass who joins in harmony' in some versions.
11 Quoted Gammon, *Desire, Drink and Death*, p.115
12 Words and music of this song were included in J Ritson, *Ancient Songs from the Time of King Henry the Third to the Revolution*, London, J Johnson, 1790. Its continuing popularity saw it reprinted in T Wright, *Festive Songs principally of the sixteenth and seventeenth centuries*, London, Percy Society, 1848 and W Chappell, *The Ballad Literature and Popular Music of the Olden Times*, London, Chappell & Co., 1859. In 1916, Gustav Holst arranged the song for four voices, Op.34, no.4
13 There were also songs that featured more specific drinks, from Newcastle or Nottingham ale to Roddam's Fourpenny ale. Gammon, *Desire, Drink and Death*, p.104
14 From the Butterworth Collection and quoted in Gammon, *Desire, Drink and Death*, p.108
15 Several ballads, often sympathetic to men, depict strife arising from the wife's desire to wear the breeches.
16 Gammon, *Desire, Drink and Death*, p.127-8
17 Quoted in V Gatrell, *City of Laughter: Sex and Satire in Eighteenth-Century London*, London, Atlantic Books, 2006, p.457
18 *Pills to Purge*, volume 6, pp.265-7 and 296-7
19 'She had rosy cheeks and dimpled chin, /and a hole to put poor Robin in' and 'At every thrust, I thought she'd burst/With the terrible size of his Morgan Rattler.' Among the trades, tinkers cured cracks in the kettle, glovers and tailors whipped out their needles, and tanners could dress any hide. Again, the occupational/sexual song has a long history. D'Urfey included several well-known songs of this genre, such as 'The slow Men of London; Or the Widow Brown,' 'The Jolly Tradesmen,' and 'The Cries of London.'
20 In the final verse 'The seventh doe she prov'd with fawn, /And to the Keeper she made great moan, /Wishing he had but let her alone, /Among the leaves so green O. In similar vein are the numerous songs involving the hunting of 'The Bonny Black Hare.' 'I says "My fair maiden, why mumble you so?/Can you tell me where the bonny black hare do go?"/Oh, the answer she gave me, her answer was "No"/But it's under me apron they say it do go/And if you'll not deceive me I vow and declare/We'll both go together to hunt the bonny black hare"' 'At which point the young maid 'laid down with her face to the sky,' while the hunter took out his 'ramrod' and 'bullets.' D'Urfey, *Pills to Purge Melancholy*, pp.197-8 in which, punning on coney (a rabbit), 'Some in the Town go betimes to the *Downs*/To pursue the fearful Hare … But my delight is a Cunny in the night, /When she turns up her silver Hair.'
21 Cited in V A C Gatrell, *The Hanging Tree*, Oxford University Press, 1994, p.125 and *Daily Universal Register*, 10 June 1785
22 R Ganev, 'Milkmaids, Ploughmen and Sex in Eighteenth-Century Britain,' *Journal of the History of Sexuality*, 16(1), 2007, pp.40-67
23 F Place, *Autobiography* cited in S Roud, *Folk Song in England*, London, Faber & Faber, 2017, p.284

24 F Place 'Collections Relating to Manners and Morals; cited in I Newman, 'Civilizing Taste: "Sandman Joe," the Bawdy Ballad, and Metropolitan Improvement' *Eighteenth-Century Studies*, 48(4), 2015, pp.437-56 at pp.443-4
25 Place, *Autobiography* cited in S Roud, *Folk Song in England*, London, Faber & Faber, 2017, p.284
26 The tune probably pre-dates the lyrics and was sufficiently well-known to be used in several ballad operas, not least Gay's *Beggar's Opera*. Muzio Clementi wrote twenty-one variations, set for piano and harp. P Dennant, 'The 'barbarous old English jig': The 'Black Joke' in the Eighteenth and Nineteenth Centuries,' *Folk Music Journal*, 10(3), 2013, pp.298-318
27 Joke was one of several well-known euphemisms for female genitalia, which appeared in song and other literary forms. Others included coalhole and cuckoo's nest. The song itself can be interpreted in different ways (some have suggested it was an anti-Catholic satire) but the emphasis on nature and the enjoyment of sex by both men and women suggests it fits well with the notions of sexuality discussed above.
28 H Mayhew, 'The Penny Gaff,' P Quennell, ed., *Mayhew's London*, London, Spring Books, 1951, pp.86-90. Mayhew also mentions 'our Cyder-cellars, Coal-holes … and such like places.'
29 Quoted in Gammon, *Desire, Drink and Death*, p.46
30 Some songs are far from straightforward. 'Still I love him' describes the poverty and harshness of married life with an uncaring man but 'still I love him, I'll forgive him; And I'll go with him wherever he goes.' There were also male songs of the 'I married a wife' genre that expressed similar sentiments – 'when I was single my pockets did jingle/I wish I were single again.'

'In Maidstone gaol, I am lamenting': Crime, punishment and socio-political comment

> So all you gallant poachers, give ear unto my song,
> It's a bit of good advice, although it is not long,
> Throw by your dog, gun, & snare, unto you I speak plain,
> For if you knew our hardships you'd never poach again.
> 'Van Diemen's Land' (aka 'The Gallant Poachers')

POPULAR SONGS, PARTICULARLY broadside ballads, were an important source of information prior to the emergence of the cheap press but they were also commercial concerns. Unashamedly, they were intended to sell and make money; and unsurprisingly, crime figured large. A 'good' murder could generate significant trade. Broadsides celebrating the execution of Courvoisier, Corder, Good and Greenacre sold in total around 1.66 million each; while that of celebrity criminals, like Rush or the Mannings, each sold in the region of 2.5 million copies.[1] Crime, particularly shocking crime, made good copy as did a high-profile execution, but there was more than sensationalism. There are insights into popular attitudes towards certain crimes and their causes, and the law and its enforcement. Even more explicit were the socio-political songs that addressed directly major problems of the day. But, while the latter were commonly, though not exclusively, critical, even radical, the former were generally conservative.

Scaffold ballads

The vast majority of crimes tried at quarter sessions or assizes in the late-eighteenth and early nineteenth century were non-violent crimes against property.[2] They were mostly mundane, received brief coverage, at most, in the local press, without becoming the subject of a popular song. The focus in song was mainly on murder and robbery with violence, though even here there was an element of selectivity. For some contemporary social commentators, such songs, with their titilating detail of gory crimes and their hero-worship of dastardly criminals, were seen as a cause of crime. This was to miss the point of many of these songs but, unfortunately, this pre-occupation with sensation has influenced later historians.[3]

Crime of violence had been part of popular culture since 'time immemorial' but the treatment was not constant over time. The 'transgressive' scaffold ballads of the late-eighteenth century contrast with the 'sentimentalized' songs produced in the early- and mid-nineteenth century. The earlier, eponymous heroes, 'Jack Chance' and 'Jack Hall' are devil-may-care rogues who die defiant, while in ballads such as 'Teddy Blink and Bandy Jack' there is a delight in thieving. The years of war against revolutionary, later Napoleonic France led to a powerful conservative reaction. Anything that appeared unpatriotic, by questioning the authority of government or threatening to undermine morality and/or patriotism, came under pressure. There was a demand from above for appropriate popular songs. 'Loyal' songs, and especially naval songs, were to be heard on the streets in the 1790s and 1800s. The old scaffold ballads, with their gory details, became as unacceptable as bawdy songs.[4] More than half of scaffold broadsides published in the first half of the nineteenth century contain no details. 'John Green' is a case in point. In others, brevity was the order of the day. 'Samuel Fellows,' who murdered his sweetheart, simply delivered 'a violent blow.'[5] A number refer to throats being slit from ear to ear as in 'The Walworth Murder Discovered,' but the account in the ballad – 'Then he drew the dreadful weapon/And cut his [son's] throat from ear to ear/And then the monster not contented/Killed his little daughter dear.' – is far less detailed than that given in the *Morning Chronicle*.[6] Given that detailed information was available in local newspaper, and used in some ballads, this points to deliberate self-censorship rather than suppression from above.

A minority (c.25 per cent) contained what might be seen as unnecessary detail, but the reason was more a desire to create a sense of shock, thereby reinforcing the moral of the story. The Harkness ballad 'Murder,' recounts the Mirfield Murders of 1847 in unusually gruesome detail. Throats cut, heads smashed in, fingers broken, no detail was spared, but the case was particularly shocking. Two of the victims were an elderly couple and the third a young servant woman about to be married. The fact that the alleged perpetrators were Irish hawkers added to the sense of outrage, which was reflected in the extensive and emotive coverage in the local press. The ballad transmitted pre-existing anger and indignation to a wider audience. Although all murders are condemned, some were deemed particularly abhorrent; so too murderers, especially if deemed to be hardened criminals or threatening 'others.'.

The portrayal of murders reflected more general discourses on criminality. Temptation, folly, immorality, at least in the form of drunkenness or greed, and godlessness were seen as root causes of crime. There was a particularly patriarchal tone to admonitory ballads such as 'The London 'Prentice Boy' in which the *femme fatale*, bedecked in silks and satins' leads the naïve hero into theft and murder before trying 'to swear away the life away of the London 'prentice boy.'[7] Poverty was not an explanation or excuse and even drunkenness was interpreted in terms of individual lack of self-control rather than a response to a harsh environment. Broadside morality was not imposed from above. Such was the nature of the trade (in terms of both supply and demand) that it was nigh-on impossible to do so. Rather in popular song was to be found popular morality.

Equally important was the depiction of the enforcement of the law, through the courts to the scaffold. By the mid-1830s murder was effectively the only capital offence. Broadsides were clear. The death penalty was the proper punishment for murder and public execution was literally justice being seen to be done. Judges, portrayed as cold and bloodthirsty in the satirical prints of Hogarth or Rowlandson, were generally represented as stern but just, ensuring that trials were properly conducted. The final act in the theatre of justice was execution. Here the state was seen to deliver justice. The scaffold also offered the opportunity for repentance and redemption and was the platform from which to deliver moral guidance. Cornelius Wood, executed for robbery and rape in 1824 was said to 'free confession make/ With shame and grief, I do confess/That I do justly die,' while in 'The Execution of Fish the Murder' the condemned man exhorts 'All young men, I pray take warning/By my sad and unhappy fate; /Don't give way to evil passions/Lest you repent when it's too late.' On the execution of Samuel Fallows, for the murder of his sweetheart/mistress Betty Shawcross, the following 'Lamentations' were printed in Gateshead.

> Repent ye youth who are astray before it be too late
> And let religion be your guide, on God your hopes let rest
> That after this you may reside in religion of the blest
> May God above then pardon me for the deed that I have done.
> .....
> My guilt lies heavy on my soul, have mercy Lord I pray,
> Accept repentance mighty Lord, into thy hands my spirit I resign.

The ballad is fascinating, not least for its total disconnect with Fallows' behaviour. Betty Shawcross already had one child to Fallows and was pregnant with a second when he, a supposedly respectable young farmer, murdered her in a particularly brutal manner, so that he could marry another woman. He exhibited 'perfect indifference' during his trial and, after sentence refused to talk with anyone about his crime, refused to repent before he mounted the gallows and died in 'sullen silence.'[8] But the moral purpose was more important than accurate news reporting. These songs provided an opportunity to repeat and reinforce advice. Men were exhorted to be sober and industrious, women to be chaste (and avoid men and drink, especially in combination), and all were reminded of the importance of church-going, honesty and industry.

The contrast between earlier 'transgressive' and later 'sanitized' execution ballads can be overstated. Gatrell's pioneering work was primarily concerned with moving beyond the simplistic and judgemental depictions of the scaffold crowd and explaining the mentalities of its members, not with providing a comprehensive survey of eighteenth-century execution ballads. In fact, moralising ballads were to be found alongside the transgressive broadsides on which he focuses. Further, there was an element of continuity that mirrors that of the bawdy ballad. Transgressive songs, such as 'The Night Before Larry Was Stretched' and (in modified form) 'Jack Hall' did not disappear and were still being printed in the mid-nineteenth century.

Transportation and prison

Despite the proliferation of capital offences in the eighteenth century, there was not a commensurate increase in the number of executions. In part this was the result of pragmatism – there were only so many corpses that could be seen, swinging in the breeze on the commons of London, particularly – but it also reflected the fact the 'Bloody Code' was predicated on the notion of discretionary terror/mercy.[9] Person and property were to be safeguarded by the threat of the death penalty, but there was no intention of executing everyone found guilty of a capital offence. Commutation of the death penalty to transportation had been a favoured option since the early eighteenth century. The most common destination was the American colonies, at least until 1776. After experimenting with a number of alternative locations, Australia was chosen as the new dumping ground.[10] In English transportation songs there is little in the way of defiance, in contrasts to Irish and Irish/Australian ballads, most notably those about Jack (or John) O'Donahue. Rarely was there a challenge to the legitimacy of the law but certain poaching songs, while sounding an explicit warning, implicitly recognised poverty as a cause of crime. Unusually, Harkness's 'The Transport's Lamentation' makes explicit the link between working-class poverty and criminality.

> Though crime is bad, yet poverty makes many a man to be
> A transport from his native land, across the raging sea.
> .....
> The rich have no temptation, but all things at command
> It is for health or pleasure they leave their native land.
> But great distress and want of work, starvation and disease,
> Makes inmates for the prison, and transports for the seas.

In many ways, transportation ballads were little more than variations on 'farewell' themes, with the obvious difference that this parting from doting parents and loving fiancées, was not voluntary. In 'The Transports' (better known as 'Farewell To You Judges and Jurries') the unfortunate convict laments leaving his 'Polly' in Liverpool; 'The Convict Maid' bemoans her separation from friends and agonizes over her mother's suffering. In such separation songs the emphasis is on the sense of loss, heightened after the relocation to Australia, by the added fear of a largely unknown but menacing destination. Details of Australia in these ballads were limited and the accounts of the experience of transportation, as in 'The Returned Convict, or the Horrors of Transportation,' highly generalized.[11] They were easily-adapted songs about un-named convicts, guilty of unspecified crimes, suffering 'dreadful' but non-specific conditions, such as 'cold chains and cold irons.' Songs written about eighteenth-century transportation to Virginia could be recycled in the 1820s simply by changing the destination to Botany Bay.[12] Similarly, the location of the original crime could be changed by an enterprising printer. 'The London 'Prentice Boy,' for example, became 'The Bristol 'Prentice Boy.' As with the execution ballads of the nineteenth century, there were warnings a-plenty to 'young fellows,' 'wicked blades' and 'gallant poachers.' Some poaching songs were more specific in naming individuals – 'Van Diemen's Land' specifies 'poor Tom Brown from Nottingham, Jack Williams and poor Joe' – but still fail to get beyond generalized descriptions of cottages 'of clods and clay and rotten straw for bedding.'

There was a broad consensus about the appropriateness of punishment for most crimes; but with one important exception: treason committed by Irishmen. The number of such ballads in the troubled years from 1798 to 1848, is small but they reveal often starkly differing attitudes.[13] An unambiguous loyalist stance is adopted in 'All Traitors,' sold by J Evans of London, with its call to rally to 'George's standard' in the fight against 'the Crops.' Each verse ends with the line 'Traitors all they must die.' Equally clear cut was 'The Soldier's Delight, Or, Croppies Lie Down.'

> We'll fight for our Country, our King, and our Crown
> And make all the traitors and Croppies lie down,
> Down, down, Croppies lie down.

However, in the Harding collection this ballad appears alongside another, printed and sold in Exeter, which is sympathetic towards the executed 'Croppy Boy.' So too are ballads, variously printed in London and Birmingham, celebrating two members of the Young Ireland movement, William Smith O'Brien and John Mitchel, both found guilty of sedition in 1848 and eventually sentenced to transportation under the hurriedly-passed Transportation for Treason Act.[14] The injustices inflicted on Ireland by 'tyrannical bad laws' are roundly condemned, and the two men are seen as martyrs in the cause of 'our dear Island "Free".'[15]

From the 1830s onwards, the eighteenth-century 'Bloody Code' was dismantled, the number of executions dropped dramatically, and new thinking about and forms of punishment came to the forefront.[16] For the early Victorians, the prison was to be the environment in which men would be ground good. Some prison ballads were a continuation of pre-execution lamentations. Richard Bishop 'in Maidstone Gaol … lamenting,' was a 21-year old murderer, saying farewell to his friends and neighbours around Forest Hill, and bereft at the thought that 'I shall Sydenham never see again;' but the main purpose of the song was to warn 'young men' not to be overcome by passion. Increasingly, ballads focussed on prison conditions and the new forms of punishment. Tommy Armstrong's 'Durham Gaol' was based on direct experience of harsh conditions – 'two great lumps of wood on which you have to lie' – harsh tasks – 'teasin' oakum, makin' balls and weavin' coco mats' – and inadequate food. 'Wakefield Gaol' also highlights hard beds and inadequate food but draws attention to the delights of cell cleaning and the risk of bullying between prisoners. 'The New Bailey Tread-mill' focused specifically on one of the most detested features of the new punishment regime. The emphasis is again on physical hardship – 'to turn this plaguey treading mill would kill a horse indeed' – and the deleterious effect on bodily strength – 'I feel the flesh desert my bones'. Strikingly, and unlike prison memoirs, there is no mention of the psychological pressures of the separate system of prison management.[17] As with scaffold ballads, the songs are essentially cautionary and conservative. 'The New Bailey Tread-mill' concludes: 'If ever I get my discharge I'll labour with good will/And taste no more of Manchester New Bailey's treading mill.'

Policemen

Although concerned with the prison regime, 'Wakefield Gaol' makes passing reference to 'the blue lobster's paw,' which brings us to the final element in the treatment of crime, namely the new police. Their introduction was controversial. There were problems of recruitment and retention, training and discipline and the popular response varied from begrudging acceptance to outright hostility in the early years. In contrast to the conservatism of execution and transportation ballads, those relating to the police are overwhelmingly critical. The shortcomings of the police – philandry, thievery, dishonesty and violence – are laid bare, but whereas *Punch* gently poked fun at the policeman's predilection for servants and mutton chops, ballad writers were less sympathetic. Constables imprisoned for stealing various items of food feature in 'The Policeman who Boned the Mutton,' 'Flyme Clarke's Wild Lament' and 'The Policemen on Drill.' An equally prominent figure is the policeman as seducer. Bet, in 'Bob the Policeman and Charming Bet' is eight-and-a half months' pregnant when she calls upon 'deceitful Bobby … don't leave me in the lurch/ But go and buy the wedding ring and take me to the church.' This he does not do and when taken before a magistrate, he denies paternity and admits he is already married. Although Bobby is told to pay 2s 6d maintenance per week, it is Bet who is left with 'a Bobby to dance upon [her] knee.' There are also several references to police violence. 'The New Policeman,' a recruit from Ireland, says 'I kick up a row for a spree, because I'm a new policeman' while another Met. constable in 'The New Police' goes further: 'I lie – swear false – break heads, egad./I'm one of the New Police.' A ballad from the late 1840s, 'The Adventures of a Policeman' brings together every shortcoming. The 'hero' works (and is dismissed from) various divisions of the Metropolitan police. In a career that lasts seven years and four months he sleeps with various women, once on duty, and fathers at least one bastard child. His thefts include goose, mutton and even a wooden leg and, all the while 'I used to break the people's head/And holloa out keep moving.' Having had 'some rigs and tossing' during his police career, he decides to buy 'a two-penny happence broom/And now [he] sweeps a crossing.' It is not surprising to find ballads warning the public of the threat posed by the police: 'If you'll be ruled by men, I'll give you my advice then,/Keep clear from all informers, and the New Police men.'

Social and political comment

Historians have looked often to social and political ballads for insights into popular attitudes in general and dissenting views in particular. As 'the voice of the poor,' ballads are seen to have an 'air of spontaneity, conviction and urgency' not found elsewhere.[18] Moreover, because of their dissenting tone, such ballads came under close scrutiny by governments, particularly around the turn of the nineteenth century. It is important to put these 'protest' songs in context. They were one part of a much larger corpus of ballads, and determining their popularity is problematic. Attractive as these songs are to later historians, did people want to sing about 'The Miseries of the Framework Knitters' or the 'Poor Frozen-Out Gardeners'? There is no simple answer but there are occasional glimpses. John Harland, the Lancashire ballad collector, talked of the songs being 'cherished and preserved in remote villages' in the 1860s, while twenty years earlier, Samuel Bamford described one particular song – 'Jone o' Grinfilt's Ramble – as 'the celebrated song ... of which, perhaps, more copies have been sold among the rural population of Lancashire than of any other song.'[19] There is a further qualification to be made. Not every social-commentary ballad was critical; some were distinctly conservative.

The long-term transformation of agriculture, through commercialization and specialization, gave rise to ballads of complaint that condemned greedy farmers and avaricious middlemen. Shorter-term factors, notably the series of bad harvests, the upheaval and privation of wars around the turn of the century and the severe post-Waterloo depression played their part in grain-growing districts, which gave rise to the 'Bread or Blood' disturbances of the early 1820s and the Swing Riots of the early 1830s. Combined with the failure of the old poor law, the harshness of the amendment act of 1834 and the longer-term hostility towards the new game laws and the corn laws, added force was given to the recurring belief that life was better 'when this old hat was new.'

By the second quarter of the nineteenth century songs celebrating rural community were largely confined to harvest-home and the like in the calendar year. There were a growing number of ballads condemning the new breed of farmer, with his new-fangled ideas, social pretensions and lack of responsibility for workers and the wider community. Enclosure and engrossment, with its detrimental impact on local communities, were condemned in 'A New Song of the Times' and 'When This Old Hat Was New,' both of which date from the early 1800s. Low wages, high food prices, and harsh work conditions were recurring themes. Songs also condemned the breakdown of social ties as a new generation of 'large families' looked to improve their homes and life-styles. The fancy dresses of farmers' wives and the piano lessons of their daughters were held up to ridicule and contrasted with the hard lot of the labourer and his family.[20] Almost as unpopular were millers and corn-factors whose manipulation of the market in corn also ran contrary to notions of a 'moral economy.' In contrast, there was some sympathy (but also a warning) for poachers who broke the game laws, and praise for 'Jack Swing,' the mysterious figure behind the rioting and anger at the corn laws.[21]

Increasingly rapid urbanization and the emergence of new modes of industrial production provided more material for ballad writers. There were songs that combine wonderment – 'The scenes of Manchester I sing,/Where the arts and sciences are flourishing' – with concern – 'Then if you get a drop on a Sunday,/To get yourself in tiff for Monday,/The raw lobster [policeman] pops you in the Bailey,/Since Manchester's improving daily.'[22]

Others were more melancholic: 'There's hardly a single place I know,/Which fills my heart with grief and woe,/For I can't find Brummagen.'[23] There were more specific concerns. The growing gulf between producer and consumer, a process which accelerated from the late-eighteenth century onwards, opened up opportunities for fraudulent behaviour. The adulteration of food was a particular target of critical balladeers, as can be seen from the following title: 'London Adulterations. Or Rogues in Grain, Tea, Coffee, Milk, Beer, Snuff, Mutton, Pork, Gin, Butter etc.' The problem was not confined to the food trades as 'A Chapter of Cheats, or The Roguery of Every Trade' made clear. Hatters, bonnet-makers, linen drapers, carpenters and wheel-wrights figure in a rogues' gallery which also included doctors and lawyers.[24] Exploitative employers were also condemned. From 'Wilkinson and His Thirteens,' in the 1790s, to 'The Cotton Lords of Preston' ballads could be excoriating.

> The working people such as we/Pass their time in misery,
> While they live in luxury/The Cotton Lords of Preston.
> They're making money every day/Yet when we ask them for more pay
> They had the impudence to say/'To your demands we'll not consent;
> You get enough to be content' -/But we will have our ten percent
> From the Cotton Lords of Preston.[25]

Although new work conditions were problematic, attention often focussed on the losers in industrialization, notably the handloom weavers.[26] Although a love song, in 'The Weaver and the Factory Maid,' emotion is heightened by the fact that the hand weaver's livelihood is being destroyed by the new steam-powered weaving; but, in sentimental fashion, love triumphs: 'if I could but her favour win/I'd stand beside her and weave by steam.' More explicit were the hardships described in 'Jone o' Grifilt Junior,' also described as 'once a very popular song' by Harland.

> Aw'm a poor cotton-wayver, as mony a one knaws,
> Aw've nowt t' ate i' th' heawse, un' aw've worn eawt
>   my cloas,
> Yo'd hardly gie sixpence fur o' aw've got on,
> Meh clogs ur' booath baws'n, un' stockins aw've none
> Yo'd think it wur hard, to be sent into th' ward
> To clem un' do best 'ot yo' con.

The references to nettles and Waterloo porridge (gruel) emphasises the woefully inadequate diet and the threat of starvation (clemming). Such are the inequalities and injustices that the once-proud weaver abandons his trade to become a humble stonebreaker on the roads.

Many of these ballads, urban and rural, were stoical, even fatalistic about the negative impact of change but some were openly defiant. There was criticism of legislation and associated institutions – notably the New Poor Law, as in 'A Dialogue and Song on the Starvation Poor Law Bill between Tom and Ben' – and support for fictional insurgent figures, such as Captain Swing or General Ludd, and radical movements, notably Chartism.[27] For the authorities, such songs were radical, even seditious; and yet their 'solutions' (implied or stated) were often conservative. There was a harking back to an older social order in which society, though hierarchical and unequal, was seen to be just and held together my mutual obligations. Many of the rural ballads expressed a wish that the centrality of agriculture be re-asserted and valued. Equally important, however, was a desire to reassert old values and restore the bonds that (or so it was believed) held society together 'when this old hat was new.'[28]

Such conservatism is consistent with that expressed in ballads dealing with sexual encounters, and crime and punishment. It is also consistent with patriotic, particularly naval balladry. 'Loyal' ballads have a bad reputation, being linked with the repressive governmental acts of the 1790s and the destruction of the vibrant but vulgar culture of 'flash' ballads. There was, undoubtedly, a tightening of government regulation in the 1790s and people like Charles Dibdin produced many hugely successful songs, glorifying the navy and its men. 'Tom Bowling' is the best-known today but it was outsold by 'The Greenwich Pensioner,' which is estimated to have sold almost 11,000 copies. As well as its memorable opening line, 'It was on the good ship Rover,' the song was known for its patriotic conclusion: 'The King, God bless his Royalty … I'll praise with love and loyalty.' However, naval ballads were a feature throughout the eighteenth century. 'The Pacifick Fleet,' was a huge success for many years after its publication in 1729. Putting the haughty Spanish in their place went down well, even if it was achieved with a little help from the Dutch. 'Rule Britannia,' with its defiant injunction to Britons never to be slaves, was immensely popular from the 1740s onwards. There was a sense of national identity, even though the distinction between English and British was not always clear.[29] The mid-century wars enhanced the profile of the navy and in the patriotic songs of the time 'valiant Jack Tar' becomes a central figure, most enduringly celebrated in 'Hearts of Oak,' 1759. 'Hearts of oak are our ships, jolly Tars are our men, we are ever ready, steady boys steady, we'll fight and we'll conquer again and again,' a song that was to be sung repeatedly over the next two centuries. Thus, Dibdin, who was employed by the governments of both Addison and Pitt, was working within a well-established tradition, albeit at a time of heightened sensitivity regarding the multifarious threats posed by the French.

The heroic portrayal of the English sailor neatly glossed over some harsh realities. 'Fair maids' were parted from their sweethearts by the press gang; 'canny Geordie' hid away at the sound of 'the tender coming.' Conditions aboard could be grim, even by the standards of the day. In some songs the treatment was humorous. Patrick O'Neal, who 'set off like a fool from Kilkenny to Dublin,' fell foul of a press gang and suffered 'half-starved and sea sick' on the journey to Spithead, though his greatest trial was conquering his hammock. This was one of a number of songs that poked fun at the ignorance of Irish recruits.[30] Poor quality food – 'rank butter and musty horse meat with weevily old biscuit' – was one of the afflictions in 'The topman and the afterguard' and then there was the strict discipline, enforced in no small measure through flogging, to the tune of 'The Rogue's March.' But this was not the image that was presented in most naval ballads, in which the indomitable masculinity of 'Jack Tar' became a symbol for the nation. Their popularity suggests that there was a substantial audience for such sentiments.

However, this is not to suggest that songs were not contested. Perhaps the best-known of these naval songs was 'Britons, strike home,' a song of considerable popularity in the eighteenth and nineteenth centuries, oft-times referred to as the third national anthem.[31] However, its history is more complex than some have suggested. The song dates to George Powell's 1695 play, *Bonduca; or the British Heroine*, with music by Henry Purcell and was commonly sung with another song from the play, 'To arms.'[32]

The chorus ran as follows:

> Britons strike home! /Revenge, revenge your
> Country's wrong.
> Fight! Fight and record. /Fight and record yourself
> in Druid's song.

The song became well-known, not simply in London as an entr'acte piece and a stand-alone concert number.[33] The outbreak of war against Spain in late 1739 (the War of Jenkin's Ear) enhanced its popularity. A one-act farce by Edward Philips, *Britons strike home; or the Sailors Rehearsal*, exploited a popular tune title, claiming that 'there is no Englishman in the kingdom but thinks it ['Britons, strike home'] the best tune that has been played for several years.'[34] And the song retained its popularity. It was claimed, at the time of the Seven Years War that 'even Children just weaned from the Breast were taught to lisp "BRITONS STRIKE HOME."'[35] Most spectacularly,

MPs – or so it is said – stood and spontaneously sang 'Britons strike home' in November 1797, when Pitt the Younger announced to the House of Commons that his attempts to negotiate a peace with France had failed.

However, the song was not an unequivocally conservative/patriotic piece. Indeed, by the turn of the nineteenth century the song had acquired radical associations, in ways that did not happen for 'Rule Britannia' or, even more so, 'God Save the King.' So problematic were these connotations that revised, loyalist versions of the song appeared. 'Britons, strike home! A New Song' (1800 or 1803) was openly anti-French and commanded Britain's 'freeborn sons take the field, The Altar and the Throne to shield.' The chorus, still called on Britons to strike home and avenge their country's cause, but the purpose was now to 'protect your King, your Liberties and Laws,' Best-known were the new words written by Charles Dibdin in 1803, which pondered forthcoming conflict.

> There some must conquer, some must die boys
> But that appals not you or me.
> For our watch-word, it will be
> Britons, strike home! revenge your country's wrong.'

But the loyalist triumph was far from complete. In 1819 at the radical 'Mr Hobhouse's dinner' at the Crown and Anchor Tavern, one of the toasts was "The source of all legitimate power – the People' accompanied by 'Britons, Strike Home' while at Henry Hunt's procession the tune was played on various occasions and the slogan emblazoned on several flags.[36] True, one of the toasts at the Davenport Conservative Dinner, 1835, 'The Conservative cause, the work of Britain's safety' was accompanied by 'Britons, Strike Home,' but the tune was played for radicals and Chartists in the north-east of England and the West Riding.[37] The contested nature of this song points to a wider, cautionary point. Songs did not have a simple or single meaning. Irrespective of authorial intent, audiences made sense of the words in the light of their values and expectations.

Some concluding observations

Crime, particularly violent crime, was a central, and profitable, theme in ballads and broadsides. Some, more so in the mid and late eighteenth century, were transgressive, celebrating devil-may-care criminals, rather than condemning them and their actions, but the enduring popularity of 'Jack Hall,' damning the eyes of all and sundry, can obscure the conservatism of many more, in which crime, especially murder, was condemned rather than excused, and punishment seen as appropriate and fairly delivered. While there was a degree of sympathy for the 'poor unfortunate,' as he made his (less often her) way to the gallows, commonly he was seen as a victim of personal shortcomings and his story a morality tale for the benefit of those who heard it.[38] Crime ballads, especially in the first half of the nineteenth century, carried implicit and explicit messages that reinforced 'conventional' morality and created a sense of shared values across society at large. Like the increasingly popular melodramas, they were, with few exceptions, conservative (and often naïve) morality tales, which, nonetheless, offer valuable glimpses into the unknown lives of that 'very large body of our fellow-citizens.'[39] The social and political songs were a more obvious challenge to the socio-economic and political order of the day, even if some of their solutions were more backward-looking and conservative than radical.

However, the days of the ballad-singer were numbered, particularly in London and the great cities and, 'the decay of the street ballad-singer ... we attribute more to the establishment of such places of amusement as Canterbury Hall and Oxford, and the sale of penny song-books, than to the advance of education or the interference of the police.'[40] It is to these new forms of entertainment that we now turn.

Endnotes

1   The murder of the aristocrat and MP, Lord William Russell, by his Swiss servant, François Courvoisier, was predictably shocking. An estimated crowd of 40,00, including Dickens and Thackeray, attended his execution in 1840. William Corder, who murdered Maria Marten in the Red Barn, in 1827,

was tried and execution in Bury St Edmunds. Within days and months there appeared broadsides and plays, some produced by local travelling companies, others appearing on the London stage. The Red Barn remained one of the most popular stage melodramas and was made into a 1930s film. Daniel Good (executed 1842) murdered his pregnant girlfriend, whose dismembered body was discovered by chance. The Greenacre case (1837) also started with the discovery of a severed head in the Regent Canal, but according to a patterer: 'Greenacre didn't sell so well as might be expected for such a diabolical out-and-out crime ... but he came so close after Pegsworth, and that took the beauty off him. Two murderers together is no good for nobody.' (Cited in J Flanders, *The Invention of Murder*, London, Harper Press, 2011, p.95) James Rush was a surprise celebrity, though double murder was unusual. The most sensational trial and execution of the year saw a married couple, the Mannings, meet their death at Horsemonger Lane Gaol. The fact that Mrs. Manning was good-looking and foreign added to the appeal of the case. As many as 50,000 people may have attended their execution, which was described, in shocked tone, by Dickens as well as being celebrated in *Punch's* cartoon, 'The great moral lesson.' The fact that the number of executions dropped dramatically after the mid-1830s may also be a partial explanation of the high level of sales.

2   See D Taylor, *Crime, Policing and Punishment in England, 1750-1914*, Basingstoke, Macmillan, 1998, chaps. 2 & 3.

3   Flanders throw-away comment about broadsides 'frequently attracting crowds of *bloodthirsty* children' is but one recent example. Flanders, *The Invention of Murder*, p.4. Emphasis added. A similar situation applies to public executions and the crowds that attended them, where the deliberately emotive accounts of nineteenth-century abolitionists have been taken as objective descriptions. This approach has been rigorously criticised in V A C Gatrell, *The Hanging Tree*, Oxford University Press, 1994, esp. Part 1.

4   K Bates, 'Morality for the masses: the social significance of crime and punishment discourse in British broadsides, 1800-1850', unpublished PhD, Keele University, 2013, which is based on an analysis of 650 broadsides, almost three-quarters featuring murder.

5   See also 'The Lamentation of Thomas Henry Hocker' which tells 'thy head I smashed thy blood it flew' but without the detail found in the report in the *Morning Post*, 27 February 1843.

6   *Morning Chronicle*, 3 January 1857. Other, more detailed, accounts focus on factual description of the wounds and the weapons used.

7   Cited in C Nunn, ''Come all you Wild Wicked Youths': Representations of Young Male Convicts in Nineteenth-Century English Broadside,' *Journal of Victorian Culture*, 20(4), 2015, pp.453-70 at pp.463-4.

8   *Lancaster Gazette*, 5 April 1823 and *Hereford Journal*, 23 April 1823. The same paper reported a week later that the family had tried the constable (with the staggering sum of £1000) to allow Fallows to escape. One paper, the *Leeds Intelligencer* alleged he had confessed to his brothers and sisters when they visited him in gaol, but this is the only such reference.

9   Taylor, *Crime, Policing and Punishment*, chap. 7

10 Taylor, *Crime, Policing and Punishment*, chap. 8

11 Detailed information about conditions in Australia in the opening decades of the nineteenth century was limited and it took a generation (or more) to find an appropriate language and imagery with which to describe the new land. Consequently, early writings and paintings were essentially a reflection of English conditions, albeit with some prominent aspects of Australia.

12 James Revel was the subject of the lengthy 'The Poor Unhappy Transported Felon's Sorrowful Account, of his Fourteen Years' Transportation at Virginia, in America' and this became 'The Unhappy Transport: Giving a sorrowful account of his fourteen years' transportation to Botany Bay, in New South Wales in February 1808 and his return home in March 1st, 1822, being a remarkable and sufficient history of the life of James Revel, the unhappy sufferer.'

13 Bates 'Morality for the Masses' refers to the crime of treason but does not consider any of the ballads mentioned here.

14 J Saville, *1848: The British State and the Chartist Movement*, Cambridge University Press, 1987. Chapter 6 gives a detailed account of the trials.

15 See for example 'Mrs Smith O'Brien's Lamentation,' 'A New Song on O'Brien's Arrest,' 'Most Lamented Lines on the Prison Torture of Mr William O'Brien,' 'Mitchel's Address' and 'Mrs Mitchell's [sic] Lament for Her Husband.' A similar situation occurred following the execution of Michael Barrett in 1867 following the Clerkenwell bombing.

16 Taylor, *Crime, Policing and Punishment*, chap. 7

17 Taylor, *Crime, Policing and Punishment*, chap. 8

18 C Elkins, 'The Voice of the Poor: The Broadside as a Medium of Popular Culture and Dissent in Victorian England,' *Journal of Popular Culture*, 14(2), 1980, pp.262-74

19 J Harland, *Lancashire Ballads and Songs*, 2nd edition, London, Routledge & Sons, (1st edition 1865) p.x and p.162. Similarly, 'Jone o' Grinfilt Junior,' which begins 'Aw'm a poor cotton weaver' is also described as 'a very popular song' in the years after the Napoleonic Wars. *Ibid*, p.169

20 This was not confined to ballads. John Clare's *The Parish* damned the new generation of farmers, as did a number of rural melodramas. *The Factory Lad* was equally severe on the new generation of ruthless factory owners and contained a scathing critique of the game laws.

21 For a more detailed analysis see R Ganev, *Songs of protest, songs of love: Popular ballads in eighteenth-century Britain*, Manchester University press, 2009, especially chapters 2 – 4.

22 'The Scenes of Manchester' in R Palmer, *A Touch on the Times*, London, Penguin, 1974, p.62-4.

23 'I Can't Find Brummagen' in Palmer, *Touch on the Times*, pp.78-80. Strictly speaking this was a song written for and performed by James Dobbs at the Birmingham Theatre Royal, but it soon appeared as a broadside. Similar sentiments are expressed in 'Liverpool's an Altered Town' and this was a song format that was easily adapted for any town or city. See also R Palmer, *The Sound of History*, London, Pimlico, 1988, chap. 2. 'Manchester's An Altered Town' is included in C Hindley, *Curiosities of Street Literature*, London, Reeves & Turner, 1871.

24 There were also songs commenting on disease, though one assumes that the catchy tune 'The Campbells Are Coming' offset the grim content of 'The Cholera's Coming.'
25 It should also be noted that 'meaning' could vary between generations. For those who lived through the 1853 strike, the song may well have had a different meaning to that of their children, who inherited it.
26 Industrial health hazards were not confined to the factories. The Sheffield metal worker, was a skilled artisan, nonetheless 'he shortens his life and he hastens his death/Will drink steel dust in every breath.' 'Tally i o, the grinders!
27 See for example 'Jack Swing,' 'General Ludd's Triumph' and 'The Chartists Are Coming.' There was nothing new in political songs. Political disputes between Whigs and Tories in the reign of Anne, the Hanoverian succession and the Jacobite risings all spawned songs.
28 A similar sentiment runs through John Clare's *The Parish*.
29 J Davey, 'Singing for the Nation: Balladry, naval recruitment and the language of patriotism in eighteenth-century Britain,' *The Mariner's Mirror*, 103(1), 2017, pp.43-66
30 See for example 'The Kerry Recruit,' though in this song, the eponymous Irishman finds himself in the Crimean War, seeing 'heads, legs and arms all scattered around' before 'a big Russian bullet she ran away with my thigh.' Anti-war sentiments are strong in 'Mrs McGrath' and 'Johnny I Hardly Knew You.'
31 The other two being 'Rule Britannia' and 'God Save the King.'
32 There was also a second song with the same title, which was essentially a love song focussing on a woman following her young man to sea, which contained the lines, 'While our rakish young fellows cry, /Britons, strike home, boys, /Briton's strike home. This was published in Chappell's *Popular Music of the Olden Times*, in which he referred to a popular old nautical song, which had been printed by both Pitt and Catnach.
33 M Vandresi, '"Britons, strike home': politics, patriotism and popular song in British culture, c.1695-1900,' *Historical Research*, 87, 2014, pp.679-702. The chorus is at p.688. Some texts have 'avenge, avenge' instead of 'revenge, revenge.'
34 E Philips, *Britons strike home; or the Sailors Rehearsal*, 1739, https://data-historicaltexts-jisc-ac-uk.libaccess.hud.ac.uk/view?pubId=ecco-0744801000&terms=britons%20strike%20home pp.8-9
35 *Westminster Journal and London Political Miscellany*, 20 October 1764, cited in Vandresi, 'Britons strike home', p.689
36 *Morning Post*, 17 May and 13 September 1819.
37 *Morning Post*, 27 April 1835, *Newcastle Journal*, 6 February 1836 and *Leeds Mercury*, 23 January 1841
38 Female criminals appeared less frequently and were often doubly condemned for transgressing the law and the norms of femininity.
39 Anon 'Street Ballads' *National Review*, xiii, 1861, p.416
40 Anon 'Street Ballads' p.416

CHAPTER 7

'Sing, sing! Why shouldn't we sing?'
Popular music in the age of the music hall

> Let's all go to the music hall,
> Where the show is gay and bright.
> Let's all go to the music hall.
> Where the stars are twinkling twice a night.
> Whether you sit in the gallery, the circle, or the pit,
> Or whether you sit in a plush red stall.
> When the busy day is done, if you want to have some fun,
> Let's all go to the music hall.
> A.V.W., 'Let's All Go to the Music Hall,'

POPULAR ENTERTAINMENT IN the Victorian and Edwardian eras is often seen to be synonymous with music hall. The enduring popularity of its songs, not to mention its re-invention in the later twentieth century, warrants close study, but there is a danger of oversimplifying a complex development and, more importantly, of overlooking other forms of popular music that were important at the time. To remedy this, the first section of this chapter provides a brief overview of the broader musical context within which music hall developed and raises the broader question of what constituted popular music. The second section outlines some of the key features of the development of music halls and singing saloons, arguing that the palatial halls, so visible in the West End of London and the major city centres, were the tip of an iceberg of venues and performers that provided an internal dynamic to the overall business, and extended its reach to a wider audience than ever attended the great halls. This is explored further in the final section which focuses primarily on the changing composition of audiences, arguing that the shift towards a more middle-class audience is easily overstated, and the limits of the direct impact of music hall understated.

Popular music-making in Victorian and Edwardian England

Popular music-making in the early decades of the nineteenth century was both diverse and dynamic as entrepreneurs responded to changing socio-economic and demographic circumstances and the growth in demand for leisure. Music hall did not spring up, fully formed in the mid-nineteenth century but evolved out of a mix of travelling showmen, bringing entertainment to the people, and publicans (and others), bringing the people to the entertainment. Ongoing urbanization changed the economics and organisation of popular leisure provision, but the pace of change was uneven across the country. The itinerant entertainer, ballad sellers and the like, continued to be important figures, well into the 1860s and 1870s, for those who were excluded, financially or geographically, from the new forms of entertainment. The relationship with other forms of musical entertainment was complex. In some cases, it was symbiotic, in others more confrontational, especially from those who railed against the commercialization and perceived inauthenticity of music hall. For many conservative, middle-class critics, music hall was destructive of both authentic folk song and improving music.[1]

The belief in music as a source of improvement and social unity underpinned, in part, the growth of choral societies and brass bands, particularly, but not exclusively, in the north of England.[2] The strength of support for the choral movement from 'the respectable lower classes' is clear, though audiences were predominantly middle class.[3] Even more so, the brass band movement, seen as 'one of the most remarkable working-class cultural achievements,' was firmly rooted in smaller, often geographically isolated, working-class communities, particularly industrialised villages.[4] Although commonly linked with chapel and temperance, there were numerous work-based bands, including the West Riding Lunatic Asylum and Arsenal F C, and many more dependent on public subscription.

Both choirs and brass bands saw themselves as vehicles of community-based improvement, which was reflected in their repertoire. The Huddersfield Choral Society, for example, was renowned for its renditions of Handel's *Messiah*. Purists might quibble at the exploitation of classical 'hits,' such as the anvil chorus from *Il Trovatore*, the grand march from *Aida* and the ubiquitous *William Tell* overture, but brass bands brought elements of classical music to a wider audience and into the realm of popular music. Indeed, by the early twentieth century, composer such as Elgar and Holst were composing specifically for brass bands.[5] But this did not necessarily mean that the popular music of the music hall was totally shunned. The Halifax Glee and Madrigal Society's repertoire included 'My Old Dutch' and 'Mrs 'Enery Hawkins.'

Across the country brass bands played regularly in local parks and at seaside resorts.[6] They were but one, albeit the most prominent, part of a range of local music-making activities that embraced concertina bands, bell-ringers and amateur orchestras.[7] There was a more irreverent tradition of music making, variously known as 'Waffen Fuffen' or ' Jiggerum, Juggerum' bands, which echoed earlier mummers' performances. Bizarrely attired, including in their ranks Zulu warriors, Red Indians [*sic*], Charlie Chaplin look-alikes and even Old Mother Riley, and with instrumentation that included watering-cans, pots, pans and kettles, bands from the West Riding of Yorkshire, when not busking, regularly appeared at charity events, such as the annual fête in aid of Huddersfield Infirmary.

There was also a continuing tradition of private music-making and singing. Cheap instruments, such as penny whistles and concertinas, became more readily available and even pianos were to be found in some working-class homes, as well as public houses. What was sung or played remains shrouded in mystery but is likely to have included a mixture of hymns, ('Lead Kindly Light,' or 'Abide With Me,') parlour songs, ('The Lost Chord' or 'Come Into the Parlour Maud,') operatic 'hits,' ('I Dreamt that I Dwelled in Marble Halls,' or 'Take A Pair of Sparkling Eyes,') and English and American-imported music hall/minstrelsy favourites, ('After the Ball,' 'Lily of Laguna,' 'Champagne Charlie,' or 'My Old Dutch').[8]

Popular music-making in Victorian England was diverse and the intermixing of genres defied neat definition.

Music Hall: chronological, geographical and organisational changes

The history of music hall in England has been chronicled thoroughly and thoughtfully elsewhere but it is important to highlight certain points directly relevant to this study.[9] The London-centric approach of earlier histories, with Charles Morton and the Canterbury in pride of place, has been replaced by a more nuanced account that recognises the diverse, broad-based and evolutionary nature of development. With the ongoing concentration of the population and an increase in disposable income as working-class living standards edged upwards, music venues, variously named 'singing saloons' or 'music halls,' sprang up in a variety of towns and cities at roughly the same time in the mid-nineteenth century. The London Music Hall Proprietors' Protection Association had a vested interest in maintaining a closed shop for the leading halls, but outside London the distinction between the two was largely meaningless and the terms were often used interchangeably. Similarly, the distinction between amateur entertainment ('free and easies') and professional ('singing saloons' or 'music halls') often breaks down on closer examination. Not surprisingly, provision was more heavily concentrated in the cities and large towns; but medium-sized towns were also involved from an early date. The Star Concert Room, Bolton, (population c.50,000 in 1841) was established as early as 1832 and by the early 1850s had an auditorium that could house a thousand people. Huddersfield (population c.34,000 in 1851) boasted the Cambridge Arms, with a similar capacity; Halifax (population c.37,000 in 1851) 'the well-patronized Canterbury.' In addition, there were smaller, pub-based, venues offering a range of musical entertainment (and more) in both towns.[10] In cities and towns there was a pyramid of provision. At the top were establishments such as Morton's Canterbury Hall in Lambeth, Pullan's Music Hall in Bradford or Thornton's Varieties in Leeds, but they co-existed with and were supported by a broader (and at times, distinctly seedy) base.[11]

In many respects, this basic pattern continued until the late nineteenth century, more so outside London, but there were significant changes in geographical and organisational terms.[12] The first wave of music-hall development had been largely centred on the towns and cities of the first industrial revolution. In the larger cities (Bradford or Leeds, for example) these were years of consolidation, while in the towns there was further expansion (such as the building of Rowley's Theatre of Variety in Huddersfield or Templeton's Varieties (later the Gaiety) in Halifax.[13] More important were three locational shifts. First, was expansion of provision in growing urban centres associated with newer industries, such as Middlesbrough (iron and especially steel), St. Helens and Warrington (glass and chemicals), Coventry (light engineering) and Northampton (factory produced shoes). Second, seaside resorts became an important location of new music halls, developing in the context of class-based resort development. Brighton and Eastbourne catered for very different clienteles; as did Morecombe and Blackpool. Even within resorts there could be clear differentiation. Scarborough boasted a more genteel north bay and a more popular south bay. Even the small resort of Redcar had two piers, the one in Coatham for the more 'discerning' middle classes. Resort-based music halls were initially concentrated along the south coast of England. In the 1880s 80 per cent were to be found there but as other resorts developed this figure fell to 50 per cent by the 1910s. Overall the percentage of music halls to be found in seaside resorts rose from c.7 per cent to c.13 per cent between 1882 and 1912. The most important element was the expansion in working-class resorts from Southend to Yarmouth and Cleethorpes and, above all, Blackpool.[14] Third, a further geographical concentration was to be found in the suburbs. The early twentieth century witnessed a dramatic increase in suburban halls in London. In 1900 there had been twenty-eight, less than a decade later the figure was forty-six, two-thirds of which were run by syndicates. The pattern was replicated on a smaller scale in Birmingham, Manchester, Leeds and Liverpool.

In organisational terms, the 1860s and 1870s saw a national network emerging. Initially, music halls relied upon local talent but the growing demand for variety, week on week, meant that artists worked in a wider regional and national context. At the same time, especially with the emergence of the *Lions comiques*, the top-of-the-bill 'star' system came into being. The Great Vance was a regular performer in London, but most years went on tour. In 1867, as the star of Vance's Varieties, he and his 'pre-eminent Party ... [comprising] several popular talented *Artistes*, appeared at Thornton's Varieties, Leeds, Brown's Royal Music Hall, Glasgow, Oswald Stoll's Parthenon, Liverpool, Manchester Free Trade Hall and the Exchange Hall, Nottingham.[15] George Leybourne's provincial tour of 1874, entitled "Past and Present," was directed grandly at 'the Principal Institutes, Lecture Rooms and Town halls in the Provinces.'[16] The reality was somewhat different. They performed at St. George's Hall, Bradford, the Mechanics' Hall, Nottingham and Pullan's Music Hall, Bradford but also at the Alhambra Palace of Varieties, Stockton-on-Tees and the Oddfellows' Hall, Middlesbrough. By the end of the year he could boast of a provincial tour 'extending over 150 days' that had encompassed not only the great cities but also smaller places such as Barrow, Huddersfield, and Margate.

Such touring was not confined to the 'stars' of the music hall. Indeed, for lesser-known performers touring was essential to make a living; and the demands could be considerable. Alf George and Nelly Glover, hardly the best-known of music-hall artists, in the late-1860s appeared as 'The Cockneys on Their Travels' in venues across the south of England (Aldershot and Portsmouth), the east (Lincoln), the midlands (Kidderminster and Walsall), the north (Huddersfield, Leeds, Manchester and Preston) as well as Scotland (Glasgow, Dundee, Leith and as far north as Aberdeen). In all they were touring for 51 weeks in 1867. They, and other largely forgotten figures such as, the duettists, Thurnhill and Fothergill, Liskard the Musical Clown, and the Ricardo family, often performing in relatively unglamorous venues, contributed to the creation of a national popular culture in the third quarter of the nineteenth century.[17]

The most striking development from the 1880s onwards was the emergence of the syndicates, as the development of music hall entered a new phase that saw the emergence of theatre chains with their plush and spacious theatres.[18] The best known, that of Edward Moss and Oswald Stoll, by the early twentieth century, comprised thirty-seven variety theatres.

Three-quarters were located across the cities and large towns of England, a quarter in London alone, with the London Hippodrome as its flagship. But they were not alone. Thomas Barrasford, Walter de Freece, Richard Thornton and Frank MacNaughten were important entrepreneurs, who reflected the new face of mass market, consumer-oriented capitalism in late-Victorian and Edwardian England.[19] Syndicates facilitated the offer of a more uniform product, greater influence on content and tone, in a bid to appeal to a wider audience, and greater control over artistes, for whom a greater degree of continuity of employment was gained at the expense of tighter contracts, which contained control over material and barring clauses to reinforce loyalty. The new, purpose-built theatres that appeared, particularly in the decades from 1892 to 1912, with their fixed seating facing the stage, were fundamentally different from the earliest music halls, having more in common with the established theatres where audiences went to see a show. There was a distancing between performer and audience, but without the fourth wall of the theatre. The audience experience changed from a participatory role in the earlier years to a more passive one. This was reinforced by the introduction of twice-nightly performances and the turns system which necessitated tighter time management, and for performers, less scope for ad-libbing and interaction with the audience.

Smaller halls, offering entertainment maybe once or twice a week, from 7 or 8 p.m. to 11 p.m., declined in number, especially in London, in the last quarter of the nineteenth century, but never totally disappeared. In the mid-1860s there were around 375 licensed halls in the capital. In 1885 the number was around 200 and fell to about 150 a decade later. Much has been made of the impact of the newly created and energetic London County Council and organisations and individuals, such as the National Vigilance League and the formidable Mrs. Ormiston Chant but their impact can be exaggerated. The high-profile and oft-quoted campaign against the Empire, Leicester Square had mixed results. Such was the scale of opposition to the decision to withhold its licence that, after a brief period, during which some hasty internal reconfiguration saw the bar separated from the auditorium, the Empire reopened. Rather than highlighting its strength of, the campaign revealed the ready availability of music venues and the importance of popular support and resistance. Health and safety considerations were more important, especially after the 1878 Building Regulations Act, but the decline of the smaller halls owed as much to the loss of support from below as to repression from above.[20]

The importance of smaller venues was equally evident elsewhere. [21] In Leeds in 1875, 362 music licenses were approved by the city's magistrates.[22] Of this total, a mere five were for 'concert halls,' that is larger venues exclusively employing professional performers. Two, the Varieties and the Princess Palace, charged for entry and were described as 'halls of very considerable magnitude and frequented by large audiences.'[23] The other three 'concert halls,' the Angel, the Rose and Crown and the Seven Stars, were little better than the much-criticized 'free and easies' which actively encouraging audience members to drink. By far the largest group of licensed music providers were the 112 pub-based 'free and easies,' variously offering music and dancing once, twice, occasionally six times a week.[24] Provision was broadly similar elsewhere. In Manchester music halls, 'some large and some small … [were] in every street, almost.'[25] J Greig, the head constable of Liverpool was more precise in identifying five music halls and 45 pubs and beerhouses licensed for music and dancing, but conceded that provision was much greater because 'the justices here have no power to prevent music and dancing in public houses, as long as good order is maintained.'[26]

Local social observers added colour to the bald statistics. James Burnley, better known to the readers of the *Bradford Observer* as THE SAUNTERER, provided a vivid picture of the diversity and dynamism of musical entertainment in the city around 1870. He distinguished between those employing professionals and those 'conducted on the "free and easy" principle.' At the top of the hierarchy was the long-established Pullan's Music Hall, in which could be heard well-performed renditions of worthy songs, such as 'The Old Oak Tree, the Monarch of the Wood,' or 'The Sea is England's Glory.'[27] Even here there was evidence of worrying frivolity, not least 'a silly song about the Grecian Bend' and the band playing 'a tune modelled upon the air "The Cork Leg."'[28] But worse was to be found at singing saloons, such as the Unicorn, where customers in the first floor singing saloon were entertained with such delights as 'Cackle, Cackle, Cock-a-doodle-doo'[29] but this was as nothing compared with 'the still lower type of singing saloons' such as the 'Dissipation Hotel … ostensibly a singing saloon but in reality … a brothel [with] simply loathsome scenes of such shameless indecency' every night.[30]

The decades around the turn of the twentieth century saw a decline in the number of smaller venues in cities like Leeds and Bradford, often due to their failure to meet stricter building standards. The licences of two long-established musical venues in Leeds, the Angel Inn, Briggate and the Beehive Inn, Vicar Lane, were not renewed because of narrow staircases and inadequate lavatorial provision.[31] Overall, there was a striking degree of consensus regarding licensing in the city. Magistrates and police were largely in agreement; and, especially in the early 1900s, the police rarely opposed any applications for music licences. Nor was there any indication of serious popular dissatisfaction with the loss of licences. This was not always the case. In nearby Bradford, there were ongoing tensions between police and magistrates and popular hostility in the 1880s and 1900s. In the 1880s a reformist magistrates' clerk, much concerned with the employment of female pianists and itinerant musicians, was at the forefront of a campaign to restrict the number of licences. Although his fears about moral decay were shared by the chief constable, the latter's selective zeal in bringing objections led to a rift in reformist ranks.[32] More importantly, accusations of 'the glaring injustices' committed by 'a few bigoted Pharisees,' reinforced magisterial resistance to police demands.[33] The issue flared up again in the early twentieth century, when a new chief constable started a 'crusade' against the smaller, older 'singing 'oils' [halls] in the city. As part of his campaign he produced the following statistics, which brought out the variations between (selected) cities, and purportedly revealed the scale of the problem in Bradford.[34]

Table 1: Music and Dancing Licences – selected cities, 1902

City	Population, 1901	Music Only		Music & dancing		Total	Ratio – total/population
		Pub	Other	Pub	Other		
Birmingham	522,000	44	7	3	26	80	1:6525
Liverpool	685,000	38	–	6	43	87	1:7784
Sheffield	381,000	114	–	2	20	136	1:2801
Leeds	429,000	113	9	7	54	183	1:2344
Nottingham	240,000	286	5	–	21	312	1:769
Bradford	280,000	361	14	2	16	313	1:895
Manchester	544,000	388	–	4	35	427	1:1274

Source: Report of the Chief Constable of Bradford, *Yorkshire Evening Post*, 29 January 1902

The 'crusade' was partly moral, partly pragmatic. The older venues, particularly, attracted 'undesirables' but were also structurally deficient. Before a packed courtroom, the chief constable opposed the renewal of forty music licences, the majority of which were well-known "singing oils" including such long-established and popular venues as the Albert Vaults, the Duchess of Kent and the King's Head in the city centre.[35] This time the magistrates were largely sympathetic and upheld two-thirds of the police objections. The magistrates' decisions were appealed, though finally upheld at the King's Bench Division.[36] Popular hostility was short-lived. Expectations had changed in terms of safety and propriety. The existence of a bar in the same room as the entertainment, which would have been unexceptionable a generation earlier when many of these "singing oils" were first licensed, was no longer deemed appropriate. Further, there was a ready supply of venues with music licences in the city. As in London, it was lack of popular support that brought the demise of the smaller venues.

Singing saloons were not simply to be found in the cities. Often relatively small, singing rooms were to be found the length and breadth of the country, from Preston to Portsmouth, from Settle to Yarmouth, co-existing with larger venues, their often-cheaper attractions prominently placarded in the streets.[37] They were also to be found in more rural settings, though most were rudimentary, in the words of one critic, little more than 'a room at the bar of a public house, with music at one end, and swearing at the other; they call it a saloon, but no respectable man and his wife could sit there for an hour.'[38]

By the turn of the twentieth century, not least as the result of the emerging syndicates, the national network of performers had been considerably strengthened. London continued to exercise disproportionate influence, attracting local talent, like J W Rowley and Walter Stockwell, who had made their names, initially in the West Riding, later regionally in the north of England, before moving south. At the same time, the big names of the London halls, Albert Chevalier, Gus Elen and Marie Lloyd among others, were to be seen in the big provincial centres and less frequently in the smaller towns.

However, two important qualifications need to be made. First, strong local traditions, notably in the north east of England, co-existed with newer forms of musical entertainment. The Shades Saloon in Newcastle brought 'concerts to our toon [with] aw the great stars down frae London' but it also offered employment to 'Mr Edward Corven, [sic] a local singer and composer.'[39] Ned Corvan, aka 'Cat-Gut Jim,' performed mainly in the Tyneside area, though he appeared at least once in Leeds and even at Wilton's in London.[40] Much of the repertoire had a distinct local orientation – 'The Toon Improvement Bill,' 'The Sword Dancer's Lament, and 'In Memory of the Hartley Catastrophe' – reinforced by the use of dialect. At the same time, Corvan happily used tunes from minstrelsy and music hall for his songs. His 'Perils of the Mine, or the Collier's Death' was set to the tune of 'Zip Coon' and 'The Rise in Baccy' to 'The King of the Cannibal Islands.' Elsewhere, the Lancashire dialect poet, reciter and comedian, William Townsley, confined his performances to a narrow area on both sides of the Pennines, while the Halifax-born, John Hartley, dubbed the Yorkshire Burns, never left his home county.

Second, many aspiring national stars never made the breakthrough and remained local, at best regional stars; and others simply did not aspire to be national figures. Ella Dean, one-time mistress and later wife of J W Rowley, aspired to be a national figure but never broke into the London scene and remained a well-liked regional star. Others cultivated a regional image and played to regional audiences. Silly Billy Elliot and Soft Tony Benson (later just the 'The Two Tykes'), were advertised as 'the greatest comedians that ever came from the county of broad acres,' and remained a popular act, but largely playing to audiences in the north of England.

Music Hall audiences

But who went to the music hall or singing saloon? Popular orthodoxy, the notion of a transition from 'pot-house to palace' between the 1850s and 1900s, carries with it a belief that early all-male 'rough' audiences were replaced by more 'respectable' and 'family' audiences. There is some qualitative, though not unbiased, evidence to support this notion of gradual embourgeoisement, but given the diversity of music halls and singing saloons, not to mention the limitations of evidence, determining audience composition is not straightforward.[41]

The music halls of London's West End were unusual in attracting people from across the social spectrum. Elsewhere in the capital the smaller halls, like many provincial halls outside the big cities, were essentially neighbourhood providers. Significantly, ambitious men like John Wilton and Charles Morton were unable to realize their dream of attracting a socially diverse audience, notwithstanding their extensive advertising. A visitor to the Canterbury observed a mixed audience:

> The majority present are respectable mechanics or small tradesmen with their wives and daughters and sweethearts … Now and then you see a few midshipmen or a few fast clerks and warehousemen, who confidentially inform each other that there is "no end of talent here."[42]

Admittedly, occasionally there was a few of 'the class of unfortunates [prostitutes]' but there was none of 'the ragged children, hideous old women and drunken old men' to be found in the gin-palaces.[43] There were important variations in neighbourhood audiences. Few in Tower Hamlets would have been able to pay 1s for a box at Wilton's in the 1860s; and even among the lower-priced seats there was a big difference between the cheapest (4d) and the dearest (8d).[44] Anstey's description of suburban music halls, written in the early 1890s, is not fundamentally different. There were 'young clerks and shop-boys … [and] respectable young couples employed in neighbouring workshops and factories' and the 'vast majority are eminently respectable.' There were 'family parties' as well as 'several young girls with their sweethearts.' Although there were 'gay young clerks and local bloods' on the fringe of the audience, their presence was offset by a trusty old matron or two.'[45]

Provincial audiences reflected local occupational structures. Significant numbers were members of the cutlery trades in Sheffield, the textile industry in Manchester and the seafaring trades in Liverpool, though people were also drawn from a range of semi-skilled occupations. Unsurprisingly, young people comprised an important part of the audience, though this diminished somewhat in the early twentieth century.[46] In those towns or cities where there were opportunities for paid employment, women were more likely to attend. Contrary to popular fears, the women who did so were, with few exceptions, respectable. In the 1860s and 1870s, there was clear evidence of social diversity in the audiences of some music halls. The Victoria in Manchester, which charged either 2d or 3d for admission, was almost exclusively working-class, though this was hardly a homogenous category. The pricing policies of other Manchester halls, where admission prices could vary from 2d to 1s, suggests that there was a wider audience, encompassing people from lower middle-class occupations.[47] In Liverpool the picture was even more diverse. Some halls (the Constellation, the Crystal Palace, Griffith's and the Metropolitan) were free; the Colosseum's admission prices ranged from 1d to 6d; the Gaiety from 2d to 1s and the Star from 6d to 1s 6d.[48] Newspaper reports confirm this. The 1d pit in the Liverpool Colosseum 'was made up of working men of the lower class … dock labourers and [other] labourers,' whereas artisans and sailors were to be found in the 6d. gallery.[49] The anonymous author of an article on 'Liverpool Life' published in 1857 noted that there were 'singing saloons for the upper, middle and lower classes [but] they are specially set apart for all these grades.'[50]

Most singing saloons were provided for and frequented by members of the working classes for whom even a 3d music-hall ticket would have been prohibitive. Admission was free, or via the purchase of a token exchangeable for a drink. Frequently, singing saloons were described as 'notorious' with 'scenes of debauchery and crime … [committed by] men, dirty, unshaven, drunk, blasphemous [and] women half-naked, riotous and obscene.'[51] However, much of this material was written and published by people with a clear reformist agenda. It suited their purpose to paint lurid pictures of immorality and criminality but not all commentators were so critical. The Alexander Hall and Singing Saloon in Manchester was 'frequented by a very respectable class of working people.'[52] Similarly, the chief constable of Leeds found little difference between the composition of the audiences in the city's big music halls and those attending singing saloons and even 'free and easies.'[53] Surveying 'poor people's music-hall in Lancashire at the turn of the twentieth century, Russell and Compagnac noted the preponderance of 'labourers, artisans, porters, navvies, street-sellers of all kind'. Although critical of the entertainment provided, they praised the members of the audiences as 'respectable and well-meaning folk; honest, straightforward, excellent workers and not deficient in … humanity.'[54]

The extent to which the advent of the syndicated music halls, especially away from city centres transformed audiences is easily overstated. Undoubtedly some new (or refurbished) music halls were more socially differentiated, as reflected in their pricing policies. The Tivoli, Manchester (the refurbished Alexandra) offered seats from 6d to 3s but also boxes from 10s 6d to £2; but the Tivoli was the exception to the rule.[55] Elsewhere there were some signs of social differentiation, The Pavilion, a suburban music hall in Lodge Lane, Liverpool, was a case in point. It was part of the Manchester-based Broadhead circuit, comprising a maximum of seventeen theatres and colloquially known as the 'Bread and Butter Tour.' Although the two shows per evening attracted different audiences, one lower middle class, the other more working class, both were drawn from the locality.[56]

The geographical and social limitations of music hall

Not everyone could directly enjoy the new entertainment. There were significant parts of the country that were geographically distant from the nearest music hall. This was particularly true of smaller towns and villages in the lightly populated parts of Devon and Cornwall, East Anglia and Cumberland and Westmorland but also applied to 'industrialised' counties such as the West Riding of Yorkshire. For inhabitants of the villages of the Calder, Colne and Holme valleys opportunities were limited. In theory, they could avail themselves of the musical delights of Leeds and Bradford, or even Huddersfield and Halifax, but in practice it is unlikely that many made the journey. Infrequently, touring companies, appearing in one of the towns or cities, might travel to nearby villages.[57] Occasionally, a small music hall sprang up locally, though the entertainment at a 'well-attended' music hall in Sowerby Bridge in 1870, on closer examination, turned out to comprise a female pianist and two female singers, one aged six.

Furthermore, even in well-provided towns and cities there remained a significant part of the population for whom even a visit to a smaller music hall was beyond their means, but this is not to say that they were not influenced by the new culture. With plagiarism rife, it was not uncommon for songs to be performed not just in the smaller halls but also, and perhaps more importantly, in other venues, such as public houses (licensed or not), singing saloons, and working men's clubs as well as in pleasure gardens and on the street or beach. Commenting in 1867 on the Great Vance's new song, 'He's a Pal o' Mine,' an anonymous contributor to *Era* was convinced it was 'sure to take as prominent a part in street minstrelsy as the other ditties he has made so famous.'[58] A quarter of a century later, Anstey made effectively the same point. Of the twenty or thirty songs sung at each music hall each year, 'perhaps two or three a year will catch the popular favour, be played on barrel-organs, whistled by street boys, adapted for burlesques and pantomimes, and overrun the entire country in a marvellous short time, until it palls upon the very villagers.'[59] A somewhat dismayed Flora Thompson noted how the latest 1890s music-hall hit ('Ta-Ra-Ra-Boom-De-Ay') spread through the countryside like an epidemic to be taken up by the villagers of Candleford Green.

> [T]he words and tune swept the countryside like an epidemic. Ploughman bawled it at the plough-tail, harvesters sang it in the harvest fields, workmen in villages painted the outside of houses to its measure, errand boys whistled it and schoolchildren yelled it. Even housewives … would attempt a tired little imitation of the high kick as they turned from the clothes-lines in their gardens singing 'Ta-ra-ra-boom-de-ay.'[60]

Nowhere was safe. In the West Riding of Yorkshire, the Honley Feast of 1893 featured long-established attractions, the inevitable 'fat woman [and] wonders of the deep sea … shooting galleries, cocoanut stalls and pea shows' and the village's highly successful brass band; but there was no escaping the new, popular music as '[t]he organs attached to the roundabouts merrily ground out all the latest popular music hall songs.'[61]

Some concluding observations

Music hall, broadly defined, was a central and dynamic element in Victorian and Edwardian commercialised popular leisure as well as being an important source of employment for a range of people needed to ensure the efficient production and delivery of on-stage performance. By the end of the nineteenth century it was entertainment 'for the people, but without entirely ceasing to be 'of the people,' particularly in the smaller venues. But it did not exist alone; it was part of a rich and diverse culture of popular music-making. Nor did it reach all; geography and economics limited direct access. Before looking more closely at the entertainment if offered, particularly its songs, we must turn our attention to popular dance.

Endnotes

1. The concerns were exaggerated and overlooked the extent to which 'improving' music was incorporated into music-hall entertainment, as will become clear later.
2. See also the attempts to bring improving music to the poorest in society via people's concerts and street-and-alley concerts.

3   D Russell, *Popular music in England, 1840-1914: A social history*, Manchester University Press, 1987, chapter 10. See also J Hargreaves, *Every Valley Shall Be Exalted: Halifax Choral Society, 1818-2018*, Huddersfield, D&M Heritage Press, 2019.
4   Russell, *Popular music*, p.162 and chapter 9 *passim*. See also T Herbert, ed., *Bands: The Brass Band Movement in the 19th and 20th Centuries*, Milton Keynes, Open University Press, 199, T Herbert, 'The Repertory of a Victorian Brass Band,' *Popular Music*, 9(1), 1990, pp.117-32, A M Wilkinson, 'The Social and Cultural History of Black Dyke Mills Band, c.1900 to c.1970,' unpublished D.Phil., Leeds Metropolitan University, 2013 and S Etheridge, 'Southern Pennine Brass Bands and the Creation of Northern Identity, c.1840-1914,' *Northern History*, 54(2), 2017, pp.244-61.
5   Elgar, *Severn suite for brass band* and Holst *Moorside Suite*.
6   C O'Reilly, '"We Have Gone Recreation Mad": The Consumption of Leisure and Popular Entertainment in Municipal Parks in Early Twentieth Century Britain,' *International Journal of Regional and Local History*, 8(2), 2013, pp.112-28
7   See S Eydmann, 'The Life and Times of the Concertina,' chapter 8 'Concertina Bands,' at http://www.concertina.com/eydmann/life-and-times/index.htm and A Smith, *An Improbable Centenary: The Life and Times of the Slaithwaite Philharmonic Orchestra, 1891-1990*, Salford, Revell & George, 1990. Slawit also had its own brass band.
8   This is borne out by a range of anecdotal, including family, evidence but see Russell, *Popular music*, especially p.148.
9   See particularly P Bailey, *Leisure and Class in Victorian England: rational recreation and the contest for control, 1830-1885*, London, Methuen, 1978, P Bailey, ed., *Music Hall: The Business of Pleasure*, Milton Keynes, Open University Press, 1986, J S Bratton, ed., *Music Hall: Performance and Style*, Milton Keynes, Open University Press, 1986 and D Kift, *Victorian music hall: culture, class and conflict*, Cambridge University Press, 1996.
10 For the Star see R Poole, *Popular Leisure and the Music Hall in 19th-Century Bolton*, University of Lancashire, Centre for North-West Regional Studies, Occasional papers, No. 12, 1982 and Bailey, *Leisure and class*. The comments on Huddersfield and Halifax are based on an analysis of the local press in an unpublished paper. This revises the earlier interpretation of Russell who argued that places such as Huddersfield and Halifax 'had to wait until the 1880s for their first halls,' while for Dewsbury and Keighley the wait lasted until the 1900s.
11 Bailey, *Leisure and Class*, has a one-line reference to the threatened 'small fry in the provinces,' (p.150) and only discusses their London counterparts in terms of their decline (p.149) He acknowledged 'the ruck of complementary institutions' in his introduction to *Business of Pleasure* (p.ix) but still downplays the fluidity of the boundary between music hall and singing saloon. Russell, *Popular music*, (p.78) notes the persistence of small-scale enterprises 'virtually indistinguishable from the concert-rooms and halls of the 1850s and 1860s but elsewhere implies that singing saloons rapidly fell away in the face of the expansion of music hall. Kift, *Victorian music hall* acknowledges the

continuance of pub-based music-halls, but her focus is restricted to the cities and large towns.
12 The following section draws heavily on CA J Crowhurst, 'The Music Hall 1885-1922. The Emergence of a National Entertainment Industry,' unpublished PhD, University of Cambridge, 1992.
13 The Northern Theatre Company took over the Grand and the Royal in Halifax in the late 1890s and opened the Huddersfield Hippodrome in 1905. A rival chain, the MacNaughten Vaudeville circuit ran the People's Palace in Halifax and the Palace in Huddersfield.
14 Resorts were a further example of the co-existence of older and new forms of entertainment. For an aspiring but impecunious music-hall performer, such as Gus Elen, a trip to Margate or Ramsgate during the season, provided an opportunity to gain experience and develop a persona, which enhanced his appeal to music-hall agents. At the same time, he brought. albeit second-hand, elements of London music hall and minstrelsy to a new audience.
15 In addition, he performed in Belfast and Dublin. Information from *Era*.
16 *Era* 26 April 1874
17 See also the emergence of the agent, whose role was greatly enhanced with the development of syndicated theatres from the 1880s onwards.
18 The legislative framework was provided by the 1856 Joint Stock Companies Act.
19 Pioneering texts include W H Fraser, *The Coming of the Mass Market, 1850-1914*, London, Macmillan, 1981, J Benson, *The Rise of Consumer Society in Britain*, London, Longmans, 1994 but see also P Gurney, *The Making of Consumer Culture in Modern Britain*, London, Bloomsbury, 2017.
20 S Pennybacker, '" It was not what she said but the way in which she said it." The London County Council and the Music Halls,' in Bailey ed., *Music Hall: The Business of Pleasure*, pp.118-40 for a critical view of P Summerfield, 'The Effingham Arms and the Empire: Deliberate Selection in the Evolution of Music Hall in London,' in E & S Yeo, eds., *Popular Culture and Class Conflict*, Hemel Hempstead, Harvester Press, 1981, pp.209-40. See also Kift, *Victorian music hall*, p.162.
21 Establishing the precise number of music providers is problematic, not least because of the number of venues that were unregulated or ignored local licensing requirements. Nonetheless, the number of licences granted for music provides a useful starting point.
22 Chief Constable's annual report in *Leeds Mercury*, 8 January 1876
23 *Leeds Mercury*, 8 January 1876
24 There were twelve in the neighbourhood of Kirkgate, attracting a combined audience of 2000 to 3000 on Saturdays and similar numbers around Briggate. 245 licences, or two-thirds of the total, were for occasional use only, such as band practices and birthday celebrations. The situation could change from year to year. The following year magistrates and police in Leeds took a firmer stance against poorly conducted 'free and easies,' reducing their number to fifty-two and only two concert halls. However, the magistrates still approved music and dancing licenses for 100 public houses and 141 beerhouses. *Leeds Mercury*, 5 January 1877.
25 Select Committee on Theatrical Licences, 1866, (305), QQ.6171, 6191, 6207, 6374-5

26 S C on Theatrical Licences, QQ. 6974-9, 6982, 6997 and 7000. A similar pattern is found in Birmingham. See the detailed reports of the Birmingham licensing sessions reported in the *Birmingham Daily Post*, 29 August 1863 and 4 September 1865.
27 The former was written by J W Cherry, the latter by J W Lake and was later included in collections of national songs.
28 Although dating from the 1820s, the Grecian Bend enjoyed a fashion revival in the late 1860s and was the subject of several popular songs. The best-known reference is in 'The Gardens Where the Praties Grow' where the 'lovely colleen' walks without a Grecian bend. 'The Cork Leg' was a well-known nonsense song, dating from c.1850 that had been sung by Sam Cowell, among others.
29 Another nonsense song that appeared in broadside form.
30 *Bradford Observer*, 26 May 1870
31 *Yorkshire Evening Post*, 11 January 1895
32 *Bradford Observer*, 19 January and 9 February 1882
33 *Bradford Observer*, 27 January 1882. The police felt they had 'simply wasted their breath.'
34 The statistics are of limited use, not least because they make no reference to capacity.
35 *Yorkshire Evening Post*, 21 and 29 January 1902
36 *Yorkshire Evening Post*, 29 January and 1 May 1902 and *Manchester Courier*, 31 January 1902
37 Reporting in the local press suggests a falling off in the last quarter of the nineteenth century, but some are still to be found in the early twentieth century.
38 SC Theatrical Licenses, Q.5388 evidence of W T Simpson
39 D Harker, *Cat-Gut Jim the Fiddler: Ned Corvan's Life and Songs*, Newcastle, Wisecrack Publications, 2017, p.15 and p.19
40 Corvan was not alone in this respect. Joe Wilson, 'probably the most popular Tyneside vocalist in "the North,"' confined himself to the north east of England and particularly to Newcastle and its immediate environs. Wilson's performances were heavily concentrated in Newcastle and local towns such as Jarrow and North and South Shields but he travelled as far south as Bishop Auckland, Darlington, Middlesbrough and Stockton. Carlisle, where he appeared on several occasions, was an exception.
41 Price policy gives some indication of the expected audience, but the most direct evidence comes from the disasters (fires, panics etc) reported in detail in the local press.
42 J E Ritchie, *The Night Side of London*, London, William Tweedie, 1857, p.70. He explained the absence of drunkenness and obscene songs to the presence of women.
43 Ritchie, *Night Side*, pp.70 and 71
44 Figures from Kift, *Victorian music hall*, table 1, p.63
45 F Anstey, 'London Music Halls,' *Harper's New Monthly Magazine*, January 1891. This was also the view of the London County Council inspector, commenting specifically on the audience at the Canterbury. Kift, *Victorian Music Hall*, p.63

46 Of the 34 fatalities at the Victoria music hall, Manchester panic in 1868, two-thirds (23) were aged between 15 and 21. A further 10 were aged between 10 and 14. Kift, *Victorian music hall*, p.65

47 The admission prices of two large halls, the London (2000 capacity) and the Alexandra (1500 capacity) ranged from 6d to 1s, considerably more expensive than the Victoria (capacity 2000) and the People's Music Hall (capacity 3000). Kift, *Victorian music hall*, p.67

48 Kift, *Victorian music hall*, p.67

49 *Liverpool Daily Albion*, 3 December 1877 cited in Kift, *Victorian Music Hall*, p.66. A similar pattern was discernible at other halls, such as the Alexandra in Manchester and the Parthenon in Liverpool.

50 'Liverpool Life' 2nd series, no. xiv, *Liverpool Mercury*, 23 February 1857

51 R Davis, Pershore Mutual Improvement Society quoted in *Barrow's Worcester Journal*, 31 May 1849 and anon. 'Liverpool Life: Its Pleasures, Practices and Pastimes,' no. xiii, *Liverpool Mercury*, 15 September 1856

52 *Manchester Times*, 11 September 1869

53 In his eyes the audiences were all 'very much of the same class of persons,' *Leeds Mercury*, 8 January 1875

54 C E B Russell & E T Compagnac, 'Poor People's Music Halls in Lancashire,' *Economic Review*, vol. x, 1900, pp.289-308 at p.291 and p.297

55 Kift, *Victorian music hall*, p.68. A similar policy was adopted by the Palace Music Hall where seats could cost as much as 5s and boxes as much as two guineas.

56 E Loudon, 'Performing the Popular: The Context and Composition of a Liverpool Music Hall,' unpublished Ph.D., University of Liverpool, 2011, esp. chapter 4.

57 The villages of Honley, Holmfirth and Marsden, for example, were visited by touring companies booked for a week in Huddersfield. For details see *Huddersfield Chronicle* 24 December 1873, 3 November 1887 and 14 February 1900.

58 *Era*, 6 January 1867

59 F Anstey, 'London Music Halls,' *Harper's New Monthly Magazine*, January 1891

60 F Thompson, *Lark Rise to Candleford*, Penguin, London, 1973 (1st published 1939), p.501

61 *Huddersfield Chronicle*, 30 September 1893

CHAPTER 8

'Dancing to the organ (in the Mile End Road)': Dance and Dancing Saloons

> Passing through the bar of the public house, you ascend a flight of stairs and find yourself in a long [dancing] room, well lit by gas. It [the orchestra] consists … of four musicians, bearded, shaggy-looking … including a fiddle, a corner, two fifes or flutes …The music itself is striking in the extreme, and at all event exhilarating in the highest degree. The shrill notes of the fifes, and the braying of the trumpet in very quick time, rouses the excitement of the dancers, until they whirl around in the waltz with the greatest velocity.
>
> Bracebridge Hemyng, in H. Mayhew, *London Labour and the London Poor*, part four, 'Those that will not work'

DESPITE THE POPULARITY of dancing in Victorian England, the emergence and development of dance saloons has been largely overlooked by writers fascinated with music hall and music-hall song. Despite being found across Victorian England, they are scarcely mentioned and, when they are, the coverage tends to focus either on London or on their insalubrity and immorality.[1] There is a similar neglect in the standard histories of music hall, notwithstanding the fact that dance, in various forms, was a major element in music-hall entertainment. The first section of this chapter, devoted to dance saloons, charts their geography but also relates their continued existence and evolution to the broader question of leisure and moral reform.

The second section focuses on dance in music-hall, stressing its diverse forms but also relating it to notions of national identity.

Dancing saloons

The term dancing (or dance) saloon embraced a wide variety of venues. Some were beyond reproach. Mr. Sinclair's 'commodious dancing saloon [in] Nelson Street,' Newcastle was the epitome of respectability.[2] Similarly, the 'excellent dancing saloon' at Ashridge, erected for use as part of the celebration of the majority of Earl Brownlow, was decorated in splendour that set it in a class of its own.[3] But these were the exception rather than the rule. Most dancing saloons were at best modest. Their reputation was lower than that of the singing saloon. Particularly in the 1860s, but also again in the 1890s, they were often depicted as 'frightful sources of demoralisation,' contributing to the threat of the 'Social Evil' (i.e. prostitution). Their name was further sullied by association with the licentiousness of their Parisian counterparts and the rowdiness of similar places in the American west – or, even worse, in Australia.[4] Especially in the ports, they were seen as a magnet for "gay" women and "fast" young men.[5] More threateningly, they were also 'dens of iniquity,' in which innocents were led astray. As Rev. Enoch Mellor of Halifax explained, in dancing saloons 'young men and women meet, loose [sic] their reason and too often … their virtue.'[6] Press coverage also focussed on the violence, often associated with foreigners, that took place in them, as in the widely-reported murder of the Spanish sailor, Antonio Lopez, stabbed to death in France's dancing saloon, Liverpool in 1862.[7]

Not everyone thought that way. *Era* defended them, railing against 'the loose and slovenly way in which Temperance facts are too often got up and promulgated as truth,'[8] More significantly, a number of senior policemen, notably, Sir Richard Mayne, the Metropolitan Police commissioner, took a more relaxed view, recognising the popularity of dancing and the more problematic alternatives. He told the select committee on theatrical licenses that he 'should not prevent people from meeting for music and dancing …[but] would rather see the people dancing at such places than drinking in public houses.'[9]

Dancing saloons were to be found across the country. Every city, from Bradford and Leeds, through Birmingham and Nottingham, to Bristol and Portsmouth had several. So too did the east end of London the major ports, such as Liverpool, Hull and Middlesbrough; and garrison towns, like Aldershot, Colchester, and Plymouth. Equally they were to be found in smaller towns, like Barnard Castle, Barnstaple and Beverley, and in the 'rural villages … [where] there is music and dancing in every little public house.'[10] Further, in a continuation of an older tradition, temporary dancing saloons were associated with fairs, to which travelling musicians were attracted. Again, the geographical spread is striking, as was their popularity. As the *Bucks Herald*, commenting on the Michaelmas Mop Fair, noted 'the public houses drove a roaring trade, particularly where a dancing saloon lent its attraction.'[11]

Many dancing saloons were in upstairs rooms in public houses or in an adjoining building; others were found above music halls.[12] Mid-century Liverpool had forty connected to public houses, in Bolton there were about ten dancing saloons attached to public houses or beerhouses, and in the east end of London, in the late 1860s, 'almost every tavern has a dancing room … ablaze with gas.'[13] Other dance saloons were opened in converted churches and chapels, in former warehouses, in part of a school for the blind and even in a lunatic asylum. Occasionally, they were to be found in the middle of 'respectable' streets, much to the dismay of inhabitants who did not take kindly to late night/early morning revelries.[14] As with penny gaffs, to which they were commonly compared, small-scale entrepreneurs of leisure utilised any vacant property with an eye to turning a profit, however small. Many were short-lived but their continuing existence was evidence of the popular demand for dancing.

There was considerable variation in the size of venues and the number of participants. One purpose-built dance saloon in Manchester had a floor of approximately 1700 square feet and could accommodate 200 people, but this was an exception.[15] The numbers attending varied from day to day and week to week. In one closely observed dancing saloon in Sunderland, the nightly numbers varied between forty and 120.[16] Across the country, mainly young working-class people attended these halls. For Mayne, 'the audiences are a very low class of people, and many of them are young.'[17] In London, 'cooks, housemaids and nurses, [were] disporting themselves in the mazy valse;'[18] factory operatives likewise in Manchester and Preston, or Leeds and Huddersfield; soldiers in Aldershot and Colchester, sailors in Hull, Liverpool and London. The popular association with soldiers and sailors confirmed the worst suspicions about dancing saloons but, although the evidence is scattered, there was little difference between the habitués of the dancing and the smaller singing saloon. Drawn from the poorest, excluded by their poverty from all but the cheapest of music halls, they took their pleasure where they could.

Almost without exception, all charged for entrance. In some as little as 1d. but more commonly 3d in the 1860s and 1870s, rising to 6d by the end of the century. Some made an additional charge if beer was required, or if additional entertainment, such as a firework display, was on offer.[19] As well as providing an opportunity to dance, many dancing saloons offered acts, not infrequently by 'nigger minstrels.'[20] The musicians were relatively few in number and, on occasions itinerants paid by the session. Pianos and fiddles were the most common instruments with the occasional cello, piccolo, harp and contra basso and even the odd concertina band to be heard. In 'a dancing-room in Ratcliff Highway,' the orchestra comprised 'four musicians, bearded, shaggy-looking foreigners ... including a fiddle, a corner and two fifes or flutes ... penned up in a corner of the room.'[21] Hemyng, Mayhew's associate, praised the music, 'exhilarating in the highest degree, as dancers ... whirl round in the waltz with the greatest velocity.' The dancing room catered for sailors and their women, but he was struck by the absence of even 'the slightest tendency to indecency'[22] In contrast, James Greenwood, a sympathetic and well-informed social commentator and journalist, painted a gloomier picture of the Three Frigates dancing saloon also on Ratcliffe Highway, which catered largely for sailors on leave. '[T]here is dancing to the music of a tinkling old piano ... which usually takes the form of a listless, dawdling waltz, [but] as a place of entertainment it is the dreariest of failures.'[23] Other observers commented on the prevalence of polkas and waltzes, jigs and quadrilles, but with virtually no reference to specific tunes. The dancing itself was described (mostly by unsympathetic observers) as little more than 'bobbing up and down' as 'men and women [were] jigging around the room' with 'plenty of vigour … but not a hint of grace [and] no accompanying sense of propriety.'[24] Mid-century dancing saloons were viewed with considerable suspicion and the negative reputation proved difficult to shake off. Writing in the 1890s, Charles Booth, another more sympathetic observer of working-class life, noted that 'of dancing, too, all classes are very fond, but it seems not easy to arrange so as to avoid the scandal which surrounds all dancing saloons.' And yet, 'the shilling balls … are eminently respectable and decorous.'[25]

The new dancing saloons, part of the growth in working-class seaside resorts, pointed to a different future, though the potential for mass social dancing was not to come to fruition until after the Great War. From Margate, Ramsgate and Southend to Bridlington and Scarborough, to Douglas (Isle of Man) and Morecombe, Southport and especially Blackpool, new facilities were developed as the combination of improving working-class real wages and cheap trains enabled young working men and women to enjoy the heady delights of a day, even a weekend, away. In Blackpool outdoor dancing platforms dated from the 1860s (Uncle Tom's Cabin) and 1870s (Raikes Hall Gardens) All-day dance music was on offer at the Central or People's Pier and the mid-1890s saw the opening of the Tower Ballroom (1894) and the Empress Ballroom (1896), both notable for their size and state-of-the-art sprung flooring. Similarly, in 'Merry' Margate, the dancing facilities offered by the old Hall by the Sea were upgraded with the construction of a purpose-built ballroom in 1898.

Critics were horrified by the way in which 'dancing saloons,' attracted a new, and less genteel, clientele. In 1893 the *Isle of Man Times* condemned the invasion of 'a howling mob of trippers of the roughest description from Liverpool, Manchester, Birmingham etc.' who frequent the 'dancing saloons and "boozing dens,"' transforming the 'fair town of Douglas into a haunt of ill-fame.'[26] There was, as the Rev. T Rippon thundered, 'something grotesque in [leaving] home deliberately at ten o' clock with the intention of dancing for three or four hours.'[27] More perceptive observers pointed to the 'magnificent and admirably constructed' pavilions, the diversity of their audiences, including 'the young and light-hearted' as well as people of 'maturer age,' and the orderliness with which events were conducted – 'the worst I have ever seen has been a little extra joviality ... [at] Bank Holiday.' They also stressed the positive economic impact of the new leisure facilities.[28]

There is one final element in the dense – but confusingly labelled – undergrowth of musical provision to be considered: the casino. There was an upmarket London scene of the mid-nineteenth century, associated with Laurenti's Casino and the Holborn Casino, and high-profile Royal Casinos in Leeds, Manchester and Sheffield, aping the London model.[29] Laurenti's, in particular, was noted for its splendour. With a high-quality orchestra, a flamboyant conductor and a large dancefloor (2400 square feet), it attracted an upper-class clientele, while the Holborn attracted the slightly less well-to-do. Other casinos had no pretensions to grandeur.[30] The Royal Casino, Liverpool, housed in a converted warehouse in a poor district of the city, charged 2d admission but offered comics, singers and dancers, as well as the opportunity to dance. 'Obscene singing [with] vicious allusions [and] gestures so indecent' were enthusiastically received by the audience, as was the dancer, whose 'petticoats are extremely short, exposing her person in a shockingly indecent manner.'[31] But there was also a fiddler who provided polkas and waltzes to which audience members, especially sailors, performed 'a giddy dance' with professional girl dancers. As another observer noted, it was 'the dancing which forms the attraction of the casino.'[32] Manchester casinos likewise offered a mixed programme of 'comic singing, instrumental performances, pantomime and buffoonery,' as well as dancing, and attracted audiences which included 'large numbers of young people of both sexes [but also including] husbands and wives, not a few with their children.'[33]

But not all dancing took place indoors. Open-air musical entertainment remained important, even in the late-nineteenth century. Itinerant musicians and singers played in the main thoroughfares and backstreets of towns and cities as well as at country feasts and fairs. As Booth noted:

> In the streets the love of dancing bursts out whenever it has a chance: let a barrel organ strike up a valse at any

corner and at once the girls who may be walking past, and the children in the gutter, begin to foot it merrily. Men join in sometimes, two men together as likely as not, and passers-by stand to enjoy the sight.[34]

It is easy to be swept away by the bright lights of Blackpool or even Bridlington – and these developments highlight the potential for mass dancing, catering for a predominantly young working-class clientele – but these venues were the exception before 1914. Most working-class social dancing took place in smaller, less glamorous venues of varying degrees of respectability from town halls, assembly halls, pubs and working men's clubs to '3d hops' in rooms adjacent to dram shops.

Dance and the music hall

Dance was an important and varied element in the entertainment provided by music hall, but it was essentially a performance to be enjoyed. There were jigs, reels and hornpipes; boot, pump and shoe dances; negro dancers and Dutch imitators; sand dances, skirt dances, rope dances, the polka, the can-can and ballet. Sometimes dance was a small part of a wider act, often a finale; other times, it was performed in its own right, either solo or duo and occasionally in a troupe.

The ability to dance was an important part in the career development of many music-hall artists. Jenny Hill, 'the Vital Spark,' was a notably vivacious dancer, particularly in her early stage career, Dan Leno started (with his brother) as a clog dancer, and Marie Lloyd not only started as a very young dancer (with her sister), but made skirt dancing a central part of her later act. The list could be extended with ease, but, as well as the stars, there were other middle-ranking stalwarts whose reputation depended in no small measure on their dancing skills. Playing to racial stereotypes, several Irish performers, such as Pat Corri, Paddy Feenan and Pat Feeney, added a jig or a reel to their jokes and songs. Feeney, 'a regular "broth of a boy" … [was] a most expert dancer.'[35] Heralded as the 'Prince of Hibernian vocalists and dancers, [he] concluded with a long-sustained and splendidly executed step dance that gained for him tremendous plaudits.'[36] But it was not just the Irish, Arthur Lloyd and J W 'Over' Rowley combined song and dance.[37] The latter, Yorkshire-born, regularly appeared as 'Lancashire Joe,' with a clog-dancing routine which 'glorified it at the expense of the quadrille, the polka, the Can-Can and every other imaginable dance.'[38]

Other acts focussed more exclusively on dancing skills, though this could be combined with the comedic (clowns or men in drag), the unusual (skipping and clog-dancing or dancing on stilts) and the grotesque (one-legged dancers and even dancers with two wooden legs). Clog-dancers, mainly English or American, but occasionally Dutch and even French, were staples of many a bill in the third quarter of the nineteenth century, especially in the midlands and north of England. The Brothers Leno were but one of a number of clog-dancing duos at the time.[39] Clog dancing was also associated with championships, local, regional and even 'world,' with the events taking place at local music halls over several days.[40] The 1880 world championship was held at the Princess Palace, Leeds between 17 and 22 May, and was won by Dan Leno. The 1898 event, reflecting a recent revival of interest in clog-dancing, took place at the People's Empire, Bow.[41] However, few champion clog-dancers became top-flight entertainers in their own right. Tom Leamore, reckoned to be as good a dancer as Dan Leno, owed his career to his ability to sing. '[P]opular though clog-dancing was … the performer could never command a really large salary.'[42] James Burns, the surprise winner in 1898, had a brief solo career, largely in provincial halls, but soon disappeared.

The most successful clog-dancing act around the turn of the twentieth century was the Eight Little Lancastrians, aka the Eight Lancashire Lads, which included the London-born Charlie Chaplin. Most of their appearances were in the halls of northern England, but they appeared several times in London and their success was based on a combination of 'pleasing vocalisation and clever clog dancing.'[43] Appearing in New Brighton in the summer of 1898 they were on the same bill as 'Tiller's Eight Diamonds.'[44] This was one of several themed troupes of formation dancers trained by John Tiller.[45] With an emphasis on straight lines and geometric figures, the troupes played variations on a basic tap and kick routine. They were best known for the 'Pony Trot' and the 'Mystic Hussars' routine. Such was their popularity that they appeared in the Royal Command Performance of 1912. The emphasis was on spectacle with 'their beautiful dresses and smart dances.'[46] They also appeared in pantomime and ballets, such as 'In Sunny Spain, or the Troubles of a Tourist' and the 'Delft Pottery.'[47]

Not unlike blackface minstrels, exotic Caledonian 'others, such as 'the MacDonald dancers, genuine experts in jigs, reels and hornpipes' or the Great Northern Troupe of Characteristics Male and Female Dancers, grander in name than number, were to be found, but with an obvious and importance difference – these troupes comprised real rather than pretend Scots or Irish.[48] Commonly described as 'wild,' 'picturesque,' even 'barbaric,' they played up to stereotypes that flattered the sense of English superiority. while entertaining audiences in a variety of venues across the British Isles. 'The Clan Johnstone Troupe of International dancers,' in their 'picturesque Highland costumes,' offered 'dancing in many forms [and gave] a picturesque effect … when the quintet join in a wild reel in the lurid glare of torches held in their hands.'[49] Led by prize-winning piper, Albert Johnstone, the 'pipe major … played on the bagpipe some of the wild barbaric stirring melodies which some people call pandemonium but is really genuine primitive music.'[50] The language is striking: what exoticism to put before an English audience! However, any sense of threat from the 'barbarian' was tempered by the fact that these troupes were aware of Scotland's place in the wider Imperial scheme, through such military spectacles as the Great Northern Troupe's 'Bonnie Scotland.' Similarly, the Clan Johnstone, stirred 'the patriotic pulse' as Pipe-Major Johnstone played "The Cock of the North," that moving melody that prompted many a gallant action at the storming of Dargai," though he followed this up with a 'lively Irish jig.'[51]

As *Era* noted 'there is nothing more popular with an English audience than a well-executed hornpipe or a lively jig.'[52] Irish troupes, such as Pat Corri's Irish Minstrels, offered a similar entertainment, combining popular songs like 'The Harp that Once Through Tara's Halls' and 'The Last Rose of Summer' with a variety of dances, the show culminating in 'a wild Irish jig, in which Mr Corri jun., attired as an old Irishwoman, is joined by Paddy Fannin and the rest of the company.'[53] The less-well known Matthews troupe, comprising four boys and four girls, danced hornpipes but also 'jigged, shouted and gesticulated in the usual stage Hibernian style,' thereby playing up to the stereotype, in *Era*'s words, of 'the reckless and exuberant Hibernian ready to tell his history, dance endless jigs and fight the whole world with ... his shillelagh.'[54] In comparison with blackface minstrelsy, Caledonian troupes were few in number and their impact less, but they were not unimportant, contributing to the diversification of popular music in England and to the creation of 'others' in the dominant popular culture of the day.

The largest and probably best-known troupes to be found in music hall were the ballet companies. The importance of ballet to music hall, particularly the Alhambra and the Empire in Leicester Square, in the late nineteenth century has been clearly demonstrated by recent research.[55] Further, as the time devoted to them demonstrates, ballet productions were important to these music halls, but, as the work of the Tiller dancers illustrate, ballets were also an important part of provincial music hall.[56] But this was not the Romantic ballet of the early nineteenth century, of *Giselle* or *La Sylphide*, nor later of *Swan Lake*, though the Empire did stage a production of the comic ballet, *Coppelia*, at the request of its leading dancer Adeline Genée. The leading ballerinas, mostly foreign and trained in the Italian school of dancing, were noted for their virtuosity; late nineteenth century ballet was more about spectacle. Rank-and-file dancers, dismissed by George Bernard Shaw as 'rows of commonplace dancers,' performed limited steps and had more in common with the drill and straight lines of the John Tiller troupes - but without the taps and kicks.[57] Notwithstanding these limitations, the exposure of flesh and unnatural bodily postures attracted the criticism of Mrs Ormiston Chant and fellow moral reformers. For the Bishop of London 'the sight of such dancing ... is a very grievous temptation.' Indeed, in his eyes, ballet was 'wholly evil ... and does great mischief to many young men,' he opined, before adding as an afterthought, and 'possibly to many young women.'[58] This did not limit the number of ballets staged, nor their popularity. There were many ballets produced. The Alhambra and Empire between them staged some 140 new ballets (or between four and five per year) in the period 1884-1915 and they were only the better-known providers. Elsewhere in London and across the provinces the attraction of the ballet was considerable. For the male members of the audience there was the sense of accessibility, if not attainability, held out, in different ways, by leading ballerinas and members of the corps de ballet. For female members, the attraction was probably more in the hope held out on the female-dominated stage of escape and a degree of independence, albeit precarious.

The subject matter of these ballets varied considerably. *In Sunny Spain* was a piece of escapism, which also included the attraction of the sanitised horror of the bull ring. *Dover to Calais, Paris* and the *Gay Mabille* offered different attractions. So too did *Ramsgate* and *By the Sea*, though the English seaside was safer and more morally wholesome. But other ballets had a more overt social/political purpose.[59] *The Revolt of the Daughters* faced head-on the question of the 'New Woman,' as did *On Brighton Pier*, with its shocking 'Lady Cyclist Galop' scene, complete with a dancer scandalously attired in knickerbockers. Other ballets, such as *Life* and *Dolly*, not unlike some contemporary melodramas, commented on the contrast between wealth and grinding poverty in the richest city in the world.[60]

Some of the most interesting ballets, paralleling a genre of music hall song, were explicitly political, extolling the virtues of the Empire, the Queen and imperialist politicians, notably Disraeli. The hugely popular *Le Bivouac*, a 'Grand Military Spectacular Ballet,' of 1885 was but one of several successful pro-imperial ballets. *The Girl I Left Behind* and *Our Army and Our Navy*, brought together the Queen and the humblest of her subjects as defenders and upholders of a 'glorious' empire. The identification between ruler and (happily) ruled was equally explicit in *Victoria and Merrie England*, which opened just before the queen's diamond jubilee. And if British history was the story of a nation's ascent to greatness, then every opportunity was taken to highlight the short-comings of other European great powers, not least Russia. *The Cross and the Crescent*, which opened in 1878 was a response to the threat posed by Russia. The audience, doubtless aware of anti-Russian sentiment in the press, greeted Russians with hisses and Turks with sympathetic cheers. In *L S D* the rulers of Europe were seen coming to London seeking British financial support. France was moderately well-received, but Russia was met with derision and instructed to mend its ways 'and not send his subjects to Siberia.'[61] Unsurprisingly, the war in South Africa produced patriotic ballets, such as *Britain against the Boer* and, especially, *Soldiers of the Queen*, which re-opened in December 1899 and ran for almost a year. The success of these imperialist ballets, like that of the jingo songs discussed later, is well known but it is easy to be misled into thinking that opinion was unanimously in favour of Imperialism. Equally easy but misleading, is the assumption that public opinion was shaped by pro-imperial popular culture. The popularity of *Soldiers of the Queen*, for example, might well have reflected pre-existing imperialist sentiments. Audience members brought with them values and assumptions with which they ascribed meaning to the spectacles before them.

Some concluding observations

Much criticised in their day and largely ignored later, dancing (as well as singing) saloons do not fit easily within the Whiggish view of music hall development. And yet they were an important part of the history of popular music, not least because they catered for a different audience – the men and women for whom music hall was too expensive, or in other ways inaccessible. Their high-profile and vociferous critics were not typical. More telling were the continuing investments of leisure entrepreneurs, large and small, and the observations of various chief constables, for whom they were very much the lesser of several evils

The opportunities to enjoy dance and dancing were considerable. Music hall entertainment offered a variety of dancers. Although much of the emphasis was on enjoyment, of the nimble and intricate footwork and the extravagant costumes, there was, in certain instances, an ideological dimension, sometimes implicit, as in the performances of certain Celtic troupes, at other times explicit, as in the imperial ballets. But it was dancing as spectacle; something to be watched. In contrast, the dancing booths and saloons offered the chance to dance the night away. There was in the dancing booth, a clear sense of continuity with the early nineteenth century. The dancing saloon, like the singing saloon and music hall, was a logical development of pre-existing leisure provision in changing socio-economic circumstances. Gradually, especially in Blackpool and on the Isle of Man in the late-nineteenth century, there emerged something that prefigured the palais de dance of the inter-war years. Here was the opportunity for working-class men and women to dance *en masse*. The shift in tone and perception was gradual but the dance hall craze that materialised after the Great War had its roots in the late nineteenth century.

Endnotes

1. The exception is L Jackson, *Palaces of Pleasure*, London, Yale University Press, 2019, chap. 4 'The Dancing Room.'
2. *Newcastle Daily Journal*, 3 April 1862
3. *Bucks Herald*, 18 July 1863
4. Rev R W Carpenter in *Hampshire Telegraph*, 26 May 1860
5. *Liverpool Mercury*, 8 March 1870. See also *Hull Packet*, 5 November 1880.
6. *Blackburn Standard*, 20 June 1860. For similar sentiments see *Sheffield Independent*, 22 Sept. 1860, *Newcastle Guardian*, 17 Aug. 1861 and *Leeds Mercury*, 6 June 1862.
7. *Liverpool Mercury*, 1 January 1862 & 26 March 1862. See also *Blackburn Standard* and *Derby Mercury* both 1 Jan. 1862, *Leeds Mercury*, 2 Jan 1862, *Newcastle Courant*, 3 Jan. 1862, *Examiner*, 4 Jan 1862 and *Morning Post*, 15 Jan. 1862. See also the shock report of a notice forbidding the carrying of knives in a Whitechapel dancing saloon, printed in German. *Morning Post*, 8 October 1872
8. *Era*, 29 December 1861
9. Select Committee on Theatrical Licences, 1866, 373, Q.1080. In contrast the chief constables of Liverpool and Sheffield gave evidence highly critical of dancing saloons.
10. S C Theatrical Licenses, 1866, 373, Report and Minutes of Evidence, Q.435. This evidence related to the county of Middlesex but there is similar evidence from as far afield as Devon and the West Riding that small pubs had dancing saloons.
11. *Bucks Herald*, 17 October 1863
12. *Leeds Times*, 5 April 1862, *York Herald*, 29 October 1864, *Bury and Norwich Post*, 17 October 1865 and *Sheffield Independent*, 3 August 1868
13. Select Committee on Public Houses, 1852/3, 855, Minutes of Evidence, QQ3950, 4437/8. *Manchester Times*, 12 September 1868, reproducing an article that first appeared in *Cassell's Magazine*.

14 The disused People's Institute was in Ancoats (*Manchester Daily News*, 7 January 1863), the lunatic asylum in Northampton (*Northampton Mercury*, 23 October 1880), the school for the blind was in Liverpool(*Liverpool Mercury*,13 March 1862) and the shocked inhabitants of a respectable row of houses were in Leeds (*Leeds Mercury*, 1 September 1882).

15 *Manchester Courier*, 29 November 1862. For example, the *Bradford Observer*, 9 March 1865, referred to a dancing saloon filled with 200 to 300 young men and women while the *Birmingham Daily Post*, 8 March 1870 reported a Liverpool dancing saloon with some 200 young people present. The City of London public house in Yarmouth reportedly attracted crowds of around 200. *Bury and Norwich Post*, 17 October 1865.

16 *Sunderland Daily Echo*, 10 February 1881

17 S C Theatrical Licences, Q.969

18 Quoted in *Dundee Courier*, 1 April 1884

19 For example, Dalton Gardens in Huddersfield charged 2d admissions but 6d when there was a firework display. *Huddersfield Chronicle*, 28 May 1870

20 J Hollingshead, *Ragged London in 1861*, reprinted London, Dent, 1986, p.36

21 P Quennell, ed., *London's Underworld*, London, Spring Books, 1951, p.61

22 Quennell, ed., *London's Underworld*, p.62

23 'Our Saturday Nights' no.xvi 'Capering Ashore' in *Manchester Courier* 16 April 1887. The sailors who dominated the clientele probably had different expectations and different opinions of the place.

24 *Western Times*, 9 February 1861, *Liverpool Mercury*, 7 August 1866 and *Bradford Observer*, 9 February 1871

25 A Fried and R Elman, eds, *Charles Booth's London*, London, Pelican, 1971, p.309

26 *Isle of Man Times*, 4 March 1893. For similar late century sentiments – dancing saloon proprietors as brothel keeper – see *Yorkshire Evening Post*. 7 Sept. 1892.

27 *Isle of Man times*, 28 November 1893. For Rippon dancing was nothing more than 'hugging set to music.' See also *Isle of Man Times* 10 February 1892, 10 & 14 January, 4 March and 28 November 1893. Such comments are illustrative of a general conservative concern with 'intemperate,' 'immodest' and 'promiscuous' dances.

28 Paul Pry 'The Morality of Douglas,' *Isle of Man Times* 5 December 1893. See also various letters in the same paper disowning the accusations of immorality in the town.

29 Jackson, *Palaces of Pleasure*, pp.103-14

30 For example, ' a singing room or casino' at Heckmondwike, *Huddersfield Chronicle*, 15 February 1868, or 'the Colorseum [sic] a sort of casino or singing room in Northgate, Halifax, *Leeds Mercury*13 March 1858 or the 'casino or music room' attached to the Old Spa Inn, Scarborough, *Huddersfield Chronicle*, 12 October 1861. The Head Constable of Sheffield, J Jackson, told the Select Committee on Theatrical Licences that 'many persons consider a casino a singing room.' Q.7268

31 *Liverpool Mercury*, 21 July 1856

32 *Liverpool Mercury*, 30 December 1869

33 *Leeds Mercury*, 7 February 1852. John Adams spoke of 'a new species of public entertainment, called a Casino, which consists of music and dancing' and which was very popular in London. SC on Public Houses, 1852/3 Paper submitted.
34 *Charles Booth's London*, p.309
35 *Era* 15 August 1875
36 *Era* 14 January 1882. Feeney started his career as a comedian, working the halls of the midlands and north of England before moving to London. *Era* 23 May 1875, 2 April 1876, 28 September 1879, 4 & 25 January & 15 August 1880, 16 April & 6 August 1881.
37 Rowley, born in Bradford, spent much of his time in Huddersfield. His ability to perform a standing somersault, which he did, often several times an evening, to the cry of 'Over, Rowley,' explains his nickname.
38 *Era* 13 August 1871
39 See for example the Brothers Travers (*Era* 18 December 1859), the Brothers Carr (*Era* 25 November 1860 & 17 September 1865) and Mr & Mrs Barker, 'clog dancers and delineators of Negro life.' (*Era* 16 February 1862).
40 George Belmont, 'Clog Dance Reminiscences,' *Era* 23 October 1897
41 *Era* 30 May 1880 and 19 February 1898
42 'A Chat with Tom Leamore,' *Era* 29 September 1894
43 *Music Hall and Theatre Review* 4 August 1899
44 *Stage* 7 July 1898
45 Other troupes included Tiller's Troubadours, Tiller's Mascots, the Fairy Troupe, the Forget-me-nots, and the Rainbow troupe.
46 *Dundee Courier* 7 January 1902
47 *Manchester Courier* 4 April & 19 December 1908 and *Sheffield Daily Telegraph* 24 February 1912
48 *Era* 18 January 1896. There were only five dancers in the Great Northern Troupe. *Era* 8 June 1896. See also 21 July 1894 and 14 December 1895. The bill at the Tivoli, London was headed by George Robey and Gus Elen.
49 *Era* 4 June 1898, 30 July 1898 and 22 April 1899
50 *Northampton Mercury*, 14 February 1902. There were various solo instrumentalists on stage including Scots and Irish pipers, violinists (including a young Paganini), concertina players (especially duet concertina virtuosi), xylophonist and others.
51 *Era* 21 July 1894 and *Bristol Mercury* 17 January 1899. See also chapter 11.
52 *Era* 14 May 1871 and see 31 July 1870.
53 *Era* 5 February 1871. The 'wild Irish jig' is not named but could well have been 'The Irish Washerwoman,' a well-known jig in the London-Irish community and later adopted as a march tune by the London Irish Rifles during the Great War.
54 *Era* 5 December 1869. Fannin's career dates from the late-1850s when he appeared as 'an Irish jig dancer and brogue singer' in Leeds and lasted for two decades. He performed across the United Kingdom and established himself as 'the most agile dancer in England.' Corri started as a comedian, became a singer of English songs ('The Miller of Dee' and 'Tom Bowling' before discovering/reinventing himself as Irish. *Era* 18 April 1858 and 18 December 1859. For the fighting Irishman image see *Era* 28 August 1864.

55 See particularly, A Carter, *Dance and Dancers in Victorian and Edwardian Music Hall Ballet*, Aldershot, Ashgate, 2005
56 Productions were put on six days a week and several ran for months to sold-out houses at several London music halls with capacities that ran from 1500 to 4000. See J Pritchard & P Yeandle, '"Executed with remarkable care and artistic feeling": popular imperialism and the music hall ballet,' in P Yeandle et. al., eds., *Politics, performance and popular culture*, Manchester University Press, 2016, pp.152-73 at p.157
57 A Carter, 'Over the Footlights and Under the Moon: Images of Dancers in the Ballets at the Alhambra and Empire Palaces of Varieties, 1884-1915,' *Dance research journal*, 28(1), 1996, pp.7-18.
58 *Era* 10 October 1885 and 27 August 1887
59 The following paragraph draws heavily on Pritchard & Yeandle, 'Executed with remarkable care and artistic feeling.'
60 Other ballets looking at London life include 'Round the Town' and 'Round the Town Again,' while 'A Dream of Wealth' was a re-working of Dicken's 'Christmas Carol.'
61 *Era* 4 January 1880. Cetewayo also makes an appearance, getting 'a genial laugh from the audience' as he dances grotesquely but he received nothing from Britain.

CHAPTER 9

'Champagne Charlie is my name': The swell, the Irish and the cockney

> From the music-halls come the melodies that fill the public mind; from the music-hall come the catch-words that fill the public mouth. But for the fecundity of the music-hall, how barren would be the land, how void the chit-chat of the drawing rooms, the parlours, the sculleries.
> George Gamble, *The Halls*, 1899

MUSIC HALL WAS a product of a modernising country, evermore urbanised, evermore commercially-oriented. It also provided an opportunity to comment on, and even shape, the broader context in which it developed through the songs, which were to be heard in the music halls and singing saloons, and which spilled out onto the streets and lanes of the country. Songwriters and publishers churned out thousands of songs, a few of which, such as 'My Old Man (Said Follow the Van)' or 'Down at the Old Bull and Bush' have survived 'the test of time' and are reprinted and replayed whenever music hall is recreated. The majority have sunk into (often well-deserved) obscurity but still survive and are readily available via the internet. Many are banal in musical terms, but in historical terms, there is merit in mediocrity.

With the ever-pressing need for novelty, the demand from performers and their agents was considerable. It was met by a multitude of songwriters, many struggling to make their way and offering a song or two to established singers, for coppers. A few became more established in the trade. Prolific songwriters, such as Joseph Tabrar, Felix McGlennon and G W Hunt claimed to have written songs by the hundreds, even thousands.[1] In addition, McGlennon had 'a circle of contributors' from whom he bought songs 'by the dozen', before revising and recycling some and rejecting others. All three men, and doubtless many other lesser known songwriters, were unashamedly concerned with making money. McGlennon saw 'the ultimate object of a song' to be getting 'published ... [and then] on to the street organ.' He went to the music hall 'to instruct myself as to the class of things that is pleasing the public ... And they like simple pathos and homely humour – something to do with the wife and mother-in-law, and so on.' The key figures 'were not the kid-gloved critics in the stalls, the eminent literary man, who do the trick for you, but the people in the pit and the gallery, who are not afraid to shout their approval or disapproval.' A successful song combined 'simple language' and particularly 'catchiness ... [for which] I will sacrifice everything – rhyme, reason, sentiment.' And, if in the eyes of critics, his output was rubbish, it was 'exactly the sort of rubbish I am encouraged by the public to write.' He took pride in his skills. There was 'great art in making rubbish acceptable.' Hunt was equally hard-nosed in his approach, as was Tabrar, who reduced popular song writing to the following formula: 'Think of a catchy refrain. Think of the d---d silliest words that will rhyme anyhow. Think of a melody and there you are.' Catchy tunes and easily learned choruses were ubiquitous; popular rhythms, especially waltzes and polkas, but also marches, were utilized; the melodic range was modest, a recognition of the limited talents of performers as well as audiences; and the music was kept relatively simple with predictable harmonies and limited use of modulation.[2]

Two observations need to be made about the limitations of printed source material, particularly song lyrics. A perusal of the pages of *Era* or the *Music Hall and Theatre Review* soon reveals often well-received songs that were not published, presumably because they were deemed to be unsuitable for the overwhelmingly middle-class sheet-music buying public, willing to spend 2s or 3s for a song to play at home. Further, printed sheet music did not necessarily capture the song as sung on stage. Additional material, such as 'encore' verses and choruses, or deliberate variations for specific audiences, were not always recorded; and the lyrics alone, often themselves ambiguous, cannot capture meaning that was imparted by tone of voice, facial expressions and other gestures, as well as patter, during actual performances. As one of Bessie Bellwood's obituarists summed it up: 'Her songs served only as skeletons, round which, and in the middle of which and, indeed, at both ends of which, she could interpolate her 'patter' and in this 'patter' was the secret of success'.[3]

Performance was critical. A well-chosen phrase delivered with a particular inflexion of the voice, or with a knowing shrug of the shoulders or a cheeky wink of an eye, not to mention ad-libs and interactions with the audience, all influenced the meaning – both intended and received – of a song or a monologue. 'Knowingness,' being in with the 'in crowd' was always important but increasingly so as attempts were made to make music hall more respectable.[4] As one frustrated observer noted in the 1880s. 'There was an unwritten language of vulgarity and obscenity known to music-hall audiences, in which vile things can be said that appear perfectly inoffensive in King's English.'[5] However, given the different elements within any audience, their different experiences and attitudes, there was no guarantee that people would get the same, let alone the 'right' message intended by lyricist or performer.[6]

Early music hall: from 'Sam Hall' to 'Champagne Charlie'

Unsurprisingly, there was a degree of continuity in terms of early music-hall entertainment and older forms. Many of the early performers, notably Sam Cowell and W G Ross, and their songs, such as 'The Ratcatcher's Daughter' and 'Sam Hall', came from the song-and-supper rooms.[7] Their repertoire drew heavily on the popular music of the early nineteenth century, including long-standing favourites such as 'A Frog He would A-wooing go' and bawdier songs drawn from less-than-reputable collections, such as the *Coal Hole Companion*, *The New Cockalorum Songster* and *Nancy Dawson's Cabinet of Choice Songs*.[8] *The Sam Cowell Comic Song Book*, which appeared in 1858, contained contemporary material – 'London's Misnomers' and '1858, A New Political Comedy

Song,' alongside older songs such as Burn's 'John Anderson My Jo,' Moore's 'The Minstrel Boy' and Dibdin's 'Tom Bowling.'[9]

Songs, specifically written for the music hall became more common in the 1850s, especially as the celebrity singer emerged. D K Gavan, 'the Galway poet,' wrote the words of 'The Rocky Road to Dublin' for 'Handsome' Harry Clifton, an early music-hall singer, best known for 'Pretty Polly Perkins.' But it was George Leybourne, signed up for the Canterbury Music Hall by William Holland, who was the trend setter. By the mid-1860s Leybourne was one of the leading *Lions comiques*, along with the Great Vance, the Great McDermott, Arthur Lloyd and 'Jolly' John Nash, who cashed in on the craze for "swell" songs.[10] Flamboyant figures with flamboyant songs, they appealed to a large audience in the lower middle and working classes, not just in the capital but also in the provinces.[11] Having watched Leybourne perform in Hull, an anonymous correspondent to *Era* praised his 'perfectly natural presentment of a "swell" given to conviviality' while capturing 'the difference between the "swell" and the fast, slangy "gent."'[12] In fact, the construction, let alone reception, of the "swell" was more complex.

'Champagne Charlie,' the best-known "swell" song, has an obvious sing-along quality and, at first sight, praises the flamboyant generosity of the hard-drinking, devil-may-care aristocrat. This is reinforced by the image on the cover of the sheet music. In similar vein, Vance's 'Cliquot, Cliquot' centres on the tipple of choice while the lyrics of his 'Slap bang! Here we are again' make clear that he's part of 'a school of jolly dogs' sallying forth at night. ''Follow my leader' cries the chief/Tonight we'll have a lark.' The emphasis on noise and disruption, cocking a snoot at authority and respectability is underlined by the cover for the sheet music of 'Jolly Dogs Galop,' which shows the eponymous 'heroes' being vainly pursued by a policeman

These are songs of liberation, even excess, that harked back to an eighteenth-century Corinthian masculinity.[13] Songs praising heavy drinking were not new but there was added bite to Leybourne's performances, which at times contained a fair smattering of anti-temperance songs. Likewise the image of the generous "toff" – Whoever drinks at my expense are treated

all the same/From Dukes and Lords, to cabmen down, I make them drink champagne — was well-established. The invitation to join the high life at no cost had a broad, masculine, bachelor appeal. So might the apparent celebration of sex. In an age of innuendo, the very name carried sexual connotations as did the (often unsubtle) flaunting of walking canes, not to mention the symbolism of champagne bottles, with corks popping and floods of liquid. And yet for all that the "swell" mixed with adoring women, his was a strangely asexual life. 'The girls on seeing me exclaim, "Oh what a champagne swell"' according to Leybourne, while one of Vance's heroes asserts 'all the pretty barmaids at those gay resorts I know/ The little darlings say that I'm a prize they'd like to clutch' but that is the end of the matter. There was sexual display, primping males showing off their fine feathers, but (at least as far as the lyrics go) little else.[14]

There was also an element of carnival in the depiction of the "swell" that spoke to a desire to be free from the constraints of everyday life, albeit for a day.[15] The extravagant style had an appeal to aspiring young men, not for the last time, with an opportunity to buy 'trendy' clothes for the first time.[16] When Arthur Lloyd sang about 'Immenseikoff (The Shoreditch Toff)' who played 'skittles, bowls and other games,' he was parodying the upper-class "swell" who in Vance's 'Slap Bang,' 'plays cricket, box and torture cocks,' but Lloyd also name-checked two firms – 'For my togs I used to deal with Poole, but now in these hard times/ I ain't now such a lively fool I get my things from Lynes/ And 'e gives them to me cheaper 'cos 'E says I shows 'em off/ And certainly I really think that I'm Immenseikoff.'

There was an element of self-parody, even an awareness of fraudulence, in the depictions of the "swell." Leybourne was well aware of his humble background and the pretence of his new life style with his contractual obligation 'every day, and at all reasonable times and places when required to do so, [to] appear in a carriage, drawn by four horses, driven by two postillions, and attended by his grooms,'[17] His flamboyant stage dress was far from a 'perfectly natural presentment.' Lloyd's outlandish "swell" costumes were self-parodic So too Vance's exaggerated figure in 'Walking in the Zoo,' and 'Adolph Simkins,' which contrasted with the realism in his 'The Ticket of Leave Man' and as the life guard in 'Matilda Baker.'[18]

The most powerful parodies, exposing the fraudulence of the "swell" and the fraility of his masculinity, came from male-impersonators, notably Nellie Power, in songs such as 'Such a Mash,' 'The City Toff' and 'Tiddly Fol Lol.' In the latter the 'party I know' has 'ten thousand a year' and 'moustachios down to here.' As well as keeping 'racehorses and hounds … he drinks champagne at the bar, smokes Intimidad cigars' [while] the duchesses all smile.' The edifice collapse in the final lines. 'But his parents gained renown as a tailor up in town, and his ancient name is Brown, tiddy, fol lol, tiddy fol, lol.'

The significance of certain songs remains elusive. Words alone are a poor indicator of overall performance. The situation is further complicated by the fact that these singers had extensive repertoires – Leybourne was said to have sung over 200 different songs in his career – and a range of characters other than the "swell." In the absence of detailed accounts of audience responses to individual songs, it is difficult to say precisely wherein lay their appeal. Leybourne in particular was well known for his ad-libbing and interaction with the audience. Responses to his concerts, particularly those given in support of a shorter working day (the nine-hour movement), strongly suggest that he spoke to a significant element of working-class society. But the *Lions comiques*, more generally, appealed to a lower-middle class audience, the young clerks

and shop assistants. However, not least for their parodying of the preening male, male-impersonators were well received by women in the audience.

The popularity of the *Lions comiques* sparked a strong reaction among 'respectable' observers, shocked by the vulgarity and inanity of this popular craze. The *Leeds Times* captured the concern. 'Songs destitute of sense, and music of harmony or sweetness, or any other musical quality … are popular now … And yet there are fools enough to crowd music-halls to hear the trash!'[19] George Leybourne was singled out for harsh criticism. 'The song ['Who's going out for a spree tonight?'] is the very essence of stupidity and the music – is not music.' Further, 'however well "Champagne Charlie" may take, and we wonder that it does take, there is a limit to human patience to which unconscious lunacy may go.'[20] Such condemnation did not dim the appeal of Leybourne and even the critics had to give ground, albeit condemning with faint praise. The *Leeds Times* again: 'We cannot but subscribe to the opinion of most who hear him, that he is one of the foremost in his department of song of the present day.'[21]

Although "swell" singers were still to be found in provincial music halls in the late nineteenth century, the craze had largely ended. Charles Coburn, whose career had started in the 1870s with 'Two Lovely Black Eyes,' had a huge success in the 1890s with 'The Man Who Broke the Bank at Monte Carlo,' a song that combined celebration of the high life with the 'lottery optimism' of the 'little man' hoping to strike lucky. The Great Vance was still performing when he appeared at the Sun music hall Knightsbridge on 26 December 1888 – only to die on stage, aged 49. Six years earlier, George Leybourne had died, penniless, at the age of 42. 'Jolly' John Nash and Arthur Lloyd were still alive, but their day had passed. Nonetheless, in his hey-day, the "swell" embodied 'a potent if slippery ideology of pleasure and social identity' which chimed well with the attitudes and aspirations of elements of both lower middle and working-class society in the 1860s and 1870s.[22]

Stage Irish and Cockneys

The "swell" was not the only character to grace the music hall stage. Often crudely stereotypical, "Irish" comics, dancers and singers were a staple of the music hall across the country from the earliest days. As with other aspects of music hall, they grew out of earlier musical experiences, but it is important to distinguish between two different audiences: Irish and English.

The Irish communities across the country in the early nineteenth century had their own entertainment, such as the 'Tom and Jerry' clubs in London in the 1830s, which provided an opportunity for working-class Irish men and women to 'spend an evening of drinking beer and singing songs together.'[23] They used their music, their songs, dances and instruments, to retain some link with and memory of 'home,' while protecting their identity as they settled to a new life in an often hostile environment. The great influx of Irish men and women fleeing *An Gorta Mór* (The Great Hunger) in the mid-nineteenth century, reinforced pre-existing immigrant communities, notably in London, Liverpool and Manchester, but created new ones in newer boom towns, such as Middlesbrough and Wolverhampton, where they formed a larger percentage of the population than in the great cities. There was never a homogenous Irish community but there were shared experiences, which created a sense of identity associated with Irish popular culture. Much of this took place informally in pubs and homes, at weddings and wakes. But for generations born in England of Irish parents there was a growing desire to see their experience reflected in wider popular culture.

Irish music, dance tunes perhaps more so than songs, became part of a wider popular culture. At the same, other forms of Irish music, were becoming more popular via the diffusion of the more respectable songs of Thomas Moore, Samuel Lover and later Percy French.[24] The expansion of music halls and singing saloons greatly increased the opportunities of Irish popular music not only for the Irish, but also for a larger host audience with different perceptions and priorities. Thus, the stage representations of the Irish served different purposes and their reception varied accordingly.

On the English stage, the Irish were variously stereotyped as argumentative and quarrelsome, jovial, if somewhat simple, loquacious, often incompetent but also sentimental.[25] One of the earliest (and most enduring) songs was Clifton's 'Rocky Road to Dublin,' a jaunty slip-jig with a catchy chorus, which combined drinking, fighting and fun as the hero 'danced some hearty jigs' albeit 'down among the pigs.' 'Finnegan's Wake,' a ballad and early music hall song of the 1850s and 1860s, celebrated the excesses of Irish celebrations. In contrast, the sentimental 'The Blind Irish Girl' played on a wider sympathy for the afflicted, whereas 'Kathleen Mavourneen,' written in 1836, before its composer Frederick Crouch emigrated to America, became popular on both sides of the Atlantic with its theme of twin separation from the singer's two loves: a woman and a country.[26] In the mid-nineteenth century it was primarily a concert piece but it rapidly gained a wider audience. In similar vein, Pat Rafferty sang of 'Norah: My Village Queen.' The pain of separation was a recurring theme in Irish emigration songs, though the best-known of this genre, 'I'll Take You Home Again Kathleen' was written by the German, Thomas P Westendorf. There was a striking constancy in the imagery in these songs. Hills were always green, mothers, silver-haired and colleens dark-eyed.[27] Social and political themes are, unsurprisingly, infrequent. McGlennon's 'Spare the Old Mud Cabin' focuses more on the plight of aged parents who escape eviction thanks to the fortuitous return from sea of their son. Yet this was the same McGlennon who was happy to set to music several of Thomas Davis poems, including 'A Nation Once Again' and West's Awake for an American audience. Given the strength of feeling aroused by the so-called Irish Question, it is hardly surprising that theatre proprietors and managers as well as performers were circumspect. As John McCormack discovered after recording 'God Save Ireland' in 1906, some songs were beyond the pale.[28]

Certain songs, such as 'The Croppy Boy,' were rarely heard in English music halls, though they featured in the annual concerts of organisations such as the Liverpool Irish Literary Society.[29] The significance of other songs was lost on English audiences, for whom 'Shan Van Vocht' was a racehorse, rather than the 'poor old woman.' But there were other venues in which song played an important part. Several melodramas, directly or indirectly, related to the injustices inflicted on the Irish. Auguste Creamer's Celtic comedy drama company offered plays such as *Coercion: or, Eileen Oge, Gallant Tipperary* and *Robert Emmett*. There could be little ambiguity about these plays – 'Bold Robert Emmett, the darling of Ireland' repeatedly laid down his life 'for the Emerald Isle.' Nor any doubt about audience responses. When Creamer's company appeared at the Stockport People's Opera House, for a week in May 1886, presenting *Arrah-na-Pogue, Kathleen Mavourneen* and *The Colleen Bawn*. it was the 'stirring and patriotic songs' that were 'received with enthusiasm by the "gods" and "pittites".'[30] Such was the concern that *Era* ran a warning piece, 'Dangerous Subjects', which singled out certain plays and songs. '*Arrah-an-Pogue* [was] the most charming and exciting of modern dramas [but] the story was rife with rebellion and patriotism from a particular Celtic point of view.' Worse, 'the song of the play "The Wearing of the Green" ... was the very essence of disaffection.'[31]

For the would-be music hall star, there was a difficult line to tread. Certain performers played safe. Pat Rafferty and Pat Casey combined comic sketches, dancing and a range of 'sentimental and humorous ditties' with no indication of social and political comment.[32] Some chose an alternative approach. Pat Rooney, a popular figure, had a repertoire, which included 'I Will Always Speak of Old Ireland with Pride' and 'Ireland Will Once More Arise from the Dust,' the latter being 'sung with immense success at Glasgow's Britannia Music Hall.'[33] Pat Feeney was a highly popular and patriotic singer but also an ardent supporter of Home Rule. His career highlights the complex, seemingly contradictory strategies needed to combine success on stage with personal political beliefs. Initially described as a comedian, within months he was being praised for his singing (at one point being described as 'the Tipperary Cuckoo,' notwithstanding the fact he was born in Birmingham) but also for his dancing.[34] He toured extensively through the country, acquiring the title 'the Shaughraun [wandering minstrel] of the Music Halls.' Early reviews spoke of the 'pleasing variety' of his Irish songs and jigs and the 'rollicking fun' of his 'caricatures of Irish life.'[35] What is more, a 'loyalty' song, sung with 'fire and force' was, according to one review of his act at the South London Palace, 'intended to show that no matter what might be said to the contrary, the men of old Ireland are as willing to die for the honour of the British flag as Englishmen, Scotchmen and Welshmen.'[36] Another London critic claimed his 'very proper idea' was 'to prove that the men who came over from Ireland have taken no small part in promoting the greatness and glory of old England.'[37] As one would-be wit put it, his song 'The rose, the shamrock and the thistle' demonstrated that 'Mr Feeney is not a *Feenyn*.'[38] In fact, this was probably a deliberate ploy, which masked a more complex figure. As an obituarist noted, Feeney 'was the most enthusiastic Home Ruler [who] in the days when Home Rule found more brickbats than sympathy in the music-halls, Pat never missed an opportunity of advocating the claim of his race.'[39] He combined 'Hibernian whimsicalities' with 'clever patriotic ditties,' championing ' with "heart and voice" the true sons of Erin.[40] Not every performance was well received. Appearing at the Canterbury, London in 1887 he was criticised for performing 'The Dove Will Fight For Freedom,' which was condemned as 'a song of rather objectionable Fenian tendencies' and 'somewhat unsuited to the audience.'[41] Nonetheless, he was generally well received in London and unequivocally so in Birmingham, Liverpool and Manchester (all with significant Irish communities) as well as in Dublin, not least because of his ongoing charity work, particularly at times of distress in Ireland.[42] The popularity of his 'patriotic' songs (and that of other pro-Irish stage productions) in England was problematic to some critics, who resorted to convoluted explanations. Despite the fact that 'The Wearing of the Green' was subversive, *Era* sought to deny the reason for its appeal by claiming that audience members were 'so carried away by the excitement to applaud the sentiments which under any other circumstance they would have most surely been the first to reprove.'[43] On other occasions, it was claimed that the audience rose above temptation. 'The people of London, and we believe of England generally, refused to take any party view ... and obstinately adhered to their original resolution of only being amused.'[44]

Irish performers, including people like Kate Carney and (the early) Bessie Bellwood, remained a key component of music hall entertainment throughout Victoria's reign and beyond. The enduring popularity of the Irish, comic, singer and dancer was firmly rooted in the appeal of the wit and verbal dexterity of those who had 'kissed the Blarney stone' while upbeat, humorous songs, stirring choruses, joyful jigs and driving reels brought considerable enjoyment to audiences across the country. The stage stereotype was part of a more complex relationship between immigrant Irish and the host communities. For English audiences, the music hall Irish confirmed pre-existing stereotypes, emphasising heavy drinking and a fondness for fisticuffs but also a naïve joviality and humour. It contributed in part to anti-Irish prejudice, in which the Irish were less civilized, uncouth 'others;' but it also made for a degree of acceptance of the good-natured, good-humoured 'Paddy.' There was a greater degree of identification on a key element of stage Irishness – the loss of village life. The sense of a lost rural community was not confined to the Irish. As urbanization proceeded apace, there was a growing divorce from the countryside, which was increasingly romanticized in art and literature as well as in various forms of music.[45]

For the smaller, but growing Irish community, the situation was different. The loquacious, jovial "Paddy" provided a convenient fiction behind which to hide, and a less threatening image to offer to a suspicious host nation. It also provided a degree of reassurance, a reminder of the resilience of those who had been uprooted and moved to a strange and often hostile world. By the end of the nineteenth century, the stereotype of the naïve country bumpkin, somewhat bemused as she or he arrives in Britain from 'the Emerald Isle,' was quite different from the lived experience of second and third generation of Irish, growing up in English towns and cities but for whom Home Rule was a crucial question. This was only partially reflected on stage. This was not to be measured simply in terms of explicitly patriotic songs. Airs that were heard in respectable English drawing rooms had a different meaning to many Irish men and women. "The Minstrel Boy" had been a popular parlour song since the late eighteenth century, but as it made its way into the music halls it became more a song of Irish resistance.[46] Nonetheless, there remained a nostalgic strand in the construction of the music-hall Irish. For emigrants hoping, however wishfully, to return home, the songs kept alive a memory of the land they had left behind, but it is was a memory that, in its fixity, became increasingly divorced from the real Ireland of the late nineteenth century. It was also a memory that had less relevance to the next generations, the London Irish, the Liverpool Irish and so forth, who had that dual identity to negotiate.[47]

In the summer of 1893, a strange transition took place. Kate Carney, the 'Champion Irish Songstress.' The singer of 'Donegal Ditties' and other patriotic Irish songs appeared on stage at Gatti's, where 'her Irish ditties met with a favourable reception' but later that evening she reappeared as 'Sarah … with matrimonial intentions [who] prefers to be conveyed to church in "a donkey cart made for two".'[48] Within months the transition was complete and she was being hailed as 'an excellent exponent of feminine life.'[49] Her subsequent success as the 'Coster Comedienne' fully justified the switch and highlighted the popularity of the 'cockney,' male and female, who had been a stalwart of music hall from its earliest days. However, the representation of the 'cockney' character evolved significantly over Victoria's reign.[50] The mid-nineteenth century 'hits,' such as 'The Ratcatcher's Daughter' and 'Vilikins and His Dinah' were essentially parodies that bore little (if any) relationship to the realities of costermonger life. They contrast with the more realistic cockney figures who appeared on the stage in the 1860s, whether Clifton's 'broken hearted milkman'[51] or Vance's 'Ticket of Leave Man,' let alone his 'Chickaleary Cove,' which combined 'cockney' and 'swell.' In the 'cockney' craze of the 1880s and 1890s 'the performer was no longer thought of as playing a role but as *being* the character.'[52] Female singers, such as Jenny Hill and Bessie Bellwood, as well as the oft-quoted Marie Lloyd, and their male counterparts, Gus Elen,

Alec Hurley and even Albert Chevalier presented themselves and were seen as quintessentially cockney.[53] Undoubtedly, appearing to be an authentic cockney (whatever that might mean!) was an important element in their success. Many working-class men and women, across the country, could and did identify with the 'cockney' characters, and their predilections and problems, as portrayed on stage. A point to which we will return in the next chapter.

Comic songs and the pleasures of everyday life

Music-hall was about entertainment and escape, however brief, from daily routines and many of the songs were, quite simply, fun. Some were simply nonsensical, such as 'What Happened to the Manx Cat's Tail' and the tongue-twisting 'She Sells Sea Shells.' In their different ways, stage aristocrats, cockneys and Irish were often figures of fun, and their songs unashamedly comic. So too were regional variants. In the north east, 'The Stage-struck Keelman' and 'He Wad Be A Noodle' were hugely successful comic songs for the Newcastle-based, Ned Corvan. Other songs, without denying life's hardships, were a celebration of life's little pleasures – from Joe Wilson's 'Thor's Comfort in a Smoke' via Gus Elen's 'Arf a Pint of Ale' to Harry Champion's 'Boiled Beef and Carrots.'[54] Camaraderie was celebrated 'Down at the Old Bull and Bush,' with Florrie Forde or at the music-hall with 'our Bessie' Bellwood. Dancing was at the heart of Kate Carney's 'Our Threepenny Hop' and Alec Hurley's 'Lambeth Walk,' while the nonsensical exuberance of the chorus of Lottie Collin's 'Ta Ra Ra Boom-De-Ay,' combined with her high kicks and the innuendo of the verses created a nation-wide hit, despite appalling respectable critics for its banality and vulgarity. Innuendo was central to many songs. Kelly Lupino's 'Queenie of the Dials' beseeched passers-by to 'squeeze me melons' while Sam Mayo 'played his concertina' in several incongruous circumstances. Gesture was also important, as (yet again) Marie Lloyd made clear – 'Every little movement has a meaning.' Many there were who would agree with her unsubtle declaration that 'A Little of What You Fancy, Does You Good.'

The 'vulgarity ... [and] stupidity' of these songs did not endear them to advocates of 'rational recreation,' who felt threatened by 'the compilation of drearily comic songsters' and by the fact that the contagion was spreading to the 'sons and daughters of the lower middle classes' who were fascinated by such 'vulgarities' as 'Pop Goes the Weasel,' 'Jump Jim Crow,' 'The Ratcatcher's Daughter,' 'The Chickalear Cove' and 'Tommy Make Room for Your Uncle.'[55] However, in their very condemnations they highlighted the success, the cross-class appeal of music hall, as well as their failure to restrict the spread of such material.[56]

Comedy could serve other purposes. It might ease pain and sorrow, particularly for the listener; it might point criticism, particularly for the lyricist. Gus Elen's 'If It Wasn't for the 'Ouses In-between' was undoubtedly humorous, from Elen's stage persona and props (watering a carrot in a pot, for example) to witty lyrics – 'Wiv a ladder and some glasses/You could see to 'Ackney Marshes/If it wasn't for the 'ouses in between' or 'And by clinging to the chimbley/You could see across to Wembley/If it wasn't for the 'ouses in between.' And there is something faintly ridiculous about the singer's rustic dreams.

> I wears this milkman's nightshirt/ And I sits outside all day
> Like the ploughboy cove what's mizzled o'er the Lea
> And when I goes indoors at night/ They dunno what I say
> 'Cause my language gets as yokel as can be.

But there is also poignancy in the lyrics. The sense of loss and/or ever-present threat is reinforced by references to specific locations. Only the decision of the London County Council to purchase 300 acres of Hackney Marshes for recreational use had saved a much-loved escape from further housebuilding. The out-of-sight Wembley was the location of a newly opened park with sporting facilities and refreshment rooms, as well as a bandstand and a music hall. But for Elen's cockney the reality of everyday life inner city life was limited space and overcrowding. It is no coincidence that the song was dedicated to campaigning journalist G R Sims.[57] Whether audiences were fully aware of this or sympathised with the critical sentiment is a moot point.

Some concluding observations

The songs considered in this chapter point to a number of important observations. The importance of escapist enjoyment is most clearly seen in the character of 'the swell.' Audiences, largely drawn from the poorer sections of society, were invited into the company of outlandish, larger-than-life characters whose extravagant lifestyle was far removed from everyday reality. There was also something aspirational in some of the 'swell' songs – the hope of buying the lucky lottery ticket or becoming 'The Man Who Broke the Bank.' The stage Irish character also offered an element of escapism into a world of joviality and sentimentality, often linked to a lost rural idyll. Many of the comic songs associated with cockney characters celebrated the pleasures of everyday life, food, drink and company but these were ubiquitous sentiments popular across the country and found in regional variants.

And yet there was always more than simple comedy and escapism. Jenny Hill, for example, combined light-hearted characters and songs with material that looked at several social issues of the day. Through a range of characters, clearly working-class women ('Knowing Servant Girl, and 'The Coffee Shop Girl'), some more specifically 'costers' ('The Flower Seller' and 'The Muffin and Crumpet Seller's Daughter), Hill (and other singers) were able to focus on a range of subjects – courtship and marriage, work and economic realities, even politics – relevant to their audiences.[58] . This raises the broader question of whether the music hall should be seen as a 'culture of consolation,' or whether it was more complex, and more subversive. The next chapter looks at social and economic issues, the following chapter at politics.

Endnotes

1. 'A Chat with Joseph Tabrar,' *Era*, 10 February 1894, 'A Chat with Felix McGlennon,' *Era*, 10 March 1894 and 'A Chat with G W Hunt,' *Era*, 17 March 1894.
2. A Bennett, 'Music in the Halls' in J S Bratton, ed., *Music Hall: Performance and Style*, Milton Keynes, Open University Press, 1986, pp.1-22
3. *Pall Mall Gazette*, 25 September 1896 cited in L Wingrove, 'Reigniting the 'vital spark': Reimagining and reclaiming the repertoire, career development and image cultivation of serio-comediennes Jenny Hill and Bessie Bellwood from 1870 to 1896', unpublished Ph.D., University of Bristol, 2016
4. P Bailey, 'Conspiracies of Meaning: Music Hall and the Knowingness of Popular Culture,' *Past & Present*, 144, 1994, pp.138-70
5. F Freeman, *Weekly Despatch*, 4 February 1883 cited in Bailey 'Conspiracies of Meaning' p.158
6. By the turn of the century, Bailey argues, this knowingness had become a second language for all classes.
7. Ross, one of the first 'one-hit wonders,' was said to have 'a truly magnificent voice' and his 'long descriptive songs … took well nigh half an hour to execute.' 'A Chat with Arthur Lloyd,' Era, 29 July 1893. See also the description in G W M Reynolds, *The Mysteries of the Courts of London*, vol.5, London, John Dicks, 1869, p.279. 'Sam Hall' was an adaptation of the eighteenth-century ballad, 'Jack Hall.'
8. See G Speaight, *Bawdy Songs of the Early Music Hall*, London, Pan Books, 1975. Among the more predictable titles are 'The Bower that stands in Thigh Lane' and 'Man's Yard of Stuff.' More interesting was the use of well-known traditional tunes. 'There's Somebody Coming' was set to the tune, 'Paddy Whack' and 'The Copper Stick,' described as 'a famous new smutty ditty never before printed,' set to 'The White Cockade.'

9   The Sam Cowell Comic Song Book 1858 can be accessed at https://archive.org/details/samcowellscomics00unse/page/n1 In addition, the collection includes such well-established songs and tunes as 'The Low Backed Car', 'Bonnie Dundee' and 'We won't go home till morning'.
10 The best introduction remains P Bailey, 'Champagne Charlie: Performance and Ideology in the Music Hall Swell Song' in J S Bratton, ed., *Music Hall: Performance and Style*, pp.49-69. In addition to those listed above, there were a whole range of singers *à la* Vance to be heard in minor provincial music halls. *Era* 11 April and 22 September 1867 for examples. These songs had their roots, in part at least, in the earlier song-and-supper rooms. One collection of Coal Hole bawdy songs was entitled *The Swell's Album*.
11 Bailey refers to Leybourne's popularity in Leeds and Bradford but his performances were well received in other cities (for example Hull, *Era*, 10 February 1867 and Liverpool, *Liverpool Mercury*, 17 July 1878) but also in smaller towns, such as Huddersfield (*Huddersfield Chronicle*, 7 March 1874), Middlesbrough (*Middlesbrough Evening Gazette*, 25 October 1870) and Sunderland (*Sunderland Daily Echo*, 28 September 1875 and 11 March 1879).
12 *Era* 10 February 1867
13 See particularly P Mason, *The English Gentleman*, London, Pimlico, 1993, chap. 7 'The Gentleman as Sportsman.'
14 Bailey asks: is this sex for those who don't want it, or sex for those who can't get it, or sex for those who couldn't handle it if they did? 'Champagne Charlie' p.62
15 See also Dickens' comments on Greenwich Fair in chapter 3.
16 Bailey refers to the link with cheap tailoring, 'Champagne Charlie' p.60
17 Cited in Bailey, 'Champagne Charlie' p.51
18 *Era* 3 June 1866
19 *Leeds Times*, 31 October 1868
20 *Leeds Times*, 8 May 1867. However, the paper conceded that 'Miss Nelly Power … is worthy of all the applause she gets.'
21 *Leeds Times*, 27 November 1869
22 Bailey, 'Champagne Charlie,' p.67. Bailey explicitly links the emergence of the "swell" to the development of capitalist society, seeing him as 'the product of a larger system of liberal capitalism that was now offering its subordinates a greater share of its economic surplus, while offering a fuller sense of membership.'
23 *Westminster Review*, 1838, p.240
24 Among Moore's *Irish Melodies*, 'The Last Rose of Summer,' 'The Minstrel Boy' and 'Endearing Young Charms' were particularly popular. French's most popular songs included the sentimental 'Mountains of Mourne' and the comic 'Phil the Fluter's Ball' not to mention the distinctly un-Irish 'Abdulla Bulbul Ameer.' Samuel Lover, the least well-known of the trio is best known for 'The Low-backed Car,' 'The Girl I Left Behind Me' and 'Molly Bawn', from his comic opera 'Il Paddy Whack in Italia.'
25 A similar pattern emerges from Mervyn Busted's analysis of references to the Irish in the Axon collection mid-nineteenth century ballads, 'Songs in a strange land – ambiguities of identity amongst Irish migrants in mid-Victorian Manchester,' *Political Geography*, 17(6) 1998, pp.627-665.

26 John McCormack made the song even more famous when he recorded it in 1911.
27 P Maloney, ''Flying Down the Saltmarket': The Irish on the Glasgow Music Hall Stage,' *Nineteenth Century Theatre and Film*, 36(10) 2009, pp.11-36.
28 T D Sullivan wrote the words celebrating the Manchester Martyrs in 1867, using an American tune, 'Tramp, Tramp, Tramp.' It was quickly taken up as the Irish national anthem and remained popular as late as the Easter Rising of 1916. It featured prominently in various anti-English lecture tours and demonstrations. G F Train who delivered a lecture 'Irish nationality and the coming downfall of the English oligarchy used the song to 'stir up the people' and in several venues 'the audience lustily joined in the chorus.' *Leeds Mercury*, 16 June 1868 and *Cornwall Gazette*, 25 June 186. In 1889 the crowd demonstrating against the imprisonment of Irish political prisoners was opened and closed by a band playing the song (*Glasgow Herald*, 11 February 1889) and when Bonar Law arrived in Dublin in November 1912 attempts to sing 'God Save the King' were drowned out by 'God Save Ireland.' *Manchester Courier*, 29 November 1912.
29 *Liverpool Mercury*, 3 December 1895. Among various songs performed that evening were 'The Croppy Boy,' 'God Save Ireland,' 'The Wearing of the Green' and 'The Boys of Wexford.' Mid-century ballads also focused on contemporary issues, notably the Manchester martyrs, as well as celebrating the heroes of the past. Busted, 'Songs in a strange land' especially pp.656-9
30 *Era* 22 May 1886
31 *Era*, 2 March 1879
32 *Era* 28 March 1896. The reference was specifically to Rafferty but applied equally to Casey. Both men started as comics before extending their act to include singing and dancing. Both toured extensively and enjoyed careers that lasted from the 1880s to the 1900s.
33 Maloney, ''Flying Down the Saltmarket' p.22. Rooney was also popular in several English cities with a large Irish population.
34 He was noted for his jigs but on several occasions delighted audiences with his set dances.
35 *Era*, 11 June 1876 and 4 August 1883
36 *Era*, 6 January 1883.
37 *Era*, 14 January 1888
38 *The Stage*, 2 September 1881
39 *Paisley and Renfrewshire Gazette*, 18 May 1889
40 *Lloyd's Weekly*, 9 January 1887 and *Era*, 12 July 1884 and 4 September 1886
41 *Era*, 8 January 1887
42 For example, in 1880 and again in 1889. The latter concert was particularly poignant. Feeney's 'great energy' enabled him to raise £2,000 'on behalf of the recent distress in the West of Ireland.' It also aggravated his already declining health and shortly afterwards he died – penniless. *Lloyd's Weekly*, 8 February 1880 and *Freeman's Journal*, 14 March and 11 April 1889. Feeney died in the May of that year.
43 *Era*, 2 March 1879
44 *Era*, 2 March 1879

45 G E Mingay, ed., *The Rural Idyll*, London, Routledge, 1989. See chapter 4 fn.12 for further references.
46 Although criticised for making Irish airs palatable to the English, several (about a third) of Moore's *Irish Melodies* were political. He had known Robert Emmett and 'Oh breathe not his name' is a lament for him. Conservative British periodicals, such as *Blackwood's Magazine*, were concerned with the subversive nature of Moore's *Melodies*. The *New Monthly Magazine* saw them as 'a vehicle for dangerous politics.' Quoted in T M Love, 'Gender and the Nationalistic Ballad: Thomas Davis, Thomas Moore and their songs,' *New Hibernia Review*, 21 (1), 2017, pp.68-85 at p.75.
47 The relationship is complex. The evidence from London in the 1940s and 1950s clearly indicates the importance of pub music sessions to Irish emigrants, seeking to preserve their 'Irishness.' However, the so-called 'authentic' music was often viewed as quaint by relatives in Ireland. For a discussion of the complex and disputed construction of Irishness in parts of post-war Britain see M Leoneard, 'Performing identities: music and dance in the Irish communities of Coventry and Liverpool, *Social and Cultural Geography*, 6(4), 2006, pp.515-29
48 *Era* 1 July 1893. See also 29 March & 26 March 1890, 23 Mat & 14 November 1891, 16 April 1892 for references
49 *Era* 16 February 1895. See also *Era* 13 January 1894 for a list of her songs – all cockney.
50 D B Scott, 'The Music Hall Cockney: Flesh and Blood, or Replicant?' *Music & Letters*, 83(2), 2002, pp.237-58
51 'The broken-hearted milkman' kept the company of 'pretty little Polly Perkins of Paddington Green' in the song of the same name.
52 Scott 'Music Hall Cockney' p.247
53 Scott argues, 'the cockney character [was] a desired image created by the music hall and perpetuated by the music hall's feeding on itself.' There is a danger of overstating both the degree of self-reflexivity and the creation of desired image devoid of real-world content, particularly in the late-Victorian and Edwardian years His argument has greater force when applied to Dick Van Dyke's toe-curling performance in 'Mary Poppins' and even to the bizarre 'cockneys' of Walford.
54 Harry Champion was particularly prolific with a range of food and drink songs: 'The Old Red Lion,' 'Another little drink,' 'Have a drop of gin, Joe,' 'Hot meat pies, saveloys and trotters,' A good blow out for fourpence' and 'Let's have a basin of soup,' Venturing further afield he also praised 'Good old Yorkshire pudden' as well as extolling the virtues of 'Gorgonzola Cheese,' though his wedding-night ditty, 'Put a bit of treacle on my puddin', Mary Ann' is somewhat ambiguous. See also Charles Coburn 'Come where the booze is cheaper,' and Harry Freeman and Harry Anderson, both celebrating 'Glorious Beer.'
55 C Mackay, 'English Songs, Ancient and Modern,' *Nineteenth Century*, December 1884
56 The sale of sheet music an indicator of popularity. Arthur Lloyd's 'Not for Joseph,' huge stage hit, became the first comic song to sell 100,000 copies of sheet music. Lloyd was associated with numerous comic songs including

'The German Band,' 'Chillingowullabadorie,' 'The Postman,' 'Dobbs in Paris,' 'Angelina Was Fond of the Soldiers,' of which only 'Married to a Mermaid' remained popular into the twentieth century.

57 P Norris, *A Cockney At Work: The Story of Gus Elen & His Songs*, London, Grosvenor House, 2014, pp.210-5

58 These examples are drawn from the detailed study by L Wingrove, 'Reigniting the 'vital spark'. As Wingrove notes both women also portrayed upper-class women, such as 'The Duchess of Petticoat Lane (Bessie Bellwood) and 'Lady Gay' and 'Miss Dashaway' (Jenny Hill).

CHAPTER 10

'A little of what you fancy': Love, marriage and other social problems

> I am a girl what's a-doing very well in the wegetable line
> And as I'd saved a bob or two, I thought I'd cut a shine
> So I goes and buys some toggery, these 'ere wery clothes you see
> And with the money I had left, I thought I'd have a spree
> So I goes into a Music Hall, where I'd often been afore
> I don't go in the gallery, but on the bottom floor
> I sits down by the chairman, and calls for a pot of stout
> My pals in the gallery, spotted me, and they all commenced to shout.
>
> Bessie Bellwood, 'What Cheer, 'Ria'

MUSIC HALL WAS the business of pleasure. Its prime functions were to entertain and to generate profits. Lyricists were largely interested in writing hit songs, not providing incisive social commentary. Performers saw themselves as entertainers not educationalists. However, the subject matter of many songs related directly to a range of mundane social and economic issues and the way in which they were treated provide insights, wittingly or otherwise, into contemporary attitudes. Many of the songs dealing with love and marriage were conventional, reflecting the dominant values of a patriarchal society in which the family was seen as the bedrock of morality and social stability. Although harsher realities intruded at times, the threat they posed was often diffused through humour. Further, the treatment of social problems, while evoking sympathy for individual victims, never explicitly challenged the social and economic order that gave rise to them; nor those who defended that order. In contrast to melodrama, music-hall song tended to be sympathetic towards the police, laughing at their human weaknesses for food and fair damsels but rarely criticising the way in which they went about their work.

Love and marriage

Love, marriage and family featured in numerous songs, though the treatment could vary considerably. While often seen as 'eternal' themes, the songs need to be understood in a more specific late-nineteenth century context in which 'natural' gender roles and institutions, in the minds of many, were being questioned, even undermined. The 'New Woman,' seeking independence, education, professional employment and even the vote was a contentious figure. Equally, if less publicised, the middle-class male 'flight from domesticity' appeared to cast doubt on an institution once seen as natural and God-given.[1] Music-hall songs celebrating love and marriage were generally conservative, upholding marriage and a 'separate spheres' ideology. This does not mean that every love song was an explicit comment. Joe Wilson's 'Sally Wheatley' was a sorrowful tale of missed opportunity and lost love. George Leybourne's 'Sarah's Gone And Left Me' comically bemoaned the sorry plight of 'a sandwich man' whose love for the eponymous Sarah, a nursemaid, is thwarted by the dastardly cat-meat man, who seduces her with a half-price skewer of meat.[2] Nonetheless, there was a general assumption that love would lead to marriage and a family life.

Love was often seen in romantic terms, foreshadowing the American popular songs of the 1920s and 1930s. In 'Love is a Mystery. Love is a Dream,' Albert Chevalier sang 'Love is romantic whatever may be said' and 'Love is the essence of life that we live.' Courtship could have its moments of harmless 'spooning', but marriage was the 'natural' outcome, even if early encounters were fun. Following 'a charming game of croquet,' Arthur Lloyd discovered 'it's naughty but it's nice,' only to find himself on the brink of matrimony within four verses. Women echoed these sentiments, though at times more whimsically. Daisy Dormer declared:

> Ain' it nice when he offers you a poppy
> Ain' it nice when he looks at you so sloppy?
> Ain' it nice when you're squeezing in the doorway
> Ain' it nice though it's colder far than Norway?'

The outcomes were predictable. 'Soon the bells, wedding bells, ring ding, dong/ Man and wife, tied for life, good and strong'.[3]

Within the family, generally speaking, mothers were seen in a positive, if sentimentalised, light, captured in Gus Elen's 'Coster Muvver.' Looking upward, pointing to heaven with cap screwed tightly in hand, he delivered a tear-jerking chorus.

> She's just the sort a muvver that a bloke wants, eh!
> Ah, when she's took'd away I won't feel wery gay,
> As far as me and 'eaven's concern'd I don't put on no side,
> But if muvver ain't a-goin' in, well this bloke stops outside.

Other songs, like 'Mother's Advice,' were more light-hearted, but even here mother as font of knowledge and support was the underlying message. Fathers in comparison, were painted less favourably. Some were lazy, as in 'We All Go to Work but Father,' others incompetent, as in 'When Father Laid the Carpet on the Stairs' or 'When Father Papered the Parlour.' Almost without exception, they were dependent on their wives. In 'Skylark, Skylark,' Arthur Lennard's 'dear little boy' pleaded with the skylark: 'If among the angels mother you see/ Ask her if she will come down again/ To poor dear Daddy and me.'[4] Such sentiments chime with the observations of people like Robert Roberts, who emphasised the central role that women played in working-class society, but they also provided a comic cover for patriarchal authority, by ridiculing individuals who failed to 'be a man.'

Marriage was eulogised, as in Katie Lawrence's 'My Old Man' with its chorus:

> My old man! My dear old man!
> Best in the world since the world began.
> In joy and tears,
> Through forty years,
> Always true and faithful to me, my old man.[5]

Georgina Leonard's 'Shadows on the Blind' paid tribute to a long and successful marriage, but couched in unambiguously patriarchal terms with its image of an old couple: 'Fifty years they've pulled together since their love tales first were told/ He is proud to love and cherish and his will she still obeys,' a sentiment given more lasting form in 'Silver Threads Among the Gold.' Marriage and family were brought together in idealised form by both Ella Retford and Daisy Dormer in 'I Want a Girl Just Like the Girl that Married Dear Old Dad.' Even in the light-hearted, 'When I Prove False to Thee,' – at which time, according to Arthur Lloyd, 'the tide shall cease its flowing' and 'the cocks will stop their crowing' – the underlying sentiment is of undying love.

Enduring love in the form of the devoted couple appear regularly. Even in Jenny Hill's harsh world the 'aged couple [who] have drifted downwards, been of all bereft' still have their love. 'Death alone can part faithful heart from heart.' In more sentimental manner, Albert Chevalier was hugely successful with 'My Old Dutch.'

> Sweet fine old gal,
> For worlds I wouldn't lose 'er,
> She's a dear good old gal,
> An' that's what made me choose 'er.
> She's stuck to me through thick and thin,
> When luck was out, when luck was in,
> Ahl wot a wife to me she's been,
> An' wot a pal!

Marriage was not always seen in positive terms. Several songs warned against it in variations of the traditional 'When I was single' complaint. In some men were trapped – 'She was one of the early birds and I was one of the worms.' More often women were the victims. 'Girls of today … don't realise how deceitful men are,' according to Vesta Victoria. Jennie Hill, 'the Vital Spark,' was among the most pessimistic.[6] A hugely successful and wonderfully exuberant performer, noted as much for her dancing as her singing, Hill portrayed a range of characters over the course of her career but much of her act focused on the lives of working-class women. The procession of down-trodden mothers and disillusioned wives combined with the unambiguously titled, though unpublished songs, such as 'I've Been A Good Woman to You,' 'Who'd Be A Mother,' 'Woe Is The Mother Who Owns Eleven' and 'A Woman's Work Is Never Done' made clear the harsh realities of working-class married life.[7] Although some critics dismissed 'I've Been A Good Woman To You' as 'inconsequential and self-satisfied,' other reports speak of the 'general and fervent expressions of admiration' called forth by her characterisation of a fierce, if lachrymose wife.[8] Similarly, her rendition of 'I'm Determined No Longer To Stand It.' at London's Royal music-hall, was 'very warmly applauded.'[9] Some songs hinted at acts of resistance. Hill was not averse to threatening various dreadful things with a rolling pin to her 'wicked and disobedient husband' but, in another song, she made clear, more radically, that she 'mean[s] to have a legal separation.'[10]

Others seemed to subvert convention through role reversal. Florrie Forde's 'Good Little Wife' was well in control of her husband. 'She calls him her 'honey' and spends all his money/ Like a good little wife should do.' Moreover, 'She makes him sift cinders and clean all the winders/ Like a good little wife should do.' The hen-pecked husband was a figure of fun, reminiscent of a Bamforth post-card, as in 'Just to Show Who Was Boss in The House.' Having been told his wife wears the trousers, Jack Pleasant's character, seeks to prove otherwise:

> Just to show who was the boss of the house
> I went and I washed all the clothes
> I scrubbed all the pans and I cleaned all the mugs
> I made all the beds and filled all the jugs
> I didn't get finished till evening

> Then she started my temper to rouse
> So I went and did the place over again
> Just to show who was the boss of the house.

Such 'comedy' songs, again, strengthened the belief that the man should be in charge by ridiculing the one who was not. Also, they could disguise a more sinister reality – domestic violence. The scandal of 'wife-beating' was a cause for concern for a small number of social reformers, who often highlighted working-class barbarity, especially in the so-called 'kicking districts' of north-west England. Popular attitudes were less straightforward. Court records reveal the prevalence of violence against women, and also a general acceptance of the need for and acceptability of male-applied discipline. The right to chastise wives, children and servants, went largely unchallenged. Only when it was taken too far was there a popular outcry.[11] Domestic violence appeared in various forms of popular culture. Melodrama lent itself more readily to serious consideration but even here domestic violence was often seen simply as the result of drunkenness. In comparison, music hall rarely addressed the question directly. However, there was unwitting testimony, notably in one of the most popular songs around the turn of the twentieth century.

Gus Elen's 'It's A Great Big Shame,' with its sub-title, 'I'm Blowed If 'E Can Call 'Isself 'Is Own,' is often cited as a humorous song, lamenting the fate of a hen-pecked husband. It is the story of a (supposedly) proper man emasculated by a diminutive, shrew-like wife of four foot two. Jim, his 'pal … as 'ad ter 'nuckle dahn [despite being] a brewer's drayman, wiva leg of mutton fist.' His physical strength ('It took two coppers for ter make 'im move along/ An annuver six to 'old the feller dahn') is contrasted with the demeaning tasks (cleaning windows and knives, scrubbing floors and 'wiv a apron on 'im on 'is knees a-rubbin' up the old 'arf-stone') that he has been forced to do. The chorus, which contains the ominous words 'an' if she belong'd ter me, I'd let 'er know who's who,' was accompanied by on-stage actions, caught on camera in the early 1930s, that made clear that the solution lies in firm, physical action. The song was reputedly a favourite among men in the gallery.[12] It proved immensely popular for

Elen and was also sung (and parodied) by men and women across the country in a wide variety of venues. *Era*, which described the song as a 'classic,' praised its 'lighter vein' with its 'savage lamentations at the miserable fate of Drayman Jim … [and his] hymeneal martyrdom.'[13] Only the *Pall Mall Gazette* 'grumbled,' taking exception to 'the introduction of the very material coke-hammer to emphasize his sentiments' on the grounds that Elen's comedic skills were such that he did not need 'such extraneous aids.'[14]

Domestic violence also appears in Marie Lloyd's 'It's A Bit of Ruin That Cromwell Knocked About A Bit.' The first chorus opens 'it's a bit of a ruin' but concludes with the singer confessing: 'Outside the Oliver Cromwell last Saturday night, I was one of the ruins Cromwell knocked about a bit.' Subsequent choruses retained the final lines but opened 'I'm one of the ruins …' Lloyd's turbulent marriage with Alec Hurley was well-known and few in the audience could have been unaware of the references. Indeed, many of Lloyd's later songs were wistful reflections on the plight of the older woman – 'You're A Thing of The Past, Old Dear' and 'I Live in Hopes'[15] – though none referenced violence directly. Violence also figured in Dan Leno's 'My Old Man.' Recounted by the wife, 'ten years … a wedded martyr,' who, having fallen for the rosy image of marriage, finds 'that matrimony means black eyes and broken noses, [while] bread and cheese is flavoured with a hob-nailed boot.' Disillusionment set in for 'not a week had we been wed, when he punched me in the head,' and 'As years go on his love for me decreases, But I'll make him suffer sure as eggs are eggs' and in the final chorus violence begets violence: 'as sure as I'm his wife, this night I'll have his life.'

Such songs, however, were the exception. Insofar as marriage was problematic, the issues were diffused via humour – as in 'Whit Cunliffe's 'The Matrimonial Handicap' – but also used to reinforce conventional morality. In Arthur Lloyd's 'German Band' the wife runs off with a strolling flautist, only to be abandoned and reduced to 'charring for a shilling a day.' The implicit (and conservative) message, that those who flaunt marriage are duly punished, is clear. Similarly, in Vesta Tilley's 'The Parson and The Cook', the errant cook, canoodling with the parson Jones, is sacked and the parson suffers the indignity of having his hair and whiskers torn. Generally speaking, errant husbands get off lightly. The various male miscreants, husbands at work or fathers in 'gay Paree,' when caught out, are exhorted only to 'Hold Your Hand Out, You Naughty Boy.' In the 1913 song, 'Don't Say a Word to the Wife,' the matter is swept under the carpet. The philandering Peter Henry seduces a girl in Brighton and, on being told he is 'the father of a fine boy,' responds in the words of the song title and explains 'there'll be trouble waiting for me if she hears about it [because] … If she finds out, you see, she'll put all the blame on me.' So "sh not a word to the wife.'

Social problems

The wider economic context, employment and its insecurities, poverty and the threat of destitution were a staple of popular culture in general. Again, melodrama lent itself more readily to treating such problems. Certain theatres, such as the Britannia, conscious of their neighbourhood audiences, offered a range of social commentary plays including *Work Girls of London, London by Night; The Streets of London; The Casual Ward*; and *The Artificial Flower-makers*.[16] It was easy to criticise their simplistic and conservative critiques.[17] As *Era*, in a review of *Sons of the Forge*, commented: 'a hero drawn from the poorer classes and the villain of the piece from the 'bloated aristocracy' will always furnish a palatable drama for an East End audience.'[18] However, there was a strong sense of injustice and a belief that society should be run on moral lines.

Music hall also featured 'social problems,' but many issues were diluted and defused through humour. The tensions created by living cheek by jowl in overcrowded rooms are treated in light-hearted fashion in three of Joe Wilson's songs: 'The Neebors Daan Belaw,' 'The Row on the Stairs' and especially, 'Keep Yor Feet Still! Geordie Hinny.' Similarly, the well-known, 'Cock Linnet Song,' (aka 'My Old Man') dealt with a very real problem (the inability to pay the rent) and a common response (a moonlight flit) but the humour of the words, and the catchiness of the tune, could detract from the seriousness of the situation. It contrasts with the more realistic but dour, temperance-inspired, 'Father, Dear Father, The Brokers Are In,' which laments the fate of starving mother and children while father drank away his wages. Albert Chevalier in 'The Jeerusalem's Dead' similarly reduces a major economic blow to any costermonger, the death of his donkey, to something comic.[19] Even accidental deaths, at home and at work, could be given a (grim) humorous twist. As the chorus of 'More Work For the Undertaker' made clear such unfortunate mishaps led to: 'More work for the Undertaker/ Another little job for the tombstone maker.'

Occasionally, the humour barely masked a more serious comment. 'The Pawnshop Bleezin'' with its jaunty tune appears initially to be comic. Based on a real incident, the destruction of Trotter's pawnshop in Newcastle in 1849, the song appears to be a humorous description of the chaos following the fire. The detail paints a different picture of anguish.

> The wimmin folk 'twas sair to see
> Lamentin' their distresses
> For mony a goon, an' white shemee,
> Was burnt wi' bairns' dresses.

And reveals a range of underlying problems:

> An' when wor Billy finds it oot,
> There'll murder be, aw hae nee doot;
> Oh dear! What garr'd me put them in?
> 'Twas a' the races an' cursed gin –
> That set my claes a-bleezin'

Before concluding:

> The world was better far aw'm sure
> When Pawnshops had ne neym, man;
> When poor folks could their breed procure,
> Without a *deed o' sheym*, man.

At a time when the London poor were coming under scrutiny, from the investigative journalism of G R Sims to the more scientific research of Charles Booth, some songs cast (or appeared to cast) an eye on the realities of the streets. A common device was to have an observer in a specific location or institution who detailed the characters before them. In 'One of The Sights of London' Arthur Lennard noted the co-existence of wealth and poverty. The 'gilded youths' around St James' contrast with the orphaned coster boy.

> He's one of the mites of London
> Cruel old London Town
> Many the mites you view as you
> Go strolling up and down
> Starving amid the splendour, tortured by hunger's
>   blights
> There's no one to help him, no mother to love
> One of London's poor little mites.

In Jenny Hill's 'Thereby Hangs A Tale,' the narrator is a stowaway, who catalogues a sorry parade of doss house characters down on their luck, the one-time lawyer, the married couple who have lost all, and especially 'Crazy Sal.'

> Muttering in a corner o'er a crust of bread
> Crazy Sal they call her, sits with palsied head
>   Hear her dreary laughter, see her skinny hands
> As the drink fiends gather round in grissly bands
>   Hear her shriek and say, 'Devils get away
> Look how they laugh and grin, Oh for God's sake,
>   Gin,'[20]

The common theme is people down on their luck and reduced to poverty, though no back story is provided, and the implicit moral is not to judge by appearances. The same theme emerges from her highly popular, 'City Waif,' though this time there are more of the street folk noted by Sims or Mayhew. The watercress seller, Sal Brown, is probably a prostitute ('some say she ain't no better, ain't Sal, than she ought to be/ P'raps she ain't, p'raps she is) but she saves the life of the waif's crippled sister. The refrain drives home the message.

> Then up comes Sal Brown at that moment and,
>   rough as she is – says she
> 'Take this money, here. Run for food boy.' Then she
>   took Kitty on her knee
> She saved the life of my sister, and though people
>   run her down
> She played an angel's part, that night, in the streets of
>   London Town.

These songs held up a partial picture of street life. They exhibit sympathy for victims, especially deserving figures such as the orphaned child, but there is little overt criticism of the existing socio-economic circumstances that created the problems. Insofar as solutions are offered, they tend to be couched in terms of individual decency. As the title of G W Hunter song exhorted, 'Give What You Can to Those in Distress.'

There was also a sense of fatalism, as in songs like 'Life Is Like A Game of Seesaw,' which ran alongside an emphasis on self-reliance as in 'A Motto for Every Man' with its chorus:

> So we will sing and banish melancholy
> Trouble may come; we'll do the best we can
> To drive care away, for grieving is a folly
> Put your shoulder to the wheel is a motto for every
>   man.

The titles of two of Harry Clifton's motto songs, 'Paddle Your Own Canoe' and 'Work Boy, Work and Be Contented' encapsulate this mentality. The chorus of the latter was unambiguous in its naive faith in hard work:

> So work boys work and be contented
> As long as you've enough to buy a meal.
> The man you may rely, will be wealthy by and bye,
> If he'll only put his shoulder to the wheel.

Scarcely more sympathetic was Gus Elen's 'Wait Till the Work Comes Round.' The song title and the opening lines of the chorus appear to combine sympathy and fatalism: 'What's the use of kicking up a row/ If there ain't no work about? But, as the scene in which he appeared on stage made clear, there was little sympathy for the unemployed. A tatty room, dirty crockery and empty beer bottles met the eye and the scene was entitled 'The Wrong-Un's Bedroom at noon.' At a time when the plight of the unemployed was a major political issue, there is little sympathy for the idea that one should 'wait till the work comes round.' Such is the burden of the song that the humour in the chorus does not ask the audience to identify with such sentiments as 'lay your head back on yer piller and read yer 'Daily Mirrer,' let alone the claim ' if you can't get work you can't get the sack/That's a argument that's sensible and sound.' But some in the audience might have taken a different view, sharing the sentiments in W P Dempsey's parody, 'Work and Be Contented.'

> Now you don't require a job,
> to obtain the merry bob,
> As frequently I fancy it's been shown;
> Many Artful Codgers thrive and by hook or crook survive
> To obtain a decent living on their own.
> In the light-fingered trade there's a fortune to be made,
> Provided you are smart as well as quick,
> And altho' it's not allowed, when you're mixed up in a crowd,
> And you see any pockets there to pick.

There were some other important exceptions. Ned Corvan's 'Sweating System' made clear that 'working men are still opprest,' while Joe Wilson's 'Ne Wark' paints a stark picture of the unemployed: 'What wretchedness, what misery.' The stark lyrics of the latter contrast with the jauntiness of the tune, 'Pretty Polly Perkins,' to which it is set. Both men drew attention to the problems facing colliers. The physical dangers were highlighted in 'In Memory of the Hartley Catastrophe' and 'Perils of the Mine, or the Collier's Death.' Poverty-driven emigration was the subject of 'Astrilly' or the Pitman's Farewell.'[21]

> Aw mind the time when collier lads cud work for
>   goold at hyem, man:
> Dash! Aw mind the time when collier lads cud
>   spend a pund each day;
> But noo the times thoor queer, man, we've nowther
>   sangs nor cheers, man;
> When we cannit raise wor beer, man, it's time te gan
>   away.

The social order, as much as the economic, was also generally viewed conservatively. While the desire for a lucky break never disappeared – that wish to be 'The Man Who Broke the Bank at Monte Carlo' – people with pretensions, living above their station were either ridiculed or condemned. With their new donkey shay, following the death of 'rich Uncle Tom of Camberwell, the central couple in 'Knocked 'Em In The Old Kent Road,' are figures of fun because they think of themselves 'carriage folk … like the toffs as rides in Rotten Row.' More savage is the critique in ''E Dunno Where 'E Are.' Market trader Jack Jones is another beneficiary of a will but this time his pretensions lead to isolation.[22]

> When I see the way 'e treats old pals
> I am filled wiv nothing but disgust
> 'E sez as 'ow we isn't class enuf
> 'E sez we ain't upon a par.

Smoking a cigar rather than a pipe, and 'wiv a top 'at on,' he ends up 'drinking Scotch and Soda on his own.' There was a 'natural' social order that to challenge was a risk.

The 'natural' gender roles of men and women were reinforced in many songs, but some performers challenged these assumptions. As Jenny Hill established herself as a major music-hall serio-comedienne in the 1870s, her repertoire contained a number of songs that challenged the position of men. So alongside songs, such as 'I'll Meet You Love Along the Line' and 'The Boy in the Gallery,' which were conventional love songs, she also sang 'Bother the Men,' 'A Fig for Men' and 'I'm Determined To No Longer Stand It.' 'Bother the Men' was originally a song performed by Mrs Howard Paul that made fun of advocates of rights for women. She appeared as 'Miss GRYM' to deliver a 'RED HOT LECTURE ON WOMAN'S RIGHTS.'[23] Jenny Hill's character, Miss Grym, appeared to be similar – an old maid to be laughed at whose arguments were nonsense – but her performances were somewhat different.[24] At the London Pavilion in January 1872, as well as singing the song, she 'upheld the rights of women and advocated their claim to wear the breeches.' Furthermore, 'the Chairman, at whom she levelled many of her remarks had rather a bad time of it.'[25] This was not an isolated incident and these outbursts enabled her to create 'an opportunity for her working-class female audience to enjoy hearing abuse leveled [sic] at men as well as the middle-classes.'[26] Later in her career Hill also commented on the contentious issue of women's education. Unlike several of her songs, this was published, suggesting that the lyrics were less likely to offend. The chorus appears to be a conservative rejection of the notion of extending female education.

> I don't believe in teaching girls
> Such trouble as the Rule of Three.
> If they only know their Ps and Qs
> They can do without your ABC.

However, her patter in performance puts things in a different light. 'Education is becoming a terrible nuisance – all the girls are getting to be such wonderful scholars that there'll soon be nothing left for men to teach us – not that they ever could teach us much, poor wretches.'[27]

Elsewhere, progressive women were treated less sympathetically. 'Happy' Fanny Field's 'The Suffragette' views 'men as simply worms' and will 'put the whole world out of joint' to get the vote.[28] Even more scathing, Jock Mills in 'The Suffragee' had no doubt that the patriarchal order was under threat. The poor 'downtrodden man' had been reduced to washing and scrubbing since his wife joined 'the Down with Men club.' Her fellow suffragettes were 'mostly old maids laid on the shelf,' and she managed to compound her treasonable and unfeminine behaviour by losing her temper, getting into a fight and being rushed to jail whilst in London protesting.[29]

This was not dissimilar from the spate of antifeminist cartoons that ridiculed and vilified advocates of female suffrage.

The Police

Another topic with strong political connotations was policing. The debate about police reform, from the early nineteenth century onwards, was highly contentious, raising questions about personal liberties and the relationship between the state and the individual. The 'new police,' not just in London, faced suspicion at best, outright hostility at worst.[30] Despite a crime fighting/thin blue line rhetoric, the bulk of police work was mundane, concerned with establishing and maintaining 'order and decorum' in public places. Increasingly, police work seemed to focus on minor offences, committed overwhelmingly by working-class men, women and children, for whom the streets were the place of work and leisure.

Old and new policemen were to be found in many forms of popular culture but with significant differences of emphasis in their treatment. There was a long tradition of mocking constables, particularly in pantomime. In the first decade of the nineteenth century, at Covent Garden, Grimaldi shut a watchman in his box, stole his lantern and sounded his rattle to create scenes of mayhem in which two buffoonish watchmen mistakenly fight each other, much to the delight of the audience.[31] The 'bobby' soon became a staple comic character in Victorian pantomime but the humour was generally benign. In the 1871 Crystal Palace pantomime, there was 'a model policeman who is always "on his beat" yet who never "runs anybody in."'[32] Cartoons, notably in *Punch*, became increasingly affectionate over time. The policeman was something of a clodhopper, but his vices were primarily a liking for beer, on and off duty, and a predilection for food and the cooks who provided it for him on his beat. In contrast, in numerous melodrama the policeman was a villain; maybe not the central villain, but a petty, spiteful figure, whose ill-treatment on stage was seen as 'gratifying and satisfactory.'[33] As an astute contemporary observer noted, there was genuine distrust and dislike of the police ... behind the hisses and laughter that points the moral for the ridiculously vicious character' on stage.[34]

Music-hall, especially in the late-Victorian and Edwardian years, had more in common with pantomime. The clumsy but good-hearted copper, with a weakness for plump cooks and plumper puddings, was very much the image conjured up by Vesta Tilley in 'It's Part of a Policeman's Lot' and 'The New Policeman;' and also in the Great Vance's 'Peter Potts the Peeler' with its chorus:

> After goose and rabbit pie
> Down area steps a stealer,
> Courting cookies on the sly
> Goes Peter Potts the Peeler.

Behind the good-natured jokes was a belief in the value of the constable. 'If it wasn't for the police … what would you do …Send for a policeman, best thing you can do' sang George Lashwood, while Maud Santley's 1897 song, 'The "Bobbies" of the Queen' put the police on a par with 'brave and bold Jack Tars … Tommy Atkins and our gallant sons of Mars.' To what extent songwriters had an eye to the growing middle-class elements of music-hall audiences is impossible to say, but such songs fitted well with the self-censorship of music-hall managements. However, there were some songs which, albeit humorously, painted a far less flattering picture. An early song, 'The New Police Act,' written in 1840 highlighted the pettiness of police action – no squibs or kites, no bell pulling and even no noise on Sundays – but the most scathing critique came in James Fawn's 'Ask a P'liceman.' The charge sheet was extensive. A nod and a wink made it clear why 'every member of the force, has a watch and chain, of course,' lifted from a helpless drunk; but in subsequent verses the critique becomes more explicit: 'He'll produce a flowing pot, if the pubs are shut or not;' and 'for advice on rapid flight, ask a p'liceman' before a final nod about his fidelity.[35] Fawn himself was praised for the accuracy of his characterisation of an ordinary policeman and the song was hugely popular and sung by many singers across the country. Unfortunately, the reviews do not make clear the precise reasons for its popularity, though it is not unreasonable (as with melodrama) to suggest it reflects a deep suspicion of police behaviour.

Some concluding observations

Though music hall was more for the people than of the people, especially by the end of the nineteenth century, certain songs addressed readily recognised issues. As with crime ballads discussed earlier, there was a conservative consensus that suggested widely shared attitudes and values. In many instances the approach was one of conservative common-sense – 'Work Boys and Be Contented.' Harsh realities could be sweetened by sentimentality ('My Old Dutch') or defused through humour ('My Old Man') Sympathy could be expressed for 'deserving' victims, without questioning the causes of their misfortunes ('Thereby Hangs A Tale'). The focus on more mundane but commonplace problems, such as finding employment, paying the rent and getting on with neighbours, created a sense of shared experiences, albeit accepted in a stoical manner; but the 'culture of consolation' argument can be overstated. The extent to which the newer, lower middle-class audiences identified with 'doing a moonlight flit' must be open to question. Further, the diversity of the material casts doubt on the validity of a single, overarching interpretation. There were songs of aspiration and inspiration, as much as of consolation and, perhaps more importantly, there were songs that had no profound message but, with their catchy lyrics and rousing and easy to sing choruses, were simply good fun that offered an opportunity to forget, however briefly, the realities of everyday life.

Endnotes

1. J Tosh, *A Man's Place*, London, Yale University Press, 1999, has some interesting comments on the 'New Woman' problem as well as the male flight from domesticity.
2. Comical thwarted working-class love was a recurring theme. Harry Clifton's 'broken-hearted milkman' lost his love to 'a bow-legged conductor of a two-penny bus'. Arthur Lloyd's butcher was thwarted by a rival who could offer the eponymous 'American beef.' See also his 'The Organ Grinder'.
3. See Ethel Victor's 'Oh! What a wicked young man you are' in which the 'wicked young man' tires of courting and decides to 'settle in life.'
4. In fact, mother did not come down, but her son joined her in heaven that night! Although dead mothers were more common, occasionally a father appeared. The

bereft son asking, in Denham Harrison's 'Give Me a Ticket to Heaven' to see his dead father was fortunate to find that he was only in hospital.

5   See also Lily Morris' 'Only a working man,' while the notion of partnership was clear in Florrie Forde's 'Man and wife should pull together' where the coupled literally and metaphorically strove together.
6   J S Bratton, 'Jenny Hill: Sex and Sexism in the Victorian Music Hall' in J S Bratton, ed., *Music Hall: Performance and Style*, Milton Keynes, Open University Press, 1986, pp.92-110, esp. pp.103-10
7   See for example *Era* 1 July 1882. The contributor praised her 'excellent' acting as she gave vent to the feelings of 'a poor but clean woman.'
8   *Era* 1 June 1879 was dismissive of the portrayal of 'a drunken wife' whereas a very positive account of the response to the song was given in *Era* 4 March 1877
9   *Era* 23 June 1878.
10 *Era* 11 February 1882 and 14 May 1881. This was of a piece with earlier songs in which she challenged the supposed superiority of men. See for example 'Bother the men' *Era* 7 January 1872 and 17 March 1872 for an attack on 'what she sneeringly called "the lords of the creation".'
11 See M E Doggart, *Marriage, Wife-Beating and the Law in Victorian Britain*, London, Weidenfield and Nicolson, 1992 and A J Hammerton, *Cruelty and Companionship*, London, Routledge, 1992
12 It has been claimed that, as well as singing along in full voice, men stood up and imitated Elen's stage actions. See P Norris, *A Cockney at Work: The Story of Gus Elen and His Songs*, Guildford, Grosvenor House, 2014, p.231-2.
13 *Era* 8 & 15 August and 26 September 1896. It also described the spectacle of 'a big hulking fellow, completely under the control of a little woman' as a 'not uncommon experience.' "7 February 1897
14 *Pall Mall Gazette* 11 January 1896
15 The song contains the memorable lines – 'For there's a lot of tunes to play on old fiddles they say, So, I live in hope if I die in despair.'
16 J Davis, 'The Gospel of Rags: Melodrama at the Britannia,' *Theatre Quarterly*, 7, 28, 1991, pp.369-89 and J Davis & T C Davis, 'The People of the "People's Theatre": The Social Demography of the Britannia Theatre, Hoxton,' *Theatre Survey*, 32, 1991, pp.137-65
17 For example, R B Peake's very successful play, 'The Climbing Boy', emphasised the 'lost boy' theme rather than focus on exploitative child labour.
18 *Era* 4 September 1870
19 Donkeys were commonly referred to as 'Jerusalem canaries,' at least by my north-London family, though I have been unable to trace the origin of the phrase.
20 A similar device, the street urchin commenting on the passing world was used to great effect in her character the City Waif and the songs that went with it.
21 See also 'Astrilly's Goold Fields' and 'Tommy Carr's Adventures in Astrilly,' though the latter warns of high prices – 'Sma' beer's ten shilling a quart in Astrilly, O!'
22 Hence the slang for being alone – 'on his Jack Jones'
23 Advert for performance at St James's Hall, Piccadilly, *Era* 18 June 1871. A similar approach was adopted in a concert in Berwick the song was performed by 'Miss Penelope Pernickity.' *Berwick News*, 19 November 1872.

24 *Era* 16 October 1870 spoke of her 'quaintly dressed old maid' in a performance at the Eastern, Limehouse.
25 *Era*, 7 January 1872
26 Wingrove 'Reigniting the "Vital Spark",' p.92
27 Wingrove, 'Reigniting the "Vital Spark",' p.95
28 The patter that accompanied the song was more equivocal but in the absence of information on performance it is impossible to say what stance she took.
29 The politics of the song is confused. While one verse refers to (suffragette) protests in London, the chorus says, 'my wife's joined the suffragists.'
30 D Taylor, *The new police in nineteenth-century England*, Manchester University Press, 1997, chap. 4
31 C Pulling, *They Were Singing*, London, Harrop & Co., 1952, pp.87-8
32 *Era* 24 December 1871. Earlier that year at the Alhambra Theatre of Varieties the audience had been regaled with the sight of 'half a dozen dogs being made to "move on" by another dog dressed as a policeman. *Era* 4 June 1871
33 Review of the 'thrilling sketch, *Men and Metal*, at the Sebright, 1892. *Era*, 16 January 1892. See also the 'loud laughter' and 'merriment and derision' that greeted the 'invariably ill-used policeman' at Crystal Palace and the Britannia, respectively. *Era* 29 December 1894 and 15 January 1898.
34 H R P Gamon, *The London Police Court*, London, Dent & Co., 1907, p.40
35 See also C P Cove's 'The Model Peeler,' the patter to which makes clear that the so-called model constable accepts bribes, lies in court and does his duty, like a man, with the help of his 'trusty staff.' With the exception of Albert Chevalier's 'The village constable,' which is an out-and-out parody expressed in 'yokel' language, the emphasis is on urban policing.

CHAPTER 11

'The Boers have got my daddy': Politics domestic and foreign

> "The Dogs of War" are loose and the rugged Russian Bear,
> Full bent on blood and robbery, has crawl'd out of his lair;
> It seems a thrashing now and then, will never help to tame
> That brute, and so he's out upon the "same old game."
> The Lion did his best to find him some excuse
> To crawl back to his den again, all efforts were no use;
> He hunger'd for his victim, he's pleased when blood is shed,
> But let us hope his crimes may all recoil on his own head.
>
> 'By Jingo' or MacDermott's 'War Song'

THE POLITICAL SONG, particularly one focussing on a specific figure, posed a conundrum for music hall managers. There was a long and successful tradition of topical songs, such as 'Is he Guilty?' which commented on personalities and issues of the day and asked the audience to respond. But, as leisure entrepreneurs sought to offer more respectable entertainment to a wider audience, they felt that they should minimize the number of contentious songs that commented on politicians and princes. Political allusions and political "gags" were deemed undesirable in the theatre and even more so in the music hall, 'where the audience is usually more impressionable, excitable and pugnacious.'[1] Managers, like James Carter Edwards, of the Theatre Royal, Hull, tried to distinguish between 'patriotism,' to which he had no objection, and 'vulgar party politics.'[2] Others were more pragmatic, simply balancing conflicting interests. In 1888 the audience at the South London Place were regaled by 'Miss Nelly Farnell … the glittering star of Erin [who] nightly champions the "grand old man" [William Gladstone] … [but] an antidote to fervid Home Rule is supplied by Mr Sam Redfearn … who dilates upon the triumphs of Beaconsfield and what he [Disraeli] did for the "glory of old England."'[3] There was also a problem for the individual performer who might be faced with a hostile audience. One solution was found by Charles Williams, 'who found favour in a political song, having reference to the Conservative and Liberal leaders by the anything but complimentary title of little pigs.'[4]

Party politics

Politicians (and other prominent figures) appeared regularly on the music-hall stage, and not just in song. There were impersonators, ventriloquists, puppeteers, even caricaturists, as well as singers. Politicians of all persuasions appeared, and the treatment varied from the adulatory to the condemnatory with varying degrees of gentle (and not so gentle) humour in between. However, as many Liberal politicians, J A Hobson in particular, bitterly complained, this was not an even field on which all politicians, or political parties, were treated equally. Generally speaking, the music-hall industry was more sympathetic towards the Conservatives and more suspicious of the Liberals who, at various times, were identified with teetotalism, censorship and Home Rule. Nelly Farnell was unusual in her praise of the Liberal leader. More of her fellow performers were critical. As Gladstone's second ministry struggled in 1884, Fred Coyne had 'a popular ditty, in which the audience, loyally and loudly interrupted by shouting the words "Take it away." The Government and Mr. Gladstone were voted to be 'useless lumber.' In the same year, when Mr Godfrey appeared as "The Grand Old Man" at the London Pavilion, 'there was sibillation in plenty.'[5] 'Jolly' John Nash's song "Put it down to Gladstone' similarly 'went excellently.'[6] In similar vein, Vesta Tilley sang 'Chalk it up to Gladstone,' though the song drew cheers and some counter-cheers.[7]

Another leading Liberal, Charles Dilke was much vilified, particularly by the arch-Tory G H MacDermott 'with a sort of nursery rhyme song,' which elicited cheering that was "something tremendous."'[8] Dilke's earlier support for republicanism made him a suspect figure in the eyes of many but it was a sexual scandal that finally brought his political career to an end when he lost his Chelsea seat in 1886. MacDermott's 'Dilke song, coming as it did … so soon after the election returns from Chelsea were published, created more than the customary excitement.'[9] MacDermott was not without his critics. Another contributor to *Era*, itself not known for its pro-Liberal sentiments, attacked him for 'pursuing a questionable policy in attacking [Dilke] in an idiotic song.'[10]

The most unpopular aspect of Liberal policy was the commitment to Home Rule, a policy which split the party itself. Music-hall advocates of Home Rule aroused hostility, notably Charles Collette, who 'sang a song of the warmest and most partisan nature with respect to the Home Rule question' at the Trocadero. The song 'create[d] uproar and cause[d] annoyance and inconvenience' to many in the audience; it was subsequently withdrawn to prevent further trouble.[11] Collette was not deterred and was singing songs such as 'What Should We Do Without Parnell?' and 'Why Don't They Give Us Home Rule?' in the early 1890s.[12] Audience sympathy for Home Rule is difficult to gauge but the popularity of Charles Coburn, who 'waved his banner on high and declared for "Home Rule for Shepherd's Bush"' and of the 'old favourite', Harriet Vernon, who, singing of 'what the public really required,' claimed 'that Gladstone shall "leave Home Rule alone,"' suggests it was limited.[13]

If Gladstone was more likely to provoke a hiss, then Disraeli was more likely to generate a cheer – and then some more. Despite (or perhaps because of) his relatively short tenure in office and his early death in 1881, he remained a popular figure in music hall song throughout Victoria's reign. Disraeli was a political outsider, a maverick whom many viewed with suspicion, but a fortuitous set of circumstances during his only substantial ministry of 1874-80 enabled him and his followers to create the myth of the man who had defended and extended British interests on the world stage, while also looking after the well-being of the country at large, through his "One-Nation Conservatism." Performing at the Victoria in 1881, Arthur Lloyd 'called forth much cheering [with a] reference to the possible return of the Earl of Beaconsfield [as Disraeli became in 1876] to political power.'[14] Popularity in life turned to near-adoration in death in certain quarters. In Harry Rickard's rendition of 'The Shining Light of England,' the mention of the late Lord Beaconsfield, as usual, called forth 'great cheering.'[15] In 'The Tablet of England,' written by Oswald Stoll and performed by Vesta Tilley in 1886, Disraeli was lauded as 'a statesman – a hero – a man!'

While much attention has been focussed on the London halls, Tory popularity was not confined to the capital. One striking example was the response to a performance by MacDermott in Day's Concert Hall in the Liberal stronghold of Birmingham in 1879. One song contained the following lines:

> We have a gallant captain,/ We will be a loyal crew
> And we'll hold together/ By the Old True Blue.

The chorus was 'taken up heartily' by the audience and 'the close of each verse followed by a whirlwind of applause.'[16] However, there were criticisms of the repeated evocation of the name of Beaconsfield. Vesta Tilley was taken to task for her 'excessively bad taste ... [in appealing] to vulgar political prejudices in the name of a Conservative leader.'[17] Praised for his dancing skills, Mr. Cairns was condemned for his 'stale [and] decidedly unprofitable' political allusions.[18] Other critics condemned the way in which appeals to patriotism were used to disguise lack of talent. Miss Minnie Jeffs 'employed her vocal resources in praise of Primrose Day and ... Lord Beaconsfield' but the 'frantic applause' owed little to 'any charm of voice or rendering as she descanted on the flag of "red, white and blue."'.[19] In sum, 'the continual mention of Lord Beaconsfield to the detriment of any other statesman, whether Conservative or Liberal, is becoming nauseous.'[20]

No other Tory politician matched Disraeli's popularity. Salisbury was one of many subjects of caricaturists and cartoonist, including the great novelty of the late 1890s, Henri Cazman's 'clever shadowography' show entitled *Medallions of Celebrities*, but appeared less often in song. MacDermott introduced a verse about him in his topical song 'What Would You Like to See?' and he featured in 'Salisbury and Gladstone,' though much of that song was directed at Gladstone's abandonment of Gordon at Khartoum.[21] Whether seen as too aloof, too prosaic or simply too unsympathetic, Salisbury never captured the imagination in the way that his predecessor had done and continued to do. Only Randolph Churchill came close to the larger-than-life persona of Disraeli. Somewhat fancifully, he was described in 'The Tablet of Fame' as being 'a pillar of state, unequalled in debate' and 'with intellect of excellence rare.' Predictably MacDermott and Nash (literally) sang his praises, as did the Tory sympathiser, Harry Rickard in 'Steady and True.'[22]

Patriotism and jingoism

Despite attempts to distinguish between political songs (unacceptable) and patriotic songs (acceptable), no clear-cut line can be discerned, not least because of the repeated elision of Conservatism and patriotism. There were many patriotic songs that focussed variously on the perceived threats to and successes of the country. Here the distinction was between acceptable and unacceptable patriotism, the latter increasingly condemned as jingoism. Much has been made of the patriotic fervour of late-nineteenth century music-hall, with the Great MacDermott's 'Jingo' song being quoted repeatedly, but there is a danger of generalizing from a highly distinctive performer, performing in particular circumstances. Since the Crimean War, Russia had replaced France as Britain's greatest threat in Europe. Renewed Russian support for the Ottoman Empire provoked a diplomatic crisis in 1878, during which battleships were despatched to deter Russian advances towards Constantinople and the straits. Despite Gladstone's campaigning on the Bulgarian atrocities of 1876, the crisis, which was resolved at the Congress of Berlin in 1878, worked to the advantage of the Conservatives, who benefitted from the upsurge of popular feeling exploited by, among others, MacDermott and the song writer G W Hunt, who spoke of 'that section of the public who were anxious for bold and patriotic action against Russian aggression.'[23]

The song was undoubtedly popular in its own right, in Liverpool as much as in London, and as a reference point in other productions, such as the 'new and fanciful ballet … Aphrodite' the opening scene of which showed Beaconsfield in his study, dreaming of Cyprus, while 'a distant chorus of "We don't want to fight"' can be heard.[24] MacDermott was not the only jingoistic singer of the day. W Johnson sung about 'The Lion and the Bear,' while 'Stand to Your Guns,' Clement Scott's 'new patriotic song' proved highly popular. To the questions 'why was Beaconsfield dear to the nation, [and] why Salisbury's cheered as her truest of sons?' he gave the simple answer: 'in the teeth of a crowd's execration, Like England – they pluckily stood to their guns.'[25]

However, that 'section of the population' that responded positively was not as large as Hunt and MacDermott claimed. MacDermott's 'War Song' went down badly in Birmingham and was less popular in several northern towns and cities, where there were criticisms of 'fanatic partisans' as exemplified by MacDermott, the *Pall Mall Gazette* and the *Daily Telegraph* and of the misuse of jingo songs by Tories at meetings across the country.[26] Parodies appeared. According to *Punch*, not only was there the well-known determination to fight but 'we've got the ink, we've got the pens/And we've got the paper too' while, more ominously the *Morning Post* reckoned 'we'll have two shillings income tax/And a d---d good licking too!'[27]

Jingoism re-appeared in the following decades and provoked similar responses. In 1885 the war in the Sudan, and especially the siege of Khartoum, sparked an outburst of ultra-patriotic songs. Vesta Tilley roused 'the patriotic feeling of the audience' as she sang 'Shall England Give In?' Henry Clark at the Trocadero gained 'Jingo applause by cheap sneers at Gladstone and by calling attention to highly-coloured pictures of General Gordon.' Charles Coburn also followed suit, but was criticized for exciting 'the feelings of the foolish and [giving] opportunity to the quarrelsome.'[28] Radicals condemned 'Jingo songs, bawled loudly by some half-drunken sots ... [and] nightly applauded by men and women who have never thought out a political problem in their lives, and could not do so if they tried.'[29] Such strident views provoked a firm defence from the likes of G B Harcourt who praised the patriotic songs of Arthur Lloyd and 'Jolly' John Nash, which they alleged were applauded by thousands, including 'drapers, grocers, and other kindred trades' assistants' rather than drunks.[30] The 'small wars' of Victoria's reign spawned various songs (including street ballads) that reflected and contributed to the growth of popular imperialism and strengthened notions of racial superiority, in which white heroes battled with savage Africans, encouraged by nigger minstrelsy.[31]

The years surrounding the turn of the twentieth century provoked an even greater outburst. A stand-off against the French at Fashoda, Kitchener's exploits in the Sudan and, above all, the war against the Boers in southern Africa, called forth songs which were sung across the country indeed across the empire.[32] The desire to show imperial unity was seen most clearly in another pro-Tory performer, F V St. Clair's 'John Bull's Letter Bag,' the lyrics of which were (allegedly) drawn from letters from Australia, Canada, Ireland and America! The song was praised for expressing 'the best patriotic sentiments … [but] with not a word of Jingo fustian in the lines.'[33]

The second Boer war gave rise to a minor flood of patriotic compositions from Tom Costello's tear-jerking 'The Boers Have Got My Daddy,' through the recycled 'Goodbye Dolly Grey,' to the lesser-known marches of Ezra Read, all celebrating aspects of the conflict.[34] Also often overlooked were the patriotic, pro-Empire Irish songs. Leo Dryden, best known for 'The Miner's Dream of Home,' and known as 'the Kipling of the Halls' sang 'Bravo, Dublin Fusiliers!' Pat Carey, in stage khaki, sang 'The Irish Are Always in Front,' with its provocative opening line: 'There's talk going round that the Irish are traitors.' Pat Rafferty, better known for his sentimental songs, defended his fellow countrymen in 'You Can't Call Them Traitors Now,' and 'What Do You Think of the Irish Now?' which contained the lines: ''You used to call us traitors because of agitators/ But you can't call us traitors now.'[35]

There was also a more general 'patriotic' songs praising Britain's armed forces, such as 'Soldiers of the Queen' and

'Sons of the Sea,' and extravaganzas, such as *Our Army and Our Navy,* (1889) and *The Girl I Left Behind Me,* (1894), which celebrated soldiers and sailors on imperial duty around the globe. There were also less obvious sources such as the 1890s musical comedy *A Gaiety Girl*, which included the song 'Private Tommy Atkins,' who was

> A-fighting for his country and his queen.
> And whether he's on India's coral strand or pouring
>   out his blood in the Soudan,
> To keep our flag a-flying, he's a-doing and a-dying,
> Every inch of him a soldier and a man.

First performed at the Prince of Wales Theatre, London, it soon ran up over a hundred performances. Haydn Coffin, as Charles Goldfield, was much praised for his rendition of 'the "Tommy Atkins" song [delivered] with all the resonant vigour and patriotic enthusiasm imaginable.'[36] But it was not just in London that the comedy was performed. There were performances in major cities in the midlands (Leicester and Nottingham), the north of England (Manchester, Sheffield, Hull and Bradford) and at various resorts from Ramsgate in the south to Blackpool in the northwest and Scarborough in the northeast. The song itself was sung in a wide range of venues: at the Sons of Temperance Cycle Club concert in Hull; at a patriotic concert in Sunderland; at a concert in aid of the Tideswell (Derbyshire) cricket club; at the East End Conservative Club in Hastings; at a concert on behalf of the Duke of Westminster's Fund for Distressed Armenians in Grandborough (Buckinghamshire); as part of a concert by "The Tennessee Darkies" in Waverton (Cheshire); and at the Cinderella Society concert and another concert in aid of the ambulance section of local volunteers at Lockwood (Huddersfield), among others in 1894 alone.

The popularity of songs such as 'Private Tommy Atkins' is striking but there was not an uncritical and unchallenged surge of patriotism sweeping the country. The second Boer war, in particular, was a divisive event and enthusiasm for war was not shared by all, as the number of anti-war parodies, such as 'Call Out The Boys of The Old Brigade' or 'Riding In The

Ammunition Van,' bears witness. For many performers there was an element of commercial calculation in their choice of songs. Gus Elen, not averse to adding a 'Dr Jim' verse in praise of the controversial figure of Leander Starr Jameson, was also happy to sing about being 'One Of The Deathless Army,' facing shells by the thousands and surrounded on all sides by cannons – the former in the oyster shop, the latter in the billiard hall.[37] Elen stood out against the tendency for comedians to 'spout doggerel and cheap Jingoism,' and was praised for treating the war from 'the comic standpoint of a Bethnal-green Boer.'[38]

Historians, notably Linda Colley, have stressed the importance of empire in creating a sense of Britishness that subsumed Irish, Scottish and Welsh identities into a broader (and greater) identity, to which music-hall contributed. Undoubtedly certain performers felt obliged (or felt it commercially wise) to conform with this notion, taking a positive view of the co-operation and unity of interest between Scots, Irish and English – the Welsh featuring less often. The Irish singer, Pat Feeney, the so-called "Irish Ambassador," sang of "The Rose and the Thistle and the Shamrock Green," to 'tremendous plaudits'.[39] At the Middlesex music-hall, the Great Northern Troupe of Characteristic Male and Female Dancers, which hailed from Scotland, made 'patriotism … the keynote … of the programme.'[40] It is not known why they choose to refer to themselves as 'Northern' rather than 'Scottish' but in the late-nineteenth century, when the popularity of empire was high, the was in certain quarters a 'voluntary suppression of separate Scottish nationality in favour of the popular concept of 'North Britain."[41] Likewise, the Clan Johnstone Troupe, appearing at the Sebright music-hall, London, appealed to patriotic sentiments.[42] Pipe Major Albert Johnstone's choice of tune was not accidental. "Cock of the North" was the march tune of the 1st Gordon Highlanders, who had played such a decisive and heroic in the battle of Dargai.[43]

The much-publicised heroism of Piper Findlater at Dargai provoked a miniature cultural storm. He himself enjoyed a brief career in music hall after his discharge from the army.[44] His exploits were also celebrated in poetry, song and musical sketches, such as the 'dramatic musical military sketch, 'One of The Boys,' which was performed across the country, from Dover to Darwen via Dudley. Among singers, Jess Burton, noted for his patriotic ballads, sang a new song about Findlater, 'What Shall We Do With Our Heroes?' while 'Jovial' Joe Culvard, 'famous ... for his faithful portrayal of the typical John Bull,' added a new verse to 'a familiar song' of his praising Findlater.[45] Although it was a Scottish regiment that triumphed at Dargai, their achievement was woven into a wider British imperial narrative. Similarly, the popular romantic military drama, which was produced in several provincial towns and cities as well as London, made its priority clear from its very title: *Our British Empire; or, the Gordon Highlanders*. Less overtly, Oswald Stoll, capitalizing upon the popularity of Piper Findlater, included him in a bill which symbolically included the well-known Irish singer and dancer, Pat Rafferty and the Welsh Quartette, who sang 'The Boys of the Old Brigade.'[46] Whether these attitudes were shared outside England is less clear cut.[47]

Some concluding observations

The development of music hall, the creation of a national network of venues and performers, contributed to an emerging popular national culture. While the focus of the industry was entertainment, music hall was not divorced from its wider political context. There were lyricists and performers who made their politics known, more often supporting the Tory party than the Liberals, more often defending the union than advocating Home Rule. They reflected political divisions in the country at large and, even if only by confirming pre-existing beliefs, contributed to the wider political life of the nation. In celebrating empire, the halls contributed to a sense of Britishness associated with its alleged achievements, ranging from military campaigns to civilizing missions, which in turn inculcated a sense of superiority over those deemed less fortunate. However, it is easy to exaggerate popular jingoism and popular patriotism. There was a degree of scepticism and indifference, the latter being particularly difficult to measure.

Looked at in their entirety, music hall songs were characterised by the diversity of subject matter and the success of the halls rested on their ability to fulfil several functions and to satisfy a range of emotions, from pathos to patriotism, even in a single evening. It offered an escape from mundane reality and, for some at least, a shared experience that helped to make sense of and come to terms with the dreariness, inequalities and harshness of everyday life. Even for those unable to go to the halls, a cheerful (or even a sad) song to be sung or whistled at work, or a barrel-organ tune to dance to at the fair or with passers-by in the street, brightened and enriched everyday life. Music hall was fundamentally about entertainment and enjoyment rather than education; and it is too easy to lose sight of this important fact.

Endnotes

1. *Era*, 'Politics on Stage,' 6 April 1889. See also the critique of the 'excessively bad taste' of Vesta Tilley in 'exciting the political feelings of her audience,' *Era* 8 December 1883.
2. *Era* 23 March 18889
3. *Era* 18 February 1888
4. *Era* 29 February 1880
5. *Era* 22 March 1884
6. *Era* 11 April 1885. Nor was this confined to the 1880s. in 1892 Harry Freeman's 'good humoured banter of Mr. Gladstone' summed up his policy 'in the phrase 'Ta-ra-ra Boom-de-ay,' thereby combining political commentary with the hit tune of the time. *Era* 2 July 1892
7. *Era* 8 November 1884
8. *Era* 6 March 1886
9. *Era* 10 July 1886
10. *Era* 29 May 1886
11. *Era* 6 April 89
12. See for example *Era* 9 May 1891
13. *Era* 3 March 1888 (Coburn) and 4 June 1887 (Vernon)
14. *Era*, 26 February 1881. Similarly, the Great Vance at the Oxford 'alluded to Earl Beaconsfield whose name was the signal for enthusiastic applause.' *Era* 8 January 1881
15. *Era* 1 September 1883. See also *Era* 14 May 1881, 11 October 1884, 28 April 1888 and 6 November 1897
16. *Birmingham Daily Globe*, 10 December 1879 reprinted in *Era* 14 December 1879. There is scattered evidence of limited popular support for McDermott in the Liberal strongholds of the West Riding of Yorkshire.
17. *Era* 8 December 1883
18. *Era* 18 July 1885
19. *Era* 28 April 1888
20. *Era* 18 July 1885
21. The line 'Poor Gordon was left to his fate' directly mirrored Conservative

political propaganda, which turned the GOM (the Grand Old Man, as Gladstone was commonly known) into the MOG (the murderer of Gordon). See for example, *The Gladstone Almanack, 1885*, London, Blackwood & Sons, 1885, price 6d.
22 *Era* 21 November 1891
23 *Era* 20 June 1878. See also 'A Chat with G H MacDermott,' in which he talked of 'national sentiment … the spirit of the moment … [and] the question of England's supremacy among nations.' *Era* 23 September 1893
24 MacDermott created 'the greatest sensation' with his jingo song at the People's Palace, Liverpool, *Era* 11 August 1878 and 6 October 1878
25 *Era* 21 July 1878
26 *Penny Illustrated Paper* 23 February 1878, *Examiner* 30 June 1877 & 16 February 1878, *Northern Echo* 7 February & 5 April 1878
27 *Punch* reproduced in *Huddersfield Chronicle* 11 May 1878, *Morning Post* 30 January 1878
28 *Era* 14 March, 2 & 9 May 1885
29 *Era* 20 June 1885
30 *Era* 20 June 1885
31 J Mullen, 'Anti-Black Racism in British Popular Music (1880-1920),' *French Journal of British Studies*, 17(2), 2012 at https://www.academia.edu/2002759/_PDF_full_text_Anti_Black_Racism_in_British_Popular_Music_1880-1920
32 For example, Mr Colverd's 'topical verse about the victory gained by General Kitchener at Khartoum' *Era*, 10 September 1898; Miss Kitty Rayburn's 'He's a bloke as I'd like to walk out wiv,' praising Kitchener and Roberts, *Era* 18 November 1899; 'the Two Bees with their ultra-jingo songs and patter' in Newcastle, *Era* 22 July 1899; Miss Amy Farrell in Plymouth appealing to the 'fiery instincts of the loyal citizens' *Era* 30 September 1899; and Miss Amy Grace's 'jingo ditty' in the military spectacular melodrama, *Under the British Flag*, performed in Cape Town, *Era* 28 October 1899.
33 *Era* 3 February 1900
34 'Goodbye Dolly Grey' was originally written for the Spanish-American war but was never used because of the brevity of that conflict It can be heard in the background in the film 'Butch Cassidy and the Sundance Kid,' which was set at the time. Read wrote The Mafeking March, The Ladysmith March, The Kimberley March, The Transvaal March and, by way of variation, The March to Pretoria as well as The Relief of Mafeking.
35 Pulling, *They Were Singing* p.79 and *New York Times*, 14 October 1900. The latter also drew attention to the publication of pro-Boer songs in several American cities.
36 *Era* 17 February 1894
37 The botched Jameson Raid (December 1895/January 1896) was an embarrassing and counterproductive incident for the British government but, initially at least, Jameson was feted as a hero in some sections of London society in particular.
38 *Era* 25 November 1899
39 *Era* 6 August 1881 and 14 January 1882
40 *Era* 21 July 1894

41 P Maloney, *Scotland and the Music Hall, 1850-1914*, Manchester University Press, 2003, p.19.
42 *Era* 30 July 1898
43 The storming of the heights of Dargai was part of the Tirah campaign (in what is now Pakistan) in 1897. Where others had failed, the Gordons carried the day. Two VCs were awarded to Gordon Highlanders for their bravery that day, one being to Piper George Findlater, who continued playing the regimental march despite being shot through both thighs. Findlater's memory was hazy and he suggested that he played "The Haughs of Cromdale." His son was also a piper and wounded in battle at Loos in 1915.
44 Findlater was extremely well received at the Empire Palace, Edinburgh where he appeared for a week, clad in tartan, pipes skirling as he played "The Haughs of Cromdale" and "Cock of the North." He toured northern England as far south as Birmingham, but critics were more impressed with the Scottish dancers who accompanied him than with Findlater's piping. He appeared once on stage with the violin virtuoso James Scott Skinner, an interesting contrast that went beyond their different instruments. Despite his fame, Findlater was also beaten in a piping competition for the Queen's medal by Albert Johnstone of the Clan Johnstone Troupe. His career was cut short when the War Office requested that he not perform at the Alhambra, London in June 1898. He was found a place in Her Majesty's household. *Era* 4 June 1898 and *Music Hall and Theatre Review* 13 May 1898
45 *Era* 8 July and 10 September 1890. Culvard also added a verse dedicated to General Gordon. In addition, performers such as A L Lloyd boosted their acts by impersonating Findlater.
46 *Music Hall and Theatre Review*, 1 July 1898
47 For a variety of reasons, from commercial self-interest to a genuine identification with empire, particularly as an opportunity for Scots, popular song collections, such as *The Scotia Music Hall Songbook* or *The Modern Scottish Minstrel*, contained several imperialist songs, such as 'Cheer Boys Cheer (for Mother England!)' words by Charles Mackay. However, the same volumes also contained more overtly nationalist Scottish songs, such as 'Hurrah for The Bonnets of Blue' and 'Caledonia.' In fact, in Harvie's phrase, there was 'a fruitful schizophrenia' whereby Scottish audiences 'applauded imperial achievements or aspirations … through Scottish involvement … [and] criticised or satirised … the English establishment.' See Maloney, *Scotland and the Music-Hall*, especially p.163 and p.171

'The Minstrels Parade': Blackface minstrelsy and the music hall

> Oh, he's got a pair of lips, like a pound of liver split,
> And a nose like an injun rubber shoe,
> He's a limpy, happy, chuckle-headed, huckleberry nig,
> And he whistles like a happy killy-loo;
> He's an independent, free-and-easy, fat-and-greasy ham,
> With a cranium like a big baboon;
> Oh, I never heard him talk to anybody in my life,
> But he's happy when he whistles this tune :-
>   (Whistles.)
>   Eugene Stratton, 'The Whistling Coon'

TO TWENTY-FIRST century eyes, the popularity of blackface minstrelsy is perplexing to the point of repugnance. However, as Michael Pickering has forcefully argued, it is essential to get beyond that 'presentism, which allows our understanding and interpretation of the past to be monopolized by contemporary values and preconceptions … [and to engage in] reflexive conversation rather than one-way monologue.'[1] A number of general points needs to be made at the outset. First, the enduring popularity of minstrelsy cannot be explained simply in terms of its dissemination of racial stereotypes. The quality of the songs – from the simple but catchy 'Jump Jim Crow' or 'Oh Dem Golden Slippers' to the sophistication of 'Lily of Laguna'; the ability of the singers, dancers and musicians; and the novelty and excitement of the overall show have to be acknowledged.[2] Second, notwithstanding these musical qualities, racial mimicry and stereotyping both reflected and contributed to a growing and persistent belief that the world was better understood in terms of racial, rather than class or gender, differences. Further, in spite of contemporary praise for the 'realism' of certain 'negro delineators,' the stage stereotypes bore no resemblance to the realities of African American life, but made imaginable an idea of 'blackness,' a 'racial pretence' that fulfilled a variety of 'white' needs, from legitimizing imperialism to providing psychological consolation.[3] Finally, while racial stereotyping was a constant and central element, its nature and reception changed over time, particularly as the broader historical context changed from the anti-slavery sentiments of the second quarter of the nineteenth century to the high imperialist views of the final quarter.

Although blacking-up was not unknown in England, blackface minstrelsy was significantly different, and by its very nature, raises questions about the function and meaning of the 'mask.'[4] Any 'mask' creates an 'other' world into which the audience is invited temporarily to leave behind their world and its values; it offers the opportunity, not simply to experience that 'other' world, but to say things that would otherwise be unacceptable. Blacking-up deliberately concealed the ethnic identity of the performer and, at the same time, created a racialized stage figure, which could either reinforce or challenge preconceptions. The most common element in the construction of 'blackness' in Victorian minstrelsy was the depiction of the negro as a carefree, easy-going, though childlike figure; someone who embodied the very opposite of Victorian bourgeois morality with its emphasis on self-control and self-improvement. This served two purposes. First, it confirmed the belief that 'whiteness' was more mature and morally superior and 'blackness' somehow both endearing and funny but also subordinate. Second, while laughing at the figure on stage, the ('white') audience was invited to laugh at its everyday self. Thus, the mask permitted a temporary escape from 'whiteness' but at the same time confirming 'blackness' as something 'other' and, implicitly at least, inferior. The belief in child-like qualities fed into sentimental images of 'smiling picaninnies,' implicitly requiring care. This in turn easily transmuted into images of the down-trodden, mistreated and enslaved 'black,' who needed the protection of the stronger and moral 'white.' Similarly, the characterisation of the negro as some form of 'noble savage' played into 'white' self-images of civilised superiority and responsibility for the less fortunate, but also allowed for more sinister images, centring on notions of 'uncivilised.' 'Carefree' could easily become lazy and irresponsible. This was the slippery slope to dishonesty and criminality. The 'savage' was no longer noble, but a figure of threat to 'white' person and property. In other words, 'blackness' comprised a bundle of stereotypes, from which certain elements might be emphasised at any given time. Although belief in the notion of negroes as objects of pity and in need of help, was strongest in the period from the 1830s to the 1850s when anti-slavery sentiments were most prominent, it never disappeared. To the contrary, it was a necessary part of the imperial story being told as more of the world map turned red. Similarly, concern with the 'savage' threat was not confined to the years of imperial conflicts in the late-nineteenth century.

Blackface minstrelsy in England

Blackface minstrelsy developed in England from the mid-1830s, distinct from and more respectable than early music hall, and achieving a cross-class and cross-gender appeal. During its heyday from the 1860s to the 1890s, its distinctiveness was clearly in view in London where the two leading troupes, the more 'English' Mohawk Minstrels and the more 'American' Moore & Burgess Minstrels performed at distinct venues, the Royal Agricultural Hall, Islington and St. James's Hall, Piccadilly.[5] However, the boundary between the two forms of entertainment was more fluid. From the 1850s music halls were looking for 'nigger' entertainers and, increasingly from the 1860s there was movement in both directions, highlighting two important and enduring feature of popular music: the search for novelty and the willingness to absorb new influences and to fuse them into something distinctive. Music hall grew out of different traditions that themselves were fluid and evolving. American minstrelsy was also a hybrid, a fusion of European musical influences, particularly English, Scottish and Irish tunes, and African, notable rhythms and dance moves. Although the emphasis in this chapter is on the incorporation of elements of minstrelsy into music hall, there was a two-way flow of material and performers.

From the outset, blackface minstrelsy was a cultural commodity within the wider popular culture. Initially the emphasis was on the individual performer.[6] The appearance of T D 'Daddy' Rice and his hit song-and-dance number, 'Jump Jim Crow' in 1836 created a sensation.[7] In the following decade there was a fundamental shift to the ensemble format that was to characterise minstrelsy into the twentieth century. Dan Emmett and the Virginian Minstrels performed in Liverpool and Manchester as well as London in the early 1840s. They were followed by a variety of troupes, including the (much copied) Christy Minstrels and the Ethiopian Serenaders, with their outstanding dancer, 'Master Juba,' William Henry Lane. His performances, combining elements of Irish jigs, American dances such as the 'Tennessee double shuffle' and what were referred to as 'authentic nigger dances,' dazzled and bemused contemporary observers.[8] The number of troupes increased, varying in size from two dozen to over 60. More importantly, they developed a distinctive and wide-ranging format. Shows initially followed a three-part pattern – overture, olio and walkabout – though later in the century the Moore and Burgess Minstrels presented a two-part show with a short (three minute) interval. Musical entertainment, in various forms, was central, they also included circus elements, such as acrobatics and juggling.[9] Over time the repertoire extended beyond plantation tunes and Stephen Foster songs to include material, such as Harry Hunter's 'The Doctor Says I'm Not To Be Worried,' not dissimilar to those found in music halls.[10] Indeed, by the 1860s, the Mohawk Minstrels included Irish, Scottish and even Old English themed nights.[11]

Minstrelsy and music hall

Songs and performers moved between minstrelsy and music hall. E W Mackney, 'that Prince of Nigger Minstrels,' was a major figure, who had established himself as a popular music hall figure in London in the early 1860s.[12] His skill as a banjo and fiddle player combined with his dancing, singing and comedy made him an outstanding all-round performer. His most popular song was 'Whole Hog or None,' which he sang (or had to sing) throughout his career. His repertoire included such predictable tunes as 'Old Dan Tucker,' 'Camptown Races' and 'The Darkies' Jubilee' but also ran to Sousa marches, such as 'Liberty Bell' and several traditional British tunes, including 'The Bristol Hornpipe,' 'Monymusk' and 'Tink a Tink,' not to mention 'farmyard imitations on the violin!'[13]

Another who moved to the music-hall stage was the renowned Christy Minstrels' dancer, Joe Brown, noted for his 'Silver Belt Jig and his Happy Uncle Tom Dance … terpsichorean specimens quite unique in their way.'[14] He too was exceptionally talented, but was not alone in appearing in music hall. Adverts for nigger' singers and dancers appeared in the *Era* as early as the 1850s, and were placed not simply from the large cities, such as Birmingham and Liverpool, but also from small, and relatively obscure places, such as Boston in Lincolnshire.[15] Amateur and semi-professional troupes, as well as duos and solo performers, were to be found. Most remain largely unknown. One of 'the greatest attractions' at the Philharmonic Hall, Islington was Barlow, 'a clever, active and quaint Nigger singer and dancer,' noted for his rendition of 'Blue-tail'd fly,' but beyond that, nothing.[16] Others left more substantial footprints in the historical record. The Alabama Minstrels, unusually African-Americans from New York, began touring in the late-1850s, spent much of the 1860s, presenting their all-singing, all-dancing rendition of 'plantation life' to audiences across the north of England and the south of Scotland. As part of their 1864 tour, they performed in Huddersfield, where interest in 'negro melodies' dated back to the mid-1850s.[17] The experience of the town highlights the popularity of minstrelsy. The (so-called) Christy Minstrels performed at the town's Gymnasium-hall and the Philosophical-hall in 1859, 1860 and 1862.[18] John Eagleton's Juvenile African Troupe and Coloured Serenaders delighted audiences in and around the town in the mid-1860s with their mixture of songs that combined Stephen Foster numbers , such as 'The Old Folk at Home' and 'Jeanie with the Light Brown Hair' with English songs, such as 'The Bloom is on the Rye' and 'Gentle Jenny Gray.'[19] Other troupes appeared in the nearby villages – the Juvenile Christy Minstrels at Kirkburton, Butterworth's Christy Minstrels at Marsden, Oliver's Troupe of Minstrels at Holmfirth – as did the home-grown Golcar Amateur Coloured Minstrels. Equally striking is the number of 'nigger' performers who appeared at the town's early music halls. The more respectable Argyle music-hall regularly engaged a range of such entertainers from individuals, such as 'G W Edwards, Nigger Vocalist, Banjo and Bones Soloists.'[20] The rival Cambridge music hall offered the Carroll troupe, 'eccentric and successful ... Niggers,' who included the locally-born Dick Crowther, as well as a blackface musical troupe, the Chirgwin family.[21] Similar acts, included the Niagara Brothers and the gifted banjo-players, the Bohee Brothers, who appeared at Rowley's Empire in the 1890s, though by then there were fewer 'nigger' acts.[22]

Blackface could be a first step on a musical career ladder. The Great Vance, Dan Leno, Gus Elen and Harry Champion all started in this way, but others went on to make their names as 'negro delineators.' One of the earliest, and undoubtedly the most idiosyncratic, was G H Chirgwin, variously known as 'The White-Eyed Musical Kaffir' or 'The Cockney Coloured Coon.' It was said of him that, 'like the pelican he stood alone' – he 'never copied anyone and no one ... attempted to copy' him.[23]

Chirgwin, whose father was a circus clown, first appeared on stage, aged 6 in 1860 as a 'negro' comedian before becoming part of the Chirgwin Family the following year.[24] In his early teens he worked the beach at Margate before joining with his brother Jack in a 'double act on "nigger minstrel" lines' that toured the provinces until the mid-1870s. His solo career started in London in 1877. In 1911 he was honoured in a jubilee concert near the end of his performing career. His musical skills were prodigious. He played the fiddle, banjo, piano, Japanese fiddle, bagpipes and Irish pipes. He was an adept dancer, and it was said to have a melodious voice and a considerable vocal range; sadly, surviving recordings do not do him justice. He was also a comedian, including 'some eccentric business with two clay pipes and a tea tray' which was particularly popular. His patter, delivered in a 'London' accent, with its quick-fire flurry of puns, had more in common with Harry Champion.[25]

Chirgwin's 'kaffir' persona was complex, if not contradictory. Although his highly distinctive make-up was allegedly an

G H Chirgwin, 'The White-Eyed Musical Kaffir' aka 'The Cockney Coloured Coon'

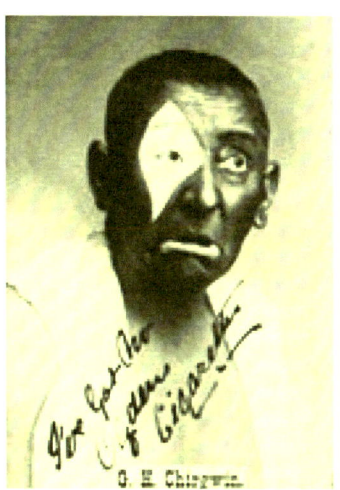

accident, it had the effect of further confusing the mask he wore. The white diamond had the effect of allowing the white-man-behind-the-mask to peep out at the audience.[26] The illusion of the blackface minstrel was further undermined by the 'cockneyisms' in his patter and his regular concluding comment, 'Could do wiv a drink,' in what was 'stock local, not mock "nigger."'[27] Here was Chirgwin telling his audience that behind the mask was the real Londoner, the man from Seven Dials and that the show/illusion was now over. The matter was further complicated by certain of his songs, which perpetuated the hybrid character, such as 'The Cockney Coon,' and 'A Good Old London Town Girl,' which asserted his and his girl's essential London-ness. Both could be read as either transcending simple racial difference and recognising a black British identity; or reinforcing them, through the 'hilarious impossibility' of black cockneys.[28]

Chirgwin was on good terms with Harry Hunter, the interlocutor and main songwriter of the Mohawk Minstrels, and performed many of Hunter's songs, such as 'Comparisons Melodious,' which he sang at a benefit concert for Hunter in 1888.[29] Chirgwin was a long-standing and consistent favourite of the music halls.[30] He was best known for two extremely popular songs: 'The Blind Boy,' partly written by G W Moore, of the Moore and Burgess Minstrels, and 'My Fiddle Is My Sweetheart,' written by Harry Hunter. 'The Blind Boy,' which

Chirgwin sang in a high falsetto voice, was unashamedly sentimental.[31]

> I am but a poor blind boy/Still my heart is full of joy
> Though I never saw the light/Or the flowers they
>   call so bright.
> I can hear the sweet birds sing/And the wild bee on
>   the wing
> Bird and bee and summer wind/Sing to me because
>   I'm blind.
> *Chorus*
> They love me, yes, they love me/And to me they are
>   so kind
> They love me, yes, they love me/Because I am blind.[32]

Similarly, 'My Fiddle Is My Sweetheart' was a mainstream music-hall song, which shows the extent to which Hunter had moved towards this genre. Again, the lyrics are sentimental, though with more than a touch of humour.

> My fiddle is my sweetheart, and I'm her faithful beau
> I take her to my bosom, because I love her so
> I clasp her gently round her neck, her vocal chords
>   I press
> I ask her if she loves me, and she answers "Yes, yes,
>   yes"[33]

More straightforward were the stage personas of Eugene Stratton, 'The Whistling Coon' and his successor, the Rochdale-born G H Elliott, 'The Chocolate Coloured Coon.' Stratton, who was born in Buffalo, had a background in circus but made a name as an Irish jig and clog dancer. In 1878, aged 17, he joined Haverley's Minstrels before coming to London two years later, where in 1881 he joined the Moore and Burgess Minstrels, working his way (literally) to the front of the stage, where, as cornerman, he sang what was to become his signature tune, 'The Whistling Coon.'

Although Stratton sang various songs, including comedy numbers such as 'The Cats in Our Backyard' and 'Polly Cockatoo,' he was best known for his "coon" songs, of which

Eugene Stratton, 'The Whistling Coon'

'The Dandy Coloured Coon' and 'The Whistlin' Yellow Gal' were the most popular.

Having made his name with the Moore and Burgess Minstrels, he moved to the variety stage because of 'the prospect of making more money.'[34] Initially he met with limited success, in no small measure because of a decision to abandon blackface. Even as a blackface singer, he was not well received at certain provincial concerts, though his popularity with London audiences remained high.[35] His partnership with Lesley Stuart resulted in a series of hit songs, including 'Little Dolly Daydream,' 'My Little Octoroon' and especially 'Lily of Laguna.' As well as highly attractive songs, Stratton's performance, as singer and dancer, were highly regarded. There was no escaping the racial stereotyping in his songs. His well-known song, 'The Whistling Coon,' is about a 'very funny, queer old coon … [who is] a knock-kneed, double-jointed, hunky-plunky moke, and he's happy when he whistles this tune.' With grotesquely 'others' features, he is clearly inferior, at best childlike, at worse like a baboon.

Even 'Lily of Laguna' is 'de same old tale of a palpatatin' niggar,' but the chorus, 'She's ma lady love, she is ma dove, ma baby love … She is de Lily of Laguna, she is ma Lily and ma Rose,' combined a sing-along tune with sentimental lyrics. The effect was further enhanced by Stratton's stage performance.[36] In addition, through its association with 'coon' songs, Stratton was an important figure in the introduction of ragtime music, not least with the controversial ragtime song 'All Coons Look Alike to Me.' Finally, he was a major influence on G H Elliott,

'The Chocolate Coloured Coon,' who took over many of Stratton's song and ensured that the popularity of this genre was sustained after Stratton's death (1919) and through the inter-war years. Elliott tended to sing more sentimental songs, such as 'By the Light of the Silvery Moon,' as well as the less overtly (or viciously) racist "Dixie" songs that had become popular in the early twentieth century.[37]

Constructing 'the nigger' in song[38]

One of the most striking characteristics of 'coon' songs across the years is the evocation of a rural arcadia, set on a southern plantation where the corn is ripe, birds singing, picaninnes playing and masters and slaves happy. In 'Carry Me Back to Old Virginny,' (written 1878), the audience is told 'no place on earth do I love more sincerely than old Virginny, the state where I was born.' In 'The Old Folks at Home,' (written 1851) the singer is 'longing for the old plantation' as much as 'the old folk at home.'[39] The (supposed) reciprocal affection between slaves and masters creates a sense of an organic, hierarchical society with everyone happy in their rightful place. Negro man are hard-working and obedient, but respected and loved.[40] 'When Old Ned die Massa [and Missis too] take it mighty hard,' we hear in ' Uncle Ned,' (written 1848), but it is the affection for masters that is most striking. 'All de darkies am a weeping, Massa's in de cold, cold ground.' (written 1852). Such reassuring images sat uneasily with the depiction of slavery in *Uncle Tom's Cabin*, which enjoyed considerable popularity in the mid-nineteenth century, and make more problematic the response to minstrelsy in England, though the evocation of a stable rural society may have had an appeal at a time when many observers were aware of the threat posed by urban society. Similarly, the image of racial harmony may have become more attractive as fears of the 'uncivilised savage' from 'Darkest Africa' became more common.

As individuals, the negro is often child-like and happy, delighting in music (the banjo-playing singer of 'Oh! Susannah'), dancing (Oh! Dem Golden Slippers' or 'De Great Cake Walk') and even gambling ('Camptown Races').[41] They are comic characters, often, dating back to the grotesque 'Jump Jim Crow.'[42] Certain physical characteristics, clearly on view on stage, are stressed in the lyrics. Sal, in 'Polly Wolly Doodle,' has 'laughing eyes and curly hair,' the subject of 'Kentucky Babe' is instructed to 'lay yo' kinky, wool head on yo' mammy's breast,' but poor 'Uncle Ned,' as well as having no teeth and being blind, has 'no wool on de top of his head.' Most blatantly, 'old fickle Ruth,' the subject of 'She's A Thoroughbred', is summed up in language more commonly associated with livestock and their breeding qualities. The lyrics detail her stereotypical characteristics: 'with big thick lips and a big, flat nose, She's inky black witch-hazel eyes and a mammoth mouth.'[43] All in all, she's 'a Thoroughbred and the best in town. She's not a regular nigger, just a chestnut brown.' Inky black or chestnut brown, it is clear that it is her physicality that defines her. As humans were seen as a higher life form than animals, so whites (especially white men) are superior to those with coloured skins.

There are also elements of the characterisation, which while still stereotypical, reflect more of a desired other. Open expressions of sentiment, especially regarding children, are to be found well before it became acceptable for white singers to do so. 'A Lovesick Nigger' and 'A Lovesick Coon' appeared at least twenty years before Bing Crosby. Fatherhood was also celebrated. 'I'm the Father of a Little Black Coon,' while in 'Poor Old Joe' the old man reflects on 'the children so dear that I held on my knee,' 'The Little Alabama Coon' is rocked to sleep: 'go to sleep, my little picaninny.' The death of a child, in particular, evoked outpourings of grief, as in 'Baby Boy Has Passed Away' and 'Close the Shutters, Willy's Dead.' The same sense of a desired other can be found in songs that dwelt on the easy-going negro, indifferent to the Protestant work ethic but it was easy to slip from wistful desire of a release from the rigours of everyday work into 'The Idler' or 'The Lazy Coon's Dream.' And it was but one further step to the negative stereotype of 'The Cunning Little Coon.'

'Coon' songs perpetuated a view of society expressed in terms of an organic, racial hierarchy. Society was contented and in equilibrium, in song at least, and everyone knew their place and fulfilled their roles. Several songs mocked the ludicrous pretentions of 'The Black Philosopher' and 'The Coon Ambassador' but behind the mockery – how could one seriously think of a black man as a philosopher? – was a fear, however poorly articulated, that the 'natural order' was not immutable. The denigration of black people on stage, by 'black' people, before a white audience was a powerful assertion of authority but which, at a time when the British Empire was coming under challenge, reflected a degree of anxiety behind the self-confidence. The myth of Dixie-land served a purpose, not just in post-Civil War America.

Minstrelsy outside the music hall

Awareness of the minstrel repertoire was not simply confined to those who attended a minstrel show or a music hall. Sheet music increased its availability, partly as prices fell by the end of the century, and partly as the second-hand music trade grew. As well as specific songs, there were a growing number of compilations. Well into the twentieth century the *People's Song Book* contained Nigger minstrel songs, alongside favourites from across the United Kingdom.[44] Earlier, Regondi produced a series of 'sixpenny concertina books,' which included '60 of Christy's Minstrels Songs' and '60 Collin's Christy's Songs.'[45] However, much more important in the dissemination of popular songs and tunes was the plethora of street musicians and itinerant performers who played a crucial role, bringing music to a much wider audience than ever attended a concert hall.[46]

Charles Mackay, commenting specifically on the 'Jump Jim Crow' craze, noted black-faced street urchins performing 'the uncouth dance ... in its full perfection on market nights in any great thoroughfare, and ... the words ... piercing above all the din and buzz of the multitude.'[47] According to Mayhew, Ethiopian serenaders, comprising the 'better class of ballad-singers,' appeared on the streets of London in the 1840s, inspired by Pell's troupe and the inimitable Juba.[48] 'Our opening chorus,' one Ethiopian serenader informed him, 'was 'The Wild Racoon Track' and we finished up with the 'Railway Overture.' In between times, came songs such as 'Old Joe,' 'Dan Tucker' and 'Going Ober de Mountain.' What he did not mention was the speed with which these songs crossed the Atlantic.[49] The sheer amateurism of the early troupes was striking – 'all thumping and whistling, for nobody knew how to play the banjo then' – as was the necessity to perform whenever and wherever money could be made. 'Regent-street, Oxford-street and the greater part of St. James's are our best places' but not always welcoming, whereas Whitechapel was more so but less lucrative. The best pitch was outside a house in which someone was ill. 'We don't move on for less than a shilling … We generally get our two shillings.' More generally, 'the gentry are our best customers,' men more than woman, and the occasional 'gent's wedding' paid well indeed. Saturday night was the time 'to get money from the working people' in the regular markets, especially in 'Cleveland-street … Carnaby-street [and] Edgeware-road.' And there was always work on the Thames steamers, outside public houses or in 'cheap concert rooms' such as the Albion in the notorious Ratcliff-highway.

There were also attractive opportunities elsewhere, 'the watering places,' or Brighton, as well as one-off but profitable events such as a review at Portsmouth to which 'we walked down … a-purpose.' A similar observation was made by a contributor to the *St. James's Magazine* in 1868, who noted 'various bands [of negro minstrels] wandering throughout the country.'[50] If Mayhew's respondents were correct, the number of 'negro serenaders' were in decline, as the returns, once 5s or 6s a day, shrunk to £1 a week; but they never entirely disappeared from city streets, as they relocated, during the summer at least, to resorts such as Margate and Ramsgate, Yarmouth, Scarborough and Blackpool. G H Chirgwin and Gus Elen were two of the more successful music-hall artists whose early career took them to the south coast as minstrels. Others, such as 'Uncle Bones' at Margate became fixtures in a lifetime career on the beach.[51] Such was the growth of seaside musical entertainment that the 'negro minstrel' became a stock figure in the satirical press. *Punch* estimated facetiously, 'twenty-three barrel-organs, eleven troupes of nigger minstrels and four blind beggars with fiddles' in Smellington-super-mare.[52] More soberly, *Cycling*, recommended Bournemouth because 'nigger minstrels are rarer than otherwhere.'[53]

The infiltration of minstrelsy into other aspects of popular music is less easy to establish but scattered evidence points to it's influence being widespread. Robert Whinham, the itinerant Northumbrian fiddler and dance master, wrote variations on the Stephen Foster song, 'Old Folks At Home' soon after it was

'Uncle Bones,'
Margate beach

heard in this country.⁵⁴ Feargus O'Connor, better known as a Chartist, boasted of having danced the 'Jim Crow hornpipe.'⁵⁵ There were also several 'Jim Crow Quadrilles,' dating from the late-1830s.⁵⁶ Unlike their American counterparts, 'Crow Quadrilles,' English 'Jim Crow Quadrilles,' did not use tunes such as 'Zip Coon,' but favoured popular English and Irish tunes such as 'Shepherd's Hey' and 'Dingles [sic] Regatta.'⁵⁷

Some concluding observations

Blackface minstrelsy was an important part of Victorian and Edwardian popular music in its own right and had a wider influence on other forms. It developed an entertainment style and a corpus of songs that remained popular in this country until the 1970s. It added to the diversity of popular music and, particularly through its association with ragtime, minstrelsy contributed to one of the major developments of twentieth century popular music – the internationalisation of popular music, which brought with it an ever-increasing 'Tin Pan Alley' influence. More broadly, through its changing stereotypes, it contributed to the way in which English society viewed itself and the world, particularly during the late-nineteenth century years of imperial expansion, in terms of (alleged) racial differences and which left a problematic legacy that was to have a significant impact after the second world war.

Endnotes

1. M Pickering, *Blackface Minstrelsy in Britain*, London, Routledge, 2016, p.3. Earlier, (p. xii) he makes the point that, like this study, his 'book operates at an analytical distance from the stereotypical images and views it discusses.'

2. See also J Mullen, 'Anti-Black Racism in British Popular Music (1880-1920).' *French Journal of British Studies* 17(2), 2012

3. See for example, Winifred Johnson, speaking of Eugene Stratton, and praising 'his Negro impersonations [as] … quite the most lifelike. [He] had never been so like a Nigger as in his "Dandy Coloured Coon."' *Era*, 'A Chat with Winifred Johnson,' 30 March 1895.

4. For a more detailed discuss see Pickering, *Blackface Minstrelsy*, chap. 4 'British Masks' and chap. 5 'Racial Mockery', on which the following paragraph is heavily dependent. See also J S Bratton, 'English Ethiopians: British Audiences and Black-Face Acts, 1835-1865,' *Yearbook of English Studies*, 11, 1981, pp.127-142.

5. Bratton, 'English Ethiopians,' p.139 Both had touring companies that traversed provincial England. The Moore and Burgess Minstrels evolved out of the touring Christy Minstrels.

6. Clearly, blackface music in England did not begin in the 1830s were Some fifty years earlier, Charles Dibdin had included 'negro impersonations' and songs such as 'The Negro and His Banjer' in his *Table Entertainments*, which were well received not only in London. The first volume of Fairburn's *Universal* Songster, a compilation of over one thousand songs, which appeared in 1825, contained eight 'negro' songs. Four of these – 'The Negro Woman's Song,' 'The Desponding Negro Slave,' 'The Negro's Soliloquy' and 'The Negro Mother' – were essential about the eponymous figure's plight. Three others affected 'negro' language but, particularly 'The Negro Drinking Song,' portrayed an infantile figure. In contrast 'Opossum Up a Gum Tree,' which was described as 'a real negro melody' was an authentic slave song, which had been popularised in England by Charles Mathews, who probably performed blackface, after his visit to America and was also associated with the distinguished African-American actor, Ira Aldridge. M Pickering, '"A Jet Ornament to Society:' Black Music in Nineteenth-century Britain' in P Oliver, ed., *Black Music in Britain: Essays on the Afro-Asian Contribution to Popular Music*, Buckingham, Open University Press, 1990 and Pickering, *Blackface Minstrelsy*, pp.1-12. For the emergence of American minstrelsy in the 1820s and 1830s see D Cockrell, *Demons of Disorder*, Cambridge University Press, 1997 and (the idiosyncratic) W T Lhamon, *Raising Cain*, Cambridge, Mass., Harvard University Press, 1998.

7. The commercialization of 'Jump Jim Crow' would have delighted Disney. There were Jim Crow hats, pipes and cigars as well as a collection of children's songs, *Jim Crow's Alphabet*, and even an autobiography – a considerable achievement for 'a lame old nigger' celebrated in a 'stupid song.' See also W T Lhamon, *Jump Jim Crow: Lost Plays, Lyrics and Street Prose of the First Atlantic Popular Culture*, Cambridge, Mass., Harvard University Press, 2003.

8. https://www.utm.utoronto.ca/~w3minstr/featured/eyewitness_juba_content.html More generally, see S J Graham's entry on Lane in Grove Music

Online https://doi-org.libaccess.hud.ac.uk/10.1093/gmo/9781561592630. article.A2285115 Moore and Burgess's star dancer was Joe Brown. *Era* 22 November 1857.

9   For more detail see Pickering, *Blackface Minstrelsy*, pp.15-7.
10 D Scott, *The Singing Bourgeois: Songs of the Victorian Drawing Room and Parlour*, Milton Keynes, Open University Press, 1989, p.90 and Pickering, *Blackface Minstrelsy*, pp.36-8
11 Pickering, *Blackface Minstrelsy*, p.31
12 *Era* 20 December 1863. He was performing at the South London music hall. Mackney started his career in Bristol in the mid-1840s. later playing Manchester, Salford, Sheffield and Birmingham before appearing in London.
13 'Monymusk. was a well-known reel or strathspey, with links to both Scotland and Ireland, and 'Tink a Tink,' which was collected by Cecil Sharp as an English country dance tune, was also included in, for example, *Scottish Dance Tunes from the Isles of Man* (!), 1804. Information from Mackney's Banjo Tutor, 1863 at https://archive.org/details/MackneyTutorCopy
14 *Era* 22 November 1857. See also 20 May 1866 which referred to 'one of those peculiar jigs which "champions" usually delight.' Brown's great rival was Wash Norton, a member of Moore & Bryant's Minstrels, who won a disputed victory in a championship 'Grand Match Dance' at the Cambridge music-hall in 1870. As well as the title a bet of £100 a side was at stake. *Era* 22 May 1870
15 The Dolphin Inn Music Hall advertised for 'a good Nigger Singer and Dancer' *Era* 9 December 1855 and again 18 October 1857.
16 *Era* 19 March 1865
17 The following references are drawn from a more thorough examination of the *Huddersfield Chronicle* and *Huddersfield Examiner* than the collection of newspaper clippings consulted by Pickering. Henry Phillip's 'Original American Entertainment' at the town's Philosophical-hall is the first recorded performance of 'negro melodies' in the town. *Huddersfield Examiner*, 24 December 1853.
18 A troupe calling themselves The Original Christy Minstrels also appeared at the Gymnasium-hall in 1872, which was somewhat surprising as the 'Farewell Visit of the Real and Original Christy Minstrels' had taken place in the town in 1869. In addition, Ramsey & Newcomb's Minstrels, an eighteen piece troupe, the Campbell Minstrels, a mere thirteen in number, the Harry Templeton troupe and Buckley's Serenaders all played in the town.
19 Pickering, *Blackface Minstrelsy*, pp.59-60
20 *Huddersfield Chronicle*, 22 January 1865 and 17 July 1864. See also 24 April 1864 ('The Great Ben Ray'), 29 October 1865 ('The Brothers Graham, Nigger Vocalists and natives of Huddersfield') and 16 January 1869 ('the oldest organized troupe of Christy Minstrels')
21 *Huddersfield Chronicle,* 10 December 1864 & 4 February 1866, and 4 February 1866 and *Era* 29 October 1865. The Carrolls and Dick Crowther were a regionally successful troupe who toured throughout the north west and north east of England but also appeared (once) in London.
22 *Huddersfield Chronicle*, 7 April 1891 and 25 September 1897
23 *Stage* 11 May 1911. This was not strictly true as there were Chirgwin imitators.

24 Biographical information gleaned from *Era* 10 October 1896, *Stage* 11 May 1911, 16 November 1927 and 27 July 1995 and *Music Hall and Theatre Review* 13 February 1897. See also S Featherstone, 'Chirgwin, George' *Oxford Dictionary of National Biography*, 2004 at https://doi-org.libaccess.hud.ac.uk/10.1093/ref:odnb/70293
25 He combined musical skill and comic ability to create another white-face stage character, an 'intensely funny … piping Scotchman whose Highland costume [was] highly ludicrous.' *Era* 7 October 1881
26 Mullen, 'Anti-Black Racism,' p.64
27 Pickering, *Blackface Minstrelsy*, p.98
28 Mullen, 'Anti-Black Racism,' p.10
29 *Era* 13 October 1888. Hunter was an important composer who wrote songs ranging from 'Dixie pastoral ('My Dear Old Cabin Home') to 'motto' songs ('Do Not Nurse Your Anger' and 'Seek To Do the Right Thing') but also included anti-feminist numbers, such as 'I've Got the Ooperzootic,' which ridiculed Elizabeth Garrett Anderson. Pickering, *Blackface Minstrelsy*, pp.37-50 and Scott, *Singing Bourgeois* pp.90-2.
30 Indeed, there was a point in the early 1880s when he was criticised for not varying his act. *Stage* 25 November 1881
31 See for example, 'Skylark, Skylark' discussed in chapter 10.
32 A 1911 recording can be heard at https://www.youtube.com/watch?v=xq3pbPrRXJ4
33 A very scratchy, and almost inaudible recording can be heard at https://www.youtube.com/watch?v=vbciBbYaDIU
34 *Era*, '"The Whistling Coon" At Home,' 4 March 1893
35 He appeared at various venues in the midlands and north of England. In 1895 he appeared twice in Hull. The first time he was 'not well received by the pitgoers in Hull' but the second was better received. *Hull Daily Mail* 27 & 28 February and 13 March 1895.
36 Pickering, *Blackface Minstrelsy*, draws attention to the incongruity of many 'coon' love songs.
37 Mullen, 'Anti-Black Racim,' p.6 and p.10
38 The following draws in part on Mullen, 'Anti-Black Racism' but the bulk of the songs quoted are from readily available well into the second quarter of the twentieth century in published community song books.
39 See also C A Whites 'I'se Gwine back to Dixie.'
40 The importance of self-control emerges clearly in motto songs, such as 'Do Not Speak the Angry Word' and 'Do Not Nurse Your Anger.'
41 See also 'Happy Little Sam,' 'The Laughing Darkie' and 'Happy Am de Boys Down Here.'
42 T Scriven, 'The Jim Crow Craze in London's Press and Streets, 1836-39,' *Journal of Victorian Culture*, 19(1), 2014, pp.93-109
43 She is also a large woman: 'And on her bed because she's stout, There's sandpaper sheets so she can't slide out.'
44 Cited in Mullen, 'Anti-Black Racism,' p.4
45 *Era* 22 December 1867. Also in the series were '40 of 'The Great Vance's Comic Songs' and '60 Standard Scotch and Irish Tunes.' Regondi was best known as a classical guitarist but was also a virtuoso on the concertina.

46 G F Rehin, 'Blackface Street Minstrels in Victorian London and its Resorts: Popular Culture and its Racial Connotations As Revealed in Polite Opinion,' *Journal of Popular Culture*, 1981, 15(1), pp. 19-38.) The seemingly minor importance of street music is misleading as it links in with a number of larger debates. The debates about street musicians (especially in London) in the 1850s and 1860s relate to question of social space, urban order and the role of the state in general and the police in particular. In broader terms the topic raises more fundamental questions about 'hearing history.' For differing attitudes towards street music see the debates on the Bill for the Better Regulation of Street Music within the Metropolitan Police District especially, *Hansard* vol.172, 17 July 1863 (Lord Fermoy) and vol. 175, 9 June 1864 (Thomas Hankey).

47 C Mackay, *Memoirs of Extraordinary Popular Delusions and the Madness of Crowds,* 'Popular Follies in Great Cities,' London, 1841, p.146 at https://vantagepointtrading.com/wp-content/uploads/2010/05/Charles_Mackay-Extraordinary_Popular_Delusions_and_the_Madness_of_Crowds.pdf

48 H Mayhew, 'An Ethiopian Serenader' in P Quennell, ed., *Mayhew's Characters*, London, Spring Books, 1951, pp.259-65

49 'The Wild Raccoon Track' was written in 1843, the same year as 'Old Dan Tucker' was popularised by the Virginia Minstrels and Dan Emmett's 'I Gwine Ober de Mountain' was published in America.

50 Cited in Rehin 'Blackface Street Minstrels,' p.22

51 In many resorts by the turn of the twentieth century blackface minstrels had been replaced by whiteface pierrots.

52 *Punch* 3 September 1898. See also its observations on Slopsea-super-mare (23 August 1882) and Starmouth (10 & 17 September and 1 October 1887). Similarly, *Fun,* 18 August 1896, included in its 'Don'ts for the Seaside' the following advice: 'Don't encourage nigger minstrels on the sands' as well as 'Don't cycle in your bathing costume.'

53 *Cycling* 16 December 1893

54 The T Armstrong manuscript is dated c.1850. G Dixon, *Remember Me: The Fiddle Music of Robert Whinham,* Wallace Music, Pathhead, Midlothian, 1995, p.54. 'Old Folks At Home' was written by Foster for the Christy's Minstrels in 1851. They appeared in England for the first time in 1857. The Armstrong manuscript also contains Whinham's variations on 'Meg Merriles' as well as original compositions, such as 'The Dolsimor Waltz' and 'The De'ils in the Fish' and 'This Is No My Ain Lassie,' both with variations.

55 *Morning Post*, 4 June 1852' O'Connor referred to it as a once-popular dance.

56 *Norwich Mercury*, 19 August 1837 and a general reference in *Era*, 16 December 1838

57 For Crow Quadrilles see Library of Congress *https://www.loc.gov/resource/sm1837.010990.0?st=gallery* For Jim Crow Quadrilles see http://richardrobinson.tunebook.org.uk/list/Tune?searchterms[andfields]=1&searchterms[simple][text]=jim%20crow nos. 1 & 3

CHAPTER 13

'Fings ain't what they used to be': The strange and lingering death of variety theatre

> Now Harry was a champion in their eyes
> With his old green tie on
> When he sung about hot meat pies
> And any, any, any old iron
> He was king of 'em all at the music hall
> Or down at the Old Britannia
> Singin' put a little treacle on me puddin' Mary Anne
> Well you can't help laughing can ya?
>
> Chas 'n' Dave, 'Harry Was A Champion'

MUSIC HALL, OR variety theatre as it was increasingly known, appeared triumphant in the early twentieth century. It was at the heart of live popular music. There was a network of theatres that crossed the land and a substantial and varied workforce, which gave it a dominant position in the commercialised popular music industry of Edwardian England. Its recently acquired 'respectability' was confirmed by the Royal Command Performance of 1912. Overall, the Great War was a further stimulus but the 1920s saw the number of theatre closures increase dramatically. There were fears that variety would go the way of American vaudeville but, rather than die, it rallied in the 1930s only to succumb finally in the 1950s.

On closer examination, the pre-war 'golden' days were less firmly based than appeared at the time. Music hall was struggling to renew itself as many of the big names were coming to the end of their careers. The evolution of 'family-friendly' entertainment ran the risk of losing a more youthful audience, and the emphasis on passive consumption made it susceptible to the threat of the new music, ragtime and jazz, coming from America in the 1900s. Novelty 'ragtime' songs abounded but they missed the point. The greatest attraction of the new music was the opportunity to dance to one of the ragtime bands, rather than to listen to witty words.[1] Technological changes, albeit in their infancy, were at best a mixed blessing. Short films might be included as a novelty turn in a traditional variety programme but, as the growth in the number of cinemas portended, film might become a powerful rival. Similarly, radio and records carried the potential to transform both the production and consumption of popular music.

Music hall during the Great War

Popular song reflected and, in part, shaped a wider coming to terms with the realities of modern warfare.[2] When war broke out in 1914 many music-hall artists, as well as impresarios, rallied to the cause, seeing it as a brief but heroic interval, to be supported and celebrated in the way that Victorian conflicts had been. Performers added a patriotic verse to songs in their repertoire and the number of specially written pro-war songs increased. 'We Didn't Want a European War' echoed the sentiment of MacDermott's 'Jingo Song,'[3] while 'Tommy is as Good a Man as Any Knight of Old' set the present conflict in a longer heroic perspective. Patronising encouragement to allies ('Good Luck, Little French Soldier Man!') coexisted with warnings to our foes ('Hands Off, Germany'). Notions of imperial unity seen in the songs of the late-nineteenth century music hall re-appeared in Florrie Forde's 'They Sang "God Save the King,"' which brought together not only an Englishman, a Scotsman and an Irishman but also a Welshman.[4] Imperial unity was extended to included 'Our Brave Colonials' and even 'John Bull's Little Khaki Coon.' 'Blokes' who had previously been seen as 'comic caper jokes,' in the eyes of Marie Lloyd, were transformed by army uniform: 'I Do Like Yer, Cocky, Now You've Got Your Khaki On.' Among the established stars, Vesta Tilley and Harry Lauder were at the forefront but other, performers, such as Gertie Gitane appeared in public to entertain the troops, some even venturing to France.[5] Yet alongside recruitment songs, such as 'I'll Make a Man of

You,' there were also songs of yearning and return. 'Keep the Home Fires Burning' appeared in 1914, 'Tell My Daddy to Come Home Again' in 1915 and 'Blighty, the Soldier's Home, Sweet Home' in 1916. Such songs became more prevalent as the initial enthusiasm for war began to wane and gung-ho recruitment songs, such as 'Your King and Your Country Want You,' no longer seemed appropriate as the conflict continued and separation and losses increased.[6] Anti-war songs were rare, but, as the war progressed, there was a distinct scepticism, most notably in 'Oh What a Lovely War,' of 1918.[7]

Most wartime popular songs, however, were not about war and its impact, but rather reflected the more mundane concerns that had been the staple of Victorian and Edwardian music-hall. Music hall, in war as in peace, was about entertainment and escape from the concerns of everyday life, including those 'temporary' adjustments necessitated by the conflict. There was a continuation of pre-war trends. Harry Champion continued to sing the praises of various dishes, such as 'Boiled Beef and Carrots' and 'Hot Tripe and Onions,' familiar, especially to his working-class London audience.[8] Such was the popularity of his 'Grow Some Taters' (1915) that it was taken up by the government as part of its campaign to encourage home-grown vegetables. Though more problematic, alcohol, especially in the form of good English ale, was similarly celebrated.[9] Champion also reprised the old motto song, 'Work, Boys, Work (and Be Contented), in 1915, but there fewer of this type of song. Ernie Mayne sang of his contribution to the war effort in 'My Meatless Day,' explaining 'I don't sell flags on the street, I go without my bits of meat.' The tone is light-hearted as is Walt Cunliffe's 'In These Hard Times.' 'Things are bad, awful bad … Food is dear, rent is dear … In these hard times you mustn't pick and choose' nevertheless there are consolations as 'every single chappie can make a girlie happy.' The upbeat tune and 'look on the bright side' message was of a piece with others of his 'bright and breezy' songs, such as 'We'll Have a Holiday in the Summertime' and 'Now That the Lights Are Low,' which extolled the new-found opportunities for spooning.

There were fewer of the old-style ('My Old Man') social commentary songs, but it was difficult to sing in the same way about the roles of women, given their increasingly visible presence in the work force. There was a shift in the depiction of women from a passive, traditional role ('The Women Who Wait') to a more positive, modern one ('What Should We Do Without Them (War Girls)?'). 'Daughters of Britain, Work with a Will' captured the change. Gone were 'the good old days with the good old ways' in which women 'drifted quietly on' and in its place a new world in which women 'work with a will … [and] learn everything they can,' including not to be 'afraid of the task we thought could only be done by men.'[10] The song was a favourite but the land army, the girl guides and the women's institute, with its wider popularity is open to question.[11] Many wartime songs that referred to women's work often trivialised or marginalised it. 'The Dance of the Fire Brigade Girls,' from the highly successful 1915 revue, *Bric à Brac*, illustrates the point well. The opening scene is set in Mummerset, where 'the houses are as picturesque as the sixteen P.G.s [Palace Girls] who appear there as firemen and other things.' Reviews do not mention 'The Dance of the Fire Brigade Girls' but focus on the 'exquisite' "Toilet of Venus" scene, the splendour of the dresses and the stand-out songs, Teddie Gerrard's 'Glad To See You Back' and Gertie Millar's 'Chalk Farm to Camberwell' and 'Toy Town.'[12] Another successful revue of that year, *Shell Out*, featured 'If The Girlies Could Be Soldiers' sung by Unity More, accompanied by a line of young women 'in the daintiest of dancing frocks and the smartest of uniforms.' She was praised for two conventional songs ('I Want Loving' and 'Little Miss Lancashire'), though most plaudits went to the comedic figure of Fred Emney.[13] Many songs were conservative, or at least ambiguous, in regard to the new role of women. This is clearly seen in Vesta Tilley's 'Where Are the Girls of the Old Brigade.' The things that 'girls are doing now,' such as driving a motor or a plough or working in munitions is 'simply wonderful, simply wonderful,' but there is a touch of the ridiculous – she 'will chase a bullock when she's told to milk a cow ' – and the reassurance that the old order has not been destroyed. The third verse notes that 'Lots of girls have done the trick, for better or for worse/confetti, and a husband and something small to nurse' while the chorus repeats that 'it's the same piece of petticoat all the while.' The matter is compounded by the fact that the song is delivered in drag. Members of the audience could laugh at or agree with the figure she presented on stage. Even a song such as

'Women of the Homeland (God Bless You Every One!)' which explicitly praised women for their war work and linked them to the men at the front through their shared 'love of home and country,' still emphasised traditional feminine qualities. Women were 'so brave but so resigned.' They sacrificed their 'dearest treasure … sweetheart, brother, son' while praying for their safe return home.

The need for escapism, exacerbated by wartime events, explains the popularity of nonsense songs. 'Sister Susie's Sewing Shirts for Soldiers' while 'Patty Proudly Packs for Privates Prepaid Paper Parcels.'[14] Verbal virtuosity was equally at the root of the success of Billy Murray's 'Which Switch Is The Switch, Miss, For Ipswich.'[15] Escapist in a different way were a number of romantic songs of varying degrees of sentimentality. Gertie Gitane made 'a direct appeal to the hearts of the public with 'There's silver in your hair, dear (But gold in your heart)' while the 'plaintive tones of her voice' was central to the success of 'When I Leave the World Behind.'[16] José Collins' 'virile sincerity' as she sang "Love Will Find a Way" made the song a hit.[17] The latter points to a shift in content discernible in these years. Old themes persisted. Mothers were still idolised by their sons ('Mother and Me'), husbands hen-pecked ('Since My Wife Joined the WAAC') and fathers incompetent ('Father's Got the Sack from the Waterworks'); but new ones emerged. The story of 'If You Were the Only Girl in the World' is well-known.[18] Robey originally planned to sing it for laughs in a traditional manner. Allegedly, at the last moment, he decided to sing it 'straight,' thereby giving him and Violet Lorraine a huge hit, which they repeated in 1918 with 'First Love – Last Love – Best Love.'[19]

Music hall and the threat of the new

Music-hall songs were also popular at the front but there were signs of change. Philip Gibbs observed members of the London Irish Rifles, at the battle of Loos (September 1915) marching to their comb-and-paper band, playing music hall songs, such as 'Hullo, Hullo! It's a Different Girl Again,' a Walt Cunliffe song from 1906; but the most popular tune was 'Waiting for the Robert E Lee.'[20] Ragtime presented an opportunity to new singers and a challenge to old.[21] Daisy Dormer sang 'Ragtime

Cowboy Joe' and the Two Rascals asked 'Are You from Dixie?' There was even a 'Ragtime Suffragette' – 'She's no household pet ... raggin' and naggin' with politics' – which combined the modernity of the latest musical craze with conservative socio-political sentiment. Alec Hurley jumped on the bandwagon with 'The Ragtime Navvy' and G H Chirgwin introduced 'The Ragtime Coon.' Despite his popularity as a cockney singer, Harry Champion felt it necessary to add to his repertoire with 'My Ragtime Missus' and 'Ragtime Ragshop,' though neither were very successful. America's entry into the war further boosted what proved to be a relatively short-lived craze. New dances (and songs celebrating them) also appeared: the tango in 1914 and the foxtrot in 1916. After all, 'In Grandma's Day They Never Did the Foxtrot,' rather then 'they were modest [and] never looked naughty' whereas 'now it's strange, what a change.' Then there were the outrageous, upbeat novelty dances – 'The Grizzly Bear,' 'The Bunny Hop,' 'The Turkey-trot' and even the 'Kangaroo Dip.'[22] The excitement of the music was heightened by its association with the exotic, in the form of the brothels and saloons from which it supposedly arose.

A more immediate threat to variety theatre came from the new revues and, most particularly, the cinema. Ominously, several big music halls – the Empire in Bradford, the Tivoli in Liverpool and the Grand in Sheffield – were converted into cinemas. Any hope that the 'good old days' of pre-war music-hall could be restored were soon dashed. The quasi-monopoly that music-hall had enjoyed before 1914 was broken. Demand for popular music, and the other elements of variety entertainment, increased but the variety theatre was no longer the sole supplier. The emergence of new competitors put pressure on theatre managers, for whom costs, at best, remained unchanged.[23] The problems were most acute in the so-called number two and number three theatres in the provinces. Some closed, some were converted into cinemas and some continued in hybrid form as cine-variety theatres. The fear was of a repetition of the American experience, where vaudeville had been killed off by RKO in the 1920s. The decline in Britain was checked in the late-1920s by two important, if somewhat surprising saviours, in the form of George Black, an early cinema entrepreneur, and Val Parnell, who showed that variety theatre could be profitable, albeit in a complex relationship, more co-operative than competitive, with other providers of popular music.[24] Black, as head of the Moss Empire chain, created a viable business model based, on the London Palladium formula, but replicated across its provincial theatres, which allowed the flagship theatre to refresh itself from the talent coming through from its revivified provincial underpinnings. His collaboration with Parnell was crucial and it was the latter who played a key role in introducing American vaudeville practices and thereby presenting a new 'high-speed variety' that offered non-stop entertainment.[25]

Not for the first time, music hall reinvented itself. The incentive to keep abreast of changes in popular culture, including slicker presentation, was perhaps greater than before but, taking a broader perspective, there was an underlying continuity in terms of overall format. The basic formula, combining singers, dancers, comedians and novelty acts on a 'balanced' bill, remained unchanged. Individual elements changed over time, though even here there was little that was truly original. 'Peg-leg' Bates was one in a long line of dancers whose performances had been enhanced by the rhythmic and percussive possibilities of a wooden leg; and even the most outrageous novelty dance act, Wilson Keppel and Betty, was part of a long tradition of 'sand dancers,' going back to figures such as Joe Brown of the Burgess and Mitchell Minstrels, widely acclaimed in the third quarter of the nineteenth century, and Messrs. Fisher and Shine, aka 'Lambro and Pedrillo,' with their 'side-splitting ... burlesque sand-dance.'[26] New performers appeared alongside established figures. George Robey's career spanned pre- and post-Great War years, as did Gus Elen and Harry Champion.[27] Similarly, George Formby, Gracie Fields and Max Miller straddled the Second World War, though none could match G H Elliott, whose career started before the first world war and finished well after the second. The importance of personality and authenticity and the use of patter and catch phrases, associated with the likes of Formby and Fields, or Miller's vulgar flamboyance, were in the mainstream of music-hall performance, not a dramatic departure.[28]

Music hall faced challenges from a variety of new formats and technologies that were transforming popular culture.

The revue, with its emphasis on coherence, in comparison to the rag-bag of acts that comprised variety, appeared in the early twentieth century but its challenge was less serious than claimed at the time. Even the highly rated *O-Kay for Sound,* starring the Crazy Gang, was glorified variety, whereas, away from the big theatres, revues were almost indistinguishable from variety. Beswick Goodgame praised Nat Gonella and His Georgians as 'the hottest modernities conceivable' but felt that their revue, *Swing It*, was 'little more than a name for linking together a team of very fine artists, each doing their own stuff in their own jolly way.'[29] More problematic was the radio, which could be enjoyed without the inconvenience of leaving home. Some artists were contractually banned from appearing on radio, others feared that the paucity of their material would be exposed; but some, notably Arthur Askey. Jimmy Jewel, and Vera Lynn, had their reputations enhanced by radio appearances. Indeed, from the late-1920s onwards there was a positive interaction between radio and variety. Variety acts, recorded before living audiences, appeared on programmes such as 'Music Hall,' and played an important part in broadening the popularity of radio.

The greatest threat came from the cinema. The pre-war practice of incorporating short films into a variety programme continued, but it soon became clear that the popularity of cinema was reconfiguring the world of popular leisure in England. Black was a key figure in variety's accommodation with cinema. Cinema could bring variety stars to town in an unprecedented manner, extending and enhancing their reputations, while attracting larger paying audiences to the benefit of cinema owners. British Pathé's *The Show's the Thing*, (1929), which starred Gracie Fields and *What the Public Wants!* presented by an affable Wilfred Pickles, gave cinema-goers the opportunity to see and hear well-known acts of the day, such as Troise and His Mandoliers, Syd Seymour and His Mad Hatters, Max and Harry Nesbitt and even the operatic baritone Denis Noble.[30] There was also a nostalgic touch as pre-war music hall stars, notably, Harry Champion and Gus Elen, were captured on film.[31] Some productions were more elaborate. *Elstree Calling*, (1930), directed by a promising youngster, Alfred Hitchcock, was described as a 'cine-radio revue' and comprised nineteen live variety acts, hosted by Tommy Handley. A similar formula was adopted in *Stars on Parade.* (1936) and *Calling All Stars* (1937).

Some artists, notably Gracie Fields and George Formby, had little difficulty in making the transition to new formats and new technology and built reputations as multi-media performers. Fields and Formby were highly successful stage performers and recording artists, with hit songs performed on radio and also available as sheet music. In addition, both starred in successful films, including *Sally in Our Alley* (1932). *Sing As We Go* (1934) and *Shipyard Sally* (1939) for the former; *Boots! Boots!* (1934), *Off the Dole* (1935), *Keep Your Seats, Please,* (1936) and *Let George Do It* (1940) for the latter. The films were flimsy but effective vehicles to showcase the stars. The versatility of Fields was brought home to the wider cinema audience, even in less successful films, such as *We're Going to Be Rich*. Set in the 1880s it referenced several music-hall favourites – 'Ta-Ra-Ra-Boom-De-Ay,' 'Two Lovely Black Eyes' and 'The Man Who Broke the Bank at Monte Carlo' – but Fields delivered the sentimental ballad, 'The Sweetest Song in All the World,' which highlighted her voice and vocal range, the self-deprecating comedy song 'Walter, Walter (Lead Me to the Altar)' and the nonsense song, 'Will You Love Me When I'm Mutton,' to which she added an unexpected degree of poignancy.[32] Cinema opened up opportunities for other domestic dancers and singers. Jessie Matthews combined stage and cinema from an early age, but it was in *Evergreen*, (1934) that she first sang her signature song 'Over My Shoulder,' along with 'Dancing on the Ceiling.' 'It's Love Again,' (1936) consolidated her standing at the forefront of stage and film musical.[33] Similarly, the dancing skills of Jack Hulbert and Cicely Courtneidge reached a wider audience through film, as in *Jack's the Boy*'[34]

The threat to variety posed by cinema became very apparent in the 1930s. There were European operettas (*Blue Danube*, 1931 and *Waltzes from Vienna*, 1934), and Far Eastern 'exotica' (*Chu Chin Chow*, 1934) but, above all, spectacular American musicals, (*42nd Street, Gold Diggers of Broadway,* and so forth). Other films highlighted the dancing skills of Fred Astaire and Ginger Rogers (*Top Hat, Shall We Dance* and *Carefree* among others). However, the most popular musical film of the 1930s was the British-made *Me and My Girl*, starring Lupino Lane in the immensely popular 'Lambeth Walk.'

The threat of 'Americanization'

Variety was inevitably drawn into wider debates about the 'Americanization' of popular culture. The debate often had a relatively narrow focus – a style of playing or dancing – but there was a wider, often unspoken, context. The relationship between Britain and America had changed significantly as a consequence of the Great War and its aftermath. A once great power was waning as another rose. Beyond such geo-political tensions were important socio-cultural differences. America seemed to be a more open and more equal society, in which there was less subservience to hierarchies and codes of behaviour. For arbiters of taste, or guardians of standards, as they saw themselves, whether in the Imperial Society of Teachers of Dancing or at the BBC, seemingly narrow concerns (for example whether the Charleston be banned from the dance floor or 'crooning' kept off air) carried considerable cultural significance that transcended the immediate musical question.

American-style entertainment was not new, but minstrelsy did not engender the same fears of cultural corruption, not least because many of the tunes had recognisable roots in Scottish and Irish music that had travelled to America since the seventeenth century, and the new songs, especially those written by Stephen Foster, were part of an equally recognisable Western European musical tradition. In contrast, the new music, both song and dance, was obviously derived more from distinctive African/African-American traditions. Some of the reaction against American cultural imports was driven by self-interest – the perceived threat to the livelihoods of English musicians – but much was driven by a belief in cultural and racial superiority, and plain snobbery.[35] The alleged musical shortcomings of 'jazz' – 'that baser cousin of music,' in the words of Sir Dan Godfrey[36] – were grounded in beliefs about proper musical forms and performance styles, but also revealed an ignorance (feigned or real) of the musicianship of ragtime composers and performers, notably Scott Joplin. In the 1920s jazz was denounced by distinguished musicians, such as Herbert Hamilton Harty, best known as the conductor of the Hallé orchestra, who spoke of 'gangs of Jazz-barbarians' whose 'jangling discords' and 'mere ugliness of sound' were responsible for 'this filthy desecration.'[37] Even more outspoken in his condemnation of the cultural and racial threat posed by jazz was Henry Coward.[38] Jazz, 'the essence of vulgarity,' was, in his opinion, primitive music in terms of structure and mode of performance. He associated it with 'the cave man and the negro of the southern plantation' and spoke of the 'banging and clanging of pots [and] pans' accompanied with debased instruments. 'The noble trombone is made to bray like an ass, guffaw like a village idiot, and moan like someone in distress.'[39] Far worse, jazz 'deadened and vulgarised taste … by popularising "toy" instruments like the ukulele and the semi-barbaric balalaika.'[40] But, as well as 'tending to sap our musical virility,' jazz threatened 'our ethical standards.' Referencing the decline of previous great empires, Coward praised first Mussolini (and Irish ecclesiastical authorities) and later Hitler for banning the tango, foxtrot and one-step and banishing 'nigger music.'[41] The speeches delivered by these men received considerable press coverage but several newspaper editorials distanced themselves. The *Hull Daily News*, for one, recognised that it was not only 'lovers of vulgarity' who appreciated jazz.[42] Indeed, there was a greater appreciation of American music, especially from the mid-1930s than commonly recognised. This points to a more important point: the fallacy of cultural contamination. The critics who talked of an alien invasion viewed audiences as passive victims, talking in terms of immunity, inoculation and even isolation, rather than viewing them as active consumers, making conscious decisions and adapting new music and dances to suit their preferences.[43] Some contemporaries were aware of this. The well-known drama critic and authority on contemporary theatre, St. John Ervine, identified a large number of 'American turns' in the London halls but noted that they were 'all excellent.'[44] Even the 'alien' Fats Waller, with his 'animalistic, jungle music, was seen as 'a part of English music hall.'[45] Reaction to American popular culture 'from below,' in the dance hall as well as in the music hall, was more positive than negative; and leisure entrepreneurs responded accordingly. 1930s music hall was also dragged into more explicit arguments about national identity. At a time of growing concern with the threats to national identity, music hall found allies in strange places. *Country Life* discovered that 'our national characteristics are nowhere so clearly evidenced as they are "on the halls".'[46] Even the scourge of the Edwardian music halls, Cecil Sharp now praised them for their 'exemplary Englishness.'[47]

Thus, somewhat surprisingly, variety theatre, apparently in serious decline in the 1920s, had refreshed and redefined itself with new talent, both home-grown and imported, to such a degree that it enjoyed a degree of public affection as the country entered the second world war; and no better symbol of this quintessential and patriotic Englishness could be found than the old-stager, Harry Champion. Reprising his pre-Great War hit, 'Any Old Iron,' in good music-hall tradition, he amended the final chorus to exhort his audience to contribute their 'old iron' to the war cause. More generally, as Mass Observation noted, music hall had a good war.

Music hall after the Second World War

The threats faced by variety theatre in the 1930s finally hit home in the 1950s. Many were long-standing. Even before 1914 it was losing a younger audience for whom the attractions of American ragtime and jazz were far greater. This problem intensified during the dance hall craze of the inter-war years and continued in the 1950s. More importantly, variety entertainment was relocating away from variety theatres, particularly from the mid-1950s with the advent of commercial television's *Sunday Night at the London Palladium*. Val Parnell's boast was bold - 'I'm offering television viewers a seat in the circle at the Greatest Variety theatre in the world to watch the finest artists that money can buy' – and he proved his critics wrong. Old and new music-hall performers appeared alongside headliners that included established stars (Max Bygrave) and new talent (Cliff Richard). The show attracted audiences of 20 million or more.[48] Parnell's claim that the biggest stars in the world could be watched at home was borne out by the experience of others. 'Who've you got at the local Empire?' Roy Hudd asked. His response: 'Me and bloody G H Elliot!'[49] To make matters worse, English audiences could also go the cinema to see the dancing skills of Gene Kelly or watch the musical extravaganzas of Rodgers and Hammerstein.

Broader social trends also contributed to the decline of variety theatre, from the bomb damage of the second world war to post-war rehousing policy. Increasingly city, and large town centres were being devoted to commercial interests. There were obvious advantages in cashing in on prime-site theatres at a time when costs were rising and competition intensifying. As entrepreneurial talent looked to television, variety theatres, especially the number two and number three theatres, were under-resourced. Their poorly maintained buildings, increasingly old-fashioned in look and their equally dated shows failed to attract investors and customers alike. In particular, the younger audience was not attracted to variety, notwithstanding the efforts to cash in on the skiffle and rock 'n' roll bandwagons. Variety contributed to the success of Lonnie Donegan and Tommy Steele, but they did not rescue variety theatre in the mid and late 1950s. Nor did sex (nude revues) and drugs (modified licensing laws) halt the decline. Variety theatre was not alone, dance halls faced major problems in the 1950s, and an increasing number of venues were converted into bingo halls.

Some concluding observations

The demise of variety theatre, as a location for entertainment, was sudden and appeared to mark the end of an era that had its roots going back to the 1850s. However, variety as a form of entertainment survived and flourished albeit in different locations. Summer seasons in the resorts, at least until the 1970s, Christmas pantomimes and other older venues such as working men's clubs offered a living for capable but middle-ranking performers, including those who were too 'blue' for television, as well as a route to greater things for the more talented; but it was radio and increasingly television that become the new home of variety. ITV's *Sunday Night at the London Palladium* held pride of place but the BBC television presented a glamorised version of Victorian music hall in *The Good Old Days* from 1953 onwards, the minstrel-based variety of *The Black and White Minstrel Show* from 1958, and more general variety programmes, such as *The Billy Cotton Band Show*. Several 'pop' stars, notably Tommy Steele and Cliff Richard, pursued careers as variety entertainers in ways that would have been entirely understandable to Gracie Fields or George Formby. Further, elements of music hall, or a remembered music hall, were to be found in popular music, from The Kinks', *Village Green Preservation Society* and Madness's *The Liberty of Norton Folgate* to the redefined Chas 'n' Dave, who saw themselves as part of a tradition going back, specifically, to Harry Champion.[50]

Much of television music hall was unashamedly nostalgic, looking back to a romanticised mish-mash of elements that barely existed in the past. However, the music hall tradition could also look forward, again embracing , or being embraced by, the new. Nowhere was this clearer than in the career of Judge Dread, whose success, particularly in the early 1970s, combined music-hall innuendo, African-Caribbean rhythms and nursery rhymes in a format that saw him banned by the BBC.[51] On the *Working Class 'Ero* album he included the George Formby number, 'Grandad's Flanalette Nightshirt.' A similar debt to music hall could also be seen in ska revival bands such as Bad Manners and Madness, to whom we will return later

Endnotes

1. There were 130, or more, ragtime bands touring in the immediate pre-war years. The Moss Empire had its own Ragtime Octet.
2. M Killgarriff, *Sing Us One of the Old Songs*, Oxford University Press, 1998 is an invaluable guide to popular song. I am also indebted to John Mullen, *The Show Must Go On! Popular Song in Britain during the First World War*, Farnham, Ashgate, 2015, though the opinions expressed here are somewhat different.
3. See also 'You Made Us Fight You, We Didn't Want to Do it.'
4. https://www.youtube.com/watch?v=Q2MQWeLfCeQ Each participant sings a 'national' song before they all sing 'God Save the King.' Amazingly, the Irishman's song is the unofficial Irish national anthem 'God Save Ireland,' the song of the Manchester Martyrs executed following the Clerkenwell bombing in 1867.
5. Harry Lauder's contribution was particularly poignant. He played a prominent role in various recruitment initiatives. His son was on active service as he appeared in a revue, *Three Cheers,* which included the song 'The Laddies Who Fought and Won,' the performance climaxing with Scottish guardsmen in full dress uniform on stage as Lauder exhorted young men to sign up. Lauder continued his performance even after the death of his son in

action, though he fainted as the curtain closed after his first rendition of 'The Laddies Who Fought' after his son's death. The better known, 'Keep Right on to the End of the Road' was written in memory of his son.

6   Mullen also draws attention to a number of 'regional' songs that referenced countries (especially Ireland but not Wales) to more specific counties and towns and which used the sense of attachment to home as part of the war effort. Mullen, *The Show Must Go On!* pp.92-9

7   The contrast with the range of songs sung by soldiers is striking. See Mullen, *The Show Must Go On!* Chapter 6. Such was the structure and control of music hall that there was less scope for anti-war songs.

8   Other songs included 'Hot Meat Pies, Saveloys and Trotters,' 'Baked Sheep's Heart Stuffed with Sage and Onions' and, more exotically 'Good Old Yorkshire Pudden,' and 'Gorgonzola Cheese.'

9   Charles Godfrey had a hit with 'Hi-tiddey-hi-ti' at a time when 'the drunken song was quite a popular feature' but which was no longer the case in 1913. *Era* 1 March 1913

10 The words were reprinted in *Landswoman*, 1 October 1918

11 For examples see *Grantham Journal*, 8 March 1919 (Carlton Scroop Company of Girl Guides) and *Western Gazette* 13 June 1919 (Charminster Women's Institute).

12 *Illustrated London News*, 20 September 1915, *Graphic*, 25 September 1915, *Illustrated Sporting and Dramatic News*, 9 October 1915 and *Tatler*, 22 December 1915

13 *Sporting Times*, 28 August 1915, Illustrated *London News* 4 September 1915 and *Tatler*, 8 & 15 September 1915

14 Imperial War Museum https://www.iwm.org.uk/collections/item/object/80021208

15 'Which switch' featured in J M Barrie's burlesque, *Rosy Rapture. The Pride of the Beauty Chorus*. The song also combined the traditional tongue-twister with a 'witty' comment on women's war work.

16 Reflecting on the blessing of life, even though poor,
> I'll leave the night time to the dreamers/I'll leave the song birds to the blind
> I'll leave the moon above to those in love/When I leave the world behind.

Within weeks of the outbreak of war Gitana sang her 'great Marching Song,' 'Violette' and on various occasions she raised money for wounded troops through the sale of autograph postcards. Touring extensively, she had a repertoire that included 'a selection of catchy songs' as well as a number of 'pretty' songs including 'Once upon a time' and 'Morning star.' *Era*, 14 October and 25 November 1914, 1, 15 and 22 March 1916, and 6 September 1916.

17 Collins, well-known before the war, played Teresa in "The Maid of the Mountains," winning praise for both her acting and singing. *Era* 27 December 1916.

18 See, for example, Mullen, *The Show Must Go On!* p.135

19 In albeit differing ways, see also Clarice Mayne, 'It's Lovely to be in Love' (1915) and Aileen D'Orma, 'Any Time's Kissing Time' (1916) and even the much-recorded stuttering song 'K-K-K Katy' (1918).

20. P Gibbs, *Now It Can Be Told*, London, Harper & Brothers, 1920. See D Taylor, *Memory, Narrative and the Great War: Rifleman Patrick MacGill and the Construction of Wartime Experience*, Liverpool University Press, 2013, pp.114-5.
21. Beyond its use of syncopation, ragtime is an ill-defined umbrella term that covered numerous players and styles. Thanks to *The Sting* (1974) ragtime has been seen as synonymous with Scott Joplin and his compositions, notable 'The Entertainer' and 'Maple Leaf Rag.' In fact, Joplin was unusual. He emphasised composed music, including worked out harmonies, and his pieces demanded considerable musical skill. More important to this study was the more homogenised and less subtle ragtime of Tin Pan Alley,
22. Marie Lloyd's 'Piccadilly Trot' was a direct challenge but failed to achieve the success of the (later) Lambeth Walk.
23. Several contemporary observers blamed the 'tax menace,' following the introduction of the theatre tax in 1916. The fact that the tax also applied to cinemas and dance halls, both of which flourished, indicates that more profound influences were at work.
24. Black built up a cinema chain in the north east of England before selling up and creating a new chain. In 1928 he was the director of the General Theatre Corporation. O Double, *Britain Had Talent: A History of Variety Theatre*, Basingstoke, Palgrave, 2012, esp. pp. 51-5
25. Time management was critical as was maximum stage usage and a general 'professionalisation' of presentation. Double, *Britain Had Talent*, chap. 4
26. *Stage*, 20 October 1882 for Joe Brown's claim to have introduced sand-dancing 25 years earlier and *Stage* 2 June 1882. There was also women sand-dancers, notably Winifred Johnson, 'A Chat with Winifred Johnson,' *Era*, 30 March 1895. Sand dancing was losing some of its popularity in the mid-1890s but the dramatic and varied dancing of Mdlle. Texarkansas gave it new life. She was particularly popular in the new resorts, such as Blackpool and Douglas, Isle of Man, but also appeared at several London halls.
27. Thanks in no small measure to the early 1930s 'Veterans of Variety' short films. See chapter 15.
28. Double, *Britain Had Talent,* Part two: Performance Dynamics. He stresses the 'constant quest' for novelty, but much presented as new was often a slick repackaging of something old.
29. *Era* 13 January and 24 February 1937
30. https://www.britishpathe.com/workspaces/df699ffd537d4e0c74710ad015dfd64d/qg4ldiTP
31. https://www.britishpathe.com/search/query/gus+elen 2020. The films do not do justice to Elen's ability. He was clearly past his best when the films were made and the limitations of camera technology forced him to modify his stage act to keep within camera shot.
32. These songs can be heard at https://www.youtube.com/watch?v=ZsxSPJ8oUCM https://www.youtube.com/watch?v=0AevoH8_5bk and https://www.youtube.com/watch?v=OZk33tWP-Tk the latter with Ray Noble and his orchestra.
33. For 'Over My Shoulder' see https://www.youtube.com/watch?v=ZjquAEjkrrs and 'Dancing on the Ceiling' see https://www.youtube.com/watch?v=PEy8OB0-6CU

34. See https://www.youtube.com/watch?v=DpGjj-9tjaw&t=36s
35. See Appleby Matthews, musical director of the Regent Theatre and conductor of the Birmingham City orchestra, *Observer*, 4 May 1924
36. D Godfrey, 'Music: An All-Pervading Influence,' *Musical Mirror*, March 1929
37. *Manchester Guardian*, 6 September 1926. As President of the Incorporated Association of Organists he delivered several speeches in which he condemned "jazz." See *Hull Daily Mail*, 5 September 1928, 2 & 3 September 1929
38. He made a major contribution to the development of choral music, particularly with the Sheffield Music Union and the Huddersfield Choral Society
39. *Manchester Guardian*, 10 October 1927; *Hull Daily Mail*, 21 September & 1 October 1927, and *Tamworth Herald* 1 October 1927
40. *Hull Daily Mail* 10 October 1927 and 22 May 1933
41. *Hull Daily Mail* 5 February 1926 and 22 May 1933. Coward also had a problem with Schonberg.
42. *Hull Daily News* 21 September 1927
43. C Waters, 'Beyond 'Americanization': Rethinking Anglo-American Cultural Exchange between the Wars,' *Cultural and Social History*, 2007, 4(4), pp.451-9 makes a similar point at p.454
44. *Observer* 19 February 1939. Ervine was a playwright in his own right but had had mixed experiences in Ireland. He also had the misfortune to lose a leg in the fighting in Flanders. He made his reputation as a critic in post-war London.
45. P Bailey, 'Fats Waller Meets Harry Champion: Americanization, National Identity and Sexual Politics in Interwar British Music Hall,' *Cultural and Social History*, 2007, 4(40), pp.495-509 quoting John Crow's review of Waller's performance at the Finsbury Park Empire in the *Spectator*, 2 September 1938
46. *Country Life*, 11 June 1938 cited in P Bailey, 'Fats Waller Meets Harry Champion,' at p.503
47. Bailey, 'Fats Waller Meets Harry Champion,' p.505
48. The show starring Cliff Richard attracted 19.5 million viewers, Max Bygraves 21 million but Harry Secombe beat both with an audience of 22 million.
49. Cited in Double, *Britain Had Talent*, p.76
50. The highly successful 21st century folk band, Bellowhead, included Harry Champion's 'The Old Dun Cow' on one of their tours/CDs. A bolder, if not entirely convincing claim has been made by B J Faulk, who claims that 'rock musicians [particularly the Beatles, the Rolling Stones and the Kinks] ... ironically appropriated the traditional forms of Victorian music hall.' *British Rock Modernism, 1967-1977: The Story of Music Hall in Rock*, Abingdon, Routledge, 2016, p.1. Originally published by Ashgate Press, 2010. See the review by D Laing, *Popular Music*, 33(3), 2014, p.573, who refers to 'a puzzling mixture of suggestive insights, assiduous scholarship, special pleading and theoretical turgidity.'
51. J Stratton, 'Judge Dread: Music Hall Traditionalist or Postcolonial Hybrid,' *Contemporary British History*, 28(1), 2014, pp.81-102

'I wish I could shimmy like my sister Kate': Dance halls and dancing between the wars[1]

> I'm looking for the Ogo-pogo, / The funny little Ogo-pogo.
> His mother was a polliwog, his father was a whale,
>
> I'm going to put a little bit of salt on his tail.
> I want to find the Ogo-pogo/ While he's playing on his old banjo.
> The Lord Mayor of London,/ The Lord Mayor of London,
> The Lord Mayor of London wants to put him in the Lord Mayor's show".
>
> 'The Ogo Pogo; The Funny Foxtrot'

WHEN MAX BYGRAVES sorrowfully announced in 1960 that 'they've changed our local palais into a bowling alley,' he signalled the end of an institution that had been central to working-class and lower-middle class popular culture for four decades, or more. Most definitely, 'Fings Ain't What They Used to Be.'[2] The advent of 'the palais' in the 1920s was dramatic and owed much to American entrepreneurship and American music, but there were other roots that reached back to the resort development of late-nineteenth century. Blackpool's ballrooms pointed the way to the future but, prior to 1914, most working-class social dancing took place in smaller, less glamorous venues of varying degrees of respectability; and therein lay a problem. Charles Booth's observation about 'the scandal that surrounds all dancing saloons' still held true in the early twentieth century.

Robert Roberts' father was not alone in believing that 'dancing rooms ... held the scum of the nation ... the lowest of the low.'[3]

The attractiveness of social dancing was enhanced by the growing number of new dances, from America and Latin America, during the 1900s. Ragtime, with its emphasis on rhythm, and its popularity increased through the Moss Empires chain, brought with it various novelty dances – variants of 'The Cakewalk,' numerous 'animal dances, and 'The Boston,' perhaps the most popular ragtime dance.[4] The tango, increasingly tamed as it moved through pre-war Europe, still shocked many and then there was the foxtrot. The excitement created by the incessant 'ragging' or syncopation, the brash, gimmicky style of playing and the emphasis on physicality and personal expression created a fundamental challenge to the traditional working-class social dancing. In the sequence dancing of the early twentieth century (as later) the emphasis was upon an agreed script for each dance.[5] There was novelty as new dances were introduced – 'The Military Two-Step' (1904), 'The Butterfly Gavotte' (1907) and, later 'The Square Tango' (1920), - but the intention remained unchanged.[6] Each couple would perform the same combination of defined steps at the same time, and in the same direction. There was little, if any, scope for freedom of expression, and this was reinforced by conventions regarding movement around the dance floor. This was to change in a short space of time with the advent of an increasing number of more spontaneous dances specially devised for couples.[7]

The influx of Americans into Europe in the latter years of the Great War gave further momentum to this musical invasion; but, at the same time, it reinforced old fears about working-class leisure, especially unchaperoned women dancing in public; and created new ones, associated with 'nigger' music and illicit drugs.[8] Sensationalist press coverage of a few high-profile London cases reinforced pessimists in their belief that English culture and morality was in grave peril. But, equally, for the entrepreneurs of leisure here was a golden opportunity.

The dance hall boom

The dance hall boom was spectacular. There was large-scale investment in new buildings, most notably the high-profile

Hammersmith Palais, but also conversions of existing halls. Chains, notably Mecca and General Theatres, were at the forefront of developments. There was a local 'palais' in almost every town, from Burnley and Nelson in Lancashire to Exeter and Exmouth in Devon but there were also numerous other venues licensed for dancing for a working-class and lower middle-class clientele.[9] In 1938 it was claimed that some three-quarters of a million people went to public dance halls each week. A year later *Mass Observation* estimated that over two-thirds of the population went dancing, with a hard core (about one in five, more likely middle-class) doing so on a regular basis.[10] Demand was bolstered by the increase in real wages between the wars and, particularly by the widening employment opportunities for working-class women.[11] The dance hall was patronised by men and women from different classes and different ages, but the most important single demographic was the young, unmarried working-class woman.

Dancing was a major element, second only to cinema, in the leisure life of the country. Although its long-term popularity was subject to short-term fluctuations, especially in the mid and late 1920s, it was largely 'recession proof.'[12] The time-honoured link between dancing and companionship and courtship was made more attractive by the infectious nature of the new music and the opportunities for self-expression, unknown to an older generation of sequence dancers. The venues, especially the purpose-built dance halls, were a further attraction. Like the cinema, they were luxurious, bright and clean, and offered an escape from the mundane realities of daily life. The entertainment itself was good value for money in comparison with other attractions.[13]

Civilizing and standardizing popular dance

The introduction and dissemination of African-American influenced music was not without its problems.[14] Ragtime and jazz, both poorly-defined but widely-used terms, had been enthusiastically received in certain quarters and roundly condemned in others. The outrage was rooted in assumptions about race and gender and found expression in a concern for the corruption of English popular music and dancing. Uncontrolled movement and inappropriate steps seemed to pose moral as well as artistic threats. For some the threats were 'jungle haunted monstrosities (J B Priestley), for others it was 'artistic Bolshevism' (Imperial Society of Teachers of Dancing) but for all critics it was a threat that had to be contained, neutralised and civilized.

Pre-war social dancing was dominated by the wealthy middle and upper classes; ballroom dancing was held in high esteem and the professional dance instructor a central figure. Even in the first decade of the twentieth century there were elite concerns that dancing standards were being eroded and action was needed to maintain and regulate them. The ISTD (the Imperial Society of Teachers of Dancers), was founded in 1904 in response to the proliferation of bad habits brought about by the degeneration of dancing into 'a mere pastime … a vulgar romp' rather than being an 'Art.'[15] The ISTD's purpose was 'to impart … throughout the country a uniform method' centred on 'dignified dance movements.' It saw its role as positive and forward-looking, 'learning … the newest dances and acquiring the most approved styles.'[16] Such was the perceived threat in the 1900s that it was suggested that the 'chief public schools … [the educators of] future M.P.s, lawyers and military officers, should teach dancing.'[17] The 'gay ballrooms where young people amuse themselves first and think about dancing style second' could not be tolerated.[18] However, the problem of "slipshod" ways of holding partners, exacerbated by the fashion for 'backless gowns,' paled into insignificance when faced with the growing number of 'freak' steps, the 'abominable hops, jumps, springs and rushes' associated with 'the American Boston and Two-step,' before the war, and, especially in the 1920s, 'the series of contortions without a vestige of grace, reminiscent of the Negro orgies from which it derives its creation,' otherwise known as the Charleston.[19] There was a danger, at least in the eyes of Philip Richardson, the editor of *Dancing Times*, that old dances like the waltz would be swept to the side-lines as new dances brought chaos on the dance floor.[20] Dance, ballroom dancing specifically, was conceived by the leading figures of the ISTD as 'Art' with an undisputed capital A. It was characterised by grace, self-control, self-restraint and properly executed steps – in other words, respectability on the dance floor,[21] Dance also carried important connotations regarding gender, class and (crudely defined) race.[22] Potentially disruptive and corrupting elements, whether habitués of working-class dance halls or African-American musicians with their 'jungle' music and dancing, had to be neutralised. Loose dancing was seen as a sign of loose morals. Both had to be resisted, civilized and standardized.[23]

Members of the ISTD, and its supporters, saw themselves as both cultural and moral guardians of a distinctive and superior English approach. As early as 1920, dance instructors, meeting at Grafton Galleries, agreed 'to do their best to stamp out freak steps.' They established a committee to determine the approved steps for a variety of dances, including the foxtrot, which had been infiltrated and put in 'grave peril' by the scandalous 'shimmy.' Driven by Richardson, the ISTD established a ballroom branch in 1924. A key figure was Victor Silvester, a winner at the first world ballroom dancing championship in 1922 and again in 1924, for whom codification and its implementation became a life-time commitment. With others he determined not simply the appropriate steps and holds but also the appropriate tempi for a range of dances, notably the foxtrot, quickstep, waltz and tango, in what was to become known as 'the English' style. Charts were produced, textbooks written and the teachers of the ISTD were the missionaries sent out to spread the gospel through lessons and competitions. Silvester led by example through his strict-tempo records and radio performances. He was not alone. Santos Casani co-operated with *British Pathé* to produce newsreel dance lessons. Intention, no matter how determined, was no guarantee of success. The would-be saviours of English ballroom dancing faced two major problems that were not entirely within their control – dance bands and their leaders, and dancers.

The creation of Victor Silvester's orchestra was a response not simply to the perceived ill-discipline of American jazz musicians, adding or extending notes at will, but also to the various ways in which dance music was played, particularly by the big-name bands, led by Jack Hylton, Carroll Gibbons, Jack Payne and Ambrose. In certain respects they shared Silvester's concern with jazz and responded by modifying 'hot' music and, in Hylton's phrase, giving it 'the British touch … which

Americans and others never understood.'[24] However, these bands prided themselves on the skill and artistic merit of their musicianship. They were less concerned with playing simply for dancing than Silvester. They were playing for themselves and for a different, listening audience; and their emphasis was on musical virtuosity, within which steady, rather than strict, tempo was observed. A further complication came from the fact that the big dance bands were to be seen as well as heard. Nowhere was this clearer than at the end of 'He Played His Ukulele as the Ship Went Down,' when Jack Hylton's band sunk as one to the floor.

The demand for 'one original dancing time and speed' underpinned the ISTD decision to determine standardised tempi.[25] The impact was limited. In 1926, Henry St. John Rumsey, a prolific writer on the subject and author of *Ballroom Dancing*, bemoaned the fact that dance bands were playing too fast for proper dancing.[26] Almost a decade later Silvester was still complaining that those bands that looked to the armchair audience were playing standard dances at 'every conceivable speed,' thereby rendering them almost undanceable.[27] Strict tempo *à la Silvester* offered a disciplined alternative, but it was as largely aimed at the myriad of bands that played for dancing across the country in dance halls, church halls and working men's clubs. These bands, semi-professional and amateur, maybe 20,000 in total, played for men and women who had come out for an evening's dancing. These were the people who 'patronise the obscure 'Bill Smith's Palais Five', because it is a real dance band which … can play all the standard dances as a dance band should play them, so that it helps them to dance.'[28]

However, even the virtues of 'Bill Smith's Palais Five' could not satisfy all paying customers, who flocked to the dance halls. Some welcomed the opportunity to put into practice the steps they had learned at a dance lesson or from an ISTD wallchart, and practiced in their bedroom. Others put off by the required conformity to prescribed steps, or simply deterred by their inability to master them, looked to simpler dancing styles, walking and shuffling in the eyes of critics. Yet others were enamoured of the 'freak' steps and not willing to conform to the instructions of 'civilizing' dance teachers or dance-hall MCs. This latter response could manifest itself in two ways.

In its negative form, there was a refusal to take up certain dances advocated by the ISTD. The most notable failure was the tango. The shockingly immoral dance from Argentina had been partly civilized in pre-war Paris and London but the process of sanitization was completed in the mid-1920s. Despite a large-scale conference of dance teachers, the tango was received with a mixture of indifference and hostility.[29] In its positive form, there was a dogged persistence to stay with dance steps proscribed by the authorities. The Charleston was widely criticised by custodians of 'the English' style. It was 'a dance with no single merit,' danced by silly and selfish men and women and resulting in bruised shins and—heaven forfend! – laddered stockings. But attempts to ban it failed dismally. MCs risked physical assault when trying to enforce Charleston bans as the fans of 'the kicking dance' asserted their right to self-expression on the dance floor. As *Melody Maker* reported, dancers at Stoke Newington 'felt so strongly that they even knocked the MC unconscious after his fifth attempt to stop them dancing the Charleston.'[30] The PCQ campaign – Please Charleston Quietly – failed as did attempts to develop a more decorous alternative in the form of the (oxymoronic) 'Flat Charleston.' Patrick Chalmers, a regular writer on dance in the *Daily Mail* in the 1920s, bemoaned 'Chaos on the Dance Floor,' but recognised that band leaders had to keep close 'to what the public's mood of the moment is demanding.'[31] And the public mood was demanding dances such as the 'Black Bottom,' because when 'the white peoples,' as he put it, 'catch the dance rhythms of the music, crooning of saxophones and tom-tom beat of drums, they find a greater exhilaration in it than they ever did in the more monotonous waltz, elaborate minuet or stately cotillion.'[32] There was no escaping the excitement of the music, the novelty of the sound and the freedom of 'freak' steps.

By the late 1930s there were signs of a reaction against the demands and sameness of the mainstream dances of the 'English style,' particularly the foxtrot.[33] The technical requirements of dancing the Charleston or the Black Bottom, even the 'English style' foxtrots and waltzes were beyond the capabilities of many would-be dancers. Others saw these dances as boring. There was a demand for simpler but more enjoyable dancing, which was met by Mecca through a series of very basic novelty dances, the best-known of which was 'The Lambeth Walk.' Effectively a return to sequence dancing, it was a stunning success, driven by the full force of Mecca publicity, combined with some help from the BBC radio and television.[34] The Chelsea Palace production of *Me and My Gal* had been on the point of closure when a BBC radio broadcast from the theatre alerted thousands to the delights of the Lambeth Walk.[35] The song was hugely successful – sales were on a par with the 1923 mega-hit 'Yes We Have No Bananas' – and the dance, with its 'jerky swagger, the 'thumbs-up gesture, and the hand-spreading Jewish 'Oi!' added to the popularity of the cheerful and cheeky-faced, Lupino, 'I'm a Cockney, born and bred', Lane.[36] The Lambeth Walk was danced in halls across the land but, continuing an older tradition, it was also danced in the streets.[37] It was one of a number of novelty dances introduced by Mecca. 'Under the Spreading Chestnut Tree,' boosted by alleged support from royalty, appealed across the respectable/non-respectable divide and lived on as a children's party dance after the war; but the equally (in)authentic cockney 'Knees up, Mother Brown,' though easy to dance, 'never made the social grade,' because according to Graves and Hodge, 'the lifting of skirts… was a little too much.'[38] Advertised as 'the latest pally dance,' the 'Park Parade' failed to achieve significant success, not helped by the relatively complexity of its steps.[39] Similarly, 'The Handsome Territorial,' despite being recorded by both Nat Gonella and Jack Hylton, soon faded from memory.

The Mecca boss, Carl Heimann, unashamedly exploited anti-Americanism by emphasizing the supposedly authentic English roots of 'The Lambeth Walk,' as a 'Cockney' dance, notwithstanding the fact that the dance was choreographed by Adele England, who openly admitted that she had made no study of Cockney culture in general or Cockney dancing in particular. She claimed to have based the steps on what she knew to be popular in the present-day dance halls. In essence, the Lambeth Walk was a simple sequence dance that harked back to Edwardian years. More interesting, is the extent to which others bought into the myth of the Lambeth Walk. For a supposedly place-specific cultural phenomenon, it quickly spread across the country, transmuting into local variations from the Margate Walk to the Blackpool Walk. However, the specific temporal context, the impending sense of threat as international tensions increased, played its part. The chirpy, defiant figure, strutting across the stage in a jaunty dance that, eventually, became a communal strut and an ebullient 'Oi!' – or 'Och Aye' in Scotland! – was well suited to the times. The cross-class camaraderie and sense of community portrayed in the film version of *Me and My Gal* was patent nonsense but in real-life dance halls in Lambeth and Luton or Leeds and Liverpool, it was easier to believe that the experience of local community was a microcosm of national unity. The commercial instincts of the Mecca bosses and their constructed popular culture was taken up by a public to a degree that surprised its creators, as for unanticipated reasons, the public took to the song and dance in an unprecedented manner.

Dance and society

Countering the threat of 'Americanization' attracted considerable attention but there were more mundane concerns for the various defenders of English dancing standards. Girls lacking buoyancy and leaden men resulted in 'aimless perambulation' on the dance floor.[40] In fact, the 'problem' reflected two important factors: the democratising of dancing and the social functions of the dance hall. Dancing fulfilled a variety of functions. The dance hall offered an escape from daily life at work and at home. The new palais offered a glimpse of a more luxurious lifestyle comparable to that of Dickens' Victorian gin-palaces. The extent to which this was achieved in the smaller dance halls is debatable. Unlike the Ritz, Manchester, Salford's 'Broadway' was described as 'only a large house, with a wall in between knocked down.' The band comprised 'a piano, drums and clarinet … and it used to be murder in there, they'd be packed, sweating cobs.'[41]

Dancing, particularly to the new music, was a form of self-expression and physical activity; but, more so, the dance hall was a venue for social interaction, providing an alcohol-free alternative to the more male and adult-oriented public house. It was a more attractive and less restrictive place for the young and single to meet members of the opposite sex. It was part of the transition to adulthood and a working life, in which one learnt such adult activities as smoking, betting and dancing. In fact, learning a few dance steps was often easier than learning the social conventions that went with young adult life. Though never exclusively for the young, the dance hall culture of the 1920s and 1930s pre-figured the more explicit youth culture of the post-second world war years.

For the young (and not so young) singles the dance hall was crucial in the often-turbulent process of meeting, dating and marrying, which remained the expectation of the vast bulk of the population. Despite the presence of MCs, charged with maintaining decency on the dance floor and the presence of parents waiting outside at the end of the entertainment – or the strict admonition to be 'home at 10 ... and not a minute later!' – the dance hall was a more relaxed and romantic place in which to meet a future partner. There was a recognised code of behaviour. It was for men to pluck up courage and ask a woman to dance, except, of course, if it was a 'ladies' excuse me,' and it was acceptable to move from partner to partner, though eventually a couple would emerge to dance together for the rest of the evening. Inappropriate behaviour was frowned upon, irrespective of the presence of MCs and bouncers.[42] Not everyone was looking for a partner – many young women, simply enjoying an evening out, dancing with each other – but many did. Inadvertently, when purists condemned dancing as 'hugging to music,' they hit upon its prime purpose for many participants.

There was a cluster of inter-related concerns about the position of women in post-war society that coloured the response to the dance hall. The re-appearance of the 'surplus woman' problem, the small but increasing number of divorces and separations and falling birth rates gave rise to fears about marriage and the family, those twin rocks on which the stability of society allegedly rested.[43] Dimly lit halls and dances that encouraged physical contact merely reinforced negative preconceptions; so too did the high-profile and exaggerated preoccupation with night clubs. To have the Home Secretary condemn them as 'plague spots' and the National Vigilance Society resurrecting the cry of 'White Slavery' in relation to the presence of 'dance hostesses,' confirmed the clubs' sleazy reputation. The fact that 'dance hostesses' could also be found in many ordinary dance halls seemingly demonstrated that the contagion was not confined to the capital. The extent to which people bought into such sensationalism is open to question. The immorality of London might appear plausible to an observer from Barnsley or Buckingham, but most were aware that the majority of local dance halls were, if not respectable, at least not 'wild.' Similarly, the claims that dancing contributed to the feminization of men (not to mention the masculinization of women), thereby threatening the institutions of marriage and the family, did not stand up to scrutiny. Entrepreneurs of leisure, conscious of the heightened awareness of licensing authorities, took measures to ensure they did not lose their licences. Other interested parties, not least parents, played their part in ensuring that 'the problem' remained something 'other' that happened in a different part of town or another city. Most importantly, for the vast majority of young people who flocked to the dance halls, beyond the immediate aim of a good night out, their medium-term hope and expectation was to meet a partner and get married. Irrespective of the pro-marriage/family propaganda of the inter-war years, there was an underlying social conservatism in that inter-war youth were not set on abolishing marriage or overthrowing the family.[44]

However, there was a more progressive attitude towards the position of women in society, of which women on the dance floor was a part. For a variety of socio-economic reasons, women were less constrained than they had been before the Great War. Irrespective of the high-profile developments, such as the enfranchisement of women, completed in 1928, or changes in the divorce laws in 1923 and 1937, there were greater opportunities in terms of work and leisure, particularly for young, unmarried women. The importance of the contribution of the dance hall is open to debate. The most positive view has been expressed by James Nott, for whom dancing and the dance hall was for women 'a wholly liberating experience [which] played a significant role in their struggle for emancipation.'[45] He argues that dancing was more than escape or exercise, offering opportunities for self-expression and enhancing self-worth. The whole experience of 'going out,' from hairstyle and make-up to clothing and footwear gave rise to an image of what being feminine meant that contrasted starkly with that of pre-war years. Dance halls, as well as being more feminine (or at least less masculine) than other leisure locations, offered women a degree of control, not least through the right to refuse a second dance, or even to dance at all in the first place. At the same time, the opportunity to develop new codes of behaviour and to construct different (or at least modified) gender roles, contributed to a broader redefinition of masculinity, following on the experience of the war, in which some of its more toxic elements were shed. However, the case can be overstated. The new freedom for women was relatively short-lived. Marriage, for practical and ideological reasons, drastically reduced women's opportunity to go out to a dance.[46] Even for single women, the expanding opportunities to create a new image could easily degenerate into the tyranny of fashion. Similarly, the 'natural' ability of women reinforced gender stereotypes. Further, many old attitudes persisted into the 1950s, at least. The dance hall phenomenon of the inter-war years was clearly important but there is a danger of allowing the novelty of change to overshadow more mundane continuity.

Dance and a common popular culture

The opening decades of the twentieth century saw a significant broadening of the range of popular music and an equally significant expansion of the means whereby this music was disseminated. Despite often exaggerated complaints about 'Americanization,' there was a process of modification, accommodation and fusion whereby new dances and new styles of playing developed and became a new norm. This process was, at times, problematic, not least in its racial stereotyping, uneven over time and region, and incomplete. Nonetheless, there could be little doubt that, by the late 1930s, a significantly different culture was in the ascendancy. The same dance music could be heard across the country via the BBC, or at the cinema, approximately the same dance steps were being attempted to the sound of numerous bands, using the same sheet music. To that extent, a common culture evolved that fused different elements from both sides of the Atlantic. Jazz music was tamed, jazz dances made less 'wild.' The old sequence dancing had been marginalised (until 'The Lambeth Walk') and the new 'English style,' of playing and dancing was less sedate, more 'wild,' than it would otherwise have been. As Hylton boasted, his style of 'symphonic syncopation … makes a subtle appeal to our British temperament … [and] is fast becoming a truly national music.'[47] In similar vein, Mecca founder, Carl Heimann claimed there was 'no differentiation between the classes' on Mecca's dance floors. And yet the evidence of the halls pointed to a different conclusion. There were meaningful regional and sub-regional variations between and within towns and cities. In most towns there were different dance halls catering for different social groups, contrary to Heimann's assertion. Even within a specific dance hall, some evenings were given over to 'Old Time Dancing,' which catered for older dancers, while others catered for younger dancers.[48] Additionally dancing was a gendered experience. The idea of 'cultures in common,' better captures the varied but complementary range of dance cultures that emerged in the inter-war years.[49]

Some concluding observations

The importance of the dance hall in working-class, and lower middle-class, popular culture is difficult to overstate. Only the cinema rivalled it in the new leisure of the inter-war years. Given the pre-war hostility to such venues, and its continuation in some quarters afterwards, the dance hall boom speaks volumes for the strength of popular demand and entrepreneurial responsiveness. The dance hall was an important venue in which adolescent rites of passage were navigated. Concerns about immorality surfaced periodically, but spoke more of the observer than the observed, whose codes of behaviour, often unnoticed by their critics, were ultimately conservative. Love and marriage, aided by popular songs of the day, survived the threat of the dance hall. It was also an important site in a growing culture war against 'Americanization' but one which demonstrated the power of the consumer. Popular leisure reformers struggled to ban, or even tame, the Charleston as long as dancers demanded it. Similarly, while the anti-American, but inauthentic cockney dance, 'The Lambeth Walk' was taken up, and adapted, with enthusiasm, attempts to get people dancing to the 'Park Parade' failed dismally.

Endnotes

1. The focus of this chapter is largely on the dance hall. There were other important venues and forms of dances, most notably the ceilidhs that were important for the Irish communities in England.
2. The original musical was produced by Joan Littlewood at the Theatre Royal, Stratford East but opened in the West End at the Garrick Theatre in February 1960. Bygrave's recording of the title song was bowdlerised for popular commercial consumption.
3. R Roberts, *A Ragged Schooling*, London, Fontana, p.179
4. P Buckman, *Let's Dance: Social, Ballroom and Folk Dancing*, London, Penguin, 1978 and T J Buckland, 'Dancing Out of Time: The Forgotten Boston of Edwardian England,' in S Dodds & S C Cook, *Bodies of Sound: studies across popular music and dance*, Farnham, Ashgate, 2013, pp.55-72
5. T A Whitworth, *A History of Sequence Dancing: Fashionable Bodies in England, 1870-1920*, Chesterfield, Whitworth, 1995 and T J Buckland, *Society Dancing*, Basingstoke, Palgrave, 2011
6. For a fuller discussion see Whitworth, *History of Sequence Dancing*.
7. J Nott, 'Contesting Popular Dancing and Dance Music during the 1920s,' *Cultural and Social History*, 2013, 10(3), pp. 439-56. at pp. 439-40
8. M Kohn, *Dope Girls: The Birth of the British Drug Underworld*, London, Granta Books, 2001
9. For details see J Nott, *Going to the Palais: A Social and Cultural History of Dancing and Dance Halls in Britain, 1918-1960*, Oxford University Press, 2015. In the early 1930s, Rochdale, with a population of c.100,000 had six dance venues before the construction of its first purpose-built hall in 1934, J Stevenson, *British Society*, London, Penguin, 1984, p.398
10. The comparative figures for working-class and middle-class respondents respectively were 76% and 67% who went dancing and 21% and 24% who went regularly. Nott, *Going to the Palais*, p.38
11. There were deprived areas (including those with employment opportunities for women) in which fewer people could afford the entry price to a dance hall but there were other areas of relative prosperity, especially those associated with the new, light industries. In addition, the fall in the cost of living enhanced the purchasing power of all wage earners.
12. Nott, *Going to the Palais*, p.25
13. Attendance at a weekday dance hall (probably about 3d) cost less than the cinema (around 6d) or attendance at a football match (around 6d to 2s). See S G Jones, *Workers At Play*, London, Routledge, Kegan & Paul, 1986, p.14
14. As early as the 1890s, the Musicians' Union was worried that European musicians were coming to the country to the detriment of their members. The focus shifted to American jazz bands (as well as foreign orchestras) after the Great War when problems were exacerbated by the success of cinema, not to mention the cheap competition from police and military bands. See M Cloonan and M Brennan, 'Alien invasions: the British Musicians' Union and foreign musicians,' *Popular Music*, 2013, 32(2), pp.277-295

15. G Butterfield, 'The degeneracy of dancing,' *Dancing Journal*, 1908, pp2-3 cited in T Creswell, '"You cannot shake that shimmie here": producing mobility on the dance floor,' *Cultural Geographies*, 2006 (13), pp.56-77 at p.65
16. See report in *Daily Mail*, 16 May 1906
17. *Daily Mail*, 16 May 1906. Eton, Harrow, Rugby and Marlborough were mentioned by name but not Winchester.
18. *Daily Mail*, 1 March 1924
19. *Dancing Journal*, 1911, p.15 cited in Cresswell, 'You cannot shake that "shimmie" here' p.65. *Daily Mail*, 26 July 1920 and 26 April 1926
20. T J Buckland, 'How the Waltz was Won: Transmutations and the Acquisition of Style in Early English Modern Ballroom Dancing,' *Dance Research*, 2018, 36(2), pp.1-50
21. In Notts' phrase 'a Terpisichorean equivalent of the "stiff upper lip."' Nott, 'Contesting' p.443
22. For a good concise introduction see Cresswell, 'You cannot shake that "shimmie" here' pp.56-9.
23. The language with which 'freak' dances were condemned was telling – they were 'ungraceful, awkward, even indecent.'
24. J Hylton, 'The British Touch,' *Gramophone*, Sept. 1926, p.146 cited in Nott, 'Contesting' p.445
25. The agreed limits were: tango to be played 30-2 bars per minute, the waltz 36-8, the foxtrot 38-42 and the quickstep 54-6.
26. *Daily Mail* 8 July 1926
27. V Silvester, 'What is your opinion?' *Dance Journal*, 1956, pp.105-6 cited in Cresswell, '"You cannot shake that "shimmie" here' p.69
28. *Dancing Times*, November 1928, p.171 cited in Nott 'Contesting' p.449
29. Other failures include the Java (1924), the Mayfair (1927), the Midway Rhythm (1928) and the Six Eight (1929).
30. Cited in Nott, *Going to the Palais*, p.130
31. *Daily Mail*, 28 April 1927
32. *Daily Mail*, 13 November 1926
33. Even in the mid-1920s H St John Rumsey was complaining that there were too many foxtrots. *Daily Mail*, 22 July 1926
34. A Abra, 'Doing the Lambeth Walk: Novelty Dances and the British Nation,' *Twentieth Century British History*, 20(3) 2009, pp.346-69
35. R Graves & A Hodge, *The Long Weekend*, 1st published 1940, London, Penguin, 19/1, p.383. See https://www.youtube.com/watch?v=Mc6XUus5IC4 not least for some fascinating French dubbing!
36. Graves & Hodge, *Long Weekend*, p.384
37. See also A Davies, *Leisure, Gender and Poverty: Working-class culture in Salford and Manchester, 1900-1939*, Open University Press, Buckingham, 1992,. p.173
38. Graves & Hodge, *Long Weekend*, p.385 and see https://www.youtube.com/watch?v=BNpP--jDbgI
39. See https://www.britishpathe.com/video/the-park-parade/query/dance
40. *Daily Mail*, 7 January 1931
41. Davies, *Leisure, Gender and Poverty*: p.90. See also R Roberts, *A ragged schooling: Growing up in the classic slum*, Manchester University Press 1976 for the hierarchy of dance halls in Salford and Manchester.

42 There was a concern that the seedier dance halls were also associated with gang violence. The evidence from Manchester and Salford suggests trouble was sporadic and not on the same scale as the pre-war Scuttler troubles. Davies, *Leisure, Gender and Poverty*, p93-4. For scuttlers see A Davies, *The Gangs of Manchester*, Milo Books, Preston, 2008
43 See also the oral testimony quoted in Davies, *Leisure, Gender and Poverty* pp.89-90
44 Nott, *Going to the Palais*, p.303, who suggests that the dance hall, as well as entrenching marriage, 'probably extended its life too.'
45 Nott, *Going to the Palais*, p.300
46 Davies, *Leisure, Gender and Poverty*, p.57, argues that the growth of commercialized leisure barely affected the weekly routines of some, especially married working-class women. See also Langhamer, 'Women and Leisure.' As well as restrictions on time as marital responsibilities increased, dancing was seen as less appropriate after marriage. Though older women, often with their daughters, returned to the dance hall, it was probably easier for most married women to incorporate the cinema into their limited leisure time.
47 Hylton, 'British Touch' in Nott 'Contesting Popular Dancing,' p.445
48 J Nott, *Music for the People: Popular Music and Dance in Interwar Britain*, Oxford University Press, 2002, p.182
49 Nott, *Going to the Palais*, p.305.

CHAPTER 15

'Let's have a song upon the gramophone': Manufactured music - records, radio and the cinema

> Away with dull care,/ The day is set fair,
> A wireless set near/ To bring us good cheer!
> …
> In Winter time/ And Summer time,
> Or leisure time/ And pleasure time,
> The daily times/ That Big Ben chimes
> Are radio times!
>
> Radio Times, 'Dan Donovan with Henry Hall
> & The BBC Dance Orchestra'

THE ROOTS OF the new technologies date from the late nineteenth century, but it was after the Great War that the spread of 'manufactured music' revolutionised the production and consumption of popular (and other forms of) music. In their different, though intertwined ways, the gramophone, the radio and the cinema transformed the way in which people listened to music, while greatly increasing its availability. For the listener, the dependence on the local music hall or park bandstand was reduced. Instead of enjoying a once-off, not to be repeated, live performance, she or he could listen to music broadcast on radio at certain times, or to a record of choice at any time. The gains in flexibility and scope had to be offset against losses of quality of the listening experience. Even with the advent of electrical recording in the mid-1920s the frequency ranges achievable on record were significantly less than those experienced in the concert hall.¹ The quality of cheaper records aimed at the mass market was modest. Similarly, the quality of broadcast music was subject to technical limitations, to which musicians had to adapt. Electrical recording reduced the need to crouch round a recording horn and increased the range of instruments that could be used, thereby reducing the heavy reliance on brass bands and military music in early recordings. There were other implications for the way in which music was produced such as the time limitations of a 12-inch record. Song writers had to work within a much tighter timeframe than their nineteenth century counterparts. Similarly, the length of a radio programme influenced what could be produced.² Nonetheless, the impact of the new technologies on popular music were far-reaching.

The record industry

Attempts at commercial exploitation of Edison's 'talking machine' in Britain dated back to the late-1870s, but it was not until the Edwardian years that major developments took place. On the eve of the Great War, there were some 500,000 'talking machines' in Britain, estimated as equivalent to one in every three houses, and some fifteen million records sold annually. By the early 1930s the number of record sales had grown by a factor of four and almost two out of three households owned a gramophone.³ Unlike the dance halls, the record industry was not recession proof. The number of acoustic gramophones available for the domestic market rose from 256,522 in 1924 to 503, 663 in 1930. Numbers collapsed in the early 1930s and, despite a rally later in the decade, the total available for the domestic market was only 40,600. Similarly, records available for the domestic market peaked at 55 million in 1930, only to fall below 20 million four years later. ⁴ These developments took place within the context of a broader 'retailing revolution' now extending to 'luxury' items.⁵

Initially, the gramophone was often an outside novelty, to be heard in assembly halls, at fairgrounds or from itinerant street 'musicians,' pushing one mounted on a barrow. Portable models, in particular, appeared in a growing number of venues, some contributing to the dance boom of these years, others providing a more sedate experience of listening to music; and yet others, more problematically, appearing *al fresco* as daytrippers took to the seaside. Gradually attention shifted to an emerging mass market among the skilled and semi-skilled working classes.[6] In 1935 one in six of the respondents to a readership survey of the up-market *Gramophone* identified as wage earners (a euphemism for working class).[7] Given *Gramophone*'s readership, this almost certainly understates the extent to which the record industry appealed across class lines, as retail prices of gramophones and records continued to fall during the 1920s. Before the war, the Winner Record Company, created with an eye to the lower end of the market, reduced the cost of its records by 40 per cent between 1912 and 1913, but at 1s 6d this was still not a cheap item. Nor was a gramophone, the price of the cheapest model was equivalent to the cost of 200 tickets for the music hall.[8] The 1920s saw increased competition and falling prices, with Decca, HMV and especially EMI to the fore. More specifically, budget labels sprang up and their records were available at the new highstreet chains, such as Woolworths, Curry's and Marks and Spencer. All in all, the growing popularity of the gramophone brought popular music to an ever-widening audience.

The broad contours of consumer taste, as reflected by record sales, are clear. From the outset some music hall stars, notably Harry Champion, Harry Lauder and Florrie Forde, availed themselves of the new technology.[9] The technical limitations of early recording techniques restricted the possibilities for ensembles, hence the over-representation of Sousa marches (particularly 'Washington Post' and 'Liberty Bell') and von Suppé overtures (especially 'Poet and Peasant' and 'Light Cavalry').[10] From the mid-1920s onwards, the new electrical recording broadened the range. A 1930 survey showed the dominance of popular dance and vocal records (roughly 50 per cent of sales), with comic songs as popular as opera.[11] Yet within these broad categories were several surprises. Among the best-selling records in the HMV/Zonophone catalogue were predictable hits – the Savoy Orchestra's 'Valencia/The Student Prince' and Gracie Fields' 'My Blue Heaven/Because I Love You' – but they were outsold by the Temple Church's rendition of Mendelssohn's 'Hear My Prayer,' which sold over 800,000 copies between its release in 1927 and 1938.[12] Given the transatlantic reach of several big record companies, certain American performers sold well in Britain. Maurice Gunsky, an American tenor, typically singing to a piano or piano and violin accompaniment, recorded songs such as 'Ramona,' 'Let Me Call You Sweetheart' and 'Girl of My Dreams,' but his most successful record was ''Why Do I Always Remember/ Lay My Head Beneath a Rose,' which sold almost a quarter of a million copies.[13] Another American, country singer Bud Billing (aka Frank Luther when not recording for Zonophone) sold over 200,000 copies of 'The Wanderer's Warning/ Will the Angels Play Their Harps for Me?' both characterised by lyrics of saccharine sentimentality and banal tunes.[14] Frank Crumit, another folk and novelty singer, sold well for HMV Victor and Decca, despite never visiting Britain. His greatest success came with Percy French's nonsense song 'Abdul, Abulbul Amir.'[15] Whimsy was very much the order of the day. The Ben Selvin Novelty Orchestra sold an estimated half a million copies of 'Dardenella,' released in 1920, but is more remembered for 'I'm Forever Blowing Bubbles,' which has survived thanks to the tribal loyalty and singing talents of generations of West Ham United fans! In similar vein, the International Novelty Orchestra (in fact the Victor studio orchestra) had success with 'The Cuckoo Waltz' and 'The Flapper Wife' in the early 1920s, but also recorded pre-war hits such as the 1890s minstrel show song, 'After the Ball' and the sentimental 'Let Me Call You Sweetheart,' first recorded in 1910.

Popular songs were covered by various artists. By far and away the most covered song was 'Sonny Boy.' Although now associated overwhelmingly with Al Jolson, it was recorded at least 40 times by artists that included well-known figures, such as Paul Robeson and John McCormack as well as lesser known ones, such as Ruth Brown and Ruth Etting. Some way behind, were songs such as ' Carolina Moon.' and 'I Can't Give You Anything but Love Baby.' The popularity of the latter was enhanced by its inclusion in the Broadway revue *Blackbirds of 1928* The inter-relatedness of popular musical culture is further underlined by two very successful and much-covered songs from the film *Broadway Melody*; the first the title song, the second, the now largely-forgotten 'Wedding of the Painted Doll,' which was covered over twenty times.[16]

Records, particularly when linked to films, were an important element in the careers of various performers who were to become household names between the wars. Dance band leaders, such as Jack Hylton, Ambrose and Jack Payne were at the forefront. Jack Payne made over 200 records for Columbia between 1928 and 1932, of which over 60 sold more than 10,000 copies, generally regarded as a measure of success at the time. 'Stein Song/Moonshine is Better Than Sunshine' sold 95,000 copies and 'When It's Springtime in the Rockies/I'm Falling in Love' over 70,000.[17] Gracie Fields and George Formby, the best remembered popular singers of the time were not alone. For example, Jeanette MacDonald, first with Maurice Chevalier and later with Nelson Eddy, appeared in several films which generated such popular songs as 'Dream Lover' (from *The Love Parade*) and 'Indian Love Call' (from *Rose Marie*).[18]

There were also some less obvious successes. Caruso's recording of 'Vesti La Giubba' sold massively. In a lengthy career, he combined operatic extracts with Neapolitan songs, exemplified by his 1933 Victor Red Label record, 'O Sole Mio/La Donna e Mobile.' Another operatically trained singer with a long recording career and considerable popularity was John McCormack. His relationship with England was complex, culminating in his decision to seek American citizenship. Like Caruso his recorded output combined operatic extracts with popular Irish songs. His earliest recordings for Odeon (London) made between 1906 and 1909 included extracts from *Rigoletto*, *Aida* and *La Boheme*, sentimental Irish airs (notably 'The Snowy Breasted Pearl,' 'Kathleen Mavourneen,' 'Killarney' and 'Eileen Aroon') and unequivocally nationalist songs ('A Nation Once Again,' 'God Save Ireland' and the 'Croppy Boy'). Given the mounting tensions in Ireland at the time, it is difficult to see the latter appealing beyond (some) members of the Irish diaspora. The balance of his repertoire changed after the Great War.[19] Operatic extracts continued to be recorded but the Irish element became increasingly sentimental, while overtly nationalist songs disappeared. His Victor Electric recordings (1925-31) contained songs recorded before the war -- 'When You and I Were Seventeen' and 'Kathleen Mavourneen' – alongside such quintessential Irish songs as 'Mother Macree' and 'The Rose of Tralee' as well as the saccharine 'Ireland, Mother, Ireland.' In addition, he recorded popular sentimental songs – 'Sonny Boy,' 'Moonlight and Roses' and 'Silver Threads Among the Gold' – as well as older songs such as 'Annie Laurie' and even 'Who Is Sylvia?' McCormack's appeal to Irish audiences is well-known but the sanitising and broadening of his popular repertoire in the 1920s and 1930s won him a larger audience on both sides of the Atlantic.

In sum, the spread of gramophone and record ownership led to an 'unprecedented availability' of recorded music but evaluating the impact of the record industry is complicated by two factors.[20] First, the data relating to record sales is incomplete and not open to simple interpretation. Given the prevalence of communal usage, the audience for any given record was greater (to an unknowable extent) than simple sales figures. Second, the impact of the record industry was intertwined, in a mutually reinforcing way, with the development of radio and film.

Radio

The expansion in radio ownership during the inter-war years was dramatic and had a profound effect on the cultural life of the nation. In the early 1920s licence holders numbered in the hundred-thousands (the precise figure is open to debate) but by the late 1930s had exceeded 9 million. As the figures in Table 1 show, the growth in the number of licence holders was dramatic, doubling in the second half of the 1920s and growing by a further factor of three in the 1930s. Improved technology – valve sets rather than crystal – and falling price underpinned the surge in ownership and the transformation from a luxury to a mass consumer good. Three out of four households, some thirty-four million people, had access to the radio on the eve of the second world war.

The most important player was the BBC but, despite its dominant position, it never enjoyed a monopoly of broadcasting. Nonetheless, the development of radio broadcasting in Britain took a significantly different form from that in America, with its proliferation of broadcasting stations. The BBC went on air in November 1922 with limited geographical coverage. Within a year eight stations had been opened, reaching roughly 50 per cent of the population, rising to 70 per cent in 1924. 1925 saw

Table 1: Broadcast Receiving Licences, 1923-39

Year	No. (000s)	Index 1930 = 100	Year	No. (000s)	Index 1930 = 100
1923	125	4	1931	3,647	118
1924	748	24	1932	4,620	149
1925	1,350	44	1933	5,497	178
1926	1,960	63	1934	6,260	203
1927	2,270	73	1935	7,012	227
1928	2,483	80	1936	7,618	246
1929	2,730	88	1937	8,131	263
1930	3,091	100	1938	8,589	278
			1939	8,968	290

Source: B R Mitchell & H G Jones, *Second Abstract of British Historical Statistics*, Cambridge University Press, 1971, p.114

eleven low-power relay transmitters brought online and the high-powered longwave transmitter at Daventry. An important breakthrough was the development of the valve set, which replaced the older crystal set with its reliance on headpieces. The valve set, while not without technical limitations, was a more attractive option. As well as operating via a loudspeaker, it could amplify weak signals and distinguish more effectively between stations.

By the early 1930s the BBC's geographical coverage in England was almost 100 per cent, but there were variations in its audience. In an age before the portable transistor radio, listening habits were determined partly by family hierarchy and partly by generational differences in non-domestic leisure activities: the dance hall, particularly, and the cinema were more strongly associated with the young and single. In the late-1930s the largest segment of the BBC's audience was (by the standards of the day) middle-aged, and while it attracted significant numbers of listeners in their late teens and twenties, these age groups were appreciably more likely to listen to commercial stations.

The BBC played an important role in bringing dance music and popular song to a wide audience, but this was not a foregone conclusion, nor was the route straightforward. The dominant figure from the outset was John Reith. He was not simply a left-over from an earlier (Victorian) age which believed in 'rational recreation' in general and music as a force for uplifting and unifying society.[21] Rather he believed such beliefs were ever more necessary in the democratising world of the early twentieth century. Universal manhood suffrage and partial (later total) female suffrage necessitated, in his eyes, the creation of a well-informed, civilized general public. Radio broadcasting, as he argued in *Broadcast Over Britain*, 1924, was to prioritise education over entertainment; to set high standards, including high moral standards, for all and to instil a sense of national harmony that would transcend the bitter divisions that scarred the country in the immediate post-war years.[22] Through the BBC, he would impose a benign paternalism. There would be freedom – freedom of access but not freedom of choice. Translated into practical broadcasting terms, this meant, among other things, that Sundays would be strictly observed, with no concessions to frivolity, and that improving, high culture would dominate the airwaves. Not for the last time, a moral entrepreneur was to find that what the public wanted to listen to was not what he believed they should hear. There was considerable tension, if not an outright contradiction, between his desire to reach as wide an audience as possible and his determination to give them what (in his opinion) was good for them, irrespective of their preferences. Similarly, the desire to educate led in one direction while the desire to unify led in the opposite. Reith was clear in his views, but the BBC was not a monolithic institution cast in his image. Important figures within the corporation, such as the head of Variety and 'enthusiastic Americanizer,' Eric Maschwitz, Cecil Graves, controller of programmes, and Archie Harding, the director of programmes for the northern region, who placed great emphasis on making radio accessible to ordinary people, had alternative visions. Not surprisingly, the evolution of radio broadcasting in the inter-war years involved a series of compromises and concessions.[23]

Music was of paramount importance to the BBC and the BBC was also a central element in the music industry as a whole. Reith and his followers were convinced of the importance of 'serious' or 'classical' music. It was to be an important element in terms of hours broadcast but, more, the BBC was to be a key provider through its own symphony orchestra, (founded 1930), under the distinguished conductor, Adrian Boult; as well as through its sponsorship of the Promenade Concerts from 1927, which was the most striking manifestation of the BBC's commitment to the musical welfare of the nation. Similarly, in broadcasting 'light music,' comprising light and comic opera as well as light orchestral pieces, the BBC contributed to its educative role. More problematic, because it was mere entertainment, was 'popular music,' a broad category including military bands and musical comedy as well as music hall and dance band music.[24]

Dance music was heard on the BBC from the outset. The Savoy Orpheans broadcast on three weekly slots from 1924 onwards. The creation of the BBC dance orchestra, initially under Jack Payne, later Henry Hall, in 1928 bore testament to the importance of 'popular' music and a determination to bring in leading practitioners.[25] However, its contribution to the dance boom was limited by the BBC's programming decisions. Further, dance music as aired by the BBC had a distinctive style that grew out of the wider debate about the threat of 'Americanization.' 'Hot' music was deemed inappropriate. Hugely successful musicians, notably Louis Armstrong and Duke Ellington, were rarely heard on the BBC and even when they were it was on regional programmes. If there were to be an American influence, Paul Whiteman and his orchestra, provided an acceptable model. From the outset, BBC dance music was to be tasteful but capable of holding the attention of the passive listener. While many in the BBC eschewed popularity in favour of 'what we ourselves think of our work,' Hall's emphasis on melody made him very popular with listeners, notwithstanding *Melody Maker*'s scathing dismissal of the 'inoffensively negative' nature of his playing.[26]

Initially, the BBC devoted relatively little time to popular music, but this had changed by the end of the 1920s. The following tables indicate the range of BBC music output. In Table 2, under the umbrella of popular music, the largest subset was that broad category that included orchestra, bands, and small groups. It is noticeable that there was significantly more light and dance music in the regional output.[27]

Table 2: Music programme time (%) by type – 1927-1930

Type	1927-9 average	1930 National	1930 Regional
Classical (all)	18	15	20
Popular (all)	25	21	36
Bands etc*	13	7	18
Dance music	16	11	20
Gramophone records	5	3	1

*Subset of light music, comprising orchestral, band and small combination (with vocalist) Source: Adapted from A Briggs, *The History of Broadcasting in the United Kingdom*, Volume 2, Oxford University Press, 1995, pp.34-5

The following figures, though not strictly comparable, show a relative decline in the amount of programme time given to dance music. Although there was a sharp increase in airtime for gramophone records in the 1930s, this was a broad category that also included classical and light classical music.

Table 3: Music programme time (%) by type – 1934, 1936 & 1938

Type	1934 National	1934 Regional	1936 National	1936 Regional	1938 National	1938 Regional
Classical	17	15	20	15	18	17
Popular	29	43	22	39	23	32
Dance	9	10	9	8	5	9
Records	8	10	11	9	7	12

Source: Adapted from A Briggs, *The History of Broadcasting in the United Kingdom*, Volume 2, Oxford University Press, 1995, pp.49 & 52

Differences of opinion over the balance between the two broad categories of 'serious' and 'popular' music to be broadcast on the BBC was not simply an internal debate, but was influenced by the competition from commercial stations broadcasting from Europe. Radio Normandie and Radio Lyon both started transmitting in 1924, followed by Radio Toulouse in 1928. The best-known and most heavily subscribed rival was Radio Luxembourg, which was on air from 1933 onwards. Pre-recorded programmes, including 'hits' of the day, were shipped to the continent for broadcast back to Britain, aimed at a key demographic (the young) poorly catered for by the BBC, particularly on Sundays.

'Light' music for the BBC was a catch-all category that embraced a range of music from light classical pieces played by orchestras as well as military and brass bands, operettas and musical comedy, dance music and popular song, which, itself could range from light classical pieces, older music-hall numbers and newer songs of the day. The compromise that emerged by the mid-1930s brought together older songs, such as 'Love's Old Sweet Song,' and pre-war music-hall favourites, that provided a nostalgic appeal to an older audience and present-day hits, such as 'Sing, Gypsy, Sing' and 'Little Man You've Had a Busy Day,' appealing to a younger audience. In addition, and acknowledging a Reithian duty to improve, there were 'gems' from the classics, including fantasias on folk songs, country dances, and sea songs , which combined elements of 'high' and 'low.'[28] Much of the music came via outside broadcasts from London hotels to seaside resorts.[29]

According to a *Daily Mail* ballot of over a million readers in 1927, the four most popular forms of 'light' music were variety and concert parties (19 per cent), light orchestral music (14 per cent), military bands (13 per cent) and dance music (10 per cent). In comparison, opera and operetta was ranked eighth (5 per cent) while at the bottom were choruses and sea shanties and chamber music (2 per cent).[30] Such expressions of public preference fed into the internal BBC debate between those in favour of leading and improving popular taste and those who believed in following popular opinion. The creation of a Revue and Vaudeville Section (1930), and the subsequent airing of series such as *Songs From the Shows*, *Music Hall*, and *The Kentucky Minstrels*, was evidence of the BBC's awareness of the need to offer a broad range of entertainment. The establishment of a

Listener Research Department under Robert Silvey in the mid-1930s further underlined the growing sensitivity to listeners' opinions. Silvey's research confirmed the strength of popular preference for variety (93 per cent), military bands (72 per cent), and dance music (65 per cent) and light music (62 per cent).[31] Listener responses also pointed to a number of (contradictory) shortcomings – too much dance music, too little dance music, poor quality dance music, and so forth – but the greatest number of complaints related to Sunday broadcasts and the total absence of light music. This presented an opportunity to the commercial stations broadcasting from the near continent. A 1937 Listener Research Department survey found a fifth of respondents listened to commercial stations during the week, rising to two-thirds on Sunday. Not all commercial stations were truly national in coverage. Radio Luxembourg came closest, but Radio Normandie struggled to get beyond London and the south of England while the Poste Parisien signal was strongest in the north of England. There were also regional variations in the popularity of specific stations, but it was clear that, taken as a whole, they appealed particularly to working and lower-middle class audiences, women more than men and the young rather than the old.[32] Unsurprisingly, popular music as a general category predominated, accounting for around 90 per cent of their airtime. In January 1937 popular songs accounted for 29 per cent of airtime, followed by light orchestral music (22 per cent), dance music (19 per cent), and comedy songs (15 per cent).[33]

Commercial station programmes had to be pre-recorded but, more importantly, this necessitated close links with the developing record companies, notably EMI and Decca. The stations, through their advertisers, made themselves more popular through association with celebrity big names. Radio Normandie, for example, offered *The Rinso Radio Revue*, with, among others, Jack Hylton and His Band, and *The Kraft Cheese Show* with Billy Cotton and his band. The response of George Formby and his fans to his appearances on *The Feenamint Laxative Show* is not recorded.[34] In retrospect, the challenge to the BBC in the 1930s appears overstated, but, at the time, it was seen to be serious when the practice of terminating (or threatening to terminate) contracts was not working and 'stars' moved to commercial stations. Although this conflict would continue into the 1960s, even a generation earlier the BBC was forced to give ground and modify its light music programming. However, one thing was clear: radio in its entirety was a major force in the popular music industry and played a central role in broadening accessibility and the range of popular music.

Cinema and the musical

The third element in this process of expansion of popular, mechanical music was the cinema. Prior to the Great War cinema had been little more than a novelty turn in a variety hall programme. Within a very short period of time the cinema emerged as a major threat to variety theatre. It shared the attractions of the dance hall – opulence and escapism – but on a larger scale. Spectacular epics, literally with casts of thousands, slap-stick comedy, often as daring as it was funny, romances, set in exotic locations with even more exotic stars, and even the fascinating novelty of documentary or semi-documentary films provide a ready explanation for its success.[35] A further element was the musical delights offered on screen. The 'all singing, all dancing' film arrived relatively late on the scene for obvious technical reasons. However, the possibilities of portraying dance on screen was realised from the outset. Initially short films simply depicted a well-known dancer, for example Annabelle Moore in *Annabelle Butterfly Dance*, (1894).[36] A more elaborate approach was adopted in *The Whirl of Life*, (1915) which told the story of the renown dancers Irene and Vernon Castle but was essentially a vehicle to show off their dances, including the foxtrot, one-step and the Castle Walk.[37] In other films dance scenes were incorporated into a broader (though often flimsy) story, as in the 1910 Danish film, *Afgrunden (The Abyss)*, which starred Asta Nielsen.[38] Filmed versions of plays or operettas also offered the opportunity to incorporate dance. *Salomé* (1923) featured Alla Nazamova and *The Dumb Girl of Portici* (1916) showcased Anna Pavlova.[39] Less common, but as with Valentino's tango in *The Four Horsemen of the Apocalypse* and, most notably, 'Maria's dance' (performed by Brigitte Helm) in *Metropolis*, dance was incorporated into and developed the central thrust of the film, the latter, combining in a nightmare scene, the erotic and the macabre.[40]

Various attempts were made to combine music and film. An interesting intermediate position was seen in Walter Forde's *You'd Be Surprised*, a 1930 musical comedy in which synchronised songs and music were added. From 1930 onwards a huge number (200 or more) of musical shorts, musicals, musical comedies and musical melodramas were produced in Britain. In addition, there were a growing number of American musicals, albeit partly constrained by the 1927 Cinematograph Film Act.[41] In cinematic, and indeed musical, terms, the quality of these films varied considerably, but the increased availability of popular music is more important. The 're-discovery' of old music hall stars – *Veterans of Variety* – led to the production of several musical shorts. Among the best known 'veterans' was Gus Elen, who came out of retirement and, at the age of sixty-nine, and recorded for *Pathé* three of his best known songs – 'It's A Great Big Shame,' 'Arf A Pint of Ale' and 'A Nice Fine Day' a.k.a. ''The Postman's Holiday.'[42] The scale and popularity of these shorts should not be underestimated. Between 1936 and 1939, *British Lion* released twenty-eight 9.5mm optical sound films as 'one-reelers,' with a running time of eight or nine minutes.[43] Each short contained three or four acts. Typically, *Variety Number 25* (November 1938), featured Reggie Bristow and His Band, playing 'Stay Out of My Dream,' Phyllis Stanley, singing 'That's My Home,' Pamela Grey and Pat Green, singing and dancing to 'This Is The Rhythm for Me' and a drum solo by Teddy Brown to 'Star Spangled Banner.'[44] Bristow appeared in eight of these shorts, with only Joe Loss and his orchestra featuring more often.. Other popular (but now largely unknown) turns were the Three Accordion Kings, the Three Radio Rogues, the Petite Ascots (dancers) and the Six Lady Harpists. And this was but the tip of an iceberg that included over one hundred shorts and newsreels of the 1930s featuring dance bands. Predictably big names, such as Ambrose, Jack Hylton and Joe Loss appeared several times but there were a range of lesser-known performers who appeared on screen: Sydney Kyte and His Band, Geraldo and His Gaucho Tango Orchestra, and Ruby Bruneau and the Hawaiian Islanders,

Not dissimilar were the musical comedy shorts produced by Monty Banks in 1930, which were about half an hour long with flimsy story lines. In *The Musical Beauty Shop*, the beauty salon owner puts on a cabaret. This pointed to one of the most used format - the 'parade of stars,' which was used throughout the decade from *Elstree Calling* (with nineteen acts, compered by Tommy Handley) in 1930 to *Calling All Stars*, in 1937 and *Music Hall Parade* of 1939. Story lines were contrived, and the film was effectively a night at variety theatre on film. Despite their cinematic shortcomings, these films, running to eighty minutes or more, brought to the scene a range of performers who would never have been seen 'live on stage' in most towns and even some smaller cities. Even much-derided 'quota quickies,' such as *Stepping Stones* (1931) and *Sing As You Swing* (1937) featured various music-hall stars of the day, while *Music Hall* (1934) featured the ubiquitous G H Elliott. A variation on this theme was to focus more clearly on individuals, (such as Jessie Matthews in *It's Love Again* (1936) and *Head Over Heels*, (1937) or Jack Buchanan in *Goodnight Vienna* (1932). Couples such as Jack Hulbert and Cicely Courtneidge, starred in *Happy Ever After* (1932) and then there was The Crazy Gang in *Okay for Sound* (1937).

Another common device was to adapt an operetta or an opera (*A Southern Maid*, 1931 and *Carmen*,1932), a stage musical (*The Maid of the Mountain,* 1932) or a novel (*The Girl from Maxim's* and *Good Companions,* both 1933), though the formula did not guarantee success. The expensively produced *Pagliacci*, starring Richard Tauber was a flop. Exotic locations helped, from the far east (*Chu Chin Chow*, 1934 and *The Mikado,* 1939) to central Europe, particularly Vienna (notably *Goodnight Vienna*, 1932 and *Blossom Time*, 1934), though a similar effect could be achieved with a make-believe setting, such as Ruritania (*The Prince of Arcadia*, 1933). The effect could be further enhanced by the inclusion of an exotic stranger – the Hungarian gypsy in *Blue Danube* (1932) or the ex-French Foreign legionnaire turned singer in the revue-style *The Song of Soho* (1930), though the latter was thoroughly rubbished by *Monthly Film Bulletin*, which thought 'the performances are poor, some of the turns vulgar, the photography bad and the film as a whole dreary.'[45] Finally, and not for the first (or last) time, musical films were set in a romanticised Ireland, as exemplified by *Kathleen Mavourneen*, (notable for being one of Maureen O'Hara's earliest films). *The Minstrel Boy* and *The Rose of Tralee* (all released in 1937) and *The Mountains of Mourne* and *My Irish Molly* (both 1938). Story lines were clichéd – Irish emigrant to America returns to Ireland to find family

– and the films little more than vehicles for well-known Irish songs. 'Danny Boy' and 'Off to Tipperary in the Morning', both featured in *Kathleen Mavourneen*.

The judgements of film critics are not to be dismissed lightly but there is a significant, if not always measurable, difference between critical and popular acclaim. Undoubtedly, some of these films were awful and not well received by audiences across the country, but the fact remains that the various British musical films of the 1930s brought to the local screen an amazing array of stars. Band leaders and their orchestras, such as Henry Hall, Ambrose, Carroll Gibbons, Nat Gonella and Harry Roy, appeared in numerous films; so too did older music hall stars, such as Harry Lauder, George Robey and Vesta Victoria; new stars, not just Fields and Formby but also Jack Buchanan, Jessie Matthews, Cicely Courtneidge and Jack Hulbert could be seen; so too could up-and-coming stars, such as Anna Neagle, and foreign singers including the African-American bass, Paul Robeson, the Polish tenor, Jan Kiepura, the Hungarian soprano, Gilla Alper and the American tenor, Franco Foresta. Even the English bass-baritone, Keith Falkner, better known for his concert performances, could be heard on film. Given the popularity of cinema and the range of musical performers to be seen and heard, this was a significant contribution to the dramatically expanding availability of popular music in the inter-war years. Further, the inter-relationship between the new technologies, records, radio and film, was mutually reinforcing and helped to sustain more traditional variety theatre.

The most spectacular musical films of the 1930s came from America. The impact of such films as *42nd Street* and *Footlight Parade* or the various *Gold Digger* films was considerable.[46] The sheer scale, the complex and stunning choreography, the innovative camera work and the array of talent put them in a class of their own. The dazzling dancing skills of Fred Astaire and Ginger Rogers featured in nine RKO films, including *Top Hat*, *Swing Time* and *Shall We Dance*. Although the cinemagoer was as much a passive recipient as the radio listener, the American 'all singing, all dancing' movie provided an unrivalled audio and visual experience, which showed up the limitations of their British rivals. *She Shall Have Music*, released in 1935, starred Jack Hylton in a clichéd story of a radio broadcast from a cruise ship. The film contained several instrumentals, including 'The Band that Jack Built' and 'Sailing Along on a Carpet of Cloud;' novelty songs, such as 'Why Did She Fall for the Leader of the Band? and 'May All Your Troubles Be Little Ones;' and an array of dancers that included the Leon Woizikowsky Ballet, the Dalmora Can-Can Dancers, Carmora – Spanish Dancing Beauty; Harlem's Hottest Hoofers and even the exotic dancer, Matheu Merryfield. But, like other British musicals, it failed to match the spectacle of its American rivals.[47] Even *The Lambeth Walk*, the 1939 version of *Me and My Girl*, failed to get beyond the statically shot stage production. The film was largely faithful to the original, though a new street scene was added and, surprisingly, the number of songs reduced to two: 'Me and My Girl' and 'The Lambeth Walk.'[48] Its naïve message of cheerful cockneys and understanding aristocrats coming together chimed with wartime sentiment, but parodies, particularly those featuring Hitler, proved even more popular.[49]

Some concluding observations

The novelty of 'mechanical' music in its various forms has rightly caught the attention of historians. The inter-war years, with their increased range and accessibility of popular music, in its various forms, witnessed a fundamental transformation in production and consumption. However, two important qualifications need to be made. First, the impact of the new technologies was limited in the 1920s. Important groundwork was done but, for example, it was not until the mid-1930s that radio became 'something that anyone could operate, offering good quality sound and interference free reception.'[50] The breakthrough 'Band Show' was first aired in January 1938 and even the upsurge in film musicals only started around 1930. Second, there was an important, though unspectacular, continuity in more traditional forms of music making. Piano sales may have declined, but there were plenty of 'joannas' in pubs, clubs and homes that remained the centre of sing-songs. Itinerant musicians and singing and dancing in the street may have diminished but did not disappear over-night. Indeed, communal singing received a boost in these years, as will become apparent as we turn to the songs of the 1920s and 1930s.

Endnotes

1. See R Pearsall, *Popular Music of the Twenties*, Newton Abbott, David & Charles, 1976 who claims that electrical recording increased the frequency range from 168-2000 cycles to 100-5000 cycles, compared with the 20-20,000 range experienced in a concert hall, p.100
2. Henry Wood reduced 'The Flying Dutchman Overture' from over ten minutes to less than eight. He performed a similar masterpiece of compression on Dukas's 'The Sorcerer's Apprentice.' Pearsall, *Popular Music*, p.94.
3. P Martland, *Recording History: The British Record Industry, 1888-1931*, Plymouth, Scarecrow Press, 2013, p.xviii
4. Figures from interwar UK Censuses of Production in J Nott, *Music for the People: Popular Music and Dance in Interwar Britain*, Oxford University Press, 2002, p.16 and p.18
5. See W Hamish Fraser, *The Coming of the Mass Market, 1850-1914*, London, Macmillan, 1981, J Benson, *The Rise of Consumer Society in Britain, 1880-1980,* London, Longmans, 1994 .and P Gurney, *The Making of Consumer Culture in Modern Britain*, London, Bloomsbury, 2017.
6. Martland, *Recording History*, p.73 and p.77
7. *Gramophone,* September 1931 cited in Nott, *Music for the People*, p.34
8. J Mullen, 'Experiencing music in the home in Britain, 1900-1925.' Paper given to Expert Workshop, From Parlour Sing-songs to Iplayers: Experiencing culture in the 20th and 21st century homes, University of Lincoln, May 2014 at https://www.academia.edu/7143472/_PDF_full_text_Experiencing_music_in_the_British_home_1900_1925
9. The revival of interest in old-style music hall in the late 1920s and early 1930s saw several singers taking advantage of the new electrical recordings. Columbia and Regal recorded Florrie Forde (1929), Ella Retford (1930), Harry Champion and Vesta Victoria (1931), Charles Coburn (1932) and Billy Merson (1933).
10. This element of 'middle brow' music continued after the Great War. Indeed, Stokowski and the Philadelphia Orchestra sold some 170,000 copies of Liszt's 'Hungarian Rhapsody No.2.'
11. Merchandising Survey of Great Britain figures cited in Martland, *Recording History*, pp.308-9
12. Martland, *Recording History*, p,310
13. Martland, *Recording History*, p,310 'Lay My Head' can be heard at https://www.youtube.com/watch?v=aSOazB31a5w
14. The wanderer, having been thrown out by his father for gambling and drinking, exhorts the listener 'don't break your dear mother's heart.' A version of 'Will the Angels' by Frank Luther and His Pards can be heard at https://www.youtube.com/watch?v=VPBMfXvi_EU Billing was probably best known for 'Barnacle Bill the Sailor.'
15. This can be heard at https://www.youtube.com/watch?v=Lv6M2omQ__U
16. See https://www.youtube.com/watch?v=YOOutukmhtw for the (black and white) film version, complete with Zanfield Dolly Girls. and https://www.youtube.com/watch?v=xmv-EuYIm-M to hear Ran Week's version. It was

also recorded by Jack Hylton and later became a staple in the repertoire of Reginald 'Mr Blackpool' Dixon and his theatre organ.
17 Martland, *Recording History*, p.323
18 'Dream Lover' can be heard at https://www.youtube.com/watch?v=-M3P2o5AowA and 'Indian Love Call' at https://www.youtube.com/watch?v=1n_bUSywN94 MacDonald was a versatile singer with recordings varying from operatic extracts (from Verdi, Puccini and Gounod) to hymns such as 'Abide With Me.'
19 McCormack recorded several songs as part of the war effort, including 'Tipperary,' 'Roses of Picardy' and 'When Pershing's Men Go Marching Into Picardy.'
20 The phrase is Nott's, *Music for the People*, p.32
21 See D Russell, *Popular music in England, 1840-1914*, Manchester University Press, 1987, Part 1
22 For a clear and concise introduction see K Laybourn, *Britain on the Breadline*, Stroud, Sutton, 1998
23 For differing interpretations see J Richards, *Cinema and Radio in Britain and America, 1920-60*, Manchester University Press, 2010 and P Scannell & D Cardiff, *A Social History of British Broadcasting*, Oxford, Blackwell, 1991, p.212
24 S Bernard, *On the Radio: Music radio in Britain*, Milton Keynes Open University Press, 1989, p.8
25 The appointment of Henry Hall was an important development. As well as his musical abilities, he was well informed about musical tastes outside London.
26 Bernard, *On the Radio*, p.15, *Melody Maker* quoted in P Scannell & D Cardiff, *A Social History of British Broadcasting*, p.210. Hall gave his audience what they wanted to a much greater degree than Ambrose or Jack Hylton.
27 For a fuller discussion see A Briggs, *The History of Broadcasting in the United Kingdom*, volume 1, *The Birth of Broadcasting*, 1896-1927, volume 2, *The Golden Age of Wireless*, 1927-1939, Oxford University Press, 1995
28 Scannell & Cardiff, *Social History*, 1991.
29 See for example the Savoy Orpheans, Henry Hall and the Gleneagles Hotel orchestra and Jack Payne and the Hotel Cecil orchestra.
30 Briggs, *Golden Age of Wireless*, p.67
31 Cited in Richards, *Cinema and Radio*, p.38. In comparison were the figures for grand opera (21 per cent), violin recitals (19 per cent) and chamber music (8 per cent)
32 Further details are given in Nott, *Music for the People*, 72-4
33 Nott, *Music for the People*, p.75. In certain areas there were significant variations. Comedy songs were much more common on Poste Parisien, dance music more frequent on Radio Luxembourg and light orchestral music on Radio Normandie.
34 Nott, *Music for the People*, p.79
35 Richards, *Cinema and Radio* provides a good overview.
36 This can be seen at https://www.bing.com/videos/search?q=Annabelle+Butterfly+Dance&docid=608043287117497300&mid=67819BE48B070119585767819BE48B0701195857&view=detail&FORM=VIRE See also the Lumiere brothers very short clip, 'Danse Serpentine' from 1896. Some shorts were more comedic, such as the

French 'Le Cochon Danseur' 1907 at https://www.bing.com/videos/search?q=dansing+pig+film&docid=608015296822906831&mid=4D-6BAA39B04CB313BA404D6BAA39B04CB313BA40&view=detail&-FORM=VIRE. Dance was used for comedic purposes by Laurel and Hardy, 'That's My Wife,' Buster Keaton, 'The Cook' and even Charlie Chaplin's bread roll dance in 'The Gold Rush.'

37 At https://www.bing.com/videos/search?q=whirl+of+life+castle+walk&ru=%2fvideos%2fsearch%3fq%3dwhirl%2bof%2blife%2bcastle%2bwalk%26FORM%3dHDRSC3&view=detail&mid=CFBF1806593EA1857427CFBF1806593EA1857427&rvsmid=DFED7F-670C893914E3BBDFED7F670C893914E3BB&FORM=VDQVAP

38 At https://www.youtube.com/watch?v=2jPI9Ujjd9A See also the German, 'Pandora's Box' (1929) which allowed the former Ziegfeld Folly dancer, Louise Brooks, to show off her skills and the American 'Our Dancing Daughters' (1929), which did the same for Joan Crawford

39 'Salomé' was based on the Oscar Wilde play (see https://www.youtube.com/watch?v=44OmwMoGWfs) and 'The Dumb Girl of Portici' (see https://www.youtube.com/watch?v=D-UtUiofa8U) was based on Auber's opera.

40 Valentino can be seen at https://www.youtube.com/watch?v=C4ELzf0u7Q8 and Helm at   https://www.youtube.com/watch?v=pJWhaRz7_VA

41 See S Guy, 'Calling All Stars: Musical Films in a Musical Decade' in J Richards, ed., *The Unknown Thirties: An Alternative History of the British Cinema, 1929-1939*, London, I B Taurus, 2000, pp.99-118

42 The films (PT85, PT96 and PT119 can be seen at https://www.britishpathe.com/video/gus-elen-3

43 http://www.pathefilm.uk/95flmdance.htm

44 https://www.youtube.com/watch?v=5KDazFVqJoI Several other Variety Numbers are available on YouTube

45 *Monthly Film Bulletin*, December 1936, p.214 cited in Guy 'Calling All Stars' at p.103.

46 https://www.youtube.com/watch?v=mwuuqBVECkw from 'Gold Diggers of Broadway' and https://www.youtube.com/watch?v=mxPgplMujzQ from 'Swing Time'

47 Pathescope released a 15-minute compilation of music clips from the film in 1936. See https://www.youtube.com/watch?v=im36di00L6Y

48 Richards, *Unknown Thirties*, p.110-11

49 For example, https://www.youtube.com/watch?v=gYdmk3GP3iM

50 Scannell & Cardiff, *Social History*, p.358

CHAPTER 16

'I like bananas': Popular songs of the 1920s and 1930s

> I don't like giggling flappers
> I don't like ancient crones
> Ah but I like bananas
> Because they have no bones
>
> I can't bear tax collectors
> Especially one who phones
> Ah but I like bananas
> Because they have no bones
>
> Alan Breeze & Billy Cotton's Band, 'I Like Bananas
> (Because They Have No Bones)'

POPULAR SONG WAS further transformed in the inter-war years as new musical influences from across the Atlantic interacted with older, local popular musical traditions. Over time, the combined influence of mass communication and a highly commercialised, transatlantic music industry gradual led to a greater degree of standardisation and homogenisation in popular music. But the boundaries of popular music remain as elusive as ever. In an age which tried to distinguish between "high-brow," "middle-brow" and "low-brow," was McCormack singing 'Che Gelida Manina' "highbrow" while McCormack singing "Danny Boy" "low brow?" Put another way, should Peter Dawson be excluded, despite the undoubted success of his "Floral Dance?" And what of Paul Robeson? The starting point for the analysis in this chapter is just under 300 songs, comprising the 182 identified in Nott's *Music for the*

People, and a further 107 included to address the limitations he notes.[1] In addition, the chapter considers communal songs in general and Irish songs in particular, based on an analysis of published community song-books.

The BBC *Yearbook* noted in 1931 'in these days ... songs are only written in the first instance as dance music, and the lyrics added after.'[2] Many new popular 'songs,' particularly in the 1920s, were little more than vocal refrains included in essentially instrumental pieces. This changed, in part, with the development of the microphone in the 1920s, which made possible a new style of singing, the controversial crooning. Singers such as Al Bowlly and 'Whispering' Jack Smith became recognized figures and songs became important in their own right. The impact of American composers, lyricists and performers, discernible in the Edwardian era, became even more pronounced, though there was something of a push-back from the mid-1930s. This in turn impacted on song content. From the hit songs of musical theatre and film to the product of Tin Pan Alley, romance was a major theme. The extent of 'moon and June' lyrics can be overstated, but there was a reaction against the more didactic elements of pre-war popular song. Similarly, the psychological and physical impact of the Great War undermined the appeal of the gung-ho jingoistic song. There were also significant elements of continuity in popular song. Pre-1914 music hall survived and adapted in a way that American vaudeville did not. Other traditions, notably choral singing, continued. Community singing, as a movement may have been short-lived, but communal singing in pubs and clubs as well as at home remained important.

The songs that were written in the 1920s and 1930s were the product of a changing society, one that was yet more urbanised and increasingly suburbanised, somewhat less undemocratic, somewhat less patriarchal; but also, a society that was conservative, adjusting slowly, conceding a little to the new to preserve much of the old. The relationship between the two was not straightforward. Popular songs were not, despites claims to the contrary, a-political entities, existing in a world of entertainment divorced from the harsh world of economics and politics, but neither were they direct, let alone coherent, responses to and commentaries on contemporary conditions.

Popular culture developed in and contributed to contemporary debates but reflected a range of different perspectives.

Love and marriage

The largest single category of popular song in the inter-war years comprised love songs, with their emphasis on companionship, happiness and marriage within a context in which marriage remained central and gender roles recognisably patriarchal. These songs were created and consumed at a time of anxious debate about gender roles and relationships. Old fears about the disruption of the 'natural' (patriarchal) society and the collapse of the institution of marriage re-emerged and collided with newer ideas and expectations, and, more importantly, with the newer realities of the socio-economic and political position of women. The tensions between a desire to return to the status quo ante bellum and a wish to create a better new world played out in different spheres, including the cultural.

Most love songs in the period, abounding with 'moons' and 'Junes' (and even the occasional 'mellow cello'), evoked positive images of happiness and personal satisfaction Love transformed life: 'What a difference a day makes' and joy was in the air as 'Zing went the strings of my heart.' Declarations of love were ubiquitous: 'I'll be loving you – always.' Mutual love was praised: 'Sweetheart we need each other.' Parted lovers wistfully pined for each other in 'When It's Springtime in the Rockies' and 'Roll Along Prairie Moon.' For all the exuberance of an Al Jolson or Eddie Cantor, reminding us that 'Yes Sir, that's my baby,' there was no doubt that marriage was in sight as 'we walk up to the preacher.' Women fell for men 'so charming, strong and tall,' while men praised the charms of their beloved, though at times in language that struggled to combine modernity with old-fashioned romance: 'Susie' was 'classy … a fair lassie' but 'Holy Moses! What a chassis!'[3]

In a minority of songs yearning was replaced by sorrow as love faded There were remembrances of past love ('I'll See You in My Dreams' and 'Deep in a Dream'), solitariness ('If You Hadn't Gone Away' and 'Dancing With My Shadow') and the sadness of promises unfulfilled ('You Forgot to Remember'). The sadness behind the façade of happiness, evoked in songs such as 'Laugh, Clown, Laugh,' brought male emotion into popular song in a way, perhaps more so in America, that provoked fears that traditional, stiff-upper-lip masculinity was being undermined.

Variations on the basic theme were played. The lure of the exotic could be achieved by changing the location to 'Sunny Havana,' 'Hindustan,' or simply 'South of the Border;' or by adding a character such as 'South American Joe' to a rumba tune. Similarly, Henry Hall's 'Play to Me Gypsy' used the still somewhat shocking tango, combining images of caravans and vagabonds, to add a sense of mystery to the lyrics. Some took a more light-hearted view of sexual encounters, such as 'Paddlin' Madeleine Home,' and 'Ma, He's Making Eyes at Me.' Others were melodramatically threatening, especially 'No! No! A Thousand Times No' and 'The Great Big Saw Came Nearer and Nearer,' in which dastardly villains were duly thwarted by heroic males. Some hinted at bawdy. 'Around the Corner and Under the Tree,' which survives as a children's song today, has more in common with the folksong, 'Gentleman Soldier,' in its evocation of casual sex. Worse was Roy Leslie's heroine, in 'She Was Only A Postmaster's Daughter,' who 'knew how to handle a mail.' Her various exploits guaranteed that the song was not played on the BBC.[4] A very few songs laughed at the conventions of female beauty, though in a way that would be unacceptable today.[5] In contrast to pre-war music hall, there were fewer warnings sounded about marriage, though dangers were highlighted in 'Seven Years With The Wrong Woman' and 'You'd Better Think Twice.' The cheerfulness of the opening verse of 'Makin' Whoopee' ('Another bride, another June/ Another sunny honeymoon') soon disappears as the happy couple are trapped, suspicious and non-communicative, though the emphasis was more on the problems of the husband, forced to wash and sew. In contrast, 'A Good Man Is Hard to Find,' for all its exhortation to 'treat your good man right,' stresses a woman's sadness and regret at being caught in an unhappy marriage.

The narrow 'love and marriage' focus was also reflected in a relative decline in the number of songs glorifying 'mother.' Sentimental songs from the immediate pre-war years, such as 'I Want A Girl Just Like the Girl That Married Dear Old Dad' and 'Daddy Has a Sweetheart (Mother Is Her Name),' continued to be sung and the saccharine treatment continued in the immediate post-war period with 'That Old-Fashioned Mother of Mine,' 'Missouri Waltz' and 'Pal of My Cradle Days,' but such songs became increasingly rare thereafter.[6]

Feel-good and comedy songs

There was a more general feel-good approach to life in the songs. In the immediate post-war years, audiences were encouraged to 'Look For the Silver Lining,' but the depression years of the early 1930s saw a flood of optimistic songs. People were exhorted to count your blessings for 'The Best Things In Life Are Free;' to look adversity in the face and 'Pick Yourself Up;' and to be positive and direct your feet to 'The Sunny Side of the Street' because the grim days will soon be over, as there are 'Blue Skies Just Around the Corner.' The significance of these songs went beyond simply morale-boosting. There was a cross-class, conservative appeal to 'The Clouds Will Soon Roll By,' recorded by Ambrose and his orchestra and heard by a wider radio audience. In times of hardship and social division, there was an appeal for social cohesion. Importantly, there was no criticism of the economic status quo and the solution, and the responsibility for finding that solution, rested with the individual.[7] There were exceptions. The lyrics of 'I'm Forever Blowing Bubbles,' were wistful. 'Fortune's always hiding' and bubbles might 'reach the sky' but 'like my dreams they fade and die.' But overall people were encouraged to believe that 'Happy Days Are Here Again.'[8]

The effects of feel-good songs were reinforced by a plethora of comic and novelty songs. Tongue-twister songs, such as 'Who Takes Care of the Caretaker's Daughter?' and 'I Miss My Swiss' would have been familiar to a pre-war audience. Nor would Harry Fay, singing 'I've Never Wronged an Onion,' sold as a comedy song foxtrot, have been out of place on the Edwardian music-hall.[9] Many comedy songs, such as 'Did Tosti Raise His Bowler Hat' and 'Follow the Swallow' were essentially instrumental novelties. 'The Ogo Pogo,' marketed as 'The Funny Fox Trot,' was one of a number of 'songs' that cashed in one a variety of dance crazes, from 'The Charleston' and 'I'm Going to Charleston Back to Charleston,' both from 1935, to 'Boomps A Daisy' in 1939.[10]

Comedy songs ranged over a variety of topics. Animals of varying degrees of cuteness featured frequently, from 'The Red, Red Robin' to 'Ferdinand the Bull.' Various vocalists exhorted their audiences, 'Let's All Sing Like the Birdies Sing,' and the Edwardian music-hall artist, Sam Mayo, found the answer to his earlier question of 'Where Do Flies Go in Winter?'[11] There were toys, ('The Toy Drum Major' and "The General's Fast Asleep'); and fruit, particularly the once exotic banana. 'Yes We Have No Bananas' was determinedly pushed, not only by the popular music composer and publisher, Lawrence Wright, but also by Elders and Fyffes, the firm of banana importers, whose business had been hit by adverse weather in Jamaica and disruptions in London docks.[12] Numerous singers (not just Shirley Temple) sang of the delights of 'The Good Ship Lollipop.' At the same time, George Formby, having failed as a tribute act to his father, and with a little help from his wife, discovered the ukulele and a new comic persona that had him 'Leaning on a Lamp Post,' 'Cleaning Windows' and even in a Chinese laundry with Mr Woo, in a manner that showed seaside humour was flourishing.

Social and political comment

In comparison with pre-war music-hall, there was little social and political comment. Policeman occasionally appeared. 'P.C. 49,' a song written in 1913 but performed during and after the Great War, depicted the unfortunate officer as a victim. On his first day 'the kids threw mud and spoiled my clothes/A dozen navvies looked at me, then punched me on the nose.' The police were still to be gently mocked, especially following the establishment of the Police College at Hendon: 'A p'liceman's the latest profession/For which one must get a degree. They're putting out feelers/For gentlemen peelers.'[13] The policeman as jovial, comic figure was more prominent. Harking back to Stan Stennett's Keystone Cops and Charles Austin's 'Parker P.C.,' Charles Penrose recorded 'The Laughing Policeman' in 1922, around whom he developed a series of sketches, which owed more to the laughing songs associated with 'Jolly' Jack Nash in the nineteenth century. The policeman as rogue all but disappeared. George Lashwood recorded 'Send for a Policeman' before the war but retained it in his later repertoire. The main thrust of the song was clear. Sending for a bobby was 'the best thing you can do.' The most positive image was to be found in Ernest Longstaffe's 1928 song, 'What's the Matter With P.C.Brown?' to which the resounding answer was 'NOTHING!' Two important changes – the advent of the female police officer and the automobile – were reflected in song. The two were brought together in 'Gertie, The Girl with the Gong' by both Harry Roy and Ambrose with their respective orchestras in 1935. The tone was light-hearted – 'If you do more than thirty, then Gertie gets shirty' – and there was little sympathy for the law which limited speeding.[14]

Excepting the inane 'Lloyd George Knew My Father,' politicians did not feature in the popular songs of the inter-war years. Baldwin may have been more successful than Disraeli, but he was hardly charismatic. More dashing were film or recording stars. The cult of celebrity was to be seen in 'They Needed A Songbird in Heaven' and 'There's A New Star in Heaven Tonight,' which followed the deaths of Caruso and Valentino, respectively. In 1930, the feats of Amy ('Wonderful Amy') Johnson were celebrated in a specially written and much recorded song, following her heroic solo flight to Australia. Equally striking by its absence was the patriotic song, perhaps reflecting a reaction against the horrors of war and an (easily exaggerated) anti-war sentiment in the country. With the collapse of appeasement at the end of the 1930s, patriotic songs reappeared, though the tone varied. There was defiance: 'There'll Always Be An England' and the loyalist 'Gentlemen! The King.' There was pride in the armed services, old and new, in 'Wings Over the Navy' and 'Lords of the Air.' There was pathos, 'Wish Me Luck As You Wave Me Goodbye' and humour, 'We're Going to Hang out the Washing on the Siegfried Line.' And there was an opportunity to refashion a modest success by a simple change of lyrics. 'Run, Adolf Run' ensured that the unlikely 'Run, Rabbit Run' would become one of the most popular songs of World War II.

As English sales figures made clear, American music was very popular. Its novelty – cleverly written lyrics and catchy tunes – explains much of its attraction, but the new culture also resonated in the different context of interwar England. It was less constrained, less hierarchical, more open to all and more optimistic. As such it appealed to those men and women whose horizons had been broadened during the war years, who wanted a better future and had no desire to return to the hidebound Edwardian days. The meaning of being a man or woman was being negotiated as much in popular music and popular literature as in "high-brow" literature and academic discourses. While traditionalists fear that masculinity was being undermined and feminised, there was greater opportunity for men to escape the mental constraints of Edwardian 'imperial' masculinity and to celebrate their joys and sorrows. Sentimental love songs, with their emphasis on shared joy in a companionate marriage – however unrealistic in practice – appealed to many women who wished to escape both the drudgery and subordination of married life. The lyrics may well have been banal but that did not mean that they did not serve a purpose. Similarly, the naïve optimism of 'Ain't We Got Fun' or 'Keep Your Sunny Side Up,' which seems so incongruous in hindsight, provided both a positive vision and an escape from the harshness of everyday life. In a different way, comic songs brought a laugh that lightened an otherwise humdrum existence. They also point to the fusion of old and new. What could be more modern than an animated cartoon, especially one starring the jazz-age flapper, Betty Boop? But 'No, No, A Thousand Times No' was an old-fashioned melodrama that would not have been out of place in the 1890s.[15]

Pubs, clubs and community singing

Attendance at variety shows, record sales and the numbers listening to the BBC's output of light music are important indicators of change but there was a substantial world of popular music, encompassing pubs, clubs and home, that cannot be measured. Yet any discussion of popular music between the wars would be incomplete without some consideration of it. Rowntree's second survey of York, *Poverty and Progress* provides an insight into the continuing importance of pub and club-based music, even at a time the numbers listening to the radio or attending the cinemas in the city had increased significantly. The same was true of *Worktown* (Bolton), the subject of *Mass Observation*'s enquiry, which noted, not only that 'Worktown people love music [and] singing' but also, and more perceptively, that 'there is nowhere else where they may sing the songs of their own choosing.'[16] According to *MO* observers, 'sentimental and old-fashioned songs go much the best … [and] the sad sort of Irish songs are popular.' However, 'mostly jazz songs are played and sung [but] the evening nearly always finishes with old-fashioned ones.'[17]

More visible, though short-lived, was the community singing movement of the mid-1920s.[18] It was part of a broader trend, dating back to the late-Victorian years and continuing into the reign of Elizabeth. At a time when 'cultural nationalism' was a matter of serious concern in many parts of Europe, not least within the Austro-Hungarian Empire, Carl Engel, noted in 1886 that 'it seems rather singular that England should not possess any printed collection of songs … while almost every other European country possesses several comprehensive works of this kind.'[19] There followed a lengthy debate about national songs, which for the most part, were seen to be synonymous with folk songs.[20] This was fiercely rejected by the indomitable Cecil Sharp who rejected the notion that a song with a known composer, no matter how popular over time, could be called a folk song. Notwithstanding this public and acrimonious spat, a growing number of people started to compile collections of 'national' songs intended to foster both patriotism and virtues such as self-reliance and constancy. The perceived need for an appropriate collection of songs for schools, and specifically boys, intensified in the immediate aftermath of the problematic second Boer War. In 1902 Cecil Sharp published his *British Songs for Home and School* and the following year saw the appearance of S Nicholson's *British Songs for British Boys* and W H Hadow's *Songs of the British Islands*.[21] The latter had a significant impact on the most influential publication, namely C V Stanford's *New National Song Book*, which in subsequent years was distributed to all but the remotest of schools. The intention of its advocates can be established with relative ease. More problematic is the extent to which these songs (and their sentiments) were taken up in schools and the wider population. In the light of later reminiscences, it is not implausible to argue that there was, at least, a core of songs that were widely known and sung before and after the Great War.

The New National Song Book subtitled 'A Complete Collection of the Folk-Songs, Carols and Rounds suggested by the Board of Education,' contained only 30 carols and rounds out of a total of 202 pieces. 168 folk-songs were presented by nation – 50 English, 50 Irish, 35 Welsh and 33 Scotch – and four songs, 'The Land of My Fathers,' 'Auld Lang Syne,' 'Rule, Britannia' and 'God Save the King,' standing alone. Some songs were less well known – for example, 'Lady Nairn's 'The Auld Hoose' or 'Weep Not I Pray' – but there is an identifiable core of songs, most reprinted in other collections, that were more widely known. These include, among the English songs, 'Come Lasses and Lads,' 'Heart of Oak.' 'The Bailiff's Daughter of Islington' and 'The Roast Beef of Old England' as well as 'The British Grenadiers;' among the Scotch songs, 'The Bluebells of Scotland,' 'The Campbells Are Coming,' Charlie Is My Darling' and 'Auld Lang Syne:' among the Irish songs, 'The Minstrel Boy,' 'The Harp That Once Thro' Tara's Hall' and 'The Meeting of the Waters;' and among the Welsh songs, 'All Through the Night,' Men of Harlech' and 'David of the White Rock' as well as 'Land of My Fathers.'[22] Stanford's song collection, and others like it, was in part a narrow reaction against commercial popular music, but it was also a more general reaction to ever-increasing urbanization, seen particularly in the English 'rural idyll' song. It was also a response to the perceived challenge to Empire through the assertion of plucky patriotism. Above all, in these collections there was an attempt to conjure up a sense of shared community which encompassed the four nations of the United Kingdom.

The community singing movement of the mid-1920s was a continuation of this trend and for its advocates there was a clear determination to create a sense of a unified, patriotic community.[23] For some, the impact of the Great War, the severe loss of life in the immediate post-war years, the severe economic slump of the early 1920s and the social tensions that culminated in the General Strike made yet more imperative the need for communal activity. At the height of the community singing movement, there was a corpus of songs that were sufficiently well known to be sung with gusto at a variety of events across the country, of which the cup final was the best known. Community singing as a movement was short-lived but communal singing continued, not just through the 1920s and 1930s and the war years but well into the 1950s, and in private as well as in public. The two most important song collections, the *News Chronicle Song Book* and the *Daily Express Community Song Book* were substantial, hard-back collections of over 200 songs, though there were cheaper, word-only versions. In addition, various publishers produced smaller but cheaper collections. One of the earliest was Hawkes & Son, *More Than Twice 55 Community Songs* (there were 115 songs in total, though eight were words only) for 6d., while Francis, Day and Hunter brought out six albums, four with thirty-two songs, two with thirty, also for 6d., in the early 1930s.

Russell talks of 'a specific "community song" genre' which denied that 'popular modernity had arrived in the musical sphere' by ignoring 'British commercial popular song of both the late nineteenth and early twentieth century and their frequently American or American-influenced counterparts of the present day.'[24] The "community song" genre, he argues, comprised national songs, such as 'John Peel' and 'All Through the Night,' a smaller number of music-hall songs specifically related to the Great War, notably 'Tipperary,' and then a variety of carols and hymns, of which 'Abide With Me' was the most popular. While these broad contours are largely correct, some modification is required. Francis, Day & Hunter included very few carols and rounds (c.5 per cent) whereas for the *News Chronicle* and Hawkes & Son the figure was about 25 per cent. There were more songs from England than from the rest of the United Kingdom, especially in the *News Chronicle* selection. American songs were a small part of the *Daily Express* collection but were twice as common in others. Music-hall songs associated with the Great War were a distinctive feature of the *Daily Express* collection, which was unique in identifying war songs. Music-hall songs featured not at all in the *Daily Express* and *News Chronicle* collections but favourites such as 'Daisy Bell,' 'Ask a P'liceman,' 'The Blind Boy' and 'Where Did You Get That Hat,' accounted for 25 per cent of the songs in the Francis, Day & Hunter song books, and the very cheap, *Every-body's Sing-Song Book* published by Herman Darewski was overwhelmingly made up of music-hall songs including 'Any Old Iron' and ''Arf a Pint of Ale.' By the mid-1930s some publishers, aware of consumer demand, were including 'modern' songs in their community song collections. Francis,

Day & Hunters' *Community Song Book*, volume 7, published in 1935, contained Wendell Hall's 1920 hit, 'It Ain't Gonna Rain No Mo'' and the Gracie Field hit, 'Sing As We Go,' from the 1934 film of the same name. Volume 8 contained three recent novelty songs: 'I Lift Up My Finger (And I Say Tweet, Tweet),' 'And the Great Big Saw Came Nearer and Nearer (to Poor Little Vera),' and 'Olga Pulloffski, the Beautiful Spy.'

Nonetheless, an analysis of the community song collections published from the mid-1920s to the late-1930s, reveals a core of some forty songs that can be categorised as follows: national songs ('Rule Britannia' and 'The British Grenadier'); English songs ('John Peel' and 'Come Lasses and Lads'); nautical songs ('The Bay of Biscay' and 'Shenandoah'); Scottish songs ('The Blue Bells of Scotland' and 'Loch Lomond'); Welsh songs ('Men of Harlech' and 'All Through the Night'); Irish songs ('The Minstrel Boy' and 'Cockles and Mussels'); but also American songs ('Marching Thro' Georgia' and 'Old Folks at Home). There is a striking degree of continuity between the pre- and post-war core songs, with the partial exception of Irish songs and the complete (and obvious) exception of American songs which did not feature at all in Stanford.[25] By featuring songs from all parts of the United Kingdom, the community song books of the inter-war years continued the notion of a shared community that embraced country and class. However, the greater emphasis on English songs strengthened the 'English' values that had been praised in Stanford: a pugnacious, if not warlike, island people but in an idyllic rural setting.

Irish songs

A further feature of these years, perhaps indicative of the need for publishers of sheet music to find new markets, were the attempts to provide more focussed collections, particularly of Irish songs. Francis, Day & Hunter had been producing specifically Irish song books since before the Great War and continued to do so thereafter. Their 1935 *Community Book of Irish Songs* contained 30 songs, of which 24 (80 per cent) had appeared in a similar publication of 1904.[26] The enduring songs ranged from the romantic ('The Gentle Maiden' and 'The Rose of Tralee'), through the romanticised Ireland ('Dear Little Shamrock' and 'Oh! Arranmore') to émigre laments ('Come Back to Erin' and

'The Irish Emigrant'). Predictably, there were comic songs, such as 'Paddy McGinty's Goat' and 'At Finnegan's Ball,' and there were a small number of patriotic songs, notably 'Rory O'More' and 'The Wearin' of the Green.'

The publication of Irish song collections is a reminder of the importance of the Irish diaspora, particularly in the cities and large towns; but Irish songs appealed to a wider audience. The recordings and radio appearances of John McCormack, of 'the strolling vagabond,' Cavan O'Connor, and even of Peter Dawson, with his 'Kerry Dance' and 'Off to Philadelphia in the Morning,' brought a range of songs, not least those of Thomas Moore, to a wider audience. In so doing, they created a particular image of Ireland. The Irishman as a jovial, if somewhat comic figures comes across in 'Off to Philadelphia,' 'At Finnegan's Ball' and 'Paddy McGinty's Goat.' The Irish 'colleen' as an innocent beauty appears in 'The Garden Where the Praties Grow' and 'The Gentle Maiden,' while an idyllic Ireland is captured in ''Dear Little Shamrock,' 'Killarney' and 'Oh! Arranmore.' It is a non-threatening image of Ireland and the Irish, one more acceptable to the non-Irish majority, especially in England but it may also be a retreat into a romanticised, if at times heroic though unsuccessful past, into which some second-generation Irish were prepared to buy.[27] Francis, Day & Hunter did include 'The Wearing of the Green,' with its references to 'the most distressful country that ever yet was seen' and 'England's cruel red' but the song ends with Ireland's sons leaving 'the dear ould isle' for a better land across the sea. There is none of the defiance and threat of 'The West's Awake,' 'A Nation Once Again' or 'God Save Ireland.' While it is true that 'the minstrel boy to the war is gone,' he fell, leaving only 'songs … for the pure and free [that] shall never sound in slavery.'[28]

Some concluding observations

Within a generation, from the eve of the first world war to the eve of the second world war, popular song became less parochial and more commercialised. Most striking, was the impact of Tin Pan Alley. Its music could be heard on stage, on radio and record, and at the cinema. It found a ready market, notwithstanding the attempts to resist the American invasion. Fears of 'Americanization' proved to be exaggerated. The older music hall tradition, showed itself to be resilient and adaptable, notably in the 1930s. Once again, there was a fusion of old and new, amply demonstrated by Gracie Fields and George Formby, whose careers embraced the stage, the recording studio and the cinema and whose repertoire ranged from the recognisably modern, sentimental love song, to the old-fashioned comic song.

Endnotes

1   J Nott, *Music for the People: Popular Music and Dance in Interwar Britain*, Oxford University Press, 2002, Appendix, pp.236-44
2   *BBC Yearbook* 1931, p.207 cited in A Briggs, *The History of Broadcasting in the United Kingdom*, volume 2, Oxford University Press, 1995, p.79
3   'If you knew Susie, like I know Susie' was a 1925 song. She also wears 'long tresses and nice tight dresses.'
4   Other verses featured 'a magistrate's daughter [who] knew what to do on the bench'
5   O Katharina. O Katharina/To keep my love you must be leaner
    There's so much of you/Two could love you
    Learn to swim/Join a gym/Eat Farina, O Katharina
6   'Me and the Old Folks at Home' (1935) is one of the few exceptions. 'His Majesty the Baby' (1935) was a novelty song poking gentle fun at the centrality of the new addition to the family.
7   D B Scott, 'Incongruity and Predictability in British Dance Band Music, *Musical Quarterly*, 78(2), 1994, pp.290-315 at p.296
8   The song took on particular significance in America when F D Roosevelt adopted it as his campaign tune.
9   Fay can be heard at https://www.youtube.com/watch?v=DFW3kJjVxY0
10 Other titles include 'Tiger Rag,' 'Do Wacha Doo' and 'La Cucaracha' as well as better-known standards, such as 'Fascinating Rhythm' and 'Sweet Georgia Brown.'
11 They went home in search of Christmas pudding!
12 Following the publication of 'I've Never Seen a Straight Banana,' Wright also offered a prize of £1000 if such a specimen could be produced.
13 C Pulling, *They Were Singing,* George & Harrap, London, 1952, p. 103.
14 For a fuller discussion of motoring and the law see K Laybourn and D Taylor, *Policing in England and Wales*, 1918-39, Basingstoke, Palgrave, 2011, chapter 7.
15 'No, No a Thousand Times No' was best known as a Betty Boop cartoon. See https://www.youtube.com/watch?v=hS4_qDTd-WY

16 *Mass Observation: The Pub and the People. A Worktown Study*, 1943, reprinted London, Faber & Faber, 2009, p.259
17 *The Pub and the People*, p.261, Richard Hoggart, writing of the 1950s, makes a similar point about the intermingling of old and new songs. R Hoggart, *The Uses of Literacy: Aspects of Working-Class Life*, 1st published 1957, reprinted Penguin, London, 2009, pp.135-144.
18 D Russell, 'Abiding Memories: The Community Singing Movement and English Social Life in the 1920s,' *Popular Music*, 27(1), 2008, pp.117-33.
19 C Engel, *An Introduction to the Study of National Music*, London, Longman, 1866, p.32 cited in S Roud, *Folk Song in England*, London, Faber & Faber, 2017, p.116.
20 G Cox, 'Towards the National Song Book: The History of an Idea,' *British Journal of Musical Education*, 9, 1992, pp.239-53
21 Hadow's collection was unusual in that it was divided into section titled, elementary, intermediate, and advanced as well as duets and choruses and melodies (without words). When rearranged in line with Stanford's collection the degree of overlap is striking.
22 Although there is a strong element of subjectivity in identifying 'core' songs, the following list is predicated on the assumption, backed up by scattered anecdotal evidence, that a large number of people knew at least the chorus and probably the opening verse of the following. As well as the four self-standing songs noted above, the full list of core songs is as follows. English: 'The Keel Row,' 'John Peel,' 'The Bailiff's Daughter of Islington,' The British Grenadiers,' 'The Roast beef of Old England,' 'A-hunting We Will Go,' 'Come Lasses and Lads,' 'Begone Dull Care,' 'Drink to Me Only,' 'Early One Morning,' 'The Mermaid, 'The Bay of Biscay,' 'Tom Bowling,' 'The Golden Vanity,' 'The Girl I Left Behind Me,' 'Heart of Oak,' 'Golden Slumbers' and 'The Lass of Richmond Hill.' Scotch: 'The Bluebells of Scotland,' 'Afton Waters,' 'Annie Laurie,' 'Charlie Is My Darling,' 'Scots Wha Hae,' 'The Campbells Are Coming,' 'Bonnie Dundee,' 'Robin Adair,' 'The Hundred Pipers,' 'Ye Banks and Braes of Bonnie Doon' and 'Caller Herrin'.' Irish: 'The Minstrel Boy,' 'The Harp that Once Thro' Tara's Hall,' 'The Meeting of the Waters' and 'Derby Kelly.' Welsh: 'All Through the Night,' 'The Ash Grove,' 'Men of Harlech,' 'David of the White Rock' and 'The Blackbird.'
23 Russell, 'Abiding Memories,' p.126
24 'Russell, 'Abiding Memories,' p128 & p.129
25 Of six core English songs in the 1920s/30s only 'Lincolnshire Poacher' did not feature before the war. Among eight Scottish core songs only 'Loch Lomond' and 'The Last Rose of Summer' did not feature in the pre-war list, while all five core Welsh songs were to be found among the pre-1914 core songs
26 Most of the songs considered popular enough for publication in 1904 that did not survive were comedy numbers that had dated badly, such as the so-called Irish coon song, 'Bedelia.' Of those that were not to be found in the pre-war collection, two at least are surprising – 'The Last Rose of Summer' and 'The Minstrel Boy,' both Thomas Moore songs.
27 More detailed research is required on this. My observation relies heavily on anecdotal evidence from older family members for whom a London-Irish

identity involved emphasising the sentimental and the comic. But see M Leonard, 'Performing Identities: music and dance in the Irish communities of Coventry and Liverpool,' *Social & Cultural Geography*, 6(4), 2006, pp.515-29

28 T M Love, 'Gender and the Nationalistic Ballad: Thomas Davis, Thomas Moore, and Their Song,' *New Hibernia Review*, 21(1), 2017, pp.69-85, S B Kress, 'The Music of the Sentimental Nationalist Heart: Thomas Moore and Seamus Heaney,' *New Hibernia Review*, 15(1), 2011, pp.123-37 and R Parfitt, "Oh what matter when for Erin dear we fall,' *Irish Studies Review*, 23, 2015, pp.480-94.

'Music while you work' ... and play: Popular music c.1940-1955

> Mother dear, I'm writing you from somewhere in France,
> Hoping this finds you well.
> Sergeant says I'm doing fine, a soldier and a half,
> Here's a song that we all sing, it'll make you laugh.
>
> Bud Flanagan & Chesney Allen, 'We're Going to Hang Out the Washing on the Siegfried Line'

THE SECOND WORLD war is commonly seen as a major turning point in the nation's history, accelerating socio-economic change and creating a sense of determination not to return to the failed decades of the pre-war years of long-term unemployment, slum-housing and gross health inequalities. The extent of change can easily be overstated. In social terms, for example, the mobilisation of women on the home front saw many enjoying new freedoms 'out of the cage,' and unwilling to relinquish them after the war but, at the same time, there were many people who saw the war as disruptive and looked to the restoration of the nuclear family, complete with breadwinning husband and homemaking wife.[1]

The war created various problems for the purveyors of popular music. Mobilisation disrupted bands as members joined the armed forces, some venues were requisitioned, others damaged during the blitz. The blackout and reduced evening-time transportation impacted on the timing of leisure provision; the relocation of troops and the later arrival of members of the armed forces from parts of Europe, the Empire and America, disrupted its geography. The latter greatly increased the influence of American popular music and dance, not least the jitterbug, and forced the BBC to modify its popular music policy. There were other positives. The growth of the war economy brought significant improvements in real wages, especially for key demographics, such as young, unmarried women, who comprised a large part of the dance hall audience. It was soon recognised that music had an important role to play in maintaining and enhancing morale and productivity as well as celebrating 'national' values. There were three distinct audiences to be entertained: members of the armed forces, including ancillary organisations, both at home and at the front; men and women at work, especially in those factories contributing directly to the war effort; and, housewives and younger household members, at home. Although found in very different geographical locations, there were commonalities in terms of the preferred music and song, which grew out of the changing tastes of the 1930s.[2] There was much that was nostalgic, for example in the songs of Vera Lynn and the continuing popularity of English bandleaders and their singers. For a decade after the war cultural continuity was the order of the day. Variety theatres and dance halls enjoyed a boom, seemingly returning to their heyday in the 1930s, and much of the popular music on radio and record, and later television, would have been more familiar to audiences of the 1930s than of the 1960s.

The BBC and forces broadcasting

The outbreak of war led to a significant structural change – the creation of a Home Service and a Forces Programme – and the consequent abandonment of the principle of mixed programming that the BBC had followed from its inception. Yet its immediate response had been modest and unimaginative, not least because of a poor understanding of its audiences and their tastes. The popularity of Radio Luxembourg, especially on Sundays, was well-known and yet it still came as something of a surprise at the BBC that troops were not enamoured of drama and religious broadcasting and much preferred to listen to Gracie Fields or Vera Lynn. Responding to listeners' complaints, the Forces Programme began transmission in February 1940, initially from 11 a.m., later from 6.30 a.m., to 11 p.m. throughout the war, albeit in different format following the rapid build-up of American soldiers in the last months of the war. Renamed the General Forces Programme in February 1944, its audience extended beyond the troops to include many on the home front. Belatedly, it was recognised, in the words of the chairman of the governors, Sir Allan Powell, that 'the BBC is out to give the men [sic] the kind of entertainment that they want—not what others think is good for them to hear.'[3] The style became more relaxed, though some thought it smacked of an officer addressing his men informally. There was more comedy and popular music, including greater use of records, resulting in more American popular music. Gradually the Forces Programme took on many of the characteristics of the pre-war commercial stations, including the request programme format. *Forces Favourites* and particularly *Sincerely Yours, Vera Lynn* proved to be hugely popular. Lynn, already a successful stage performer and recording star, was both artistic and artless. As the iconic 'forces sweetheart,' her repertoire combined a generalised sentimentality ('Safe in My Heart,' 'I'll Walk Beside You' and 'Love's Old Sweet Song') with songs of the moment ('When They Sound the Last All Clear,' 'That Lovely Weekend' and 'We'll Meet Again') and of place ('The London I Love', 'A Nightingale Sang in Berkley Square') and songs of optimism ('It's A Lovely Day Tomorrow'). Her songs were carefully chosen to convey a message of reassurance to counter the siren-voiced 'Lili Marlene' and her allegations of soldierly infidelity, made on German broadcasts into Britain.[4] While many of her songs harked back to an idealised pre-war past, she also evoked a sense of community and held out hope for a better future. Undoubtedly feminine, but not glamorously feminine, she brought sincerity and sentiment, especially filling the emotional space of separation.[5] Some 20 per cent of the British population tuned in to her programme and yet there were only twelve episodes of *Sincerely Yours*. There were fears that her songs were undermining troop morale at a time when the Nazis were in the ascendancy, especially in North Africa.[6] Basil Nicholls, Controller (Programmes) was in no doubt. The BBC should excise 'crooning, drivelling words, and slush,' as well as innuendo, in favour of 'marches and cheerful music of every kind.'[7] Lynn was not the only victim. Male crooners were deemed to lack the necessary 'virility' and, continuing a longer-standing concern with 'Americanization,' dance music was closely scrutinised. In summer 1942, the BBC decided to 'encourage a more virile and robust output of dance music.'[8] Victor Silvester was held up as a paragon of virtue. Geraldo was deemed too American and was replaced by the more British Jack Payne. Harry Roy's 1944 tour of the Middle East demonstrated that dance music was very much in demand by the troops. The BBC responded by introducing *Variety Cavalcade*, alongside the longer-running *Variety Bandbox*, featuring Ted Heath and Joe Loss and singers, including Helen Clare, an ENSA performer, best known for songs such as the mawkish but defiant 'Coming In On A Wing and A Prayer' and the oft-sung 'I'll Walk Beside You.'

Music While You Work

Maintaining civilian morale and improving productivity were central to the war effort and politicians, notably Ernest Bevin, and broadcasters alike looked to devise suitable programmes. *Workers' Playtime*, first broadcast in 1941 'from a factory canteen, somewhere in Britain,' was a one-hour variety programme, offering light relief at work. Better known for its comedians, it also featured singers such as Anne Shelton, Betty Driver, Eve Boswell and Julie Andrews. More innovative was *Music While You Work*, which ran from summer 1940, as part of a wider campaign to improve productivity. Initially two thirty-minute programmes were broadcast daily, at 10.30 a.m. and 3 p.m. with a third added at 10.30 p.m. for night-shift workers. The guide-lines were clear. The emphasis was to be on rhythm and repetition, even monotony, rather than subtlety or artistic merit. A jig or a quick-step was deemed the most suitable in terms of rhythm. Volume was a key consideration and singing, to be included sparingly should be well-known and of a sing-along nature without breaking up the overall tempo of the show.[9] Denis Wright, the show's co-producer was unambiguous. There was no place for slow foxtrots, tangos, or waltzes. There would be no 'dreamy numbers of any sort' and 'no vocals of the sob-stuff order.' Instead there was to be 'PLENTY OF SNAP and PUNCH; RHYTHM of a straightforward kind; CLEAN CLEAR-CUT MELODY [and] BRIGHTNESS of all sorts.'[10] But some songs could be too up-beat. The Ken Mackintosh band, from Halifax, made only one appearance. Their rendition of 'Deep in The Heart of Texas' was deemed unacceptable when an enthusiastic drummer's 'rim shots' sounded like bullets being fired when played through loud-speakers. In all some 500 bands appeared, the majority performing more than once. There was considerable variety – dance bands, brass bands, military bands, light orchestras, and instrumental ensembles. Big name band leaders, such as Victor Silvester and Joe Loss appeared several times, but the most featured ensemble was Trois and His Banjoliers, whose career had started in the mid-1920s and continued until his death in 1957.[11]

Music While You Work was deemed to be most appropriate for factories characterised by low-skill and repetitive manual labour, especially munitions factories. It was essentially a top-down imposition of music, at best a paternalistic intervention, with no consultation with workers or their representatives. Nonetheless, the programme was popular, with workers, which spoke more of the tedium of much factory work than anything else. It remained a mainstay of BBC radio throughout the war and remained on air until September 1967.

Dancing (and singing) the war away

After an initial downturn in September 1939, within weeks dance halls enjoyed an unprecedented boom in popularity, notwithstanding the disruptions brought about by the blitz, the black-out and the restrictions on public transport.[12] Across the country, local authorities granted more licences for dancing and new venues were found to meet the growing demand. Seaside towns, Blackpool, in particular, were transformed into all-year resorts.

The wartime boost to purchasing power, especially for young, unmarried women, enabled thousands of them to indulge in one of the most popular of working-class leisure activities and at a time when the dance hall was one of the few opportunities for pleasure.[13] There was also a psychological dimension to the attraction of dancing. The allure of peacetime dancing was enhanced during the war. There was something defiant about going out dancing when there was a real risk of injury or death during air-raids. There was a morale-boosting sense of collective solidarity in the face of hardship and danger. And with an awareness of the risk of an early death, there was a 'live for the moment' mentality, which further enhanced its popularity. The dance boom was well under way but received a further boost from the arrival of American troops and their music from 1942 onwards. The American Forces Network and later the Allied Expeditionary Forces Programme, though intended solely for a military audience, brought new sounds to the ears of the civilian population. The AEFP programme reflected the makeup of the allied forces. Around 50 per cent was American but 40 per cent British. The American Band of Supreme Allied Command, better known as the Glen Miller band, led the way. Although not considered by many to be a great bandleader, he appeared frequently on a range of BBC programmes and was responsible for numerous popular instrumental and vocal numbers: 'In the Mood,' Chattanooga Choo Choo,' American Patrol,' 'Pennsylvania Six Five Thousand' and 'String of Pearls' among others. However, the music and dances of the 1930s remained popular. As well as the old favourites, the waltz, the foxtrot and the quickstep, there was also a boom in Old Time dances, such as Quadrilles and the Lancers.

The disruptions caused by blackout requirements and increased shift work led to more afternoon dances at the local palais, which may have encouraged greater social mixing. More women were to be found as mobilization increased and younger girls, some barely in their teens, appeared in the dance hall. The movement of men and women because of the war effort impacted on social diversity. Army camps expanded, bringing together men from different parts of the country. Young women in the land army or ATS, found themselves far from home and there a growing number of people from across the world. Most attention has focussed on African American GIs, but they were but the most high-profile element in a highly varied mix of nationalities. Dancing was seen to be important, for them, and dances, either with local, semi-professional musicians or gramophone records, were organised in various venues. The outcome was not some happy melting pot. There were real tensions. There was suspicion of and hostility towards outsiders 'stealing our women,' there were tensions between the different armed forces, and there were internal tensions, most notably along racial lines in the American army, but also along class lines particularly in the RAF. Nonetheless, there was a greater awareness of differences in customs and culture and an acceleration of the rate of cultural diffusion. The speed with which people came to know of the Andrews Sisters or Glen Miller owed much to the peculiar circumstances of the war.

Looking more specifically at dances, two trends stand out: simplification and diversification. The former was largely due to an influx of essentially social, rather than serious, dancers, for whom mastery of steps was a secondary consideration. The drop in standards, as seen by dancing teachers, was exacerbated by the sheer numbers on the dance floor and the subsequent development of 'crush' dancing, which limited the scope for properly executed steps. In addition, novelty nights and novelty dance competitions became more common. 'The Hokey Cokey,' known in pre-war years, became a hit as a music-hall song and dance routine from 1942 onwards. The actions were easy to learn, and any number could join in, likewise, 'Knees Up Mother Brown.' Similarly, the conga, popularised by American troops, required little in the way of dancing skill. Its simple format – 1, 2, 3 kick – was easy to master and, again, the communal nature of the dance allowed for mass participation. Not for nothing was the catch phrase of the day: 'I came, I saw, I conga'd.' Other popular dances encouraged mass participation while, at the same time, offering the possibility of greater artistry. The Big Apple was essentially a circle dance for couples, performing, to the cry of a caller, steps such as 'Spank the Baby,' 'Pose and a Peck' and 'Truckin'.' The most spectacular but controversial dance was 'The Jitterbug,' which was derived from the 1930s 'Lindy Hop.' It was quickly condemned as yet another primitive dance, in which the exuberance of the participants demonstrated a lack of control that was, at best immodest, at worst, immoral. To make matters worse, for older critics at least, it had its own dress code and language. This, of course, added to its attraction to the young. Some dance halls banned the jitterbug, some dance teachers sought to tame it but, as with the Charleston a generation before, the response from below was crucial. The jitterbug was not universally popular. Indeed, on the crowded war-time dance floors there was limited space for more flamboyant steps and the real risk of retaliation at anti-social dancing. Nonetheless, the jitterbug survived but was transformed into the jive, which proved to be one of the lasting legacies of these years.

Song, like dance, was a morale booster. Shortly after the outbreak of hostilities, Radio Luxembourg (September 1939) went off air, shortly followed by Radio Normandie (January 1940). This strengthened the position of the BBC but added to its responsibility to entertain and reassure. Part of the response, an emphasis on continuity, was well exemplified by the continued broadcasting of *The Kentucky Minstrels*, a show that dated from the early 1930s.[14] It fitted well with BBC notions of respectability and family-oriented entertainment. Its sentimentalised and idyllic 'other' world, where songs were 'crooned by the plantation darkies,' was both nostalgic, harking back to a day when things were (allegedly) simpler, certainly less urban, and happier, and reassuring, offering 'proper' songs that contrasted with the American monstrosities of the present. The inclusion of hymns (notably 'Abide With Me') and quasi-religious and uplifting songs (for example Sullivan's 'Lost Chord') strengthened these appeals. It was a format which fitted well in a new world in which a different barbaric enemy threatened. The recording stars of the 1930s also appeared in several BBC variety programmes, and the concerts organised under the auspices of ENSA. The songs they sang during the war were predictably varied, combining themes of love and marriage that had become so dominant in the 1920s and 1930s with more specific recognition of the present day and its problems.[15] Heroism, the determination to fight on, was captured in 'Coming in on a Wing and a Prayer' and the American, 'Praise the Lord and Pass the Ammunition,' written in response to the attack on Pearl Harbour. Others made fun of the conflict. The transition from civilian to army life was mocked in Irving Berlin's 'This Is the Army Mr Jones' and 'Kiss Me Goodnight Sergeant Major,' with its plea: 'Sergeant Major be a mother to me.' Limited army fare provides the inspiration for 'The Quartermaster's Stores,' while George Formby invited people to 'Imagine Me on the Maginot Line,' and assured them that 'I Did What I Could With My Gas

Mask.' The latter enabled him to exploit his successful formula of silliness and suggestiveness.

> The lady living next door, Mrs. Hicks
> She heard the sirens blow one morn at ten to six.
> She dashed outside in nothing but her nicks,
> But she knew what to do with her gasmask.

Others, 'Roll Out the Barrel' or 'Bless 'Em All' were cheerful sing-alongs that owed much to music hall tradition.* In different vein were the rousing numbers of the Andrews Sisters, who appeared on the Forces Programme and the BBC Home Service, notably with 'Boogie-Woogie Bugle Boy' and 'Don't Sit Under the Apple Tree.' Despite worries about the impact on army morale, sentimental songs were popular, from the more upbeat, 'You Are My Sunshine' to the more wistful, 'I'll Be Seeing You' and 'White Cliffs of Dover.' The poignancy of separation was captured by Vera Lynn. 'Even though we're parted,' she sang in 'Lili Marlene,' 'Your lips are close to mine… Your sweet face seems to haunt my dreams.' And, as ever, there were nonsense songs. 'Mairzy doats and dozy doats' crossed the Atlantic and lightened the mood and survived as a party puzzle before transmuting into a children's song.

Images of patriotic factory workers, singing along to *Music While You Work*, plucky Londoners singing in the underground as they escaped German bombs, and of Vera Lynn singing to the troops in Burma have become part of a foundation myth of contemporary Britain, which obscures more than it reveals of wartime conditions. However, when due allowance is made for the less glorious side of wartime – the less than wholehearted commitment to factory production, even in industries contributing directly to the war effort and the black market, to take but two obvious examples – morale on both the war and domestic fronts held up well, even during the difficult months between Dunkirk and El Alamein. The reasons were many but singing and dancing were among them. The BBC prided itself on 'a good war,' but, according to *Mass Observation*, music halls, pubs and clubs had a better one.

---

*   'Bless 'Em All' was also widely parodied as 'F*** 'Em All.'

The BBC and popular music after the war

The BBC was never a monolithic institution but there were many influential figures, not least the new director-general, Sir William Haley, who believed in the Reithian creed of improvement, within a cultural pyramid that had the (newly formed) Light Programme as its broad base and the Third Programme as its narrow peak, and who saw 'Americanization' as a threat to be resisted.[16] The BBC had built up a mass audience during the war but without knowing much about it beyond a generalised image of a largely uneducated, 'low brow' mass, comprising ex-soldiers, returning to work, and their wives, returning to home.[17] Many radio producers remained uninterested in popularity, even viewing it as a sign of failure, but there was no returning to pre-war practices, rather a stumbling, often reactive, response towards a new future. There was a gradual acceptance that radio was often simply background to other activities and many people simply wanted to be entertained.[18] Of necessity, and with varying degrees of enthusiasm, certain features of mass culture had to be adopted. In its annual report for 1951/2 it was conceded that 'the Light programme is designed for those who enjoy the most popular kind of entertainment,' still clung to the notion that it could 'interest its listeners in more serious matters.'[19] In the first decade after the war, the BBC saw itself primarily as a family-centred, domestic leisure activity, which brought the best of music hall or the working man's club but without the vulgarity and innuendo. The long-running *Kentucky Minstrels* (again) fitted the bill to perfection.[20]

In a period when much attention was focussed on seeking to restore the patriarchal nuclear family after the disruptions caused by the upheavals of war, the BBC played its part particularly in programmes such as *Housewives' Choice*. It ran from March 1946, had a large audience (over eight million at its peak in the 1960s) and generated over 3000 requests a week, giving it a quasi-democratic flavour. The actual selection was made by the overwhelmingly male compères, who fronted the programme. The first tune played, and a recurring favourite, was 'Greensleeves,' but the selections offer a partial reflection of changing tastes. The Andrews Sisters were oft-requested in the late 1940s but by the mid-1950s local favourites, such as

Ruby Murray or Jimmy Young, vied with American stars, such as Perry Como.[21] Similarly, *Family Favourites* was unremittingly family-centred, to such a degree that, initially at least, there no rude or offensive songs (and certainly not 'noisy jazz') and no mention of fiancées, let alone of girlfriends. Certain songs were played on a regular basis. Pat Boone's 'I'll Be Home' and Ella Fitzgerald's 'Every Time We Say Goodbye' had an obvious appeal; as did Anne Shelton's somewhat more suggestive, 'Lay Down Your Arms (And Surrender to Mine).'

The records selected for play on air cannot be seen as an accurate measure of popular taste, but they do indicate some broad trends. There was an element of wartime nostalgia (Vera Lynn, Flanagan and Allen and the Andrews Sisters), a hint of pub-based entertainment (Russ Conway) but also of the new (Elvis Presley). There was also a strong suggestion of the 'entertain and educate' mentality. Kathleen Ferrier, singing 'What Is Life to Me Without Thee?' from Gluck's *Orfeo ed Euridice*, gave yearning a classical form. Although recorded in 1929, the Manchester Children's choir's version of Purcell's 'Nymphs and Shepherds' remained a firm favourite. Other, more accessible 'high-brow' pieces included the finale of Bruck's violin concerto, the intermezzo from Mascagni's *Cavalleria Rusticana* and the duet, 'Au fond du temple saint,' from Bizet's *Pearl Fishers*.

Looking across the range of programmes on air, music for ballroom dancing and from big bands predominated. Although current hit songs featured on air, they were often packaged up in big band arrangements played by various regional orchestras.[22] Henry Hall, an established favourite, had a regular spot until the late 1950s. *Tip Top Tunes* featured Geraldo, while Victor Silvester provided strict tempo tunes in *Memories for You*. The revival of interest in old-time dancing found a response in *Those Were the Days* and *Time For Old Time*. One of the most popular shows, which ran for many years on radio before transferring to television, was *The Billy Cotton Band Show*. The programme encapsulated the BBC's determination to repackage (some) American music and make it acceptable for a British audience, much as earlier American dances had been civilized. Cotton was a successful band leader in the inter-war years, but he was strongly influenced by music hall. His repertoire ranged from big band favourites (covering Paul Whiteman's 'It Happened in Monterey' and 'Play to Me Gypsy'), through sentimental numbers ('My Heart Belongs to Daddy' and 'Did You Ever See a Dream Walking') to music-hall nonsense ('With Her Head Tucked Underneath Her Arm') and American comic songs ('Smile, Darn Ya, Smile' and 'Eleven More Months and Ten More Days'). Cotton's cheery cockney persona (complete with trademark opening call: 'Wakey, Wakey') was of a piece with earlier music hall. His band played a range of American tunes but in a style that would have been recognised by Jack Payne, and this was enhanced by the singing of Alan Breeze, Kathie Kay, and Alma Cogan. In many respects the programme highlighted the strengths and weaknesses of the BBC's approach. Its long-standing opposition to 'crooners' and the unwillingness to name band singers made it difficult to promote band music at a time when personalities were coming more to the fore. The determination to resist creeping 'Americanization' reinforced this problem. There was a growing disconnect between this type of show and the musical tastes of younger generations born in the 1940s. And yet, as the viewing figures bear witness, there remained a considerable audience for this type of music throughout the 1950s and even into the early 1960s.

Radio Luxembourg

The emergence of commercial radio stations located on the continent and broadcasting English-language programmes was a problem for the BBC in the 1930s. Their content and style were effectively a critique of BBC programming. Radio Normandie, which broadcast to the whole of the south coast, adopted American-style programmes (hit records and soap operas) and American-style presentation; as did Radio Luxembourg adopted a similar approach but had a greater geographical reach. The competition was greatest on Sundays. Advertising Institute survey figures suggest that Luxembourg attracted a large audience, especially among lower wage earners and their families.[23]

Radio Luxembourg had been a significant rival to the BBC before 1939 and the rivalry resumed in 1946. In 1951 its English programmes switched to medium wave (208 metres) from where as, 'the station of the stars', it broadcast from 6 pm each day. Although its claim of a four million audience in Britain was probably an over-estimate (and the BBC counterclaim of one million an underestimate), anecdotal evidence suggests it was eating into the core Light Programme audience, women in particular. As early as 1949 it had broadcast a Sunday evening *Top Twenty Show*, hosted by Pete Murray, which was based on record sales rather than sheet music sales.[24] However, he also hosted a more conventional hour-long Saturday-night dance music programme, featuring the Russ Morgan Orchestra. There were also programmes devoted to the ballet, Irish and Scottish requests as well as several regular doses of religion.

The substantial family audience that Luxembourg built up in the first decade after the war was lost in the mid-1950s as television, and particularly commercial television, moved into variety. A rethink was required, which fortuitously coincided with the transformation of American popular music. In 1956 it introduced a half-hour slot of taped rock 'n' roll music, compèred by Alan Freed. Later Benny Lee fronted *Record Hop*, which featured the latest records from Columbia and Parlophone. From 1960 Luxembourg became more heavily focussed on the teen market. Within a few years it had switched almost entirely to programmes playing pop records. Unlike the BBC, which was constrained by the needle-time arrangement with the Musicians' Union and the record companies' licensing agency, Phonographic Performance Limited, Luxembourg had no limits on record time. Even in the mid-1950s, and more so afterwards, the BBC was seen not so much as 'Auntie' but as 'Grandma.' Yet, despite its undoubted appeal to a youth market, Luxembourg found itself facing stiff competition from other pirate radio stations, notably Radio Caroline, which played chart hits unconstrained by the company links found on Luxembourg. From a consumer point of view, the transformation of Luxembourg and the appearance of Caroline offered access to a range of music that was less frequently played on terrestrial radio and television.

Popular music and television

Television was a major challenge to variety theatre and radio. In the first decade after the war the BBC had shown relatively little interest in developing television, though it broadcast *Come*

Dancing from 1949 onwards, turning it into a competition in 1953. Parliament's decision to allow the licensing of commercial television created a very different environment. Both channels looked to variety. ITV with its *Sunday Night at the London Palladium* and BBC with its Saturday night *Billy Cotton Band Show* and *The Black and White Minstrel Show*. These were immensely popular shows that attracted audiences of 20 million or more. Both were a manifestation of a music-hall tradition that can be traced back to the mid-nineteenth century, but by the third quarter of the twentieth century music hall was no longer subversive. Like minstrelsy, it had been domesticated and was being served up to a middle-class and middle-aged audience. On both channels televised variety seemed to be modernizing. Cliff Richard topped the bill on *Sunday Night at the London Palladium* and Tom Jones appeared on *The Billy Cotton Band Show* but, particularly in the case of the latter, there was a touch of desperation as they looked to rock 'n' roll to give new life to a tired and dated format. *The Billy Cotton Band Show* finished in the mid-60s, *Sunday Night at the London Palladium* at the end of that decade. Despite complaints at the time, it was almost a further decade on before *The Black and White Minstrel Show* was taken off screen.

There was an opening for programmes specifically aimed at the buoyant teen market. Reflecting concerns with the preservation of live music, the earliest programme, BBC's *Hit Parade* was a series of covers by its in-house musicians. The more innovative *Six Five Special* still had a backing band comprising session musicians. On ITV's *Oh Boy!* original performers appeared live, but reflecting their growing importance, records were at the centre in *Juke Box Jury* and *Cool for Cats*. Even when bands or soloists appeared in their own right in *Ready Steady Go* and *Top of the Pops*, they mimed to their records.

Dancing and dance halls in the 1950s

The wartime boom in dancing continued for more than a decade after the end of the war. The harshness of 'austerity Britain' has been well rehearsed, but these years also saw greater security of employment and a modest rise in real wages. The nature of the recovery meant that this increased purchasing power was spent on traditional leisure activities. These were boom years for the cinema, football matches and the dance hall. Demand exceeded supply as the crowded dance floor bore witness, but this was not a deterrent. Indeed, as the country left the harshest years of austerity behind, the early signs of mass affluence provided a further fillip to dancing and the dance industry. The number of licensed venues increased in almost every city and large town, the number of professional and semi-professional musicians grew, and the numbers participating on the dance floor almost certainly reached an all-time high. The standard dances remained popular but there was a revival of old-time dancing, especially in the north of England. Square dancing was introduced from America in the early 1950s and the jive proved itself resilient in the face of attempts to ban it. The dance hall retained its importance in terms of social interaction, while the emergence of a jive culture, complete with a dress code and jargon of its own, enhanced opportunities for self-expression and emergent independence from adults. Old and new co-existed with relatively little friction. In shared venues, half the evening could be devoted to standard dancing, half to jive; or the dance floor itself could be (informally) divided to cope for quick steppers and jivers alike. Even when different halls catered for different dancers there was little sign that the bubble was about to burst. Yet, in a short period of time things changed dramatically – the local palais had indeed been turned into a bowling alley, or worse. Ballroom dancing, even in its very modest form of 'crush dancing,' was increasingly seen as old-fashioned. There were new, more exciting venues – night clubs and discotheques. There were more exciting (and more solo) dances to do – 'the twist, the stomp, the mashed potato too. Any old dance that you want to do, but let's dance,' as Chris Montez sang. And there was a wider range of venues in which to socialise. The local hop, especially in the village hall or school assembly room, was simply square. Milk bars and coffee bars, with their juke boxes full of new music, much from America, were cool. Even hanging out at home, listening to the latest record on the new portable, Dansette, record player was preferable. The dance floor was now the preserve of the serious ballroom or sequence dancers.

The record industry

The post-war record industry was dominated by four major companies. EMI, Decca, formed in the 1930s, Philips and Pye. Recorded music was to be heard in the streets and in the dance halls, especially during the war years when there were fewer musicians available. It was also to be heard on the juke boxes found in 1950s arcades and coffee bars and, increasingly, on the radio, especially the commercial stations.[25] The 1956 Copyright Act was an important relaxation of the law which led to a rapid growth in the use of records in a variety of public places.[26] The post-war years saw important technological changes in the record industry. The old 78 rpm shellac records were replaced by 33 or 45 rpm vinyl over the course of the 1950s. The quality of recordings was transformed by the development of stereophonic systems from the middle of that decade. The price of records fell at a time when portable record players came on to the market.[27] Youth purchasing power was also increasing and record sales soared. Total production quadrupled between the mid-1950s and the late 1970s. The rate of change was greatest in the years 1955-62.[28]

Table 1: UK Record Production (million units by type)

	78s	45s	33s
1955	46.3	4.6	9
1962	1.9	55.2	20.4

Source: S Frith et. al. *The History of Live Music in Britain: 1950-1967*, Routledge, London, 2013, p.149

Although majority British owned, the major companies were part of large, multinational entities and this was an important element in the American dominance of popular music in the late 1940s and early 1950s. American records probably accounted for two-thirds of the 1950s hits in Britain.[29] The list of successful American singers is impressive – Doris Day, Jo Stafford and Teresa Brewer as well as Perry Como, Frankie Laine, Nat 'King'

Cole and Guy Mitchell, not to mention Dean Martin and Frank Sinatra. But there were important British figures. Vera Lynn, 'the Forces sweetheart,' remained popular as did Alma Cogan and Anne Shelton. Among male singers Jimmy Young and particularly David Whitfield were the most successful.

The war and its aftermath largely explain the popularity of 'The Homing Waltz' and 'Auf Wiedersehen Sweet Heart' (both by Vera Lynn) and Anne Shelton's 'Lay Down Your Arms;' and also 'The Happy Wanderer,' the international hit by wartime orphans, the Obernkirchen Children's Choir. The pre-war preoccupation with love and marriage continued – literally so in the title of one of Alma Cogan's hits – with Mario Lanza ('Because You're Mine'), Guy Mitchell ('Truly, Truly Fair') and Al Martino ('Here in My Heart' and 'Spanish Eyes') at the forefront. But there was also a strong element of frivolity in several novelty songs, including 'Nellie the Elephant' (Mandy Miller), 'The Runaway Train' (Michael Holliday) and 'Never Do a Tango with an Eskimo.' (Alma Cogan).[30] There were, however, signs of change. American singers, such as Slim Whitman, Jim Reeves and Frankie Laine hinted at the greater changes that would come from the 'discovery' (and commercialization) of country and western, blues and gospel music. Also hinting at a new world of celebrity and star-struck fans, 'The Prince of Wails,' 'The Nabob of Sob,' the unlikeliest of stars, Johnny Ray, made his name with the aptly titled 'Cry' in 1952.

Some concluding observations

Despite the disruptions and change caused by war, popular music continued along familiar lines. Dance halls enjoyed a boom as more people than ever before took to the dance-floor, whenever they could. The bands of 1930s and their singers remained popular and gave a reassuring sense of continuity and community at a time of great uncertainty. ENSA concerts and new radio programmes brought familiar names and familiar sounds to both war and home fronts. Although easily mythologised in retrospect, popular music contributed to the maintenance of morale and productivity and helped to create a sense of a common purpose and a shared culture. There were changes. The position of the BBC was strengthened and its approach to popular music modified, even though its response was often cautious and out of touch with popular opinion. Pre-existing trends, notably the growing influence of American music, were accelerated.

In broad terms, in the post-war years, there was a determination not to return to the failures of the early 1930s, but in terms of popular music there was no fundamental break with the past. There was something very familiar about the 1950s, whether it was the big bands on the BBC, the big stars in variety or just the local palais or pub. Richard Hoggart noted how many of the older songs lived on (and had meaning) decades after they had first appeared. His account of club singing, where working-class people enjoyed the music they wanted, makes this clear.[31] As in *Worktown*, 'an evening's playing will comprise a majority of songs from the last twenty years ... but will include a substantial sprinkling of earlier tunes.'[32] The latter included 'the seriously emotional,' such as 'Silver Threads Among the Gold,' Lily of Laguna' and 'My Old Dutch' and 'the amused and mocking,' such as 'Hold Your Hand Out You Naughty Boy,' 'Any Old Iron' and 'Yes, We Have No Bananas.' Reluctantly, Hoggart concedes that more recent songs have become an accepted part of an evening's entertainment: 'Shepherd of the Hills' and 'Auf Wiedersehen' having been joined most recently by 'Oh, My Papa' and 'How Much Is That Doggy in the Window.' Old and new co-existed but, perhaps more importantly, there was a process of selection whereby songs 'gain complete entry into the canon,' and these were songs, which 'touch old chords ...[and] values which people still like to cherish.'[33] However, in the mid-1950s, there were signs of a new mass culture – skiffle and rock 'n' roll – that so worried Hoggart and which will be the subject of the next chapter.

Endnotes

1. Welfare reform forward looking as it was, was predicated on a traditional model of family.
2. Sentimental songs from the Great War, such as 'Keep the Home Fire's Burning' were also popular.
3. P Rayner, 'When Radio Was King: The BBC Light Programme, Listenership and Taste, 1945-1955,' unpublished PhD, Cardiff University, 2001, quoted at p.129
4. S Barnard, *On the Radio: Music radio in Britain*, Milton Keynes University Press, 1989, p.22
5. C. Baade, 'Sincerely Yours Vera Lynn,' *Atlantis: A Women's Studies Journal*, 30(2), 2006, pp.36-49. Lynn portrayed the same image in a number of films, 'We'll Meet Again,' 'Rhythm Serenade,' and 'One Exciting Night.' K Guthrie, 'Vera Lynn on Screen,' *Twentieth Century Music, 14(20, 2017, pp.245-70*
6. Rayner, 'When Radio was King,' p132. It was 18 months before she had another solo programme.
7. Rayner, 'When Radio was King,' p.133. The singing of female crooners generally was condemned by MPs and BBC moguls as the 'caterwauling of an inebriated cockatoo.' More appropriate was the lower, strong voice of Anne Shelton.
8. BBC internal memo cited in C Baade, ''The dancing front': dance music, dancing, and the BBC in World War II,' *Popular Music*, 25(30, 2006, pp.347-68 at p.357
9. M Korczynski & K Jones, 'Instrumental music? The social origins of broadcast music in British factories,' *Popular Music*, 25(2), 2006, pp.145-64 at p.149
10. Cited in Korczynski & Jones, 'Instrumental music?' p.149
11. Pasquale Troise was born in Naples in 1895 but came to London in the 1920s and joined the London Radio Dance Band. He then set up the Selecta Plectrum Mandoline Orchestra, a name he changed in the early 1930s. He was a successful stage performer and recording artist before the war and an obvious choice for 'Music While You Work.' I have been unable to trace a wartime performance. The following is from 1950. https://www.bing.com/videos/search?q=troise+and+his+mandoliers&&view=detail&mid=FD-8577BAC0F24767A43DFD8577BAC0F24767A43D&&FORM=VRD-GAR&ru=%2Fvideos%2Fsearch%3Fq%3Dtroise%2Band%2Bhis%2Bmando-liers%26FORM%3DHDRSC3
12. This section draws heavily on Nott, *Going to the Palais*, Oxford University Press, 2015, chapter 2
13. Cinema-going became less popular, according to *Mass Observation*, but the pub retained its attraction, albeit largely for a male clientele.
14. M Pickering, *Blackface Minstrelsy in Britain*, Abingdon, Ashgate, pp.186-212
15. There was also an element of gatekeeping on the BBC to ensure that inappropriate songs were denied airtime. ''Santa Claus Is bringing You Home For Christmas' was one such victim.
16. The purpose of the Light Programme was to interest listeners in the world at large 'without failing to entertain them.' BBC Yearbook for 1947 cited in Rayner, 'When Radio was King,' p.37

17 Under Reith the BBC had shown little interest in audience research. The Listener Research Unit was only set up in 1936. This lack of concern was part of a mindset which saw the BBC providing what its audience needed rather than responding to what its audience wanted.
18 The concern with 'tap listening' dated back to the 1930s and was still going strong in some parts of the BBC in the 1950s.
19 Rayner, 'When Radio was King,' p.193
20 'Have A Go' hosted by Halifax-born Wilfred Pickles is the best example of capturing the atmosphere of a northern club.
21 Somewhat surprisingly, 'The Eton Boat Song' was also requested but whether it was truly popular is a moot point. Virtual none of the programmes have survived. https://andywalmsley.blogspot.com/2015/08/on-light-part-4-when-housewives-had.html
22 S Barnard, *On the Radio*, p.39
23 There was also Radio Paris, Radio Toulouse and Radio Hilversum. For details of the Advertising Institute's surveys see A Briggs, *The History of Broadcasting* volume 2, Oxford University Press, 1995, p.253 and p.337
24 The BBC viewed sheet music as music to play and, therefore, superior to records which were merely music to listen to.
25 There were c.15,000 juke boxes in Britain in 1959. A Horn, *Juke box Britain: Americanisation and youth culture 1945-60,* Manchester University Press, 2009, p.62 and chapter 3 for the concerns surrounding them.
26 See S Frith, et., al., *The History of Live Music in Britain, volume 1: 1950-1967,* Routledge, London, 2013, chapter 6.
27 K D Tennent, 'A distribution revolution: Changes in music distribution in the U.K. 1950-76,' *Business History*, 55(3), 2013, pp.327-47, at pp. 333-4. As Tennent makes clear there were a variety of factors involved, including the increased competition that followed from the removal of retail price maintenance.
28 T Gourvish & K Tennent, 'Peterson and Berger revisited: Changing market dominance in the British popular music industry, c.1950-80,' *Business History*, 52(2), 2010, pp.187-206 at p.191. In 1955 the total production stood at 60 million units compared with 250 million in 1979. In the early 1960s 45s accounted for c.70 per cent of production, by the early 1970s 33s accounted for c.60 per cent.
29 Gourvish & Tennent, 'Peterson and Berger, appendix 2, p.206
30 The list can easily be extended. Both Lita Rosa and Patti Page asked, 'How Much Is That Doggie in the Window?' Alma Cogan wondered 'Where Will the Dimple Be?' and Max Bygraves, when not singing about pink and blue toothbrushes, could set a twee love song in 'Gilly, Gilly, Ossenfeffer, Katzeneller, Bogen, By the Sea!'
31 R Hoggart, *The Uses of Literacy*, 1st published 1957, reprinted Penguin, London, 2009, chapter 5, 'The Full Rich Life, c. Illustrations from Popular art – Club-Singing,' pp.129-44. See also the importance of family sing-songs for the Davies family in the 1950s, discussed in chapter 19.
32 Hoggart, *Uses of Literacy*, p.136
33 Hoggart, *Uses of Literacy*, p.144

'Don't You Rock Me, Daddy-O': Skiffle and rock 'n' roll

> Put your glad rags on and join me hon'
> We'll have some fun when the clock strikes one
> We're gonna rock around the clock tonight
> We're gonna rock, rock, rock, 'till broad daylight
> We're gonna rock, gonna rock around the clock tonight
>
> Bill Haley and His Comets, 'Rock Around the Clock'

THE 1950S WITNESSED several short-lived musical crazes: calypso, cha-cha-cha, mambo, skiffle and the one that did not go away, rock 'n' roll. In part the ephemeral nature of popular music reflected a long-standing business model based on novelty and change. In part it reflected a shorter-term reaction against the influence of Tin Pan Alley and Denmark Street, and the dominance of dance bands and crooners in post-war Britain. The highly influential skiffle movement emerged from the self-consciously counter-mainstream trad jazz boom and second folk revival.[1] It fed into the rock 'n' roll craze, which marked a major departure in English popular music. Both skiffle and rock 'n' roll highlight the complex interaction between musical traditions in and between America and Britain, and the importance of syncretic moments which shaped 'the dominant musical tradition of our time' in a way that is not obscured by a misleading contrast between 'Afro- American music' and 'European music.'[2]

The music was central to the debate about the problematic nature of youth culture, and wider social anxieties about marriage and family.[3] The 'teenager' was not created in these years but the size of that cohort, its growing purchasing power and its interest in things American, gave it particular prominence.[4] Unskilled, working-class youths, especially, had more disposable income and more freedom than ever before, in the years between leaving school, aged 15, and getting married, or in the case of young men, doing national service. Whether as indiscriminate and irresponsible consumers of trash culture in milk bars and coffee bars, or as a violent gang member, from the Teddy Boys with their flick-knife or knuckle-duster, to riotous mods and rockers, teenagers, and their cultures, were perceived as a generation apart, posing social, cultural and moral threats.[5]

Skiffle

The origins of skiffle are complex and obscure. The term was used in early twentieth century America and applied to 'do-it-yourself' jazz bands, often using unusual and improvised instruments, which had much in common with the 'Jiggerum Juggerum' bands found in England from the late nineteenth century onwards. It was a democratic, 'bottom up' music that emphasised amateur participation and enthusiasm. It was simple, often crude, but joyous. It opened up opportunities for music-making (and for some, money-making) to a wide range of mainly young people, who, lacking the ability and/or the opportunities to become a member of a dance band, wanted to make rather than simply listen to popular music. There was also the opportunity to dance, free of the constraint of ballroom rules. Inspired by Lonnie Donegan, and others, there was a proliferation of skiffle groups, most very short-lived, which fed into rock 'n' roll and also paved the way for the 1960s beat boom.

Equally important, were the indisputably American origins of songs that were at the heart of skiffle. The Vipers recorded 'It Takes a Worried Man' and 'Pick A Bale of Cotton;' Chas McDevitt 'Greenback Dollar' and 'Freight Train;' and Lonnie Donegan 'Rock Island Line,' 'Cumberland Gap' and 'Midnight Special.' Teenagers, who had never even been train-spotting, sang of 'Casey Jones' and 'The Wreck of the Old 97;' and even of the 'Last Train to San Fernando,' though without realising that it referred to Trinidad rather than California. The novelty of 'white' men singing 'black' music can obscure the fact the skiffle also drew on hill-billy/country traditions, associated with Jimmy Rodgers, Woody Guthrie, Hank Williams and the Carter family, and which had a ready audience in some parts of the country, particularly the 'Nashville of the North' that was Liverpool.

American folk music arrived in a variety of ways. There were informal links, including semi-mythical merchant seamen bringing records into Liverpool. The presence of American troops and access to the American Forces Network (AFN) further broadened interest during and after the war. More specifically, wartime collaboration between the BBC and CBS gave rise to programmes such as the ballad opera, *The Martins and the Coys*, aired in August 1944. A piece of wartime propaganda, the feuding hill-billy families put aside their differences to defeat Hitler. The programme featured Burl Ives, Woodie Guthrie, Pete Seeger and Sonny Terry. Guthrie sang 'Nine Hundred Miles' and, in keeping with the overall purpose of the programme, 'All You Fascists Bound to Lose.' The gradual foregrounding of American culture continued in the 1950s. Alan Lomax worked with the BBC on several programmes that embraced blues, trad jazz, English and Irish folk song and calypso. More influentially, Lomax, with his group the Ramblers, became an advocate for skiffle, describing it as 'the people's alternative to Tin Pan Alley.'[6]

If the folk revival was one route to skiffle, trad jazz was another. Skiffle emerged as interval music during concerts, notably by Ken Colyer's jazz band but also Chris Barber's. It helped popularise the music of bluesmen (Lead Belly, Big Bill Broonzy, Muddy Waters, Sonny Terry and Brownie McGhee, and Lonnie Johnson) and gospel singers (Sister Rosetta Tharpe).[7] The break with jazz came in 1955 with Lonnie Donegan's *Backstairs Session*, EP, though he had recorded 'Rock Island Line' a year earlier. This was followed by his rapid rise to prominence with hit records in 1956, such as 'Cumberland Gap,' and 'Gamblin' Man.' In the same year Donegan was booked for a fourteen-week tour on the Moss Empires variety circuit, which took him to major towns and cities alongside a ventriloquist, comedy cyclists, a calypso pianist and 'Mundy & Earle – A Boy, A Girl and a Gramophone.' As the headliner, he had a 35-minute slot in which he and his group performed 'Wabash Cannonball,' 'Lost John' and 'Nobody's Child' and the inevitable 'Rock Island Line.'[8] His performances reportedly electrified his audiences and, not just in the case of George Harrison and Paul McCartney, inspired many to take up a guitar and learn three or four chords.

Skiffle was more than a one-man story. Various skiffle groups enjoyed modest commercial success. Wally Whyton and the Vipers, the City Ramblers, Chas McDevitt with Nancy Whiskey, as well as Beryl Bryden and Betty Smith were at the fore. Success was to be measured as much in juke box plays, in milk bars and coffee bars, as in record sales and chart appearances. By the late-1950s there were some 15,000 juke boxes in Britain, with their numbers increasing at 400 a month.[9] Initially found in fairgrounds and seaside amusement arcades, increasingly they moved onto the high street across the country as they shed their reputation for seediness. Cultural critics, notably Richard Hoggart, had little time for the coffee-bar culture but its popularity among teenagers was beyond dispute.[10] Belatedly the BBC presented a specialist radio programme, *Saturday Skiffle Club*, which regularly featured Chas McDevitt and Johnny Duncan, and later (February 1957) it televised *Six-Five Special,* with its heavy emphasis on skiffle, including amateur performers. Even Billy Cotton felt there was an opportunity in recording Lonnie Donegan's hit, 'Puttin' on the Style.'

More important than chart success – and skiffle never dominated the pop charts – was the upsurge in sales of cheap guitars and the creation of numerous amateur skiffle groups to be heard in youth clubs, church halls, pubs and clubs, at some cinemas and dance halls, especially at record-based lunchtime sessions, and even in school halls.[11] Estimates suggest there were between 30,000 and 50,000 skiffle groups in the late-1950s.[12] For every successful amateur or semi-professional skiffle group, performing on a local circuit, there were an unknown number more, who played for pleasure, and a few shillings, on an occasional basis at a garden fete or local carnival.[13] For the majority of young men (and it was overwhelmingly young men taking part) it was no more than a leisure-time activity.[14] For a minority it was the start of a career in music. Alexis Korner, a major formative influence when he played with Lonnie Donegan in Ken Colyer's jazz band, moved into electric blues, while Martin Carthy made his reputation (along with Dave Swarbrick) in the English folk revival. The Quarrymen went on (with certain changes in personnel) to become *the* beat group of the 1960s, while the lead singer of the Kool Kats and the guitarist in the Candy Bison skiffle groups, Rod Stewart and Ronnie Woods respectively, went on to highly successful pop careers.

The response to skiffle was varied. The "Skiffle or Piffle" debate, if such it can be called, rumbled on through 1956 and 1957. The trad jazz community was dismissive. Ken Colyer asserted it had 'not produced any worthwhile talent ... and [had] no originality.' Alexis Korner acknowledged its 'commercial success' but dismissed it as 'musically ... mediocre.' Graham Boatfield, writing in the *Jazz Journal* was even more scathing. The Colyer skiffle group was dismissed, in a phrase that combined both musical and racial elitism, as 'a bankrupt pier-show of black-faced minstrels' while class prejudice emerged as Donegan's singing was compared to 'a number of intoxicated hillbillies returning from some over-length orgy.' *Melody Maker* was almost bland in comparison, opining that skiffle is the dreariest rubbish to be inflicted on the British public since the last rash of Al Jolson imitators.'[15] To a large extent, the comments reflected the conservatism and insularity of those judging the musical tastes of the young , which was predicated on the belief that dominant popular music of the day was (again) being degraded. Skiffle had its defenders, including Paul Oliver, writing in *Music Mirror*, who saw it as a means to the end of a better knowledge of blues and jazz, and Steve Race, writing in *Melody Maker*, who praised it for encouraging amateur music making – and for keeping worse records out of the charts.[16] Alan Lomax, more perceptively, drew attention to the British antecedents of American folk music as part of skiffle's appeal, as well as praising its participatory nature.[17] Others saw it as relatively harmless, even positive in terms of encouraging active participation, at a time when television was threatening to encourage yet more passivity. There was also something almost wholesomely British about the leading practitioners. Donegan's singing was enthusiastic and uninhibited. His introductions were funny and there was an endearing cheekiness about his performances. Above all, like Buddy Holly later, there was a simplicity and approachability that gave the impression that he was not that different from his audiences, who could, if they wanted, perform like him. Equally, the more folk-derived sound of Chas McDevitt and Nancy Whiskey had a good-natured and unthreatening quality. Likewise, the Vipers offered the novelty and excitement of American music but with none of the threat that was to be associated with rock 'n' roll, which had arrived in the country at more or less the same time as the skiffle craze took off.[18]

Rock 'n' Roll

If skiffle was music played by men born in the 1930s for an audience born in the 1940s.[19] Rock 'n' roll was for and by a new generation; except that Bill Haley was born in 1925 and had enjoyed a lengthy career as a yodelling cowboy before becoming an unlikely founding figure of and ambassador for rock 'n' roll. Rock 'n' roll, as it developed in America, despite its sanitisation and commercialization by the major record companies, was novel and exciting for a young white audience. It was also diverse, drawing on a variety of popular traditions, including country, blues, and gospel. In its first flourishing, c.1955-60, there was no all-embracing formula to capture Haley along with Elvis, Jerry Lee Lewis, Little Richard, Buddy Holly, Eddie Cochrane, Gene Vincent, and the Everly Brothers. Outraged American conservatives, secular and religious, cared little for distinctions and condemned it, not simply as 'a musical eccentricity' but as 'a communicable disease,' threatening, in their eyes at least, both the musical and moral wellbeing of the nation. This commercially-communicable phenomenon aroused hysterical condemnation and adoration in almost equal measure as radio and television stations, along with record and film companies, sought to exploit it to the full. The "cultural contagion" spread across the Atlantic. Rock 'n' roll was given airtime on Radio Luxembourg and AFN, though barely on the BBC Light Programme, and it was played on the growing number of juke boxes.[20] *Blackboard Jungle* brought it to a cinema near you, and record sales literally brought it home for numerous families. Though Elvis never managed more than a brief stop-over at Prestwich, Bill Haley (1957), Jerry Lee Lewis and Buddy Holly (1958), Gene Vincent and Eddy Cochrane (1960), and Little Richard (1962), all toured the country bringing live music to their fans.

The responses to rock 'n' roll were varied and throw light on a country that was still living with the economic and social consequences of the war. For the young (and not so young) the attraction of the music lay in its excitement, its lack of restraint and its promise of something better – at least, more American. Sensationalist press accounts of vandalised cinema seats exaggerated the extent of hooligan behaviour and misrepresented much good-natured exuberance. Nonetheless, for more conservative commentators, here was the embodiment of all that was wrong with 'Americanised' youth: out-of-control teenagers with too much time on their hands, too much money in their pockets and not enough discipline. In the late summer and early autumn of 1956, the so-called *Blackboard Jungle* "riots" began, reaching a peak in September at a showing at the Trocadero cinema in the Elephant and Castle, London.[21] '[A] fourth-rate film with fifth-rate music,' according to the up-and-coming politician, Jeremy Thorpe, was able to 'pierce the thin shell of civilization and turn people into wild dervishes.'[22] The meeting of delinquent youth and degenerate culture sparked a moral panic that led to a series of knee-jerk bans of the film across the country and produced instant judgement on the generation gap that, allegedly, had been exposed. Although the panic in the popular press soon subsided, the announcement of a tour by Bill Haley and His Comets saw the press stoking fears of trouble ahead. In fact, the tour was both successful and largely without incident.[23] In part, this was due to a careful public relations campaign, which stressed the god-fearing, family-orientation of the group. Haley was accompanied by his wife and his manager by his 77-year-old mother. The links with Britain were stressed. Haley's mother came from Ulverston; and he openly professed his love of English literary and musical culture. Haley's friendly, avuncular persona also helped.[24] But, in no small measure, success was due to the excitement about the music that contrasted with the measured reassurance of the dance bands. The very crudeness of the guitar and saxophone breaks gave it a sense of spontaneity. Further, Haley's form of rock 'n' roll had its roots, recognisably, in Western Swing and cowboy music, which already had a following in Britain. Similarly, the jiving, which had given rise to trouble in the inappropriate setting of cinemas showing *Blackboard Jungle*, was nothing new to wartime and post-war generations that had seen the jitterbug evolve into the jive in many dance halls across the country. Finally, and somewhat paradoxically, Haley's on-stage patter and the group's slapstick routines had more in common with that stalwart of the BBC, Billy Cotton and, unsurprisingly appealed across the alleged 'generation gap.' *Stage*, not noted for its sympathetic coverage of American rock 'n' roll, saw Haley and the Comets as 'essentially a comedy outfit meant to be seen as well as heard' and recognised that they were 'certainly calculated to make people happy.'[25]

If Bill Haley did much to make rock 'n' roll acceptable, and for many of its fans this was not something to be sought, there was no escaping his atypicality: Elvis Presley or Little Richard he was not! The pelvic-thrusting gyrations and smouldering good looks of the former were never let loose on the British public, while the latter's high-energy performance and camp persona was not seen live in Britain until 1962, by which time first-generation, commercialised rock 'n' roll had passed its peak. In 1958 two rock 'n' rollers in their twenties toured Britain. Jerry Lee Lewis was 23, Buddy Holly 22. The contrast between the two was considerable. The bespectacled Holly never lost the wholesome 'boy next door' image and his distinctive guitar style never seemed to be beyond the scope of the enthusiastic amateur. The long-haired, Lewis, with his extravagant, iconoclastic stage act and overt sexuality was something else. His style owed much to his Pentecostal church background, with its emphasis on exuberance, physicality and emotional display. and to an intensity born of a 'Christ-haunted' tension between his personal faith and his public career as a secular musician.[26] His high-energy music, notably 'Whole Lotta Shakin' Going On' and 'Great Balls of Fire' were extremely popular.[27] *Stage* conceded that 'lovers of rock 'n' roll probably appreciated the performance of this man without inhibitions,' but felt others found it 'all very puzzling – and scary.'[28] But it was immorality, rather than hedonistic music, that brought the tour to an abrupt end when it was revealed that he was married to his 13-year-old cousin.

In contrast the whirlwind Holly tour, also in 1958, passed without scandal. *Stage* continued its critique of rock 'n' roll performance by noting his 'weird gyrations … shivering and shaking, jumping and strutting' but noted that his set, which included 'Oh Boy!' 'Peggy Sue' and 'That'll Be the Day,' had 'the teenagers screaming with delight and applauding for more.' To the amazement of one of their correspondents 'The Crickets … turned out to be lively, entertaining and a little overwhelming.'[29] Reports in the provincial press highlighted their popularity with an overwhelmingly young audience.[30] The 1960 tour headlined by Eddie Cochrane and Gene Vincent was, with one exception, incident free. A stage invasion, fist fights in the aisles and destruction of theatre seats in Dundee led both the *Aberdeen Evening Express* and *Stage* to talk of a rock 'n' roll riot but the small-scale disturbance was not repeated elsewhere. Several papers commented on the good-natured enthusiasm of the audience. The *Coventry Evening Telegraph* reassured its readers that there had been 'no frantic scenes' and the audience had 'dispersed for late buses rather than … waiting to mob their heroes.'[31] Reports across the country referred, somewhat condescendingly, to "scream-agers", whose noise threatened to drown out the music but recognised their popularity with a young audience in a way that baffled older reporters.

Without touring the country, Elvis Presley was the dominant figure in the American rock 'n' roll invasion, with a stunning number of chart hits in the years before he went into the army. His breakthrough, 'That's Alright (Mama),' was with Sun records, but his commercial success came after his move to RCA. Following 'Heartbreak Hotel,' he had hits with 'Don't Be Cruel,' 'Hound Dog,' Blue Suede Shoes,' 'Love Me Tender,' 'All Shook Up,' 'Teddy Bear,' 'Jailhouse Rock' and 'King Creole.' While there can be little doubt about the commodification of Elvis, 'a white man who had the negro sound,' in the words of Sam Phillips, equally there can be little doubt of his popularity.[32] Reports of his stage performances provoked earnest discussion on the BBC Home Service about the peculiar effect this type of music had on the young but it did not stop 'Aunty' giving him some airtime. Nor did it stop Elvis imitators taking to the stage in an attempt to cash in on his popularity.

Unsurprisingly, driven by hard-headed record producers through to wannabe rockers, home-grown 'stars' emerged, trying to cash in on what many thought would be a short-lived craze. It is easy to dismiss English rock 'n' rollers of the late-1950s as pale reflections of their American counterparts, but this is misleading.[33] First, it assumes that Tommy Steele or Cliff Richard simply wanted to be an English Elvis or Little Richard. Second, it overlooks both good British performers, such as Adam Faith and Johnny Kidd and the Pirates, and the saccharine sell-outs, the Bobbys and Johnnys, in the Billboard charts. (Suffice it to say 'Pat Boone' and to remember his pedantic desire to correct Fats Domino's grammar when covering 'Ain't That A Shame.'[34]) Third, it fails to appreciate how the emergence of amateur rock 'n' roll groups led into the beat boom of the 1960s.

There was always an ambiguity about Tommy Steele. He might have been billed as 'Britain's answer to Elvis Presley,' but he was also 'the boy from Bermondsey.'[35] His route to rock 'n' roll came via the country music of Hank Williams and skiffle, though during his years in the merchant navy he became aware of Elvis Presley and Buddy Holly. His dramatic rise to fame owed much to careful management by John Kennedy and Larry Parnes. Like Bill Haley, he was promoted as the wholesome face of rock 'n' roll. His undoubted enthusiasm and affability lent itself to a clean-cut, non-threatening image, at a time when the popular press was happy to link rock 'n' roll with teenage delinquency and immorality.[36] The smiling, besweatered Steele constantly played down an suggestion of being (or wishing to be) a sex symbol.[37] 'Rock With The Caveman' was the hit that set him on a career that saw him topping the bill at Sunderland Empire, no less, by November 1956. But no-one who listened to the words, let alone saw him perform it on stage, could have missed the element of parody. This was end-of-the -pier entertainment that owed more to a longer music-hall tradition, as did his born-in-Bermondsey 'cockney' authenticity. Steele, himself, made known his wish to be more than a rock 'n' roll performer and several observers noted at the time that he had 'a talent beyond the ability to satisfy a passing phase' and to become 'a first-class entertainer.'[38] His star billing at the 1957 Royal Variety Performance was an important staging post in his career and a reflection of his appeal to a wider audience. His subsequent recording career showed a continued desire to broaden his appeal, with novelty songs such as 'Nairobi' (1958), 'Hiawatha' (1959) and 'Little White Bull' (1959), from the film *Tommy the Toreador*. In 1963 he starred in the West End musical, *Half a Sixpence*, signalling the successful transition he wanted to an all-round entertainer. Nor was he alone in moving into a revived and relocated variety tradition. Lonnie Donegan recorded 'Does Your Chewing Gum Lose Its Flavour (On the Bedpost Over Night)?' in 1959 and 'My Old Man's a Dustman' in 1960. Cliff Richard followed a similar career path. 'Move It,' seen by some as authentic rock 'n' roll, had brought condemnation from the *New Musical Express* for his 'violent hip-swinging and crude exhibitionism,' and provoked one television critic to ask: 'Is he too sexy for television?'[39] A year later he was appearing in more innocuous form in the film *Expresso Bongo*, intended as a satire but popular with teenage fans taken by the music.[40] The transformation to a British Ricky Nelson was completed with records such as (the prescient) 'Bachelor Boy' and 'Summer Holiday,' the latter becoming the title song of the film, released in 1963.

It was easy to proclaim the death of rock 'n' roll c.1960. Buddy Holly and Eddie Cochran were literally dead, Elvis had been in the army and was creating a new entertainer image and repertoire. Little Richard had (re-)discovered religion – halfway through a tour of Australia – and Jerry Lee Lewis was still struggling to overcome the scandal that ruined his 1958 tour. This is to overlook the extent to which rock 'n' roll was taken up by numerous amateur groups from the mid-1950s onwards. Aided by the publication in 1957 of Bert Weedon's *Play In A Day*, guitar tutor, and the availability of relatively cheap, especially mail order, guitars, amateur performers, in their thousands, had formed skiffle groups, which in turn spawned rock groups. These were the roots of the 'beat boom' of the 1960s.

Revolting youth? Continuity and change in 1950s popular music

Skiffle and early rock 'n' roll undoubtedly had a significant impact on the development of popular music in Britain but the extent to which it helped give rise to a distinct youth culture is more debatable. There was an element of incomprehension (feigned or otherwise) on the part of certain older commentators but there is less evidence of a generation gap than one might believe from some commentators.

The shock of a constructed 'black' music, moving from the margins into the 'white' mainstream,' so powerful in America, was not experienced to the same extent in Britain. Further, entrepreneurs and impresarios adopted charm offensives, distancing themselves and their proteges from riotous images in favour of a more acceptable boy-next-door demeanour; and this was reflected in the lyrics of the songs. Behind the problems of 'Wake Up, Little Susie' (failing to get home on time from the movies) or 'Fool's Paradise' (the disappointment of those blinded by love) was a desire for love and matrimony. It was no coincidence that 'Peggy Sue got married not long ago.' Even Marty Wilde, singing 'Bad Boy,' was complaining about being misunderstood. The bad boy was only 'a good boy in love,' and who could condemn that? This was reinforced by the known wishes of Tommy Steele and Cliff Richard to broaden their appeal as family entertainers. There was a further factor. The new music was not quite as shocking as some suggested. There was a pre-existing audience for American popular music, from the wartime bands, jitterbugging and jiving, to the country and cowboy music of the 1950s, which found in rock 'n' roll, particularly that of Buddy Holly and the Everly Brothers, a recognisable and enjoyable musical form. They might not have gone to the Southampton Gaumont, the Stockton Globe or the Wigan Ritz – that was for their kids – but parents were happy to listen to a local group singing 'That'll Be The Day' and 'Bye, Bye Love' in their local pub or club.

Popular music changed in important ways in the second half of the 1950s but there were also elements of continuity. 1956 saw Lonnie Donegan enjoying great success with

'Rock Island Line' and Elvis had his first top-ten chart hit with 'Heartbreak Hotel' but Anne Shelton was more widely popular as she exhorted her soldier sweetheart to 'Lay Down Your Arms (And Surrender to Mine).' Ruby Murray ('Softly, Softly'), Tony Bennett ('Stranger in Paradise') and Jimmy Young ('Unchained Melody') all had number 1 hits with records that owed little to the new musical crazes. Even during 1959, when Elvis, Buddy Holly and Cliff Richard topped the charts, so too did Jane Morgan ('The Day That the Rains Came Down'), Shirley Bassey ('As I Love You') and Bobby Darin ('Mack the Knife'). And then there was Sheb Wooley's 'Purple People Eater,' demonstrating the enduring appeal of the nonsense song.[41] A similar picture emerges from the best-selling album charts. Lonnie Donegan, Bill Haley and Tommy Steele all reached number one; but so too did Nat 'King' Cole. Elvis had four number one albums, as did Frank Sinatra. The most successful albums in the late 1950s were film musicals. *Carousel*, *Oklahoma* and *The King and I* in 1956; *West Side Story* 1957, *My Fair Lady* and *South Pacific* in 1958.[42]

Some concluding observations

Skiffle and rock 'n' roll brought distinctively new sounds to popular music in the 1950s. They offered a clear alternative to the dance bands and crooners, but rarely dominated the pop charts, let alone album sales and the wider world of popular music. Further, many of the stars of 'first generation' British skiffle and rock 'n' roll followed a route into popular entertainment that would have been familiar to George Formby or Gracie Fields, while their successors appeared bland. Nonetheless, a new generation of record-buying consumers, as likely to buy cheap cover copies from Woolworths as the more expensive originals, emerged and laid the base for the revival of the record industry that was struggling to recover from the collapse of sales that dated back to the 1930s. More importantly, the late 1950s saw an upsurge in popular music-making. Do-it-yourself instruments were at the heart of skiffle. Cheap guitars and a Bert Weedon tutor facilitated the explosion in amateur rock 'n' roll bands, experimenting with a variety of new musical forms, many from America. This was the seed bed from which the British beat boom was to emerge and to which we turn next.

Endnotes

1. Denis Mitchell, producer of the BBC's *Ballads and Blues*, aired in 1953, spoke of 'folk singers and jazz musicians find[ing] a common platform in modern and traditional folk music from both sides of the Atlantic.' https://genome.ch.bbc.co.uk/45bb2079d7bc466d8324c3e0c4e916a9
2. P Tagg, 'Open letter: 'Black music,' Afro-American music' and 'European music,' *Popular Music*, 8(3), 1989, pp.285-98, esp. conclusion p.295. Tagg was referring specifically to America but the point also applies to Britain. Contrast with Bradley who, talking of 'codal fusion,' refers to a 'European code' with an emphasis on harmony, based on triadic chords, rather than rhythm and even melody and in which improvisation is rare and the 'distinct and separate … Afro-American code' is characterised by, among other things, an emphasis on rhythm, including rhythmic variation, blue notes, the use of call and response and improvisation. D Bradley, *Understanding Rock 'n' Roll: Popular Music in Britain, 1955-1964*, 1992, chapter 3. Tagg rejects the 'supposed pair of opposites "black" or "Afro-American music" versus "European music,' claiming that in musicological terms the key elements of the former (rhythm, blue notes, call and response and improvisation) are not unique to 'black' music. Bradley makes clear that he does not believe in a 'pure Africanism at the fountainhead of everything' but appears to reject the notion that Afro-American music was already a form of codal fusion.
3. See also the flurry of publications giving advice on child-rearing and parenthood, including Dr B Spock, *Baby and Child Care*, 1946 and J Bowlby, *Child Care and the Growth of Love*, 1953
4. In 1931 in England and Wales there were 3.4 million people aged between 15 and 19. This figure was not exceeded until the mid-1960s when the estimates for 1966 showed 3.7 million people in this age category. As a percentage of the total population, 15-19-year-olds were a larger segment of society (8.5 per cent) in 1931 than 1966 (8 per cent). B R Mitchell & P Deane, *Abstract of British Historical Statistics*, Cambridge University Press, 1962, p.13 and B R Mitchell & H G Jones, *Second Abstract of British Historical Statistics*, Cambridge University Press, 1971, p.6.
5. D Kynaston, *Family Britain, 1951-57*, 2009 pp.379-80. S Cohen, *Folk Devils and Moral Panics: The Creation of the Mods and Rockers*, 1972 is the classic study of the latter disturbances. The reality was far less melodramatic and there were contemporary commentators who painted a more nuanced and favourable picture. See for example, Hilda Marchant 'The Truth about the "Teddy Boys"' in *Picture Post* cited in Kynaston, *Family Britain*, p.381
6. In 1957 he published *The Skiffle Album, featuring Skiffle and Folk Songs popularised by Alan Lomax and the Ramblers*, which contained a wide range of songs, American, British, old, and new.
7. M Dewe, *The Skiffle Craze*, Aberystwyth, Planet, 1998, esp. chapter 1.
8. B Bragg, *Roots, Radicals and Rockers: How Skiffle Changed the World*, London, Faber & Faber, 2017, p.267
9. A Horn, *Juke box Britain: Americanisation and youth culture, 1945-60*, Manchester University Press, 2009, p.62 and p.169

10 R Hoggart, *The Use of Literacy*, London, Chatto & Windus, 1957, especially 'The Juke Box Boys,' chapter 8 part A.
11 For a more detailed account of the growth of skiffle in northern cities see, J P Watson, '"Beats Apart": A Comparative History of Youth Culture and Popular Music in Liverpool and Newcastle-Upon-Tyne, 1965-1965,' unpublished Ph.D., University of Northumbria, 2009, chapter 4 'Popular Music in the North of England.' £10 was relatively cheap for a guitar in the mid-1950s but still a considerable sum of money for many, equivalent to at least £200 today. Mail order guitars cost as little as £6 6s (c.£125)
12 Bragg, *Roots, Radicals and Rockers*, p.303 but no source is given.
13 See Dewe, *Skiffle Craze*, chapter 6 and Bragg, *Roots, Radicals and Rockers* refers to an estimate of 'between thirty and fifty thousand active skiffle groups at the height of the craze in 1957,' p.303
14 Both Neil Kinnock and Michael Howard were reportedly in skiffle groups in their teens, as was Max Clifford, a singer and guitarist in the now-forgotten Dominoes. Dewe, *Skiffle Craze*, p.134
15 Quotations taken from Bragg, *Roots, Radicals and Rockers*, p.190 and p.305. Bragg does not give full references.
16 Bragg, *Roots, Radicals and Rockers*, p.191 and *Melody Maker*, 2 March 1957 cited in Dewe, *Skiffle Craze*, p. 129
17 A Lomax, 'Skiffle: why is it so popular?' *Melody Maker* 31 August 1957 cited in Dewe, *Skiffle Craze*, p. 131
18 It appears to have escaped public notice that the group took their name from Raymond Thorp's 1956 novella, *Viper: The Confessions of a Drug Addict*.
19 Lonnie Donegan was born in 1931, Chas McDevitt in 1934 and Wally Whyton in 1929.
20 There were very few outright bans but, by the use of green labelling, the BBC severely restricted airtime for rock 'n' roll. S Barnard, *On The Radio: Music Radio in Britain*, Milton Keynes, Open University Press, 1989, p.37
21 To a large extent the 'riots' were the product of sensationalist press coverage. While there were incidents of damage to cinema seats, there was more exuberant dancing, inside and outside of cinemas.
22 Cited in Kynaston, *Family Britain*, p.655. Bill Haley and His Comets dominated the soundtrack of the film, particularly the opening track, 'Rock Around the Clock' and 'See You Later Alligator,' which played a key part in the unfolding of the story. In addition there were two songs by the Platters ('Only You' and 'The Great Pretender') and two by Freddie Bell and the Bell Boys ('Teach you to Rock' and the highly subversive 'Giddy Up a Ding Dong!')
23 G A Mitchell, 'Reassessing 'the Generation Gap': Bill Haley's 1957 Tour of Britain, Inter-Generational Relations and Attitudes to Rock 'n' Roll in the Late 1950s,' *Twentieth British History*, 24(4), 2013, pp.537-605
24 Haley had been involved in controversy in America when he was targeted by followers of the notorious white supremacist, Asa Carter. Mitchell, 'Reassessing' p.583
25 *Stage*, 14 March 1957
26 The same tension was true of Little Richard. See C Mosher, 'Ecstatic Sounds: The Influence of Pentacostalism on Rock n Roll,' *Popular Music and Society*,

31(1), 2008, pp.95-112, C Motley, 'Hell Hounds, Hillbillies and Hedonists: The Evangelical Roots of Rock 'n' Roll,' *Religions*, 2016, http:// www. mdpi.com/journal/religions/special_issues/Contemporay-Culture and R J Stephens, '"Where else did they copy their style but from church groups?" Rock 'n' Roll and Pentecostalism in the 1950s South,' *Church History*, 85(1), 2016, pp.97-131

27 Both were recorded on the Sun label. Lewis also recorded country numbers such as 'Fools Like Me' and Hank Williams' 'You Win Again', though with distinctive piano breaks. His career did not recover from the scandal for another four years, though he continued recording with Sun throughout
28 *Stage* 29 May 1958. Their reporter seemed as much concerned with his 'weird antics,' noting he 'frequently combed his long wavy blond hair, pulled his socks up and scratched himself.'
29 *Stage* 6 March and 3 April 1958. *Stage* also referred on several occasion to the successful home-grown talent in the show – Des O'Connor.
30 For example, *Newcastle Journal*, 7 March and *Mexborough and Swinton Times*, 22 March 1958
31 *Aberdeen Evening Express* 22 February, *Stage* 25 February and *Coventry Evening Telegraph* 29 January 1960
32 D Harker, *One For The Money: Politics and Popular Song*, Hutchinson, London, 1980, chapter 3 'Thank God for Elvis Presley?' It is also the case that this boom provided openings for the likes of Fats Domino and Ray Charles.
33 See for example, Barnard, *On The Radio*, p.34
34 It is claimed that Boone wanted to record it as 'Isn't that a shame.' The anecdote may be inaccurate but there is no doubt that Boone presented white America with a range of acceptable covers, as to his credit, he now freely confesses.
35 *Stage*, 31 January 1957
36 This involved, among other things, highly publicised meetings with (alleged) debutantes.
37 Colin McInnes famously described him as 'every nice young girl's boy, every kid's favourite elder brother, every mother's cherished adolescent son.' Cited in G A M Mitchell, 'A Very 'British' Introduction to Rock 'n' Roll: Tommy Steele and the Advent of Rock 'n' Roll Music in Britain, 1956-1960,' *Contemporary British History*, 25(20, 2011, pp.205-225 at p.215
38 *Melody Maker* 22 December 1956 and *Stage* 23 May 1957
39 D Kynaston, *Modernity Britain, 1957-1962*, London, Bloomsbury, 2013, p.194
40 The film, which was based on a stage play, featured several songs by Cliff Richard, an instrumental piece by The Shadows but also two traditional airs – 'Loch Lomond' and 'The Irish Washerwoman.' Its satirical message appears to have been lost on celluloid.
41 Strictly speaking, 'Purple People Eater' was released in 1958 and was also recorded by Judy Garland in the same year.
42 Other successful albums include 'Pal Joey' and 'High Society' but also 'The Duke Wore Jeans.'

'Twist and shout': Illusion and disillusion in the 1960s and 1970s

> People try to put us down (Talkin' 'bout my generation)
> Just because we get around (Talkin' 'bout my generation)
> Things they do look awful c-c-cold (Talkin' 'bout my generation)
> I hope I die before I get old (Talkin' 'bout my generation)
>
> The Who 'My Generation'

IN THE LATE 1950s the popularity of singers such as Elvis, Buddy Holly and Eddy Cochran gave rise to talk of another American invasion that threatened English popular culture, and to fears that home-grown popular music was little more than a pale reflection. In fact, within a decade it was 'the Brits' invading America. The incentive to do-it-yourself music-making from skiffle and rock 'n' roll, and the discovery of rhythm and blues and country and western music, were building blocks in the development of a new (and commercially highly successful) sound, but which, for all its distinctiveness, also owed something to older traditions. For many contemporary commentators, the beat bands not only challenged older forms of popular music but also embodied in performance and lyrics, attitudes and ideas that were fundamentally at odds with the 'Establishment.' Popular images of 'Swinging London' comprise bright young things, confident, successful and affluent enough to support their extravagantly stylish life-style in defiance of the values of an older generation. In examining these claims, the focus in this chapter is deliberately narrow: Liverpool and the Beatles, and London, and the Who and the Kinks.[1]

Liverpool: from the Quarrymen to the Beatles

Liverpool was a much-divided city – along class, gender, ethnic and religious lines – and beset with economic problems that manifested themselves particularly in above-average youth unemployment in the post-war years. Being a member of a band could be a source of income and even an escape from a life of limited opportunities. It also offered a chance to create a new identity, which, perhaps, went beyond harsh social divisions and prejudices.[2] The scale and diversity of popular musical provision in 1950s Liverpool was striking. Its position as a major port, as well as its proximity to Ireland, brought a wide range of people and their cultures. Consequently, there were many active musical communities, sometimes separate but often overlapping; sometimes exclusive but often feeding off each other.

American music, in various guises, was a long-standing part of the city's cultural mix. It was greatly strengthened, during and after the second world war, by the presence of the large American base at Burtonwood, the entertainers brought over for the GIs and the broadcasts from AFN (the American Forces Network). Swing music was immensely popular during and immediately after the war. There was also a following for country music, particularly associated with Jimmy Rodgers, dating back to the 1930s This was strengthened by the films of the 'singing cowboy,' Gene Autrey (including *The Sagebrush Troubadour, Red River Valley* and *Comin' Round the Mountains*) and by the airtime given to Hank Williams. 1950s Liverpool was 'the Nashville of the North.' There were a variety of clubs, as well as Burtonwood, at which country groups, such as the Dusty Road Ramblers or the Ranchers, played.[3] A local country-style singer Ronnie Wycherley, later better known as Billy Fury openly acknowledged his debt to American country music. Local awareness of American popular music was broadened by the trad jazz revival and, particularly, the emergence of skiffle. Skiffle was less exclusive than jazz and was to be heard in inner-city youth clubs and suburban dance halls.[4] There were also 'Doo Wop' influences and rhythm and blues groups, such as the Roadrunners. The growth of a largely informal network of performers, audiences, and venues provided a supportive framework within which rock 'n' roll and the Mersey sound grew.

There were also other important musical influences. The city had a substantial Irish community and, although sectarianism was a serious and ongoing problem, its cultural influences were felt widely. Similarly, Liverpool had a well-established African Caribbean community, concentrated in Toxteth, which again exerted a musical influence beyond Liverpool 8. Lord Woodbine was a well-known and influential Trinidadian calypso singer. External stimuli were also important, notably Lonnie Donegan's appearance at the Liverpool Empire (November 1956) and Buddy Holly's at the Liverpool Philharmonic Hall (March 1958), but the key element was the proliferation of grass-roots bands, numbering as many as 250 in the early 1960s. It was an environment in which a more distinctive and original musical style could arise. The 'beat boom' did not suddenly materialise. Its roots were firmly in the late-1950s and early-1960s, the latter years easily dismissed as musically barren.

The Beatles loom large over any account of popular music and popular culture in and after the 1960s. Here the focus will be on their musical evolution from their origins as a skiffle group, the Quarrymen, to their early years as the Beatles. In the earliest days, like many other groups, they were essentially a Lonnie Donegan cover band. Increasingly, especially after Paul McCartney joined, they became more of a rock 'n' roll band, covering American hits. Among major influences, the Crickets and the Everly Brothers were at the forefront, though their repertoire also included Fat's Domino's 'Ain't That A Shame.'[5] During their residencies in Hamburg, particularly, at the Star Club, they became more than simply a cover band. The influence of rhythm and blues in their repertoire was clear, with songs such as 'Roll Over Beethoven' and 'Sweet Little Sixteen,' but they were learning and experimenting with a new musical genre.[6] Although one of a number of similar Liverpool groups, and for much of the time not the most highly regarded, the Beatles developed a more distinctive style and sound. They also started writing their own material, mainly through the Lennon/McCartney partnership. The breakthrough came in 1962/3. After the failure of 'My Bonnie,'[7] 'Love Me Do,' released in November 1962, was a modest chart success.[8] Aided by an appearance on 'Thank Your Lucky Stars,' their next single, 'Please, Please Me,' released in January 1963, narrowly failed to make number 1 in the hit parade but achieved sufficient recognition to get the Beatles a place on tour as support, initially for Helen Shapiro, later Tommy Roe and Chris Montez and finally Roy Orbison. This was followed by three number 1 hits, 'From Me to You,' 'She Loves You' and 'I Want to Hold Your Hand.' Their position was consolidated by two very successful LPs (*With the Beatles* and *Please, Please Me*), released in the same year. Success was based on a distinctive amalgam of Motown ('Chains' and 'You've Really Got a Hold on Me'), rhythm and blues ('Roll Over Beethoven' and 'Money') and their own compositions, which were, initially, mainly optimistic, here-and-now, love songs, such as 'I Saw Her Standing There,' Do You Want to Know A Secret,' 'All My Loving' and 'I Wanna Be Your Man.'[9] The outcome was a novel and exciting sound, and a confident performance style, which if not iconoclastic, cocked a largely good-natured snook at authority.[10] Their distinctiveness caught the attention of Maureen Cleave, one of the first London-based journalists to pick up on the their emergence. 'The darlings of Merseyside,' as she described them, 'know exactly what they can get away with ... They stand there bursting with confidence and professional polish.'[11]

An important element in their emergence onto a national stage was BBC Radio. Between January 1963 and December 1964, they appeared on *Saturday Club* on ten occasions, the first just after the release of 'Please, Please Me.' Equally important, for the Beatles, the BBC and its audience, was *Pop Go the Beatles*, a series of sixteen programmes broadcast in the summer of 1963.[12] To have a programme in their own right, albeit introduced with an excruciating version of 'Pop Goes the Weasel,' was clearly important and it gave them a vehicle for their songs. Additionally, and importantly in the development of popular music on the BBC, it provided them with an opportunity to offer covers of American music still relatively uncommon on air. This included rock 'n' roll numbers ('That's Alright Mama,' 'Lucille' and 'Long Tall Sally') and a variety of rhythm and blues numbers ('Memphis Tennessee' and 'I Got to Find My Baby') and soul songs ('You've Really Got a Hold on Me' and 'Soldier of Love)' There were also guest appearances from a range of artists, including well-known pop singers, such as Johnny Kidd and Brian Poole, as well as Cyril Davies' Rhythm and Blues Stars and the Graham Bond Quartet, but also the middle-of-the-road Bachelors. The combination of radio and television appearances and chart successes brought about the transformation from local, Liverpool group to national and international stars.

This transformation was reflected in their repertoire. The album *Beatles For Sale*, released in December 1964 includes songs by Buddy Holly ('Words of Love'), Chuck Berry ('Rock and Roll Music') and Carl Perkins ('Honey Don't' and 'Everybody's Trying to Be My Baby') and was described by Lennon as their 'country and western LP.' This was clearly not the case with *A Hard Day's Night*, (1964), which foregrounded the Lennon/McCartney song-writing partnership as did *Rubber Soul* (1965), *Revolver* (1966) and particularly the concept album, *Sergeant Pepper* (1967). The musical inspirations were diverse: Motown ('You Won't See Me' and ''Got to Get You into My Life'), Greek and Indian music ('Girl,' 'Within You, Without You' and 'I Want to Tell You') but also music hall ('Your Mother Should Know,' 'When I'm Sixty Four' and 'Good Day Sunshine').

Though less diverse than their musical influences, several themes are explored in their lyrics. Unsurprisingly, many are songs about love but they are more reflective and less brashly confident than their first hits ('And I Love Her' and 'Michelle').[13] 'You've Got to Hide Your Love Away' captures a sense of loss but combined with a masculine fear of being laughed at, that is reminiscent of the Everly Brothers' 'Cathy's Clown,' 'I'll Cry Instead,' another song about lost love, also reflects a fear of being ridiculed but with scarcely hidden anger, including a threat to break hearts. Others, even more reflective, deal with loneliness. 'The Fool on the Hill' is alone but is in fact a wise 'innocent,' whereas 'Nowhere Man' is isolated 'in his nowhere land making all his nowhere plans.'

Disturbingly, the listener is asked 'isn't he a bit like you and me?' Equally, bleak is the landscape of 'Eleanor Rigby' full of 'all those lonely people.' But while the question is asked – 'where do they all come from? – no answer is given. Similarly, 'She's Leaving Home' is about parental lack of comprehension, rather than an explanation of actions.

Also pertinent is the sense of place and an accompanying sense of loss. As early as 1963, in 'There Is a Place' the unnamed location is a way of escaping the world 'when I feel low, when I feel blue.' 'In My Life,' is a more explicit and sorrowful reflection on the past, 'the 'people and things that went before,' which 'I'll often stop and think about.' Places have 'changed, some forever, not for the better [and] some have gone' while 'lovers and friends, I still recall, some are dead, some are living.' 'Magical Mystery Tour' is predicated on remembrances of a day-trip to Blackpool, while 'Penny Lane' and 'Strawberry Fields Forever' reference memories from childhood, though the latter is not straightforward in that 'nothing is real' and 'living is easy with eyes closed/Misunderstanding all you see.' As well as people and places disappearing, there is also a sense of the passing of an older social order. In certain songs there appears to be a harking after a patriarchal order, with man the provider and woman the homemaker ('Hard Day's Night' and 'When I Get Home.') In the former, the male singer 'work[s] all day to get the money,' in the latter he has 'a girl who's waiting home for me.' In others, a more matriarchal world of love with stronger, supportive women ('She's A Woman' and 'Another Girl') Thus, for all their innovativeness in musical terms, there was in their lyrics – in part at least – a conservatism about a disappearing Liverpool, even before they left it in summer 1963, though their social observations did not go beyond a sense of something being wrong and/or lost. Unlike both the Who and the Kinks, there was no attempt to bring together in an album a sustained and coherent commentary on society.

Although by far and away the most successful Liverpool group, the Beatles were not alone in popularising the Mersey sound. Freddie and the Dreamers, ('I Like It' and 'How Do You Do It?) and The Searchers ('When You Walk in the Room') had once been more popular than the Beatles on Merseyside.[14] Nowhere was the sense of local identity stronger than in the songs of Gerry and the Pacemakers. 'Ferry Across the Mersey,' affectionately praised Liverpool ('the place I love and here I'll stay') and 'You'll Never Walk Alone,' which, despite being an American show tune (from *Carousel*), became an anthem for Liverpool FC and then for the city following the Hillsborough tragedy.

At the time, the Beatles were seen as the embodiment of a break with the past. Some historians have made similar claims. Simonelli talks of 'the original golden age of British rock and roll … ushered in by the Beatles.'[15] Others have sought to debunk what they see as a myth. Sandbrook dismisses the idea of the 1960s as a turning point, while Fowler dismisses the Beatles as little more than family entertainment.[16] While justifiably reacting against the mythologizing of the Beatles, both judgments are problematic. It would be folly to deny the Beatles' roots in earlier music, especially in the distinctive milieu of post-war Liverpool, but there was something more than evolution to their music in 1962/3, let alone in 1964/7. Their music was evolving, syncretic and distinctive and proved hugely successful, and not only in Britain. It also provided a model for others and, as such, was a significant addition to the range of popular music. Similarly, to deny that the Beatles were at the cutting edge of youth culture seems perverse, even though they incorporated older elements into their music.[17] But they were prepared to modify their appearance and tone down their stage act. They also followed the path to the London Palladium and the Royal Command Performance in 1963, even if they did ask (some) audience members to 'rattle their jewellery.' They may have been a more consensual band than the Rolling Stones, but they were more than family entertainment.[18]

London: The Who and the Kinks

Liverpool dominated coverage of popular music in the early and mid-60s, but the beat boom manifested itself across the country, not least in London. Despite toppling the Beatles from number one in the charts, the Dave Clark Five, at the forefront of the so-called 'Tottenham Sound,' lacked originality. Clarke was hardly the most innovative drummer of his day, and 'Glad

All Over' was not notable for its musical or lyrical qualities. Of greater interest, are the Who and the Kinks.

The roots of the Who are to be found in the trad jazz revival and skiffle but, like several other bands, they were influenced by rhythm and blues and Motown. Initially closely associated with London, they extended their geographical appeal, and soon became (along with the Small Faces), the face and music of the Mod subculture. Pete Townshend in particular stressed the cultural and political significance of popular music, seeking 'to defy post-war depression … articulating the joy and rage of a generation struggling for life and freedom.'[19] There was a sense of opportunity – 'I could go anyway … I could live anyhow … I could go anywhere' – and optimism, as 'Never gonna lose, the way I choose.' Increasingly as this optimism waned, their act sought to 'communicate aggression and frustration.'[20] In 'I Can't Explain' there are 'funny dreams, again and again,' while the things you've said have got me real mad' but, repeated constantly, is the refrain, 'I can't explain.' Best remembered for the line 'I hope I die before I get old,' 'My Generation' was more about frustration as 'people try to put us d-down.' It was a generalised sense of grievance rather than a clearly articulated critique, and yet, Townshend was clear. Popular music 'clicks your social conscience – makes you think about life.'[21]

Townshend's attempt to 'think about life' in a more sustained manner led to *Tommy*, hailed as the first rock opera, which first appeared as an album in 1969. *Tommy* is at times vague, at others difficult to comprehend, and at others absurd. Yet, not least because of its spectacle and songs, such as 'Pinball Wizard' it was very successful. It owed much to the musical ambitions of Kit Lambert, the personal difficulties besetting Townshend and, as a result, the new age mysticism of Meher Baba.* Townshend stressed the importance of 'the play between self and illusory self' and there are several scenes, notably involving the Acid Queen, which relate to Townshend's particular problems. However, the significance of other incidences – the cruelty of 'Cousin Kevin' and the abusive Uncle Ernie in 'Fiddle About' – is less obvious in terms of Townshend's life, let alone wider societal concerns.[22]

---

*   Dismissed as Ali Baba, by fellow band member, Roger Daltrey.

In contrast, *Quadrophenia* is firmly focussed on the Mod experience of the mid-1960s, albeit from the distinctive perspective of 1972/3 when the album was produced. Townshend's intention was 'to provide narratives and analyses of youth culture.'[23] *Quadrophenia* is a tale of frustration and failure. Jimmy, the central character, is at odds with his parents and their values but, for all yearning for something better, and for all the promise seemingly held out by the Mod lifestyle, Jimmy's journey to self-discovery ends in failure. The picture Townshend paints has familiar scenes of Mods in Brighton but bears little relation to the affluent image of Carnaby Street and 'Swinging London.' 'Dirty Jobs' talks of 'the man who looks after the pigs' and 'the man who drives a local bus.' Jimmy is an unglamorous dustman. Life is monotonous and unsatisfying. 'Every year is the same and I feel it again. I'm a loser, no chance to win,' according to 'I'm One,' and 'loneliness starts sinking in.' The world of 'The Helpless Dancer' is threatening. Work is merely a means to an end – maintaining a Mod lifestyle, though even here there is a sense of doubt. 'I got to move with the fashion,' Jimmy sings in 'Cut My Hair;' and fashion includes 'Zoot suit, white jacket with side vents five inches long' but although he's 'dressed right … [he] just can't explain why that uncertain feeling is still here in my brain.'[24] Moving to Brighton is not the fulfilment of his hopes. While the beach might remain for Jimmy 'a place where a man can feel he's the only soul in the world that's real,' the reality is something very different, as Ace Face, the eponymous 'Bell Boy' makes clear. 'Some nights I still sleep on the beach/Remember when stars were in reach' but 'then I wander in early to work/Spend days licking boots for my perks.' The clearest statement of failure comes, however, in the track 'I've Had Enough.'[25]

> I've had enough of dancehalls
> I've had enough of pills
> I've had enough of street fights
> I've seen my share of kills
> I'm finished with the fashions
> And acting like I'm tough
> I'm bored with hate and passion
> I've had enough of trying to love.

The album's accompanying photo-essay, featuring working-class youths from Battersea reinforces the sense of failure to break out from a world characterised by 'dirty jobs,' low pay and deeply entrenched inequalities.[26] Townshend, who often commented on the strong links with fans, said he had created a working-class hero with whom they could identify. In this light, the undoubted success of *Quadrophenia* reflects the failure of the Mod dream, rather than the success of 'Swinging London.'

The Kinks also emerged from a musical mix of skiffle, rock n roll, rhythm and blues, and music hall.[27] Their first commercial record was the Chuck Berry number, 'Long Tall Sally,' and their first hit single, the blues-derived 'You Really Got Me.'[28] They enjoyed considerable chart success in the mid-1960s with songs of varying degrees of social commentary from the music-hall style parody, 'Dedicated Follower of Fashion,' the critique of smug prosperity in 'A Well Respected Man' and 'Mr Pleasant,' to the bleak realism of 'Dead End Street.' They sought more sustained social commentary, notably in the three albums, *(The Kinks Are) The Village Green Preservation Society*, (1968), *Arthur, or The Decline and Fall of the British Empire*, (1969) and *Muswell Hill Hillbillies*, 1971. To a greater degree than The Who or the Beatles, they offered a wide-ranging critique of 1960s Britain, which exposed the *absence* of fundamental change in the supposedly 'revolutionary decade of the '60s, as a result of persistent social and economic inequalities. Increasingly the 1960s, and particularly its emphasis on classlessness, was seen as a fraud. As with the Who, there was a sense of having been cheated.

Although seen, particularly by American audiences, as quintessentially English, their Englishness was elusive, even contradictory, not least because of the technique and tone of their 'story-telling,' including multiple voices and the use of irony and ambivalence, if not ambiguity.[29]

The Kinks, particularly the Davies brothers, were firmly rooted in London working-class life, as it adjusted to postwar modernization, including, in their case, relocation from central London to Muswell Hill. Musically, it was a pub-based, piano-centred culture; politically it was linked to the Labour party.[30] Their songs commented on the world that grew out of post-war social reform. Although 'Not Like Everybody Else,' the Kinks did not simply revolt against an older generation.

Like the Who, they provided a critique of an over-sold, 'You've Never Had It So Good,' 'Swinging London' view of the country in the 1960s. Theirs was the perspective, not of the successful art college student, but of the 11+ failure factory worker. For Dave Davies, the Kinks' success owed much to being able 'to communicate the struggle of the working man [*sic*] trying to survive in a greedy and purely materialistic society.'[31]

The harsh realities of working-class life are recurring themes in their songs. The inhabitants of 'Dead End Street' are 'strictly second class.' The squalor of their accommodation in a 'two-roomed apartment on the second floor' with 'a crack up in the ceiling and the kitchen sink … leaking,' is matched by their sparse diet, 'a Sunday joint of bread and honey' and the threat of 'the rent collector … trying to get in.' A similar bleakness pervades the later 'Scrapheap City.' Counterpoised against working-class poverty is middle-class/suburban prosperity, in which material advantage is undermined by the hypocrisies with which it is riddled. The eponymous 'Well Respected Man,' seems 'oh so good, oh so fine … oh so healthy in his body and his mind' as he's 'doing the best things so conservatively.' Beneath the veneer of respectability 'his father pulls the maid,' his mother 'passes looks … at every suave young man,' while he 'adores the girl next door' and is 'dying to get at her.' The owner of a 'House in the Country' is 'oh so smug … [but] he's socially dead.'[32]

There is an ambivalence about the Kinks' attitude to both past and present. Their flamboyant, at times Beau Brummel appearance, set them apart from the staid young men who dressed like their fathers, and had more in common with the image of the Who. The world of their 'Dedicated Follower of Fashion,' was 'built 'round discotheques and parties.' The 'pleasure seeking individual … flits from shop to shop.' His clothes are 'never square,' for one week he is in 'polka dots, the next week … in stripes.' However, he is also 'fickle,' 'a butterfly,' seeking 'flattery' as much as fashion. Vanity, 'he thinks he is a flower to be looked at,' becomes ridiculous when he pulls his frilly nylon panties right up tight,' while still believing that he is a 'dedicated follower of fashion.' There is also a real sense of the loss of the past, real or imaginary. In 'Where Have All the Good Times Gone,' Ray Davies pleads 'let it be like yesterday, please let me have happy days.' In 'Autumn Almanac,' he extols the virtues of an older working-class tradition of 'my football on a Saturday, roast beef on Sunday ... and Blackpool for my holidays,' even though the Davies would more likely have gone to Ramsgate or Margate. Particularly in the commercially unsuccessful, *The Village Green Preservation Society*, Ray Davies evokes a nostalgic image of rural England that has brought comparison's with Orwell's conservative patriotism. The past is viewed (literally) in affectionate terms in 'Picture Book,' and 'The Last of the Steam Powered Trains' celebrates not simply a fast-disappearing mode of transport, but also a fast-disappearing way of life. The eponymous 'Village Green Protection Society' preserve 'the old ways from being abused' and, along the way stand up for 'strawberry jam ... draught beer,' and oppose the modern monstrosities of the 'office block and skyscraper.' At the same time as asking God to save 'Vaudeville and Variety,' Donald Duck is included in the list of worthies. Disconcertingly, the Preservation Society is also 'protecting the new ways for me and for you.'[33]

This ambivalence towards the past is even more apparent in *Arthur, or The Rise and Fall of the British Empire*, which grew out of a request from Granada Television for a 'rock opera.' The television production never materialised but a twelve-track album did. Although Arthur is the central character, the story is spread over three generations and the multiple voices undermine the notion of a central, authoritative perspective.[34] The opening track, also released with modest success as a single, 'Victoria,' combines praise, (Arthur is 'free' and 'life was clean' in the land of his birth), with direct criticism ('sex was bad and obscene and the rich were so mean') and satire ('From the West to the East [of the Empire], From the rich to the poor, Victoria loved them all.) Churchillian sacrifice, again in the name of freedom, is invoked but, as the final song, 'Arthur,' makes clear, for all his ambition and hard work, Arthur 'all the way was overtaken by the people who make the big decisions' as 'the world's gone and passed [him] by.' To make matters worse, the alternatives (emigration as represented by his son) and suburbia (as represented by his grandson) are flawed. And yet, ambivalent again, 'Shangri-la' is more than a satire on suburbia. There is, however muted, a celebration of the small pleasures of this escape from poverty, more Arnold Bennett than George Orwell, in which 'you're in your place ... and know where you are.' More importantly, 'you need not worry, you need not care,' even if 'you can't go anywhere.'

Muswell Hillbillies provides the most sustained and coherent critique of contemporary England. The opening track, 'Twentieth Century Man,' sets the scene. 'This is the age of machinery, a mechanical nightmare,' that has erased 'the green pleasant fields of Jerusalem.' Davies sings of being 'a paranoid schizoid product of the twentieth century,' a theme taken up in the unambiguously titled second track: 'Acute Schizophrenia Blues.' It is also a world of insecurity and inequality ('Slum Kids' and the later 'Demolition) in which the little man (and woman) has lost out. Davies rails against urban improvement in a manner reminiscent of Clare's earlier condemnation of enclosure. For both, the little guy lost out in the name of progress. There are also echoes of Orwell's *1984*. 'Uncle Son,' echoing 'Arthur,' is 'just a workin' man' following 'simple rules' and with 'simple plans,' but he is told what to do by politicians, generals, preachers and even trade unionists. In more than one song 'civil servants and people dressed in grey' are the villains of the piece.[35] Several songs emphasise either the pressure of work ('Alcohol' and the later 'Have Another Drink') or its tedium ('Oklahoma USA' and 'Scrapheap City'). The alternatives offer little hope of improvement. 'Work is a bore' for the girl in the factory but 'in her dreams she's far away in Oklahoma USA.' The dreamy 'Holiday' seems to offer the opportunity to leave behind insecurity, sedatives and sleeping pills but it is a flawed arcadia, 'the sea's an open sewer ... [and] I'm breathing through my mouth so I don't have to sniff the air.' There appears to be some consolation in older culture. 'Give me William Shakespeare ... I'll take Rembrandt, Titian, Da Vinci and Gainsborough,' but in the present there is little more than Granny's 'Cuppa Tea' and a sense of defiance. In the final track, 'Muswell Hillbilly,' Davies faces the move to the 'identical little boxes of Muswell Hill with his 'photographs and memories' and a determination that they're never gonna kill my cockney pride.'

In fact, Davies' confidence in the past does not last long. In a track on the 1975 album *Schoolboys in Disgrace*, 'No More

Looking Back,' ostensibly about a girl he had once known, he is clear that 'yesterday's gone and that's a fact ... look straight ahead that's the only way it's going to be.' The most explicit condemnation of the 1960s is found in 'Working in the Factory,' from the 1986 *Think Visual* album, which reprises many earlier themes. For the 11+ failure there was no thought of a professional career, but 'they sold us a dream but in reality/ It was just another factory.' Music 'gave me hope back in 1963 ... but then the corporations and big combines/Turned musicians into factory workers on assembly lines.' There was a sense of profound disillusionment about the 1960s, which they shared with the Who. Ray Davies later wrote, 'the sixties were a con, the establishment still ruled the country.'[36] If there was consolation to be found in the music and the lifestyle, it was short-lived, though for Davies the resilience of an older working-class culture provided not simply a fall-back but also a resource.

However, there was an important contrast between the two groups. In contrast to the more aggressively masculine image of the Who, the Kinks offered an alternative masculinity, a greater awareness of gender identities (especially 'Lola'). They also offer a degree of sympathy, albeit in conservative terms, for the problems of women, though at times they appear as the cause of men's misfortunes. The 'sinner ... who used to be a winner' in 'Alcohol' is partly undone by 'his selfish wife's ambition' and later by 'the floosie [who] made him spend his dole.' More often, women, usually young, struggle with a Hogarthian world beyond their control. The threats of the 'bright lights, big city' are seen in 'Big Black Smoke,' in which 'the fairest purest girl, the world has ever seen,' at least according to her parents, ends up, exploited by the men in her life, sleeping in 'caffs and coffee bars' and spending every penny on 'purple hearts and cigarettes.' A stage further on, 'Little Miss Queen of Darkness,' similarly exploited, ends up 'in a little discotheque,' being 'oh so friendly to every fella that she met,' but 'sadly dancing on.'' Lifestyle, and by implication class is the dominant consideration in 'Two Sisters.' The affluent world of the unmarried Sylvilla, who 'looked into her mirror ... and her wardrobe,' is contrasted with the domestic drudgery of Percilla, who 'looks into the washing machine ... [and] the frying pan.' But despite being jealous of her sister's liberty and luxury, Percilla 'saw her little children and then decided she was better off than the wayward lass that her sister had been.' Domesticity and the family triumph over an emancipated lifestyle, in a way that reflects Davies social conservatism. Even the bluesy 'Holloway Jail,' with its sympathetic depiction of 'the living hell' of prison for a mother and child, is predicated on a traditional woman-as-victim theme. The 'young and ever so pretty' lady who went to gaol is now 'old and pale … [as] she wastes her life away sitting in that prison cell' but there is ironic sympathy for the male singer for whom life, 'now she's in jail, [is] giving me hell.'

Some concluding observations

The beat boom of the mid-1960s has acquired almost mythical status in recent years but behind the hyperbole were several innovative groups, whose skills in terms of music and lyrics profoundly influenced the course of late-twentieth century popular music. However, for all their novelty, their musical achievements grew out of a range of earlier musical influences. Rather than a simple reproduction of the sounds of earlier bluesmen or rock 'n' rollers, there was a process of fusion and development. In addition, to the musical innovations, several songs provided comments on contemporary society. The extent to which this can be seen as a generational revolt against 'the Establishment,' is open to debate. The experimentation of the Beatles, whether in terms of drugs' culture or Indian music, complemented the sense of alienation and isolation in several of their songs. More explicitly, both the Who and the Kinks expressed the aspirations of their generation, particularly working-class youth, and yet both came to the pessimistic conclusion that the promises of the '60s were false. There was a sense of change, but no change. In 'Won't get fooled again.'. 'We were liberated from the old, that's all, And the world looks just the same.' The new boss looked just like the old. The con could happen again, but instead of the defiant song title ('Won't get fooled again'), the chorus is less confident. 'I'll get on my knees and pray we don't get fooled again.' There was also a sense of local community under threat, particularly in the songs of the Kinks, but also the Beatles, and of sorrow at the erosion of older values. The 'Swinging London' of Carnaby Street and the King's Road meant little to the working-class youth of Battersea, let alone Billingham. There was more than a division between the beneficiaries of the new affluence and new youth cultures and those left behind. There was an ambivalence about both the present that was emerging and the past that was (often literally) disappearing during the 1960s.

The advent of these new groups, notably the Beatles, and the response of their fans, was dramatic. However, as with rock 'n' roll, there was no wholesale musical takeover. When 'Love Me Do' and 'Please, Please Me' entered the hit parade, they were outsold by Frank Ifield ('Lovesick Blues' and 'Wayward Wind') and battled with the bland pop of Mark Winter ('Venus in Blue Jeans' and Bobby Vee ('The Night Has a Thousand Eyes'). Even later, 'Pinball Wizard' shared the charts with Mary Hopkin ('Goodbye'), Dean Martin ('Gently on My Mind') and Sarah Vaughan and Billy Eckstein ('Passing Strangers'). The singles charts, however, were not synonymous with popular music. As the album charts reveal, popular tastes were more broadly based. As in the 1950s, film musicals, notably *South Pacific*, but also *The Sound of Music* and *West Side Story* were extremely popular. So too were Frank Ifield, Jim Reeves, Val Doonican and Andy Williams. Equally important were a variety of community-centred forms of music that were not captured in any of the charts. Pub-centred singing was in decline during the 1960s but variety clubs, particularly in the north of England, flourished. When the Batley Variety Club opened in 1967 the headline act was the Bachelors. In following years, performers as diverse as Gracie Fields, Shirley Bassey and Roy Orbison appeared on stage. The Irish diaspora supported a different, flourishing music culture, not only in places with an established Irish community, such as London, Liverpool and Tyneside, but also in those with more recently arrived immigrants, such as Coventry and Luton. Similarly, post-war immigration, especially from the Caribbean and south Asia, brought new music that was largely unknown in chart terms.

Endnotes

1. There were important developments in other major cities and towns, notably Birmingham, Manchester, and Newcastle, some of which will be considered in the following chapters.
2. K Gildart, *Images of England Through Popular Music: Class, Youth, and Rock 'n' Roll, 1955-1976*, Basingstoke, Palgrave, 2013, chapter 3, especially p.64. There is a danger of romanticising the extent to which music brought together people across racial lines. See chapter 21.
3. For details see J P Watson,'" Beats Apart": A Comparative History of Youth Culture and Popular Music in Liverpool and Newcastle-upon-Tyne, 1956-1965, unpublished PhD, 2009, chapter 5
4. The Cavern, initially a venue for jazz and folk music, famously banned rock 'n' roll.
5. They also included the well-known Liverpool folksong, 'Maggie Mae.'
6. *Live! At the Star Club in Hamburg, 1962*, released as a double-LP in 1977 shows clearly the influence of rhythm and blues but also the diversity of their repertoire, which included 'A Taste of Honey,' 'Falling in Love Again,' 'Bésame Mucho' and an up-beat version of 'Red Sails in the Sunset.' The rhythm and blues influence comes over in their performances on BBC radio (Saturday Club and Pop Goes the Beatles) in 1963 and 1964, including 'Johnny B Goode' and 'Memphis Tennessee' as well as the Cricket's 'Crying, Waiting, Hoping.' There are only two Lennon/McCartney songs included.
7. It seemed an ill-chosen song for the English market. In Germany, in contrast, it reached no.5 in the hit parade.
   Sheik of Araby' and 'Ain't She Sweet.'
8. A Lennon/McCartney number, the song was simple but with a distinctive blues harmonica and harmonies that suggest a debt to the Everly Brothers.
9. As well as the rawness of the sound, there was a naive directness about lyrics, such as 'my heart went boom/as I crossed the room.' This phase finished with *Help!* and the abandonment of touring.
10. Lennon and Harrison in particular were fans of George Formby.
11. M Cleave, 'Why the Beatles Create All that Frenzy,' *London Evening Standard*, 2 February 1963 cited in I Inglis, '"I Read the News Today, Oh Boy!": The British Press and the Beatles,' *Popular Music and Society* 33(40, 2010, pp.549-562 at p.552
12. This was part of a wider emerging awareness of northern culture in the BBC, though it is worth stressing the extent to which Liverpool carved out a distinct identity that set it apart from 'the North,' especially as dominated by Manchester. See P Atkinson, 'The Beatles on BBC Radio in 1963: The "Scouse" Inflection and a Politics of Sound in the Rise of the Mersey Beat,' *Popular Music and Society*, 34(20, 2011, pp.163-175.
13. 'Can't Buy Me Love' is an exception to this observation.
14. They were joined by The Swinging Blue Jeans ('Hippy Hippy Shake'), Billy J Kramer and the Dakotas ('I'll Keep You Satisfied') and the Merseybeats ('Wishin' and Hopin') all offering variants on the optimistic love song.
15. D Siminelli, *Working-Class Heroes: Rock Music and British Society in the 1960s and 1970s*, Plymouth, Lexington Books, 2012, chapter 2. The quotation is at p.31

16   D Sandbrook, *White Heat: A History of Britain in the Swinging Sixties*, London, Abacus, 2006, p.748, and D Fowler, *Youth Culture in Modern Britain, c.1920 to c.1970*, Basingstoke, Palgrave, 2008, p.174
17   See, for example, 'For the Benefit of Mr. Kite.' The reference is to a poster advertising the forthcoming appearance of Pable Fanques' circus in Rochdale in 1843.
18   O Heilbronner, 'The Peculiarities of the Beatles,' *Cultural and Social History*, 5(1), 2008, pp.99-115 refers to the Beatles as a 'consensual band representative of English society in the early and mid-1960s' at p.99
19   P Townshend, *Who I Am*, London, Harper Collins, 2012, p.4 and p.340 cited in K Gildart, *Images of England Through Popular Music: Class, Youth and Rock 'n' Roll 1955-1976*, Basingstoke, Palgrave, 2013, p.89 and p.105
20   Siminelli, *Working-Class Heroes*, chapter 4, the quotation is at p.72
21   Cited in Gildart, *Images of England*, p.105. This sense of failure is also found in 'Substitute' issued in 1965.
22   For a more detailed analysis see C J McGowan, 'Harmony and discord within the English 'counter-culture', 1965-1975, with particular reference to the 'rock operas' Hair, Godspell, Tommy and Jesus Christ Superstar,' unpublished Ph.D., Queen Mary college, University of London, 2011, chapter 9.
23   K Gildart, 'Class, Youth and Dirty Jobs: The Working-Class and Post-War Britain in Pete Townshend's "Quadrophenia"' in P Turschwell, ed., *Quadrophenia and Mod(ern) Culture*, Basingstoke, Palgrave, 2017 on which much of the following paragraph is based.
24   Later, but in similar vein, 'I work myself to death just to fit in.'
25   There is an element of ambiguity in the final track 'Love reign over me.'
26   There is a further twist. The filming of *Quadrophenia* coincided with the 1978/9 'Winter of Discontent' and captures some of the sense of betrayal of the 'old' Labour Party, though the image of Mods in the mid-1960s is more nostalgic than in the original album.
27   This can be heard in several songs but especially *The Village Green Preservation Society*. It is also clear in Davies' 'Mr Flash' in the album *Preservation Act 2*, who is clearly modelled on Max Miller. Generally, see P G Sullivan, '"Let's Have A Go At It": the British Music Hall and the Kinks,' in T Kitts & M J Kraus, eds., *Living On A Thin Line: Crossing Aesthetic Borders with the Kinks*, Rumford, RI, Rock and Roll Research Press, 2002, pp.80-99
28   Ray Davies, who was greatly influenced by Big Bill Broonzy, later referred to 'You Really Got Me' as 'north London blues.' M Doyle, The Kinks: *Songs of the Semi-detached*, Reaktion Books, London, 2020, p.54
29   N Baxter-Moore, '"This Is Where I Belong: Identity, Social Class and the Nostalgic Englishness of Ray Davies and the Kinks,' *Popular Music and Society*, 29(2), 2006, pp.145-165
30   Family sing-songs incorporated music hall, film musicals, ballads and folk music. Doyle, *The Kinks* , p.39.
31   D Davies, *Kink: An Autobiography*, London, Boxtree, 1996, p.134 cited in Gildart, *Images of England*, p.130
32   See also 'Mr Pleasant' in which material success ('your brand new limousine, twenty-four inch TV screen') is offset by Mrs Pleasant 'flirting with another young man.

33 There was also a debt to Dylan Thomas, *Under Milk Wood*. Doyle characterises *VGPS* as Pop Art fantasy. Doyle, *The Kinks*, p.130

34 A Palmer, '"In Land that I Love": Working-Class Identity and the End of Empire in Ray Davies' Arthur or the Decline and Fall of the British Empire,' *Popular Music and Society*, 37(20, 2014, pp.210-232

35 See particularly 'Here Come the People in Grey.'

36 R Davies, *X-Ray. The Unauthorised Autobiography*, London, Viking, 1994, p. 311 cited in K Gildart, 'From "Dead End Streets" to "Shangri Las": Negotiating Social Class and Post-War Politics with Ray Davies and the Kinks,' *Contemporary British History*, 26(3), 2012, pp.273-298 at p.292. See also C Fleiner, 'The Influence of Family and Childhood Experience on the Works of Ray and Dave Davies,' *Popular Music and Society*, 34(3) 2011, pp.329-350

'Woke Up This Morning:' How we got the (rhythm and) blues – and found some soul

> Got my mojo working, but it just won't work on you
> Got my mojo working, but it just won't work on you
> I wanna love you so bad till I don't know what to do
> I'm going down to Louisiana to get me a mojo hand
>
> I'm going down to Louisiana to get me a mojo hand
> I'm gonna have all you women right here at my command
>
> Muddy Waters, 'Got My Mojo Working'

AS THE FEARS aroused by jazz in the inter-war years bear witness, popular music in Britain was considered in terms of 'whiteness' and discussed in terms of the threats posed by alien, uncivilized forms of music and dancing. 'Black' or 'negro' music was seen as essentially 'other,' something that 'had an impact on,' rather than 'being part of' indigenous popular music, despite the longstanding presence of black communities and black musicians in Britain. Black-face minstrelsy in the nineteenth century, even more so, *The Black and White Minstrel Show* in the twentieth century, reinforced this sense of 'otherness.' The fact that 'negro minstrelsy' owed much to popular music brought from Britain and Ireland and, in turn, offered its own 'Irish' and 'Scotch' shows, did nothing to undermine this simplistic, racialised division between 'black' and 'white' music. The growing awareness of American popular music, from ragtime onwards, further reinforced this view, not least because American popular music had been re-constructed along racial lines from the late nineteenth century onwards. Part of the purpose of this and the next chapter is to demonstrate how the once 'other' became a central part of popular music in the latter part of the twentieth century.

Although widely used, terms such as 'the blues' and 'rhythm and blues', are elusive, giving rise to often bitter, but ultimately sterile, debates about what constituted authenticity and what was a bastardised or commercialised form of the music. Given its diverse roots in African rhythms and songs, work songs and field hollers as well as European balladry and hokum; given the blurred edges with boogie-woogie and ragtime; and given important regional variations, notably between the Mississippi Delta and Texas, it is more appropriate to use blues (and by extension, rhythm and blues) as a convenient umbrella term, rather than a precise definition. Similarly, given the commercial awareness of the earliest known/recorded bluesmen and blueswomen, it makes little sense to seek out and prioritise 'pure' or 'authentic' blues in terms of freedom from the corrupting influence of commercialization. Finally, the desire to find and preserve the 'true' blues (or any other music form) makes a nonsense of the ways in which popular music develops as circumstances (social and economic but also technological) change. Thus, a further purpose of this chapter is to move beyond such arguments and to focus on 'syncretic moments' and to argue for a developmental process of imitation, experimentation and fusion out of which new musical genres evolved.

Discovering the blues in post-war Britain

Awareness of the blues in Britain before, and even during, World War II was limited to a small number of aficionados. The situation changed after the war in no small measure as a result of the trad jazz revival, skiffle and the second folk revival. The interest in traditional jazz, and the desire of men such as Ken Colyer to recreate an 'authentic' New Orleans sound, led to a growing interest in its black roots. Blues were of interest because they were seen as 'the simplest form of jazz.'[1] There were record recitals of 'race' music and even formal lectures by such men as Paul Oliver, but the blues were very much a niche interest. The emergence of skiffle further increased awareness and interest. However flawed Lonnie Donegan's introduction to 'Rock Island Line' might have been, it brought Lead Belly's name to a wider audience than ever before.[2] Albeit approaching from a different direction, the second folk revival also played its part, most notably through the work of the Ballad and Blues Association and of Alan Lomax in London, which culminated in *Ballads and Blues*, produced for the BBC in 1953, with its aim of providing 'folk singers and jazz musicians … a common platform in modern and traditional folk music from both sides of the Atlantic.' Thus, Big Bill Broonzy was heard along with Ewan MacColl and A L Lloyd but also Humphrey Lyttleton, Seamus Ennis and Cy Grant.

The broadening of awareness of the blues was a slow process. Immediately after the war, there were only a small number of records from America, many brought in informally.[3] There were a few minor record labels in Britain and the specialist record shops in London (Dobell's) and the larger cities (Hessy's in Liverpool and Collet's in Manchester) but they were not readily accessible for the majority of the population.[4] The BBC very occasionally aired a programme which included blues music, such as Lomax's three-part series, *The Art of the Negro*, but, as with its policy towards jazz, this was confined to the Third Programme.[5] Finally, the opportunities to see live musicians was restricted by the understandable but restrictive stance of the Musicians' Union, which was not relaxed until 1957. Nonetheless, a growing number of bluesmen toured Britain. Josh White and Lonnie Johnson in were among the first, but among the most influential were Big Bill Broonzy, John Lee Hooker, Memphis Slim, and 'Champion' Jack Dupree.[6] Sonny Terry and Brownie McGhee, who appealed to part of the burgeoning folk club scene, also became regular visitors. For would-be British blues bands, tours gave some of them an opportunity to work with and learn from established American stars. The relationship was often difficult, not least because of the limited knowledge and ability of novice bands, but working with someone even as critical as Sonny Boy Williamson, 'taught … a lot about feel and emotion, and also … improvisation.'[7] Growing interest, as much on continental Europe as in Britain, led to the annual American Folk Blues Festival, which brought an array of touring African-American blues musicians to several British venues, between 1962 and 1972.[8] More importantly, Granada television decided to broadcast a 45-minute recording of the 1963 show – *I Hear the Blues* – which was followed up by a second programme, *The Blues and Gospel Train* in 1964.

These tours were important in raising awareness of the blues among British audiences, but it was a particular version of the blues that was anachronistic, inconsistent and heavily gendered. Sister Rosetta Tharpe was an undoubted star of *The Blues and Gospel Train* but the only woman in the cast list. Similarly, *I Hear the Blues* had only one female performer – Victoria Spivey.[9] The blues were constructed in terms of the anguished male, in and of a rural environment and uncontaminated by any taint of commercialism. Lead Belly, Big Bill Broonzy and Muddy Waters could all be presented as – and more importantly were happy to play the part of – this archetypal blues singer.[10] Consequently, women were marginalised, their often humorous and downright lewd songs expunged from the canon, and their popularity and commercial success denied. At the same time, the southern plantation image was totally at odds with the lived experience (and musical preferences) of 1960s African-Americans. The suffering, noble savage was an image that fitted well with a nation that prided itself on its role in abolishing the slave trade, without coming to terms with its contribution to the Atlantic slave trade and the extent to which British prosperity was rooted in slavery. Although more attention was paid to 'authenticity' than ever was the case with Victorian minstrelsy, the construction of the bluesman was effectively another re-working of older tropes, though ones in which participants were happy to connive.[11] On a lighter note, it gave rise to incongruities such as the sight of Rosetta Tharpe's high-heels and Matt Murphy's electric guitar in an ante-bellum set for *The Blues and Gospel Train*.[12]

Murphy's anachronistic guitar leads to a final point about the music itself. In a debate about 'authenticity,' on both sides of the Atlantic, purists emphasised the importance of the acoustic guitar. In so doing, they blinded themselves to changes that had taken place following the large-scale migration from the southern states to cities such as Chicago and set themselves up for disappointment when Lonnie Johnson sounded like an Ink

Spots' tribute act and Muddy Waters played an electric guitar. British commentators, coming from jazz scholasticism and the preoccupation with authenticity, struggled, but eventually succeeded in accommodating Muddy Waters, B B King and John Lee Hooker in a tradition that included 'timeless artists [such] as Blind Willie Johnson, Barbecue Bob and Lewis Black' and their music, which went 'right back to West Africa in its primitive, almost chanting, ultra-rhythmic accompaniment.'[13] There remained a grave suspicion of commercial exploitation. Rhythm and blues, the term increasingly used to describe the urban music of black mass migration, was still seen as 'a reprehensible bastardization of a fine folk form', in Albert McCarthy's words.[14]

The gradual growth of interest in rhythm and blues was a feature of late-1950s Britain. Broonzy, King and Waters gave it a degree of respectability as its popularity gradually grew. Skiffle and rock 'n' roll transformed attitudes and expanded audiences, bringing a new generation in touch with blues on a scale not previously experienced. Within a short space of time, men (and it was overwhelmingly men) who had listened in awe to the stars of *The Blues and Gospel Train* were themselves performing at the National Jazz and Blues Festivals alongside American artists.[15]

The 1960s rhythm and blues boom and its aftermath

London, 'the new Chicago,' according to *Melody Maker*, was the focus of much contemporary attention, but the rhythm and blues boom involved clubs and groups across the country. In London, the Eel Pie Island Hotel and the Crawdaddy Club (in Richmond) became well-known venues but more influential were the Marquee and the Flamingo. More importantly, rhythm and blues clubs were to be found not only in the major cities but also in smaller towns. By the end of 1963 estimates suggested some 2000 were in existence. The accompanying emergence of home-based rhythm and blues groups had an important impact on the evolution of popular music.

The first developments came from blues purists, notably Alexis Korner and Cyril Davies. They supported Muddy Waters on tour in 1958 and their London Blues and Barrelhouse Club became an important venue. Their band,

Blues Incorporated, provided opportunities for a wide range of aspiring performers, and their 1962 album, *R & B From the Marquee*, was highly influential, though never a commercial success. The 12-track album was evenly divided between American numbers, including 'I've Got My Mojo Working'[16] and 'Hoochie Coochie Man,' and compositions by band members. In 1962 Davies, more committed to Chicago-style blues, left, unhappy with the suggestion that their repertoire should be extended to include more popular Chuck Berry and Bo Diddley songs and their line-up augmented by horns. The short-lived Cyril Davies All Stars included Long John Baldry and Jimmy Page alongside members of Screaming Lord Sutch's Savages! Following Davies' death, the All Stars, led by Long John Baldry, were renamed as the Hoochie Coochie Men, and included in their number a young Rod Stewart and a keyboard player by the name of Reg Dwight.

If Blues Incorporated was a southern blues incubator, the northern equivalent was John Mayall's Blues Breakers from Manchester. Like Blues Incorporated, the Blues Breakers was a fluid organisation, which attracted a string of important musicians. Eric Clapton joined in 1965 and was a key figure in their influential album, *Blues Breakers and Eric Clapton*. The debt to American bluesmen was clear – 'Ramblin' On My Mind'[17] (Robert Johnson), 'Steppin' Out' (Memphis Slim) and 'It Ain't Alright' (Little Walter) – but there were four of Mayall's compositions and a joint effort with Clapton ('Double Crossing Time'.) Clapton left almost immediately to form Cream, with Ginger Baker and Jack Bruce. His replacement, Peter Green, a gifted instrumentalist and singer/songwriter, became better known as a member of Fleetwood Mac.

Another influential early group was Geno Washington and the Ram Jam Band, which started playing in the early 1960s when Washington was stationed at RAF Bentwaters, Suffolk. Their repertoire was eclectic, including 'Que Sera Sera,' but mixed rhythm and blues and soul.[18] There were similarities between its music and the Rolling Stones, who were by far the most successful English band to emerge from the early '60s boom. Skiffle provided the entree to the blues for several members, Blues Incorporated offered a first opportunity to perform in public and in Brian Jones they had a wealth of information and records from which to develop their act. After a debut performance at the Marquee, they gained a residency at the Crawdaddy before going on their first tour. The line-up stabilised in 1963, after Bill Wyman and Charlie Watts joined, and they released their first record before undertaking a bigger national tour in the same year. In the early days they were, self-confessedly, imitative, with Chuck Berry ('Come On,' 'Bye Bye Johnny' and 'Carol'), Willie Dixon ('Route 66' and 'I Just Want to Make Love to You') and Muddy Waters ('I've Got My Mojo Working' and ''I Can't Be Satisfied') particular favourites, though this did not stop them drawing on other sources, (Lennon/McCartney 'Wanna Be Your Man' and Holly/Petty 'Not Fade Away,' for example) and including a few of their own compositions.[19]

Initial responses to British rhythm and blues bands in general were often negative, encapsulated in Sonny Boy Williams claim that 'they wanted to play blues so badly … and they did.' Allegations about 'white imposters' were part of an essentialist claim that only 'Negroes' could sing the blues.[20] As one critic in *Jazzbeat* bewailed, 'groups such as the Rolling Stones are taken seriously and … several thousand teen-age fans … believe they have heard some authentic rhythm and blues.'[21] Later judgements still referred to the 'whitened versions of African American rhythm-and-blues' offered by the Stones.[22] Precisely what is meant by 'whitening' remains unclear, but to move to a non-judgemental and dynamic view, the Stones can be seen as moving from imitation, through experimentation to the creation of a distinctive approach that made sense to them and their audience.[23] This was clear in their distinctive rendition of 'The Last Time' and especially 'Not Fade Away,' in which Buddy Holly met Bo Diddley in London.[24] Equally important were the experiments in song writing. While never matching Lennon/McCartney, the Jagger/Richards duo produce some important and successful songs, particularly 'I Can't Get No Satisfaction,' which was covered by both Otis Redding and Aretha Franklin.[25] Even more striking was the success that the Stones had in America, where interest in blues music had been in decline for several years. As part of the 'British Invasion,' British rhythm and blues bands rekindled an appreciation of a music and musicians who had sunk into obscurity. Muddy

Waters claimed that 'before them people [in America] didn't know anything about me ... Then the Rolling Stones and all those other English bands came along, playing this music, and now the kids are buying my records and listening to them.'[26] Although the Stones were to experiment (with mixed success) with other musical forms, they never totally abandoned their rhythm and blues roots and in 2016 produced a cover album, *Lonesome & Blue*, that featured songs by well-known figures, such as Little Walter, Willie Dixon and Howlin' Wolf, and lesser-known performers like Magic Sam and Eddie Taylor.

The Stones were not alone. The Yardbirds, who took over the residency at the Crawdaddy Club, drew heavily on Chicago blues singers, such as Howlin' Wolf and Muddy Waters. *Sonny Boy Williamson and the Yardbirds*, the album of the tour, was recorded in December 1963 at the Crawdaddy Club. *Five Live Yardbirds* was a cover album of well-known blues numbers, but the instrumental breaks allowed guitarist, Eric Clapton to show off his ability, particularly in duets with Keith Relf (harmonica) on 'Smokestack Lightening' and with Paul Samwell-Smith (bass guitar) on 'Here 'Tis.'[27] The Animals, with a distinctive singer in Eric Burdon and an equally outstanding keyboard player in Alan Price, produced a string of blues-inspired singles – 'Boom, Boom,' 'See See Rider' and especially 'House of the Rising Sun' – as well as a more upbeat version of Nina Simone's 'Don't Let Me Be Misunderstood' and Sam Cooke's 'Bring It On Home.'[28] Among other groups, Them, with another distinctive singer in Van Morrison, the Spencer Davis Group and the Moody Blues covered a range of blues standards, ('Dimples,' 'Bright Lights, Big City' and 'Route 66') with Motown songs and their own blues-influenced compositions. Similarly, the Small Faces, in their early work, were influenced by rhythm and blues. The success of groups such as this bear witness to the extent to which more mainstream pop music was being infiltrated, but this transition also created internal tensions. This was clearly seen in the career of Manfred Mann. The group had its origins in the Mann-Hugg Blues Band, which had backed Sonny Boy Williamson, with mixed success. Teaming up with Paul Jones, a good friend of Brian Jones of the Rolling Stones, as lead vocalist, they become Manfred Mann. Their first album, *The Five Faces of Manfred Mann*, contained blues numbers, such as 'Hoochie Coochie

Man' and 'I've Got My Mojo Working,' but their singles, ('5-4-3-2-1,' 'Do Wah Diddy Diddy' and 'Sha La La') were increasingly pop-oriented, which created tensions with Jones and bass-player Jack Bruce. Both left – Bruce to become a member of Cream, Jones to set up his own Blues Band.[29]

The height of the rhythm and blues boom was largely over by the late 1960s, though Fleetwood Mac, with the distinctive presence of Peter Green, proved to be almost as long-lived as the Stones. However, later groups, such as the Jam and Style Council, with Paul Weller as the common factor, even Squeeze acknowledge their (partial) debt to rhythm and blues. Jules Holland later formed his highly successful and influential Rhythm and Blues Orchestra in the 1980s, while Bill Wyman's Rhythm Kings have been touring since the early 1990s. More generally, elements of rhythm and blues migrated into much mainstream pop music, and, notwithstanding the fears of bastardization and the cries of dilution, popular music since the 1960s, has been profoundly influenced by it in its numerous commercial variants.

Soul Music – America hits back

One of the most interesting and important musical figures in Britain was Clive Powell, better known as Georgie Fame.[30] His route to prominence was in many respects unsurprising. Inspired by skiffle and early rock 'n' roll – from coffee bar juke boxes to Elvis on screen in 'Jailhouse Rock' and Buddy Holly live at the Ritz, Wigan – he played boogie-woogie piano in a local dance band, did a season at Butlins, before moving to London, gigging in various Soho pubs and clubs. His first breakthrough came with the Marty Wilde Big Beat Show, as backing pianist for the likes of Billy Fury and Dickie Pride. More importantly, during the 1960 Eddie Cochrane/Gene Vincent tour, he discovered the music of Ray Charles and switched to the Hammond organ. His second breakthrough came with a residency at the Flamingo Club in 1962, which was to last until 1965. There, and while on tour at various American military bases, such as Chicksands and Alconbury, and at northern clubs, such as the Twisted Wheel in Manchester, he encountered a range of musical influences. His first album, with the Blue Flames, *R & B At the Flamingo*, lived up to its title with tracks such as 'Baby Please Don't Go,' 'Parchman Farm' and 'Night Train' but also included Smokey Robinson's 'Shop Around.' By 1966 and the third album, *Sweet Things.* the soul influence was clear in versions of Sam Cooke's 'The Whole World's Shaking' and Rufus Thomas's 'The World Is Round.'[31] Even more strikingly, he was the only white artist on the 1965 Tamla Motown tour, headed by the Supremes and including Smokey Robinson and the Miracles, Martha and the Vandellas, the Earl Van Dyke Six and an almost unknown fifteen-year old by the name of Stevie Wonder. In fact, the tour was less than successful outside London venues but the mid-1960s still witnessed the growing popularity of soul music.

Soul music in America had emerged from an amalgam of gospel and rhythm and blues. Its roots went back to the days of slavery and the post-Civil War success of the Fisk Jubilee Singers, who toured Europe, visiting London in 1873, and regaling Victoria with songs such as 'Steal Away to Jesus' and 'Go Down Moses.'[32] It was a tradition that remained strong in the twentieth century. Groups such as 'The Blind Boys of Mississippi,' 'The Blind Boys of Alabama' and especially the Staple Singers were all prominent in black communities during the quarter century after the second world war. The crossover to secular and more mainstream, white music (and from this the crossover from America to Britain) was complex and problematic. Groups like the Drifters, originally a doo wop group with Clyde McPhatter as the lead singer, or solo singers such as Lavern Baker and Ruth Brown made some impact but the most important figure from the 1950s was Ray Charles, who combined jazz and blues but also country and western music.[33] It was, however, the Berry/Gordy Tamla Motown 'production line,' with its intention of giving a sense of black identity to ghetto kids, as well as making money, that churned out a stream of chart successes between 1964 and 1967 and made household names of the Supremes, Martha and the Vandellas, and Smokey Robinson and the Miracles.[34] Other key figures included Sam Cooke, whose musical career, aroused much criticism at times, despite his 'double-voiced' performances of what has been termed 'ethnically marked music.'[35] Problematic in a different way was the explicit support given to the civil rights movement by Nina Simone

('Mississippi Goddam') and Aretha Franklin (notably the chart success, 'Respect') and the assertion of black pride by James Brown (especially 'Say It Loud').[36] Although racial tensions were less apparent in Britain, it was difficult to divorce such singers and their music from wider racial politics.

Soul singers were not confined to American performers. Dusty Springfield, who started her career as a member of a folk-pop group, was a major figure in the popularisation of Motown. Several groups moved from rhythm and blues to soul – Georgie Fame and the Blue Flames, the Spencer Davis Group and the Small Faces – while the Jamaican duo, Bob and Marcia, took one of Nina Simone's better known songs, 'Young, Gifted and Black,' into the charts for ten weeks in spring 1970.[37] Further, imported soul records, the more obscure the better, were at the heart of the dance-oriented Northern Soul scene which encompassed not only well-known venues, such as Wigan Casino, The Twisted Wheel and Blackpool Mecca, but also The Shades in Northampton and The North Park Club in Kettering.[38]

The appeal of rhythm and blues and soul

The popularity of rhythm and blues and soul is clear but raises some interesting questions. Put simply: why should the music of troubled slaves on plantations in the southern states of ante-bellum America appeal to the relatively well-to-do youths of suburban Britain? How could the Mississippi Delta be relocated on the Thames, let alone the Tyne? That there was an appeal cannot be doubted. Ray Davies, Eric Clapton and John Steel, of the Animals, gave voice to a wider felt sense of identification.[39] Part of the attraction may have been found in that combination of fear and fascination that had helped blackface minstrelsy maintain its popularity. In that respect, the ante-bellum southern plantation construction offered a semi-sanitised and safe depiction. There was suffering in the songs, but it was less problematic and threatening for being in a different time and place. The argument should not be overstated[40]. In early-1960s Britain, there was an awareness of racial injustice and its victims, however idealistic and naïve in hindsight. The plight of Civil Rights marchers was to be seen on British television. Martin Luther King's campaign, notably his 'I Have A Dream' speech received wide media coverage as did his assassination. Similarly, Aretha Franklin and James Brown were high-profile figures, whose music was part of, not simply a backcloth to, the civil rights movement. Additionally, the scurrilous arguments, particularly in Smethwick, during the 1964 general election gave further immediacy to the issue of racism in England. It is easy to be dismissive of the white, suburban make up of rhythm and blues club members, but the post-war generation had grown up in a society that was more ethnically mixed than ever before. Paul Oliver, the highly-regarded writer on the blues, looking back on the 1960s from the vantage point of the 1990s , noted that 'the music of a segregated minority was a symbol of the gulf between themselves and the values and attitudes of their parents.[41]

The music provided one means of coming to terms with ethnically-mixed, post-imperial Britain, at a time when many members of older generations appeared (and indeed were) wedded to outmoded ideas of the Empire and its inferior races. Post-war changes, the accelerating loss of Empire, the humiliation of Suez, the Notting Hill riots and the growing number of New Commonwealth migrants gave rise to debates about the meaning of Englishness.[42] The comfortable sense of national identity and cohesion that grew out of the (often mythologised) experiences of the second world war was visibly crumbling in the 1950s and early 1960s. A range of commentators, often sympathetic to improving 'race relations', still shared a 'Them and Us' view of society, in which there were 'white' hosts and 'black' visitors, and in which the latter were expected to conform to the values and codes of behaviour of the former. Thanks in no small part to the 'People's War,' the white working-classes were no longer a 'race apart' and had been incorporated into the national community. The new 'race apart' were those immigrants from the Caribbean and south Asia who were clearly identified by the colour of their skins.[43] For many in the wartime and pre-war generations, for whom society had been overwhelmingly white, such formulations may have made sense, but for some of the post-war generations, growing up in a society that was becoming year-on-year more ethnically diverse, they did not. Over time shared musical interests helped foster a wider awareness of and sympathy for 'others' in society. Northern 'Soulies', irrespective of ethnicity, looking back from the 1990s, stressed friendliness and the way in which the scene provided a safe environment.[44] However, hindsight can sanitise the past. Welcoming new musical cultures did not necessarily bring acceptance of a new, more diverse society. Eric Clapton's oft-quoted drunken rant, in which he voiced his support for Enoch Powell, demonstrates that it was perfectly possible to like 'black' music but not like the presence of 'black' people in the country.[45]

There were also more immediate reasons for the popularity of rhythm and blues and soul that related to the novelty of the music and the experience of clubs and concerts. In an age when pop music seemed dominated by safe but homogenised music, from the post rock 'n' roll Cliff Richard to Adam Faith, not to mention Bobby Vee, there was something raw, and therefore seemingly authentic, about the sound of John Mayall and Cyril Davies or Ray Charles and Aretha Franklin. There was something exciting about the guitar driven rhythm and blues of the Yardbirds and a depth of feeling to the singing of Georgie Fame. There was something spontaneous about the performance of Mick Jagger or James Brown. Paul Oliver's conclusion that rhythm and blues was music to dance to was fundamentally correct.[46] In fact, part of the attraction, contrary to the belief that blues was simply about suffering, was that the music and the lyrics, blues and soul alike, encompassed a range of emotions, including not least unashamed pleasure.

Some concluding observations

The growing interest in the blues and the subsequent rhythm and blues boom, and soul, more so than the advent of ragtime and jazz, had a major impact on popular music in this country. Arguments about 'authenticity,' interesting for the light they throw on contemporary attitudes, obscure the fact that the mid-1960s in particular saw, a period of initial imitation, experimentation and development of a distinctive British approach that embraced rhythm and blues and soul. These developments were part of a wider and complex African musical diaspora that links parts of Africa, Europe and America, and the Caribbean. London particularly, but also Liverpool, Birmingham and Manchester, were important meeting places for differing musical traditions in which the complex reworking of other music by the dominant culture created 'a circuit of production and exchange.'[47] Further, from a more individual perspective, this experimentation and evolution was part of longer career trajectory, not necessarily involving a return to blues roots, and embracing other musical genres, notably soul but also ska, from which was created a multi-faceted 'alternative authenticity,' rather than imitation of other cultures, which defied simple categorisation.[48] More broadly, the involvement with different musical cultures from African, African-American and African Caribbean sources was part of a process of adjustment whereby *all* generations had to confront questions of identity, and to which we now turn.

Endnotes

1. Mezz Mezzrow, "Blues are the pattern for authentic jazz,' *Melody Maker*, 27 March 1948, p.2 cited in R F Schwartz, *How Britain Got the Blues: The Transmission and Reception of American Blues Style in the United Kingdom*, Abingdon, Routledge, 2016, p.21
2. Billy Bragg notes that 'Rock Island Line' was not written by Lead Belly, the line itself didn't go to New Orleans and there were no toll gates but, other than that, there was nothing wrong. B Bragg, *Roots, Radicals and Rockers: How Skiffle Changed the World*, London, Faber &Faber, 2017, p.3
3. Technically their importation remained illegal until 1960.
4. Production was limited to 99 copies to avoid the imposition of Purchase Tax, at 33.3 per cent on imprints of 100 or more.
5. AFN and Radio Luxembourg played more blues music, but the extent should not be overstated.
6. Dupree was an important popularizer, especially in the north of England, where he lived (Halifax) and played in local pubs and clubs for about a decade from the mid-1960s to the mid-1970s.
7. Cited in Schwartz, *How Britain Got the Blues*, p.150. The band in question was the Yardbirds.
8. The tours continued in Europe until 1985. The British venues included predictable places – London Hammersmith, Manchester Free Trade Hall and, with no sense of irony, the Colston Hall, Bristol. In addition to the major English cities (Bradford, Newcastle, Leicester, Birmingham, and Sheffield) performances were also held in Bournemouth, Boston, Darlington, Hemel Hempstead and Sunderland.
9. Victoria Spivey, aka Queen Victoria, was a talented multi-instrumentalist, singer and dancer whose recording career lasted from the mid-1920s to the

early 1960s. Among her accompanists on record were Louis Armstrong, Lonnie Johnson and (in 1962) Bob Dylan. For her performance on *I Hear the Blues* see https://www.youtube.com/watch?v=Gnqi5b5CAvw

10   From his first tour in 1951 Big Bill Broonzy was more than happy to play up to an 'authentic' image, being billed as 'one of the great Mississippi Delta Men,' even though, as several commentators have noted, his playing style had more in common with Texas bluesmen, such as Blind Lemon Jefferson. Authenticity claims could create problems. An attempt to produce an album of Lead Belly songs by John Lee Hooker collapsed when it transpired that he did not know any Lead Belly songs! For the construction of Lead Belly as the paradigmatic bluesman, see R Cole, 'Mastery and Masquerade in the Transatlantic Blues Revival,' *Journal of the Royal Musical Association*, 143(1), 2018, pp.173-210, at p.180. More generally, Cole stresses how the blues revival 'forced African American artists into assuming the mask of black face minstrelsy,' at p.174

11   The same could be said of the construction of Jimi Hendrix's image with its highly sexualised and wild traits.

12   Cole, 'Mastery and Masquerade' especially pp.184-7

13   Review of John Lee Hooker 'Hoogie Boogie' b/w 'Whistlin' and Moanin' Blues' in *Melody Maker* 24 May 1952 cited in Schwartz, *How Britain Got the Blues*, p.56

14   Albert McCarthy was a well informed and well-regarded jazz and blues critic who edited several specialist publications in the 1940s and 1950s.

15   The 1964 festival saw Memphis Slim, Jimmy Witherspoon and Mose Allison perform alongside (among others) the Rolling Stones, Manfred Mann, the Yardbirds (including Eric Clapton), Georgie Fame and the Blue Flames and the Graham Bond Organisation.

16   https://www.youtube.com/watch?v=STjn0ZM5JiI

17   https://www.youtube.com/watch?v=qEhjcqzdoxU

18   'J Stratton, 'Melting Point: The Making of British Black Music in the 1950s and 1960s' pp.27 -45 at p.36 in J Stratton and N Zuberi, eds., *Black Popular Music in Britain Since 1945*, Abingdon, Routledge, 2014

19   For 'Come On' see https://www.youtube.com/watch?v=-OLkVbDA3OQ and 'I Just Want to Make Love to You' https://www.youtube.com/watch?v=UV7aIJs4NFk

20   The singing of Long John Baldry and Eric Burdon showed that at least some white men could sing the blues.

21   Cited in Schwartz, *How Britain Got the Blues*, p.142. Interestingly in an interview with *Melody Maker* (2 May 1964) Jagger was quite explicit: '… don't listen to us. Listen to the men [sic] who inspire us.' And asked: 'Why get your information second-hand when it's fairly easy to buy it new?' Similarly, Keith Richards described the early Stones as 'a white London imitation of South Side Chicago blues.' Cited in D Allen, 'Feelin' bad this morning: why the *British* blues? *Popular Music*, 26(1), 2007, pp.141-156 at p.143.

22   J Stratton, 'Popular Music, Race and Identity,' *The Sage Handbook of Popular Music*, London, Sage, 2015, pp.381-400 at p.395. Stratton specifically refers to a version of 'Poison Ivy' by the Australian band, Billy Thorpe and the

Aztecs who 'whitened the Rolling Stone's whitened version of the original.' Thorpe's version is clearly pop but the difference between the Stones and the Coasters is less obvious. For Thorpe's version see https://www.youtube.com/watch?v=WrHoEx7cpDM, the Stones at https://www.youtube.com/watch?v=h9rTWPsJh6o&list=RDh9rTWPsJh6o&start_radio=1&t=8 and the Coasters at https://www.youtube.com/watch?v=ZRfRITVdz4k

23 Interesting J Stratton elsewhere makes the point that the Stones were 'trying to make sense of the music and utilise it for a different cultural purpose.' Stratton, 'Melting Point' pp.27 -45 at p.35.

24 For the original version by the Crickets see https://www.youtube.com/watch?v=NN2L84dvoag, and the Stones at https://www.youtube.com/watch?v=gIKfN3CuFXA. The debt to Bo Diddley can be seen via https://www.youtube.com/watch?v=7XsSQG6GDrQ

25 The Stones at https://www.youtube.com/results?search_query=i+can%27t+get+no+satisfaction+the+rolling+stones, Otis Redding at https://www.youtube.com/watch?v=CpmZWUPrCgo and Aretha Franklin at https://www.youtube.com/watch?v=3r4rsp_1NQ0

26 Cited in Allen, 'Feelin' bad this morning,' p.143

27 For 'Smokestack Lightning' see https://www.youtube.com/watch?v=1IHrXlxoWKU and 'Here 'Tis' https://www.youtube.com/watch?v=AdBWokA8Hjc

28 For 'House of the Rising Sun' https://www.youtube.com/watch?v=0Fy7opKu46c, 'Don't Let Me Be Misunderstood' https://www.youtube.com/watch?v=Bw7RTUEZMyg and 'Bring It On Home' https://www.youtube.com/watch?v=8EoS7GDSu0U

29 For 'Hoochie Coochie Man' see https://www.youtube.com/watch?v=SYK2vO_S1XA. Compare with 'Do Wah Diddy Diddy' https://www.youtube.com/watch?v=43vOAw2sAFU and 'Sha La La' https://www.youtube.com/watch?v=Xz2CXDFmz5w

30 The following paragraph draws heavily on K Gildert, *Images of England Through Popular Music: Class, Youth and Rock 'n' Roll, 1955-1976*, Basingstoke, Palgrave, 2013, chapters 2 and 3.

31 Baby Please Don't Go https://www.youtube.com/watch?v=TiAN8rAqYgg and The Whole World's Shaking https://www.youtube.com/watch?v=5vG0sISL9QY

32 Fisk College was established in Nashville after the Civil War by the American Missionary Association and its touring choir was a crucial source of funds. Even before this, interest in gospel music had seen the publication of 'Slave Songs of the United States' in 1867, which included 'Roll Jordan Roll,' Jacob's Ladder' and 'Deep River.'

33 In particular, the two-volumed *Modern Sounds in Country & Western Music*, 1962 had a major impact on both sides of the Atlantic, as a black man sang the white music of Hank Williams (for example, 'Take These Chains From My Heart' and 'Your Cheatin' Heart') and Don Gibson, ('I Can't Stop Loving You') to a lush orchestral sound and backing singers.

34 For example, Supremes 'Baby Love' https://www.youtube.com/watch?v=9_y6nFjoVp4 Martha and the Vandellas 'Dancing in the Streets' https://

www.youtube.com/watch?v=CdvITn5cAVc Other groups include the Marvelettes, who had the first Motown number 1.
35 M Burford, 'Sam Cooke as Pop Album Artist – A Reinvention in Three Albums,' *Journal of the American Musicology Society*, 65(1), 2012, pp.113-78
36 Mississippi Goddam https://www.youtube.com/watch?v=LJ25-U3jNWM Respect https://www.youtube.com/watch?v=6FOUqQt3Kg0 Say It Loud https://www.youtube.com/watch?v=9bJA6W9CqvE
37 At https://www.youtube.com/watch?v=ubDVUQon5BE
38 See D Nowell, *The Story of Northern Soul*, London, Portico, 2015
39 M Doyle, *The Kinks: Songs of the Semi-Detached*, Reaktion Books, London, 2020, pp. 32, 51-2
40 Cole, for example, talks of 'vicarious identity politics' among white fans. for whom 'a primitive racialized alterity [was] a perfect antidote to the flourishing mass consumerism of the so-called affluent society,' 'Mastery and Masquerade,' p.196.
41 P. Oliver *Story of the Blues*, London, Pimlico, 1997, p.193 cited in Allan, 'Feelin' bad this morning,' p.144,
42 Britishness and Englishness were often used interchangeably – by the English. Even in the 1950s, there was a growing awareness of distinctive Scottish, Welsh and Irish identities, though the latter was considerably complicated by the existence of a border on the island of Ireland and a community in the north that often seemed more British than the British.
43 C Waters, '"Dark Strangers" in Our Midst: Discourses of Race and Nation in Britain, 1947-1963,' *Journal of British Studies,* 36(20, 1997, pp.207-38
44 L Back, 'Voices of Hate, Sounds of Hybridity: Black Music and the Complexities of Racism,' *Black Music Research Journal*, 20(2), 2000, pp.127-49
45 See also Back, 'Voices of Hate' and the discussion of skinhead reggae.
46 Oliver, *Story of the Blues*, p.193
47 Stratton, 'Melting Point,' especially p.28. Stratton draws heavily on P Gilroy, *The black Atlantic: modernity and double consciousness*, London, Verso, 1993
48 Allen, 'Feelin' bad this morning,' p.154

'Islands in the Sun': Calypso to reggae

> This town (town) is coming like a ghost town
> All the clubs have been closed down
> This place (town) is coming like a ghost town
> Bands won't play no more
> Too much fighting on the dance floor
>
> The Specials, 'Ghost Town,'

PARTICULARLY SINCE THE turn of the twentieth century, popular music in England had been influenced by various musical innovations from America. African-American musicians had been seen in a variety of venues and media, but they were essentially visitors. The advent of African-Caribbean music was fundamentally different. Migrants from the various islands came over, particularly after the second world war, bringing with them their musical traditions. Not since the mass immigration of the Irish in the mid-nineteenth century, had there been a similar cultural importation. In both cases, there were initially two broadly defined, but not undifferentiated, communities – host and immigrant – but, with the passing of time, greater social interaction, including marriages, blurred the distinction and created a more complex society, which raised crucial questions of individual and collective identity. What did it mean to be black and British? What did Britishness mean in a multi-cultural country?

African Caribbean music and dance had a profound impact on English popular music. Musicians attracted to and experimenting with different musical forms, and entrepreneurs looking for new commercial opportunities facilitated its dissemination. Demand was fundamental and there was a growing and diverse market for popularised versions of ska and reggae, for Jimmy Cliff and Bob Marley, Steel Pulse and Aswad, the Beat and the Specials, let alone Madness and UB40. As a consequence, music which was once denounced and derided, as boring, repetitive or worse, became one of the major influences on late-twentieth century popular music. However, this cultural intermixing and development of new musical forms was intimately related to wider social changes, in part responding to, in part shaping them.

Sound systems

Sound systems, developed in post-war Jamaica as a response to particular circumstances, were established in England in the mid-1950s and retained their importance through the following decades. With their distinctive bass sound and DJ/record-based culture, they were, in many respects, at the top of the musical hierarchy.[1] Considerable attention has been focussed on London, with its various competing sound systems, but they were to be found in every African Caribbean community across the country, in the big cities (Birmingham, Bristol, Leeds and Manchester) but also the smaller towns (Huddersfield, Reading and Wolverhampton). Records, imported from Jamaica or licensed from abroad, were central, with novelty, especially pre-releases, at a premium. Equally important was the role of the DJ. In the intimate atmosphere of the dance hall, DJs and audience were not simply physically close but also interacting. There was an opportunity to comment on their lived experience and in a language of their own. Patois, precisely because it was not received English, was a powerful way of articulating grievances, making sense of a hostile and otherwise incomprehensible world, and developing an individual and collective sense of pride and worth. Sound systems became sites of self-awareness, resistance and protest.

Calypso: Lord Kitchener, Harry Belafonte ... and Lance Percival

Insofar as Caribbean music was known in immediate post-war England, it was Trinidad and calypso that came to mind. Trinidad had a distinctive, Catholic carnival tradition and its music evolved out of a variety of influences from European quadrilles, Venezuelan string bands and Cuban *son*, not to mention American rhythm and blues later.[2] Furthermore, calypso and protest went together, not least since the 1940s with anti-Americanism and the growing demands for independence.[3] However, from the carefully choreographed arrival of Lord Kitchener on the *Windrush* in 1948, with his newly-written 'London is the place for me,' through the celebration of West Indian cricket success, such as 'Cricket, Lovely Cricket,' (1950), to the appearance of the Trinidadian All Steel Percussion Orchestra at the 1951 Festival of Britain celebrations, an image for public consumption was created of fun-loving but essentially harmless (almost childlike) musicians.[4] This was deceptive – and largely deliberately so. There was a tradition of innuendo that shocked broadcasters and politicians. Marie Bryant's 'Don't Touch Me Nylons' was banned by the BBC and had Lt. Col. Marcus Lipton asking questions in parliament about 'indecent records.'[5] More importantly, there were a range of calypsos that dealt with the more mundane realities of life. 'Nora,' for example, was the lament of a homesick Trinidadian about to abandon London. The affable Lord Kitchener was highly critical of racially prejudiced London. 'The complexion of your face/Cannot hide you from the negro race.' Thus, he sang, in a mixture of sadness and bitterness, 'You can never get away from the fact / if you're not white you're black.'[6] Similarly, in 'If You're Brown,' he lamented, 'if you're white well everything's all right/If your skin is dark, no use, you try/You got to suffer until you die.' There was also defiance, not least in the independence song 'Black Power' with its demand for 'black dignity' and a chorus repeatedly echoing 'black power.' Lord Invader's response to the 1958 riots was also unambiguous:[7] 'Teddy Boy Calypso (Bring Back the Cat O Nine)'.

Such songs were heard by a minority. Cheerful calypsos might be heard at the Café Royal and the Hurlingham Club, and steel pans at an Oxford Commemoration ball, but the overall 'white' audience was limited.[8] In English popular music, calypso owed more to the Jamaican-American, Harry

Belafonte, dubbed the 'King of Calypso,' despite the fact (which he freely acknowledged) that he had never won a competition for either road song or tent song in Trinidad. Indeed, his calypso owed more to Jamaican mento. Nonetheless, a series of records – 'Island in the Sun,' 'Matilda,' 'Banana Boat Song' and 'Jamaica Farewell' – established his name in both Britain and America.[9] Calypso was a short-lived craze, briefly reappearing in comic form with Bernard Cribbins' 'Gossip Calypso' and Lance Percival's 'Woe Is Me (Shame and Scandal in the Family)', both of which were minor chart hits.[10] Probably the biggest, but unrecognised, calypso chart hit was a version of a song recorded by the Mighty Dictator and, later the Duke of Iron. Johnny Duncan's version of 'Last Train To San Fernando,' however, is remembered as a bluegrass number.[11]

The most lasting legacy of Trinidadian carnival, was the Notting Hill Carnival, which came be traced back to an indoor (and televised) *Caribbean Carnival* in 1959, organised by Claudia Jones, following the Notting Hill Riots of the previous year.[12] As well as the Trinidad All Stars and Hi Fi steel bands, the carnival featured the Trinidadian calypso singer, Mighty Terror, whose repertoire was varied. His popular 'Chinese Children Call Me Daddy,' referring to an affair his wife had had, was deemed obscene in some quarters, while 'Patricia Gone with Millicent' was shocking for its subject matter, lesbianism, but in 'Negro Know Thyself,' which he had recorded in the early 1950s, he made clear that 'negro people must all unite ... [to] save ourselves from iniquity.'[13] His presence in the 1959 'Caribbean Carnival' was an important signifier of an emerging sense of black identity in an often openly racist society, but the impact of calypso in England was relatively short-lived. Trinidadian music was soon to be overwhelmed by ska, rocksteady and reggae from Jamaica.

Ska

The emergence of ska in early-1960s Jamaica was dramatic. It grew out of restricted access to the American music market, rivalry between competing sound systems and entrepreneurial flair.[14] Theophilus Beckford's 'Easy Snappin' was recorded in 1959 and a year later the seminal 'O Carolina' by the Folkes brothers, featured the drumming of the Rastafarian Count

Ossie, was released.[15] Within a short space of time individuals, such as Prince Buster, Jimmy Cliff and Desmond Dekker, and groups, such as the Maytals and the Skatalites were producing records which were heard, not simply in Jamaica but also in England. Although often seen as less political than reggae or calypso, there was social comment in Derrick Morgan's 'Starvation' or the Maytals 'Tough Times' and political comment in Skatalites 'Independence Ska.' With a (relatively) large market, especially in London, a network of specialist retail shops sprang up and, more importantly, the new music was heard in cafes, dance halls, at house parties and in clubs via the distinctive sound systems.[16] As Jah Vego, of the People's Record Store in Ladbroke Grove, observed, 'so many places ... wouldn't let black men in. So we have to do our own thing, keeping dances in houses, in basements, in the shebeens, or in school dinner halls.' The absence of any available big hall effectively necessitated the growth of the sound system business.[17]

Ska, with its links to Rude Boy culture in downtown Kingston, was successful in Jamaica, but its impact in England was less apparent. The BBC showed as little interest in ska as it had in calypso, arguably less, and its production and distribution was confined to small independent labels and retailers. On the few occasions that a ska (or ska-light) record appeared in the charts, it was as a novelty number. The idiosyncratic Migil 5 had a top-ten hit with a bluebeat version of 'Mockin' Bird Hill' in 1964. Almost at the same time, the Jamaican-born Milly (Small) reached number two in the charts with 'My Boy Lollipop.'[18] A lightweight, feel-good song that played into the 'black as exotic' trope, it is nonetheless of interest for two reasons. Firstly, it highlighted the movement of songs between America, the Caribbean and England. Chris Blackwell, looking to create a mass market for commercialised ska, took a 1950s American rhythm and blues number and transformed it into a commercial success.[19] Secondly, it pointed to emerging awareness of new musical genres. Millie was backed by an all-white group, the Five Dimensions, which included Georgie Fame. At a time when there were few opportunities to hear ska outside immigrant communities, he was experimenting with ska and playing with a range of African and African-Caribbean musicians at the Flamingo and Roaring Twenties clubs. Fame played with Prince Buster on 'Wash, Wash' and the latter's 'Al Capone' sealed the link with Mod subculture, as white 'Rude Boys' emerged in London. Fame was by far the most serious and most able English exponent of ska.[20]

By the mid-1960s ska lost much of its popularity in Jamaica. Rocksteady, briefly, and reggae became dominant. Ska retained a following among black Britons, but it was increasingly seen as 'old man's music' by a generation born in England, many of whom looked to roots reggae. Before looking at this, Two Tone and the ska revival of the late 1970s/early 1980s needs to be considered.

Two Tone and the ska revival

Two Tone emerged in the late-1970s, in part a reaction against 'heavier,' and more exclusionary roots reggae. It was music to dance to for people who 'want to jump around a bit.'[21] There was also a commercial incentive to create a larger market that encompassed black and white audiences. Additionally, there was a wider, social and political aspiration, which grew out of new experiences. Particularly in inner-city locations, such as Handsworth or Brixton, the generation born in the early and mid-1960s had grown up in an ethnically and culturally mixed community, in a way that their parents had not. From this arose a desire to find a common voice, particularly for black and white working-class youths, at a time of increasing racial hostility. The Selecter's singer, Pauline Black observed clear in an early interview in 1979: "We like to give people something to dance to and enjoy themselves. They can listen to the words, listen to the beat.' As she later stated, 'you're here to dance and then to think.'[22] The Two-Tone record label logo summed the multiracial ideal of black and white, separate but adjacent and connected. So too did the mixed race (and gender) line-ups of the Selecter, the Specials and the Beat. As Ranking Roger, of the Beat, made clear: 'All you got to do is to look on stage and you see unity.'[23] Madness, the only all-white band on the Two Tone label, also aspired to this ideal – though not without problems as the result of some of their followers – as did, a little later, UB40.

A significant element in their repertoires were tributes to earlier ska and reggae stars. The Specials first album, for example contained covers of Toots and the Maytals' 'Monkey Man,' the Skatalites 'You're Wondering Now' and Dandy Livingstone's 'A Message to You, Rudy.' There was, as several media observers noted, social and political commentary on aspects of contemporary society.[24] They addressed a range of social problems, notably the soul-destroying nature of work, or of the lack of it, as in the Beat's 'Get A Job,' or giving voice to a more generalised despair, as in the Selecter's 'Time Hard,' and especially, the Specials' 'Ghost Town.' There was a clear political dimension to their music, most explicitly in the Beat's 'Stand Down Margaret.' However, their principal focus was on the various manifestations of racism, from violence on the streets to police harassment. One of the starkest songs was 'Concrete Jungle,' by the Specials, in which 'animals are after me … it ain't safe on the streets.' Thus, 'I have to carry a knife because there's people threatening my life' and 'I can't dress the way I want I'm being chased by the National Front. In 'It's up to you' they made clear that there was a choice to be made. For 'Black' and 'White' the choice was 'Unite! It's up to you, or fight!' Or, in 'It doesn't make it right,' just because you're black or white 'it doesn't mean you've got to hate him/It doesn't mean you have to fight/It doesn't make it alright.' Not dissimilar was the Beat's 'Monkey Murder.' Their involvement in Rock Against Racism and the Anti-Nazi League was the logical outcome.

For a brief period between late 1978 and 1981, Two Tone attracted much attention. The Selecter, the Beat and the Specials had several chart hits, the latter's included 'Ghost Town,' which topped the charts for three weeks in July 1981.[25] There were a few television appearances in which ska provided the sound backdrop. BBC's *Play For Today* on 26 October 1982. Leslie Stewart's, *Three Minute Heroes*, was not well-received by the critics but brought a new audience into contact with the music.[26] There were also two major Two Tone tours in 1979 and 1980, though they gained a degree of notoriety as a result of violence at some gigs. The Two-Tone dream never fully materialised, particularly in the short run. Its popularity reflected an 'unprecedented degree of rapport that had built up between black and white youths,' but, without doubting the sincerity of Pauline Black, Ranking Roger and others, there was a naivety about their approach and a failure to appreciate changes in part of the anticipated audience. Their gigs were attended by well-intentioned white people and the musicians themselves genuinely believed they could bring together black and white youths, but the anticipated common ground was an illusion and the ska revival petered out in the early 1980s.[27] In the longer term, the Two-Tone bands remained on the road. There were changes in both personnel and repertoire, notably the rapping of the re-formed Beat's Ranking Junior, but the basic approach – music to dance to and lyrics to think about – continued and appealed not only to their fans from the 1970s but also to younger generations, some of whom had not been born at the time of the original tours.

Reggae

Ska's popularity in Jamaica was relatively short-lived. The Skatalites disbanded in 1965 and, fortuitously, the ska beat slowed during the summer heatwave in 1966. More important were new influences from American soul to Latin American dance rhythms.[28] With greater emphasis on the electric bass guitar and its clear rhythm, and with more socially and politically aware lyrics, rocksteady appeared in 1967. The following year Toots and the Maytals released 'Do the Reggay.'[29] Desmond Dekker, Jimmy Cliff and particularly the Wailers became the face of Jamaican music across the world. Without downplaying the appeal of music and lyrics, the dramatic growth of reggae owed much to entrepreneurial zeal, notably in the person of Chris Blackwell.

The popularity of reggae, especially among the young, second generation African Caribbean people, was considerable, but existed largely below the radar of the BBC and the pop charts. Independent record retailers distributed imports from Jamaica and independent labels developed in England. As with ska, the sound system was central, at house parties and in various clubs across the country.[30] In mid-April 1969, Desmond Dekker and the Aces reached number one with 'The Israelites' and followed this with another chart hit, 'It Mek.' In the summer months, Max Romeo's 'Wet Dream' fluctuated up and down the charts before reaching number 10 in mid-August, despite (or perhaps because of) a ban by the BBC, while the Pioneer's 'Long Shot Kick De Bucket' and

Jimmy Cliff's 'Wonderful World, Beautiful People' were both chart hits from October through to December.[31] Reggae had arrived and so too had Trojan records.[32] Between 1968 and 1971 a series of pop reggae albums and singles were produced by the label, including Dave and Ansell Collins, 'Double Barrel' and Bob and Marcia 'Young Gifted and Black.'

In the 1970s reggae became a world-wide phenomenon with Bob Marley as its poster-boy. Variously known as the Wailing Wailers or the Wailing Rudeboys, the Wailers were well-known in Jamaica and had progressed from ska, through rocksteady to reggae.[33] Changes in personnel led to a renaming as Bob Marley and the Wailers, but more importantly there was a change of style and tempo with a clear eye on commercial success. They were greatly helped by Chris Blackwell and Island Records.[34] The 1973 tour deliberately included several universities (Essex, Lancaster, Manchester and York) and polytechnics (Hatfield, Leicester and North Staffordshire) and one education college (Middleton St George) as well as an appearance on *The Old Grey Whistle Test* on BBC2, to broaden appeal. An elaborate marketing strategy was developed and refined. The early Wailers-as-rebels, associated with 'Catch a Fire' and 'Burnin'' became a more 'hip' image by the time of (the renamed) 'Natty Dread.'[35] The 1975 tour proved to be the breakthrough and was confirmed by the chart success of the single 'No Woman, No Cry.'[36] Although criticised in some quarters for making musical compromises, there can be little doubt that Marley brought reggae to the attention of a wider audience than ever before, including many who then went on to explore its roots.[37]

In all, there were seven tours and linked albums and singles, from *Catch a Fire* and *Burnin'* both 1973, to *Uprising*. 1980. Among the tracks released were 'I Shot the Sherriff' and 'Get Up, Stand Up,' (1973), ''No Woman No Cry' and 'Revolution,' (1974), 'Exodus,' 'Three Little Birds' and 'One Love/People Get Ready,' (1974), ''Is This Love?' (1978) and 'Redemption Song,' (1980). Marley's impact in terms of chart success was mixed. On the one hand, there were seven top ten records but his most successful singles, 'One Love' and 'Buffalo Soldier' were issued after his death; as was his only number one album, *Legend*. Nonetheless, the album *Exodus* enjoyed sustained success being in the charts for over a year, though ironically, Eric Clapton achieved a top ten hit with 'I Shot the Sherriff.' However, the impact of Marley and the Wailers cannot be measured simply in terms of chart successes. His message, which denounced oppression, encouraged resistance but called for unity, found a wide audience. His voice, both melodic and sincere, his passionate involvement in politics, and a series of well-honed publicity campaigns turned him into an important cult figure. The extent to which inner-city black youths in London, Birmingham or Manchester identified with the idea of a return to Africa is debatable, but his references to Babylon spoke to many black youths who saw themselves as being in internal exile in the land of their birth. He also appealed to alienated white working-class youth, offering a more inclusive vision than that found in roots reggae.

It was a measure of the growing popularity of reggae that the BBC, belatedly and (with the exception of John Peel) reluctantly started to broadcast it, albeit more on local stations, such as Radio London (*Reggae Time*) and Radio Birmingham (*Reggae, Reggae*). Pirate stations, notably Capital Radio, especially David Rodigan's *Roots Rockers* show, London Weekend Radio, the People's Community Radio Link (Birmingham) and Dread Broadcasting Corporation, the first black-owned radio station, were more important in bringing reggae to a wider audience from the 1970s onwards.

While the growing popularity of reggae in general terms is beyond doubt, there were important internal tensions and divisions. Marley's commercialised reggae was rejected by those, for whom King Tubby, Big Youth, Burning Spear, Black Uhuru and the Gladiators were seen as more authentic. On the other hand, the increasingly macho roots reggae, and sporadic incidence of violence, alienated others who looked more to 'sweet' reggae and the soul scene, particularly in the person of Aretha Franklin. With James Brown and Stevie Wonder, she was linked with the civil rights movement in America and heightened awareness of the plight of the African diaspora.[38]

British reggae

The popularity of Jamaican-born ska and reggae musicians acted as a stimulus to British-born bands, though there was a persistent belief that, almost by definition, British reggae was inferior. The experience of racism, whether in the form of police harassment, educational exclusion or above-average unemployment, the sense of being in exile made Jamaican-imported reggae attractive in the first place and provided stimuli to the development of distinctive British forms of reggae.

Aswad, Misty in Roots and Matumbi all came from London, but there was considerable variation between them. The more commercialised, reggae light of the latter brought them an appearance on Top of the Pops and a minor hit, 'Point of View,' in October 1979. This contrasted with the Rastafarianism of Misty in Roots' 1979 album, *Live at the Counter Eurovision*, which included 'Ghetto of the City' and 'How Long, Jah.' Aswad were the most prolific and best known of the three, having first come to notice as the backing band on Burning Spear's *Live* album in 1977. In songs like 'Back to Africa' (1980), they echoed the Garveyite pan-Africanism of Burning Spear. 'Africa is her name/A place where we'll be free once again.' There was an imperative to 'Free ourselves from all persecution/Got to get free from this wicked Babylon.' Other songs, 'Three Babylon,' 'It's Not Our Wish (That We Should Fight)' and 'Sons of Criminals' were more focused on immediate problems but there was the same sense of suffering and alienation.[39]

Much the same could be said of the Birmingham-based Steel Pulse, who in the late-1970s and early-1980s released several hard-hitting singles and albums. There is anger in 'Ku Klux Klan,' where 'I come face to face with my foe/disguised in violence from head to toe.' There is contempt for the cowardice of the KKK but also a determination to act: 'do as they do/In this case hate thy neighbour.' 'Babylon' is the source of ruin where 'the hustlers of life have hooked and drained you from the man … you used to be' but the answer is to 'return Rastaman, where you came from/The land of your fathers.' In the unambiguously titled, 'Babylon Makes the Rules,' those in charge make 'my people suffer … my people are in a mess but nobody wants to know.' There is frustration, 'count the times we've been let down,' but also defiance. 'We must recapture our culture.' The most damning critique comes in 'Handsworth Revolution.' Deprivation, 'phoney laws' and hatred are all that Babylon brings. 'Cause there is still hunger/ Innocent convicted/Poor wage, hard labour/Only Babylon prosper and humble suffer.' But 'blessed with the power of Jah Creator/We will get stronger and we will conquer,' and the song ends 'Handsworth Revolution.' Finally, in 'Tribute to the Martyrs' the idea of being part of a wide-ranging historical struggle is made clear. As well as referencing Martin Luther King and Malcom X, Marcus [Garvey] and [Steve] Biko, the song also praises Toussaint L'Ouverture, the leader of the successful slave rising in Haiti that led to independence in 1804. Mention is also made of the Morant Bay rebellion of 1865, the brutal suppression of which left a lasting and powerful legacy in Jamaican popular culture.

The existence of a distinctive British reggae was even more apparent in the 1980s with the emergence of DJs associated with the Saxon sound system in Lewisham, London. Among the more successful were Tippa Irie, ('Complain Neighbour,' 'Police Officer,' 'Don't Like Police,' 'Hello Darling,) and Smiley Culture ('Cockney Translation,' and 'Roots Reality'). 'Cockney Translation' starts as if it were a dictionary:

> Say Cockney fire shooter. We bus' gun
> Cockney say tea leaf. We just say sticks man

but it progresses to something more

> Cockney say grass. We say outformer man ...
> Cockney says Old Bill we say dutty Babylon ...

Significantly, neither speak received English, both exist outside mainstream society, but, whereas Rasta culture was essentially exclusive, here was a black British identity that could be inclusive, at least with other sub-cultures. In that respect, there was a continuity of aspiration with the Two-Tone bands previously discussed.

Lovers' Rock

Even at the height of roots reggae in England, a significant number of young black people either did not identify with it, or openly rejected it, looking for an alternative in 'sweet' reggae or soul. For many second-generation African Caribbean youths, Motown meant more than Marley. Janet Kay enjoyed reggae 'but didn't feel part of the Rastafari movement, of roots and back to Africa … I didn't feel it related to my life and my surroundings.'[40] Lovers' Rock, a fusion of soul and reggae, emerged in the mid-1970s with Louise Mark's 'Caught You in A Lie.' Its first major chart hit was Janet Kay's 'Silly Games,' in 1979, but it can be traced back to earlier romantic rocksteady and reggae singers. Despite its debt to Philadelphia and Kingston, there was a distinctive British flavour and it was very much the music of a British-born black generation.[41] Initially associated with south London, it found adherents across the country, notably in Birmingham, Bristol and Leeds; and, again, it was the sound systems in clubs and dance halls that guaranteed its popularity.

The disconnect with roots reggae, itself developing a harder edge, has been explained partly in class terms – a middle-class, suburban rejection of disreputable reggae culture and an inner-city, working-class move to hip-hop – and partly in gender terms, a rejection of hyper-masculine reggae for a more feminised form, Lovers' Rock. The dance hall was a heavily masculine venue, with the selecters' cry of 'Ladies a your time now!'[42] For some women there was 'Rasta-for-*him*, not Rasta-for-I.'[43] However, Lovers' Rock was more than a 'female sanctuary.' By capturing the extent to which emotional turmoil was an issue for black men as well as women, it appealed to and was performed by both men and women. Beshara, 'Men Cry Too/Man A Reason,' a chart hit in 1981, openly challenged the notion that 'true' men never cry. Further, in Lovers' Rock, the erotic and loving complemented the political rather than standing in contradistinction.[44] As well as providing an emotional outlet, it also offered, to both men and women, another alternative one to be found in the cities of America rather than Africa.[45] There was no contradiction between Lovers' Rock and politics. Brown Sugar's 1977 single, 'I'm in love with a Dreadlocks' combined the romantic ('so in love, so in love, so in love' and 'never felt this way before') with a less overtly aggressive political ('they say he shouldn't lock his hair/And talk about the clothes he wears').[46] More explicitly, Walford 'Poko' Tyson of Misty in Roots, made clear that singing about 'love and women' could be combined with 'progressive protest music.'[47] The dance hall, as ever, was a complex venue, but one in which rebellion, enjoyment, the opportunity to dance and the chance to meet a partner were all important.

The popularity of Lovers' Rock went largely unappreciated at the time.[48] It was overlooked, even dismissed, by fans of roots reggae, for whom their concern with suffering led to a narrow definition of 'authentic' black music, in which there was no room for 'frivolous' Motown-inspired music.[49] Yet Lovers' Rock was an important part of the culture of second-generation black Caribbean immigrants and 'probably expressed far more organically what it meant to be black and British than any amount of roots.'[50]

White reggae

In the early 1960s there were relatively few white musicians interested in and capable of playing ska or reggae. Georgie Fame was the oft-quoted, notable exception but there were other groups who enjoyed some standing. Coming from a soul background, the Huddersfield-based Inner Mind, with Ian Smith, performed at all the major reggae venues across the country and were sufficiently well thought of to appear alongside the Pioneers, Desmond Dekker, Derrick Morgan and the like in the late-1960s. Ultimately, they enjoyed short-lived success, losing out to the attractions of the sound systems, but as the audience for reggae diversified and expanded, and more white musicians became attracted to it, the number of white reggae bands grew as a hitherto largely ignored music moved into the mainstream. In commercial terms at least, the most successful were Madness and UB40, though, the Clash, the Ruts, and even Bad Manners all built up a following.

From their earliest days as the Bodysnatchers, later the North London Invaders, Madness's interest in and debt to rocksteady and reggae was clear. Their final name and the first single, 'The Prince,' were clear tributes to Prince Buster, while 'One Step Beyond' was a cover of one of his records. The only white group signed by the Two-Tone label, they had been the backing group on tour for the Specials, the Selecter and Toots and the Maytals. However, their commercial success owed more to dance-oriented, pop songs ('Baggy Trousers' and 'Our House') albeit with a ska beat.[51] Indeed, as their career developed, their music articulated a sense of white Englishness, more akin to the Kinks, as well as showing strong links with music hall. Their early career was also marred by a significant neo-Nazi presence at several their concerts.[52] The career of Bad Manners was not dissimilar. Their commercialised ska sound is clear in various tracks, including 'My Girl Lollipop,' a re-working of Millie's 1960s hit, and 'King Ska Fa' but, with the possible exception of 'Inner City Violence,' there is no social commentary. Increasingly the band depended on novelty numbers, such as 'Can Can' and 'Tequila' and they played for a white, and often right-wing, skinhead audience.

More serious in their commitment to reggae were UB40. From the mixed community of Balsall Heath, Birmingham, group members had grown up with various musical forms including reggae. Their chosen name made clear the harsh economic conditions that beset them. The band had a dual purpose: to play reggae and to get off the dole. Their first album, *Signing Off,* demonstrated their success on both counts. It was based on an accessible but reggae-based musical style combined with songs that addressed current issues. Their debt to reggae was clearly seen in their 1983 album, *Labour of Love*, with its covers of Eric Donaldson's 'Cherry Oh Baby,' the Melodians' 'Sweet Sensation' and Jimmy Cliff's 'Many Rivers to Cross;' though the most successful track was 'Red, Red Wine,' based on Tony Tribe's reggae version of the Neil Diamond song. *Signing Off* with its distinctive cover, featuring Unemployment Benefit Attendance Card, UB40, addressed several major social and political issues.[53] 'Little by little' condemned income inequality. 'Poor boy sleeps on straw/The rich boy sleeps in bed' but worse, 'the fat boy fills his belly/My poor boy's a dead.'[54] 'Burden of Shame' was equalling scathing. It condemned of British imperialism, not least the neglect of 'the cries of an African son' but made clear that, while 'there's a soldier's hand on the trigger … it's we who are holding the gun.'[55] The most outspoken, and directly political, critique was reserved for Margaret Thatcher in 'Madam Medusa,' with its references to 'tombs of ignorance, of hate and greed and lies' and 'the evil tree of knowledge.' The innocent are scourged and there is 'silent suffering … through the land,' while 'in her bloody footsteps, speculators prance.' This was music to dance to and lyrics to ponder.

Also, more serious in their relationship to reggae were the Clash with covers of popular roots songs such as Junior Murvin's 'Police and Thieves' and Willie Williams' 'Armaggideon Time.' The lyrics of several of their songs reflected a shared experience of limited opportunities ('Career Opportunities'), the threat of extremism ('English Civil War') and a more general sense of frustration, notably in 'White Riot.' The song, which grew out of Joe Strummer's experience of the 1976 Notting Hill riot was condemned for its incitement to violence: 'White riot, I want to riot.' Although black and white share common problems, the former 'don't mind throwing a brick,' while the latter 'go to school where they teach you how to be thick.' More importantly, and foreshadowing latter divisions, 'white riot' was a cry by the white dispossessed for 'a riot of our own.' Although the Clash were prominent in the Rock Against Racism campaign, they were unable to reconcile punk's contradictory stance on race. The Ruts, from south London, were another heavily committed, reggae-influenced punk band. They also played on several occasions as part of the Rock Against Racism campaign, not least as part of the Misty In Roots Unite collective in Southall. 'Babylon' was burning 'with anxiety … positively smouldering with ignorance and hate.'[56] Southall, which had a significant south Asian population (and a small African Caribbean one) was the scene of particularly ugly scenes on 23 April 1979. Racially motivated violence had been on the increase since 1976, when Gurdip Singh Chaggar was stabbed to death by white youths outside a public house. A forthcoming election, the provocative presence of the National Front, and widespread protest, resulted in vicious conflict between demonstrators and the Metropolitan police's Special Patrol Group, which resulted in the death of Blair Peach and the clubbing of several leading protesters. The events of that day had a profound impact on opinion and raised serious questions about policing in London.[57] The Ruts' protest, 'Jah Wah' referenced the assault on Clarence Baker, the Anti-Nazi League leader, 'the blood and the madness … [and] the blood on the streets that day.' 'Jah War,' with its explicit reference to the police, 'hot heads came in uniform/thunder and lightning in a violent form,' was too much for the BBC, which banned the song.[58]

Second only to Bob Marley for reggae record sales in the 1970s, ignored, when not banned, by the BBC, despite his popularity, and castigated by the musical press, was Alex Hughes, better known as Judge Dread. His career shows, yet again, the importance of fusion between different musical genres. His approach, which appalled purists and the BBC alike, but which attracted a considerable working-class and punk following, showed that having a popular formula can make familiar music, which might otherwise have remained alien and unappreciated, and thereby encourage further exploration. Having lived with an African Caribbean family in Brixton, he acquired a love for and knowledge of ska and reggae. Hughes took his name from a Prince Buster track, in a career that spanned over a quarter of a century. During this time he had a series of successful records, combining ska and reggae rhythms with 'adult' nursery rhymes, parodies of pop hits and music hall songs. His first record, released by Trojan records, was inspired by Prince Buster's less-than-decorous 'Big Five.' In Hughes' 'Big Six,' bluebeat meets a distinctly blue boy, a formula he repeated on 'Big Seven.' 'Big Six' was a hit in Jamaica, but when he appeared in Kingston, like Charley Pride's first appearance at the Grand Ol' Oprey, his skin colour silenced the crowd. His diversity is easily seen. Alongside a version of 'Rudy A Message to You,'[59] he covered Mike Sarne's 'Come Outside' and Doris Day's 'Move Over Darling' in a manner reminiscent of Marie Lloyd's (alleged) version of 'Come into the Garden Maud.' 'Grandad's Flannelette Nightshirt' was from the George Formby songbook and 'Y Viva Suspenders' was Max Miller to a cod-Spanish tune. For all that, he had more reggae hits in Britain than Bob Marley.[60]

Reggae-lite and reggae-as-resource

As with rhythm and blues, reggae's impact was felt more widely in mainstream pop music. Marmalade had had a number one hit with the quasi-Caribbean 'Ob-Le-Di Ob-La-Da,' but even more cynical was Jonathan King, promoting the Piglets 'cod-Caribbean knees up,' 'Johnny Reggae,' which owed as much to music hall as to ska or reggae.⁶¹ Also avowedly commercial was Musical Youth's 'Pass the Dutchie.' It sanitised the lyrics, as the 'kouchie' (ganga pipe) in the Mighty Diamonds' version became the 'dutchie' (cooking pot), it made more commercial the tune, and introduced a packaged group of cute kids.⁶² For other artists, reggae influences were incorporated into a more distinctive sound. The Police, for example, claimed, somewhat pretentiously, to have 'reggae influences in [our] vocabulary [... which] became synthesized into our infrastructure until it was utterly part of our sound and you couldn't really call it reggae any more.⁶³ Their 'substantially refined' white reggae, is discernible not only in 'Roxanne' and 'Walking on the Moon' and (less obviously) 'Message in a Bottle.' Despite a two album tribute, *Reggatta Mondatta: A Reggae Tribute to the Police,*' there remains much force in Gilroy's tart observation that the Police 'inverted the preconceptions of Rasta ... served, within pop culture at least, to detach reggae from its historic association with the Africans of the Caribbean and their British descendants.'⁶⁴ Alternatively, ska and reggae could be viewed as contributing to a wider range of musical resources to be drawn upon, to a greater or lesser extent as artists saw fit. Elvis Costello, for example, was happy to incorporate reggae but as one of a number of genres upon which he drew. 'Watching the Detectives,' on his highly acclaimed debut album 'My Aim Is True,' utilises a reggae beat but there are few hints of reggae on other tracks.⁶⁵

Some concluding observations

British society changed significantly in the post-war, post-imperial decades. Although white Britons consistently exaggerated the number of immigrants from the Caribbean (and south Asia), new commonwealth immigrants constituted a significant minority in society, not least because like the Irish in the nineteenth century, they were concentrated in particular districts of certain towns and cities. The music, in all its variety, that came with them was one part of the complex interactions, within and between generations, that characterised these years. Music was both reactive and proactive. It provided an opportunity to express both hopes and fears, a way to make sense of the world and create a sense of identity, both collectively and individually. Further, this process of change took place in a dynamic, evolving environment, which saw greater awareness and interaction in all spheres of life, and which gave rise to new perceptions and attitudes. The once exotic, marginalised, even ridiculed, became more widely accepted and valued as it was afforded a place in the mainstream. In terms of popular music, African Caribbean influences had a profound effect. For much of the 1950s and 1960s, only the occasional novelty calypso or ska song was heard outside immigrant communities. A decade later, reggae had acquired a national (and international) audience and was being played by an ever-widening number of British bands; but ska and reggae meant different things to different communities and different generations.

All migrant communities have coping strategies, many of which involve the preservation of cultural activities linked to home. Unsurprisingly, music and dance play an important role. The first post-war generation came from various islands, each with its own traditions. Although more people came from Jamaica than any other island, it was the carnival and calypso associated with Trinidad and Tobago and the Bahamas that predominated. Calypso opened up commercial opportunities without losing its ability to criticise. Its impact was curtailed partly by its association with comedy but more importantly by the growing influence of Jamaica and its music in the African Caribbean communities in England in the 1960s. Despite this, calypso had shown that an imported musical style could have an impact on the domestic music scene.

Through imported records and visiting performers ska and reggae provided an important link with family in Jamaica as well as its social and political developments. The former was soon eclipsed, first by rocksteady and then reggae. A new generation might condemn ska as 'old man's music' but for the old men it retained its importance as a means of preserving an identity in a hostile environment. However, for a generation, particularly of young black men, less willing than their parents to tolerate the frustrations and injustices of a racist society, reggae, with its close links with Rastafarianism, offered a better way of understanding and reacting against the society in which they had grown up. Although Jamaican reggae was commonly seen as superior, more authentic, black British bands gave reggae a distinctive turn that related to Tottenham as much as Trenchtown. However, the black audience for reggae had its limits. Its pan-African vision, the macho tone and incidents of violence alienated not only the aspiringly respectable suburbanites but also inner-city young men and women who found the soul scene more attractive. As Rastafarian influences declined in the late 1970s, the new reggae of Smiley Culture offered a new vision of being black British.

Commercial considerations also played an important part in the evolution of African Caribbean music. In contrast to America, black British communities were relatively small and dispersed. There was, irrespective of any other considerations, a pressure to develop a wider market by appealing to white audiences, which was discernible from the days of Melodisc records in the 1950s, but which became more powerful in subsequent decades. Ska and reggae had attracted a white, Mod following from the early 1960s, when Georgie Fame had been playing at the Flamingo and Roaring Twenties clubs. By the mid-1960s, fans of 'this new sound' were confident that 'bluebeat [ska] is here to stay,' even if they over-egged their argument with the claim that 'the Beatles have been well and truly squashed.'[66] The fragmentation of the mod movement in the late 1960s and the emergence of the skinhead and later punk subcultures saw a continuing, but complicated relationship with reggae and Rude Boy culture. Shared experiences at school and in out-of-school leisure, and a shared sense of exclusion from mainstream, white, middle-class society, led to common musical interests.[67] Groups like the Viceroys ('Work It') and the Versatiles ('Children Get Ready') attracted skinhead followers.[68] Symarip's 'Skinhead Moonstomp' unambiguously had a target audience.[69] The ska revival was predicated on the belief that there was common ground between black and white youths, especially in the inner cities. In terms of broadening appeal to a new white audience, Two Tone succeeded: in bringing together black and white, less so. In part this was due to the growing interest in reggae, in part to the diverse and contradictory elements in punk. Madness, even more so Bad Manners, attracted National Front and British Movement sympathisers, while certain punk groups were openly white-supremacist.[70]

Hard-headed economics, albeit combined with artistic and political intent, was also behind the reformulation and rebranding of raggae. Bob Marley and the Wailers took it in a different direction and to an international audience. Similarly, UB40 developed a highly successful form of reggae that grew out of their experiences and brought both the music and the message to a considerably wider audience. This led to resentment in some quarters. 'Reggae music invent by the Jamaicans/UB40 tek it and make the most million,' according to Macka B.[71] Others, were even more cynical, in their appropriation and exploitation of reggae, but it would be misleading to talk simply in these terms. For some groups there was a conscious wish that went beyond simply commercial considerations to bring ska and reggae to a wider audience. Further, there is an important thread, linking most of the ska/ska-revival and reggae bands, that explains their considerable popularity. Theirs was music to enjoy, music to dance to, but music also combined with thought-provoking lyrics that expressed a range of emotions and offered hope for a better future.

Endnotes

1. L Bradley, *Sounds Like London,: 100 Years of Black Music in the Capital*, London, Serpent's Tail, pp.213-5, William 'Lez' Henry, 'Reggae, Rasta and the Role of the Deejay in the Black British Experience, *Contemporary British History*, 26(30, 2012, pp.355-73, P Gilroy, *There Ain't No Black in the Union Jack*, London, Routledge, 1992, esp. pp. 216-7, 252-5 and 261-5, and P Ward, 'Sound System Culture: Place, Space and identity in the United Kingdom, 1960-1989,' *Historia Contemporánea*, 57, 2018, pp.359-76
2. S Dudley, *Carnival Music in Trinidad*, Oxford University Press, 2004, especially chapter one. A similar carnival/calypso tradition was also found in the Bahamas.
3. See for example the Mighty Sparrow's 'Jean and Dinah,' aka 'Yankees Gone,' which exceptionally won both the Road March and the Calypso King competitions, and Lord Invader, 'Rum and Coca Cola,' (not the bowdlerised version by the Andrews Sisters).
4. The Percussion Orchestra repertoire included Brahms's 'Cradle Song,' The Tennessee Waltz' and 'Put Another Nickle in (the Nickelodeon)'
5. L Bradley, *Sounds Like London*, p.50. 'Don't Touch Me Nylons' https://www.youtube.com/watch?v=LBuI_7OGqhI
6. 'If You're Not White, You're Black' https://www.youtube.com/watch?v=566gtlESMxs

7   'Black Power' https://www.youtube.com/watch?v=KtFwJtWUR1w This contrasts with the sadness in 'If You're Not White' where he observes 'you hate the name of Africa/the land of your great grandfather/the home where you really belong.'
    youtube.com/watch?v=Dda8NBHpEaM
8   See also Bradley, *Sounds Like London*, chapter 2 'Are They Going to Play Music on Dustbins: How London learned to love the steel pan.'
9   Belafonte was a talented musician, producing a wide range of material including chain gang songs ('Swing Dat Hammer' 1960) and 'Many Moods of Belafonte,' in which he collaborated with Hugh Masekala and Miriam Makeba. He also had a distinguished career as a civil rights campaigner.
10 This pairing is unfair on Percival who was an able calypso singer, regularly performing on 'That Was the Week That Was,' and well regarded by Trinidadian calypso singers.
11 Duke of Iron https://www.youtube.com/watch?v=mMyNcMG7Ryk cf Johnny Duncan https://www.youtube.com/watch?v=W_4thzXTrrw
12 The early history of the Notting Hill carnival is disputed. There were street parties in the mid-1960s, with a jump-up street parade turning into a parade in 1966, but it is claimed that the first true street parade took place in 1973, while in 1976 its character became more Jamaican with the first appearance of sound systems.
13 'Negro Know Thyself' https://www.youtube.com/watch?v=5afZZffWpYo
14 J Heathcote, 'Urban Spaces and Working-Class Expressions across the Black Atlantic: Tracing the Routes of Ska,' *Radical History Review*, 87, 2003. Soul Jazz records, *Studio One Jump Up: The Birth of a Sound* contains the sound of Jamaican R & B and early ska, including artists such as Clue J and the Blues Blasters, Derrick Morgan and the Maytals.
15 https://www.youtube.com/watch?v=gxhkE6Qj7NA
16 Heathcote, 'Urban Spaces and Working-Class Expressions' and Ward, 'Sound System Culture'
17 L. Bradley, *This is Reggae: The Story of Jamaica's Music*, New York, Grove Press, pp.115-6
18 'My Boy Lollipop' https://www.youtube.com/watch?v=dwrHCa9t0dM
19 'My Boy Lollipop' was the fourth highest single in Jamaica in 1964, outselling (at number 5) Prince Buster's 'Wash, Wash.' J Stratton, Chris Blackwell and "My Boy Lollipop": Ska, race and British Popular Music,' *Journal of Popular Music Studies, 22(4), 2010, pp. 436-65*
20 The Beatles' 'Ob-La-Di Ob-La-Da,' Paul's 'granny shit,' according to John Lennon, was not their greatest track. J Stratton, '" Ob-La-Di Ob-La-Da": Paul McCartney, Diaspora and the Politics of Identity,' *Journal for Cultural Research*, 18(1), 2014, pp.1-24. Stratton argues the song is more complex, particularly in terms of musical influences which embrace ska and music hall.
21 Linval Golding of The Specials, *Black Music*, February 1980 cited in S Jones, *Black Culture, White Youth: The Reggae Tradition from JA to UK*, Bassline Books, 2016, p.105.
22 *Coventry Evening Telegraph*, 3 November 1979 and *New Musical Express*, 23 February 1980 cited in Jones, *Black Culture, White Youth*, p.106
23 *Black Music*, October 1982 cited in Jones, *Black Culture, White Youth*, p.107

24 See for example, the comment in *Stage* (11 June 1981) on the Beat. 'Lyrically, [their] material deals with such issues as unemployment and persecution.'

25 'Ghost Town' was displaced at the top of the charts by Shakin' Stevens' 'Green Door.' The Selecter eight hits included 'On My Radio,' Three Minute Hero' and 'Missing Words.;' The Beat, '"Tears of a Clown,' Mirror in the Bathroom,' 'Too Nice to Talk To' and 'Hands Off She's Mine.' On 17 November 1979, The Selecter and The Specials were in the top ten, alongside Dr Hook, Abba and Sad Café.

26 *Play For Today* was screened after the 9 p.m. news. On 26 October 1982 viewers enjoyed the pre-watershed delights of 'The Last of the Summer Wine' and 'Terry and June.'

27 Stratton takes a harsher line, dismissing Two Tone as 'a nostalgic white reaction against the demands for equality being made by the second-generation Black British.' J Stratton, *When Music Migrates: Crossing British and European Racial Faultlines, 1945-2010*, London, Routledge, 2019, p.125 See also his 'Skin deep: ska and reggae on the racial faultline in Britain, 1968-1981,' *Popular Music History*, 5(20, 2010, pp.191-215) His reference to 'a white yearning for time past with little conflict' ('Skin deep' p.208) misrepresents the attitudes and aspirations of many who attended those gigs and supported Two Tone at that time, though this critique is based on personal recollection and anecdotal evidence.

28 R Steffens, 'Rock Steady' Groves Music Online, https://doi-org.libaccess.hud.ac.uk/10.1093/gmo/9781561592630.article.23629 and   S Davies, 'Reggae,' Grove Music Online, https://doi-org.libaccess.hud.ac.uk/10.1093/gmo/9781561592630.article.23065

29 Toots and the Maytals, 'Do the Reggay' https://www.youtube.com/watch?v=cwTcoHapkGY

30 See for example, Ward, 'Sound System Culture' for details of Huddersfield, West Yorkshire.

31 'Israelites' https://www.youtube.com/watch?v=HA1ZRIQuHy4 'It Mek' https://www.youtube.com/watch?v=5JXwN1HrnFY 'Wet Dream' https://www.youtube.com/watch?v=C79spWeuakU 'Long Shot Kick De Bucket ' https://www.youtube.com/watch?v=zA78G52P3QY 'Wonderful World, Beautiful People' https://www.youtube.com/watch?v=dckyG-fXSdw Dandy 'Reggae in Your Jeggae' also released in 1969 was less (commercially) successful.

32 For Trojan records see M de Koningh & Laurence Cane-Honeysett, *Young, Gifted and Black*, London, Omnibus Press, 2018

33 Their first album, the Wailing Wailers, included 'Simmer Down,' 'Rude Boy' and 'One Love' but also 'What's New Pussycat.'

34 This was part of a broader strategy to sell reggae to a white audience, including films, such as *The Harder They Come*, the soundtrack of which featured Jimmy Cliff, Desmond Dekker, Toots and the Maytals, the Melodians and the Slickers, and later *Countryman*, which was dedicated to Bob Marley and the Wailers.

35 The original title was Knotty Dread with its sense of Rasta militancy

36 For further details see Jones, *Black Culture, White Youth*, especially pp.67-73.

37 See for example in M Alleyne, 'White Reggae: Cultural Dilution in the Record Industry,' *Popular Music and Society*, 24(1), 2000, pp.15-30

38 There were various musical links including Marley's cover of the civil rights anthem, 'People Get Ready' and various recordings of 'Young, Gifted and Black.'
39 See for example 'Sons of Criminals.' 'So foreign true, this poverty/ Oh I, and I did feel the pain/For some many years, just blood sweat and tears.' Or 'Three Babylon' with its line 'three Babylon try to make I and I run/they come to have fun with their long truncheons.'
40 Bradley, *Sounds Like London*, p.219
41 L A Palmer, 'Men Cry Too: Black Masculinities and the Feminisation of Lovers Rock in the UK,' in J Stratton & N Zuberi, eds., *Black Popular Music in Britain since 1945*, refers to it as a product of 'transatlantic cultural networks where Philly soul met Jamaican rub-a-dub with a dose of British pop.' at p.120. See also. Bradley, *This is Reggae*, who describes Lovers' Rock as 'a genuinely black British musical style,' p.440 and Bradley, *Sounds Like London*, chapter 6.
42 Palmer, 'Men Cry Too,'p.115 fn.1. For a statement of Lovers' Rock and the female voice, see D Hebdige, *Cut 'n' Mix: culture, identity and Caribbean music*, London, Routledge, 1987, p.135. See also Jones, *Black Culture, White Youth* pp.55-7
43 Bradley, *Sounds Like London*, p.228
44 L A Palmer, "LADIES A YOUR TIME NOW! Erotic politics, lovers' rock and resistance in the UK,' *African and Black Diaspora*, 4(2), 2011, pp.177-92
45 Hebdige, *Cut 'n' Mix*, specifically referring to black British girls stresses the importance of Aretha Franklin and Diana Ross as role models.
46 'I'm in love with a Dreadlocks' https://www.youtube.com/watch?v=K8fP-fmsDfw See also Horace Andy & Tappa Zukie, 'Natty Dread a Weh She Wants' https://www.youtube.com/watch?v=f324Xs0C3hA Gregory Isaacs 'Dreadlocks Love Affair.' https://www.youtube.com/watch?v=L4XRPg6MxSI
47 Cited in Palmer, 'Ladies A Your Time,' p.189
48 Young black women bought records but not in the shops that contributed to the compilation of the hit parade.
49 It was a view largely accepted by the music media, some sociologists and social historians (the present writer included) who, at the time, interpreted 'the black experience' in terms of 'educational deprivation, poverty, unemployment and antisocial behaviour.' The phrase was used by the British Film Institute, describing two British-made films by black directors, *Pressure* (1975) and *Burning An Illusion* (1981) and cited in Bradley, *Sounds Like London*, p.242.
50 Bradley, *This is Reggae*, p.441. He also delivers a nice sideswipe to the 'mainstream media, who were now skanking as if their lives depended on it, [which] chose to rubbish it as not be authentic (i.e. black) enough.' Since writing the first draft of this book, Steve McQueen's *Small Axe* has appeared on BBC TV. The importance of Lovers' Rock is strikingly presented in the second film.
51 Gilroy is more scathing accusing Madness of hijacking ska and declaring it white. *Ain't No Black*, p.226

52. Again, Gilroy is scathing seeing these London-based white reggae bands attracting 'young racists' with their 'patriotic nationalism.' *Ain't No Black*, p.226. For a more nuanced view see M Worley, 'Oi! Oi! Oi!: Class, Locality and British Punk,' *Twenty Century British History*, 24(4), 2013, pp.606-36
53. The album also included four instrumental tracks, including 'Signing Off' and 'Reefer Madness.' There is also a version of the well-known 'Strange Fruit.'
54. Their first single 'Food For Thought' drew attention to famine in Africa.
55. There is a belief in change, 'stone by stone/Rich man's mountain comes tumbling down.' which contrasts with the more pessimistic tone of their hit single, also include on the album, 'King,' which refers to 'your people now' as 'chained and pacified.'
56. 'Babylon Burning' https://www.youtube.com/watch?v=zCkNu9OxThc
57. Generally, see, E Cashmore & E McLaughlin, *Out of Order? Policing Black People*, London, Routledge, 1991; specifically, National Council for Civil Liberties, *Southall 23 April 1979: The Report of the Unofficial Committee of Enquiry* (1980) and *The Death of Blair Peach: The Supplementary Report of the Unofficial Committee of Enquiry* (1980).
58. 'Jah War' https://www.youtube.com/watch?v=01zIS6oYqec
59. 'Rudy (A Message to You)' https://www.youtube.com/watch?v=neUol8ObS7U
60. J Stratton, 'Judge Dread: Music Hall Traditionalist or Postcolonial Hybrid?' *Contemporary British History*, 28 (1), 2014, pp.81-102
61. 'Ob-La-Di Ob-La-Da https://www.youtube.com/watch?v=Lu2mEkhcrQA For a more general discussion of the song see Stratton, ''Ob-La-Di Ob-La-Da': Paul McCartney, Diaspora and the Politics of Identity.' 'Johnny Reggae' https://www.youtube.com/watch?v=4wShL3lIkro The phrase is Paul Du Noyer's, cited in J Stratton, 'The Travels of Johnny Reggae: From Jonathan King to Prince Far-I; From Skinhead to Rasta,' *Communication and Critical Cultural Studies*, 9(1), 2012, pp.67-86 at p.68
62. Mighty Diamonds 'Pass the Koutchie' https://www.youtube.com/watch?v=kpPQSsi9sw8 and Musical Youth 'Pass the Dutchie' https://www.youtube.com/watch?v=dFtLONl4cNc
63. Sting interview cited in M Alleyne, 'White Reggae: Cultural Dilution in the Record Industry,' *Popular Music and Society*, 24(1), 2000, pp.15-30 at p.25
64. Gilroy, *Ain't No Black* p.227
65. There are hints in 'Less Than Zero' and 'Sneaky Feelings' but not in tracks such as 'Alison,' Red Shoes' and 'No Dancing.' For his, and others, involvement with soul, see A Marks, 'Young, Gifted and Black: Afro-American and Afro-Caribbean Music in Britain 1963-88,' in P Oliver, ed., *Black Music in Britain*, Milton Keynes, Open University Press, 1990, pp.102-117, esp. pp.112-3. Marks, like Gilroy, sees this as distracting from real reggae.
66. C Hamblett and J Deverson, *Generation X*, London, Tandem Books, 1964 cited in Gilroy, *Ain't No Black*, pp.221-2
67. Acknowledged, for various reasons, by Bob Marley and his backers. See his 'Punky Reggae Party.'
68. 'Work It' https://www.youtube.com/watch?v=wuCvd6zLfl1 and 'Children Get Ready' https://www.youtube.com/watch?v=qrs5EfdvOW8

69 'Skinhead Moonstomp' https://www.youtube.com/watch?v=PWvRr8XxDhU
70 See for example 4-Skins 'Master Race,' The Exploited 'Class War' and Criminal Class 'Blood on the Streets' and 'Fighting the System' but see Worley' Oi! Oi! Oi!' for a nuanced analysis of punk. Others explicitly rejected this, notably the Business with 'Oi Against Racism and Political Extremism but Still Against the System.'
71 Born in Wolverhampton of Jamaican parents, Macka B was greatly influenced by Jamaican toasters, such as Big Youth and Prince Far-I. The quotation is included in J Mullen, 'UK Popular Music and Society in the 1970s,' *French Journal of British Studies,* xxii, 2017, pp.1-14 at p.7

CHAPTER 22

Conclusion: Mummers to Madness-the broader picture

> Enjoy yourself it's later than you think
> Enjoy yourself while you're still in the pink.
> The years go by as quickly as a wink
> Enjoy yourself, enjoy yourself
> It's later than you think.
>
> Madness, 'Enjoy Yourself (It's Later Than You Think)'

Continuity or change?

EIGHTEENTH CENTURY MUMMERS, setting out on their village perambulations at Christmas or Easter, performing their often limited repertoire of 'traditional' songs and dances on pipes and tabors, maybe a fiddle, to a small, parochial audience, were a world away from Madness, on tour across the country, singing a mixture of ska-inspired and music-hall-influenced hits, old and new, accompanied by electric keyboard and saxophone, to a stadium audience that ran to thousands. Various 'revolutions,' socio-economic and cultural, transformed the context in which popular music operated. A range of technological developments, pioneered in the late nineteenth century and applied increasingly across the twentieth, transformed the production and consumption of music.

Until the early twentieth century, live performance was central, whether it be for a professional music hall artiste or an itinerant barrel-organ player, or even for the amateur performer at home or in an ale house. Their instruments were acoustic, but volume was at a premium, whether playing at a fairground or in a dancing booth. Singers, likewise, needed to generate sufficient volume to capture the attention of an early music hall audience, or drown out its chatter. The invention and development of the microphone allowed for the development of new styles of singing; the development of electrified instruments, notably guitars and keyboards, and the use of amplifiers made easier the task of filling a room with sounds and made possible new sounds. Indeed, recording techniques developed to such an extent that by the late 1960s a band could make a musical sound that could not be recreated on stage. Alongside this professional music-making was an important, but easily overlooked, tradition of amateur music making, often of surprising quality. For those with the wherewithal (or good fortune) to acquire an instrument and the ability to play it, there were a range of relatively (and increasingly) cheap instruments – fiddles, whistles, pianos, concertina, guitars. And there was also the most accessible and portable musical instrument – the voice.

If the production of music was transformed by technology, so too was its consumption. Until the turn of the twentieth century, live performance was also central to the listening experience, irrespective of venue. Thereafter, the situation changed fundamentally. The advent of radio, television and film greatly increased the range and quality of available music and the convenience with which it could be heard. No longer was it necessary to go the local variety theatre, or even the local working man's club. The development of the wax cylinder, records (78, 45 and 33 rpm), cassettes and compact discs made music repeatable and portable, even if there was a price to be paid in terms of sound quality. The sound quality of recorded music was steadily improved as gramophones morphed into music centres. By the 1960s records were at the centre of popular music consumption. There was still an important role for live performance, not least because of the collective experience, but the quasi-monopoly position it enjoyed c.1900 had been undermined.

And yet for all these dramatic changes, and the very different periods and contexts in which popular music developed, there was an important element of continuity in terms of the range of functions it performed over the two centuries covered by this book. Both individually and collectively, it provided means of exploring and expressing a range of profound emotions. It could entertain or educate. The physical and emotional experience of singing, playing or dancing, created opportunities for self-expression and self-discovery of social and political identities. Such were the complexities of performance, for performers and audience members, and the differing meaning ascribed to or derived from a performance, not to mention the limitations of evidence, especially in the earlier years, that its specific significance and impact will remain a matter of ongoing debate. However, there is an underlying continuity in terms of artistic, social and political functions associated with popular music and of the recurring issues explored by it.

Some possible patterns, broader themes and unanswered questions

The often-serendipitous changes that took place and the sheer untidiness of popular music, which defies clear-cut definition, categorisation and explanation, makes generalisation hazardous, but it is necessary to stand back from the detail considered in previous chapters. Two overviews suggest themselves, which offer framework within which to explore the two-way interaction between popular music and society. The first, more descriptive, focuses on the music-hall/variety tradition. Most of the basic elements of Victorian and Edwardian music-hall were pre-figured in late-eighteenth and early-nineteenth century England and the emergence of music hall, as a location as much as a form of entertainment, in the 1840s and 1850s was a logical development of popular entertainment in the changing socio-economic context of early Victorian England. Although there was more to nineteenth-century popular music than music hall, it stood stage centre. The protracted decline of variety theatre in the twentieth century reflected its adaptability and tenacity. But if the nineteenth century had witnessed a concentration of elements previously found in distinct locations, the twentieth century saw a relocation (and romanticisation) of music hall in radio and television, as well as a dispersal of certain elements into other forms of popular music. The development of popular dancing was not dissimilar. The portable dancing booths of the eighteenth century were superseded by the dancing saloons and, more so, dance halls of the nineteenth and twentieth.

The second, more interpretative, would focus on interactions between different musical traditions and emphasise the importance of musical accommodation and fusion. It sets the development of English popular music in a context that embraces musical interchange and adaptation both within the nations (and regions) of the United Kingdom and, increasingly, within the Atlantic cultural trade network through which American, African-American and later African-Caribbean music influenced the development of popular music from the 1840s onwards.

The emphasis on cultural interaction raises several important questions relating to authenticity and appropriation. Whether related to Northumbrian piping, American blues or Jamaican reggae, claims that there is an essential or pure form are difficult to reconcile with the diverse roots of these (and other) genres and their continuing evolution in terms of repertoire, playing style and instrumentation. Purist cries of 'betrayal,' be directed at Muddy Waters or Marley, let alone Dylan, fail to do justice to musical dynamism and creativity. They also fail to recognise the economic realities facing many musicians. More importantly, they overlook the way in which musical 'compromise' (or fusion) created a wider market for that music and a gateway to its antecedents. Seeking to confine a musical genre to its 'authentic' form is the equivalent of preserving in aspic a museum specimen. Similarly, claims such that 'white men can't sing the blues' or 'only the Irish can play the union pipes' both oversimplify the history of these (and other) genres and overlook clear evidence to the contrary. More problematic is the relationship between cultural fusion, cultural appropriation and commercialization. There are some clear-cut examples of insensitive appropriation and misrepresentation of African American and Irish popular music, for example, but should early Elvis or UB40, for example, be seen simply as appropriators of African American blues and African Caribbean reggae? Or should they be seen as developers and popularizers, bringing hitherto little-known music to a wider audience and thereby extending the bounds of popular music? Similarly, should they be criticised for making a commercial success of music that had been performed sung by black artists for years with little recognition or reward? Or should they be seen as part of a long tradition of commercial popular music, traceable back to the eighteenth century?

The popularisation of rhythm and blues or reggae, and the emergence of new audiences raises questions about the meaning ascribed to popular music and its relationship with identities, from the individual to the national. On a number of occasions, particularly the years of the French and Napoleonic wars, the age of high Imperialism and during the second world war, popular music, in part at least, was explicitly linked with national identity, couched in terms of Englishness or Britishness that offered an image of unity that transcended regional and class, though not always religious, differences. The patriotic songs of the 1790s and 1800s, the jingoistic songs of the late-Victorian years and stoical yet sentimental songs of Flanagan and Allen, or Vera Lynn, were active attempts to construct and manipulate a national identity; but they were not always successful. There was not a single interpretation of 'Britons, strike home,' nor a uniform response to MacDermott's 'Jingo Song.'

Indeed, the extent to which men and women thought (and sung) in national terms should not be overstated. Notions of England dissolve in the face of north/south rivalries but even these regional cultural identities were fissiparous. The Pennines was (and still is) an important physical and cultural barrier, while the followers of 'Trelawney's Army' had little love for their supposedly fellow west-countrymen in Devon. Local rivalries point to the persistence of parochialism in modern, urban society, not fundamentally dissimilar from earlier customs in which local identity and parochial superiority were asserted. Though the old parishes were swamped by the rapidly growing towns and cities, the traditions of communal singing in a variety of venues, including working men's clubs, pubs, football terraces as well as the home, created a sense of localised community. The 'village' survived in town and city. This sense of local identity was also true of various youth sub-cultures, particularly after the second world war. They were characterised by distinctive musical styles, as well as distinctive appearance, which distinguished themselves from the status quo, both socio-political and cultural, but also from each other.

It is no coincidence that many of these groups had very strong local ties to specific districts, particularly in London.

Similarly, many of the minority immigrant communities never bought into this English national identity. Indeed, for the Irish from the mid-nineteenth century and West Indians later, music was a source of identity and as a means of coming to terms with living in a hostile 'host' environment. With succeeding generations, this process became more complex as hyphenated, dual heritage identities developed. For generations born in England it was difficult to talk meaningfully of home in Tralee or Trinidad but there was not a uniform response. For some the preservation of distinctive 'traditional' music and dance was of paramount importance in maintaining a distinct identity. But for others there was no such imperative. On the contrary, it was a culture that could be modified and popularised to the point that 'Danny Boy' and 'The Wild Rover,' or 'O Carolina' and 'Cherry Oh Baby' became part of a shared, communal songbook.

Popular music also contributed to a more personal sense of identity. At the risk of over-intellectualisation, certain, though not all, popular songs addressed a variety of issues, from the highly personal (love and marriage) to the societal (class relations and law enforcement). It would be naïve to treat popular songs as unproblematic indicators of values and attitudes, not least given the commercial influences at work, but it would be equally naïve to assume that they had no meaning to their various consumers. Meaning was most clearly seen in social-commentary or political songs, condemning callous factory owners or tyrannous rulers, but even the most insipid 'love and marriage' song of the 1930s or 1950s carried an ideological content with which the listener could engage, in one way or another.

The meaning, or ideological content, of songs leads to a consideration of popular music, in its various forms and venues, as a site of tension and conflict. Throughout the two hundred years considered in this book plebeian music and dance was viewed, largely from above, as problematic. The prospect of young people, especially from the working classes, enjoying each other's company with limited or no supervision aroused fears in the breasts of moral reformers, even sympathetic social observers, not to mention generations of parents. And these were fears that could be stoked by overzealous pamphleteers and unscrupulous journalists. In recurring panics about the corrupting influences of popular music, the same themes recur. Dances are at best clumsy and inelegant, at worst, unrestrained, salacious or indecent. Songs are inane, suggestive, if not downright lewd and subversive of authority. And these shortcomings were compounded by being associated with foreigners, from the licentious French, the foppish Italian to the animalistic 'negro.' Such were these fears that various expedients were used to control the threat to morality. Some were unsubtle in their use of the law and the police; others were more imaginative in attempting to tame savage song or dance with decorous, respectable alternatives; neither tactic was particularly successful. The key was in the title: 'popular music.' As long as a dance or a song was popular, for whatever reason (including the very fact that someone was trying to ban it), it was difficult for authorities, in whatever form, to suppress it. Moral reformers preached to the converted, while those whom they sought to convert largely ignored them. Moralistic entrepreneurs, seeking to make respectable the content of the acts on stage, had limited influence, even within, let alone beyond their theatres. The BBC could ban Judge Dread from their airwaves, but they could not stop people buying his records in large numbers. Police (not the band) were too few in number, and too aware of the dangers of antagonising large crowds of men and women enjoying themselves, to act in any but the most serious breaches of the peace; and many magistrates were well aware of this too.

More to the point, fears were often grossly overstated or untypical. From eighteenth-century ballads, through music-hall favourites to twentieth-century pop songs, many were conservative in sentiment, supportive of marriage and 'traditional' gender roles, and condemnatory of crime, especially crimes of violence. Likewise, many dancing saloons in the nineteenth century and most dance halls in the twentieth, were more decorous, more respectable and more self-policed than lurid accounts of depravity would have us believe. This did not mean that there were not tensions. Young men and women went to dances, in part at least, to meet a partner and all that that entailed.

'Come lasses and lads, away from your dads,' was a sentiment that echoed down the ages, even though their concerned parents had done the same. Alcohol was consumed, often excessively and illegally, at nineteenth century fairs and twentieth century village hops, but the practice was widely tolerated. Other harmful substances, some legal some not, were consumed, but, as in the case of cigarettes, these were often tacitly approved rites of passage. The privatisation of music consumption after the second world war may have reduced some of these problems, though the number of hastily opened bedroom windows suggests that it was not just music that was being consumed. Successive generations, literally and metaphorically, made 'a song and dance,' particularly about rites of passage associated with the transition to adulthood that they themselves had been through, but whatever the fears of reformist critics, there were widely-accepted and widely-observed popular codes of behaviour. The high-profile panics of the past, the cries of generational conflict and moral collapse, should not obscure the fact that consensus was as much a feature of popular music as confrontation. There is little evidence to suggest a widespread abandonment of societal norms. Indeed, in a broad sense, and not least driven by commercial imperatives and the need to appeal to a wide audience, the contours and contents of popular music were shaped in no small measure by the norms and values of society at large.

While much can be learned about popular attitudes in times past through the study of popular music there is much that remains unknown. We will never know how many people attended the music halls, singing saloons and dance saloons of Victorian England. We will never know the number of people who heard a music hall hit as it was sung or played in the streets, on the beach and at the fair. Nor will we know how many people played a tune as the sheet music was passed around and sold second hand, or how many people listened to (rather than bought) the hit records of the twentieth century. And how do we put figures on the singing, dancing and playing that took place in workingmen's clubs, public houses and homes? More importantly, how do we capture the totality of a performance in the absence of physical presence? Music and lyrics might be available in a variety of forms, but they are only part of the overall experience. How are we to explore the meaning given by audiences, themselves not homogenous, to a performance? Performances were often complex, with implicit as well as explicit meaning, which audiences could 'read' in a variety of ways that remain hidden to the historian.

It would be wrong to end on a negative note. As well as establishing the broad outlines of the evolution of popular music in modern England, this study has explored the broader contexts within which it developed and with which it interacted; and in so doing, has shown the varied and important functions of popular song and dance. Easy to dismiss as lightweight, inauthentic and ephemeral, 'popular' music was precisely that – popular; and in exploring the reasons for this popularity it is possible to gain insights into important aspects of everyday life in times past. However, a sense of proportion is called for. Popular music was produced and, more importantly, consumed, not for the benefit of later historians, but for enjoyment at the time. Remember Madness: 'Enjoy yourself! It's later than you think.'[1]

Endnotes

1 *Prince Buster, Suggs and Georgie Fame, 'Enjoy Yourself'* https://www.youtube.com/watch?v=WE8FATuziSc

Late-eighteenth/early-nineteenth century tunes

SPACE PRECLUDES THE inclusion of all the tunes mentioned in chapters 2 and 3. The following tunes are among the more 'popular' and most were to be found in numerous collections across the country. The tunes are arranged in the order in which they are first mentioned.

As noted in the main text, there was no fixed version of each tune. As noted in the main text, some tunes had multiple names (e.g. 'Brighton Camp' or 'The Girl I Left Behind Me') and also varied in terms of notation. Others (e.g. 'Cheshire Rolling Hornpipe') had versions in different keys and time signatures. How these tunes were played at the time is unknowable, but it is unlikely that most performances matched the later reconstructions, in television plays and films, which feature musicians of considerable skill! The tunes are as follows.

Shepherd's Hey

King Charles of Sweden

Pease upon a Trencher

APPENDIX

Planxty John O'Connor

Turlough O'Carolan

Sir Roger de Coverley

Packington's Pound

Sellenger's Round

Nancy Dawson

Soldiers Joy

Brighton Camp (aka The Girl I left Behind Me)

The Flowers of Edinburgh

The Irish Washerwoman

The Rakes of Mallow

Off She Goes

White Cockade

The Downfall of Paris

Haste to the Wedding

APPENDIX

John of the Greeny Cheshire Way

Cheshire Rolling Hornpipe

Cheshire Rolling Hornpipe

407

The Trumpet Hornpipe

The Friendly Visit

Tripping Upstairs

Rollicking Irishman or Yorkshire Lasses

General Index

A

Aldershot, 110, 127, 128
Allied Expeditionary Forces Programme, 290
Alper, Gilla, 264
Ambrose, and His Orchestra, see Dance bands
American Forces Network (AFN), 290, 307, 310, 322, 354fn
Americanization, 7, 224, 231fn, 241, 244, 245, 257, 282, 288, 294, 296, 304fn, 318fn
Andrews Sisters, The, 291, 293, 294, 295, 379fn
Animals, The, 348, 351, 355fn
Anti-Nazi League, The, 365, 374
Askey, Arthur, 222
Astaire, Fred, 223, 264 and see Film Musicals
Aswad, 360, 369

B

Babylon, 368, 369, 370, 374, 382fn, 383fn
Bad Manners, 228, 372, 373, 378
Baker, Ginger, 346
Baker, Lavern, 350
Baldry, Long John, 346, 355fn
Ballads, 13, 21, 26, 28fn, 54, 55-9, 64fn, 66fn, 106, 189, 192, 338fn, 391; Child, Francis, 56; Percy, Thomas, *Reliques of Ancient English Poetry*, 56, 57 and see also Broadside ballads
Bamford, Samuel, 22, 30fn, 33, 94
Barrasford, Thomas, 111
Barrel-organ, 119, 130, 193 209, 385
Barrie, J M, *Rosy Rapture. The Pride of the Beauty Chorus*, burlesque, 229
Barrow, 110
Bassey, Shirley, 317, 336
Bachelors, The, 325, 336
Beat, The, 360, 364, 365, 381fn and see Two Tone
'Beat Boom,' 1960s, 306, 314, 316, 317, 323, 327, 335
Beatles, The, 8, 231fn, 308, 322-7, 330, 335, 336, 337fn, 347, 338fn, 378, 380fn, 383fn
Beckford, Theophilus, 362
Beggar's Opera, The, 26, 35, 45, 83fn
Belafonte, Harry, see Calypso
Bellowhead, 231fn
Bellwood, Bessie, 143, 152, 153, 154, 157fn, 161fn, 163
Ben Selvin Novelty Orchestra, 252
Bennett, Tony, 317
Berry, Chuck, 325, 330, 346, 347
Beshara, 371
Betty Boop, 276, 282fn
Big Youth, 368, 384fn
Billing, Bud, aka Luther, Frank, 252

Birmingham, 59, 66fn, 71,91, 102fn, 109, 114, 123fn, 127, 129, 151, 186, 188, 194.195fn, 201, 212fn, 231fn, 337fn, 353, 354fn, 360, 368, 369, 371, 373
Black, George, 220
Black, Pauline, 364, 365
Black Uhuru, 368
Black and White Minstrel Show, The see BBC television
Blackface minstrelsy, Chapter 12; 40, 134, 197fn, 227, 298, 341, 351; Alabama Minstrels, 201; Burgess and Mitchell Minstrels, 221; Christy Minstrels, 200, 201, 214fn; Ethiopian Serenaders, 200, 208, 214fn; Mohawk Minstrels, 199, 200, 203; Moore and Burgess Minstrels, 200, 203, 204 211fn;Virginian Minstrels, 200. See also Elliott, G H, "The Chocolate Coloured Coon,' 204, 205, 221, 263; Harry, Hunter, 200, 203; 'Master Juba,' 200; Mackney, E W, 200, 212fn; Rice, T D 'Daddy,' 200; Stratton, Eugene, 'The Whistling Coon,' 197, 204-6, 211fn
Blackboard Jungle, 311, 312; riots 311
Blackpool, 109, 129, 131, 137, 190, 209, 230fn, 241, 267fn, 285, 326. 332. 351
Blackwell, Chris, 363, 366, 367, 380fn
Blind Boys of Alabama, The, 350
Blind Boys of Mississippi, The, 350
Blues, 301, 307, 309, 310, 318fn, 325, 335, 338, 342-5, 346, 347, 348, 350, 351, 354, 355fn, 357fn, 388 and see Rhythm and blues
Blues Incorporated, 346
Bo Diddley, 346, 347, 356fn
Bob and Marcia, 351, 367
Boer war, see War
Bolton, 108, 127, 276; *Star Concert Room, The*, 108; *Worktown* (Bolton), 276, 277, 302

Bond, Graham, 325, 355fn
Boone, Pat, 295, 314
Booth, Charles, 129, 138fn, 139fn, 171, 233
Bowlly, Al, 270
Bradford, 19, 108, 109, 110, 113-4, 119, 127, 139fn, 158fn, 190, 220, 354fn; Pullan's, 108, 110, 112
Brass bands, 11, 51fn, 106, 107, 250, 259, 289
Breeze, Alan, 269, 296
Brewer, Teresa, 300
Brighton, 23, 43, 109, 170, 200, 329
British Broadcasting Corporation, 224, 228, 240, 244, 254-7, 259-61, 286-9, 290, 292, 293, 294-6. 307, 308, 310, 312, 324, 337fn, 343, 361, 366, 368, 375, 391
BBC Radio: Force's programme, 286-90, 231; Home service, 286, 293, 314; Light programme, 294, 297, 303fn, 310; Third programme, 294, 343
BBC Radio programmes: *Art of the Negro The*, 342; *Ballads and Blues*, 318fn, 343; *Family Favourites*, 295; *Forces Favourites*, 287; *Housewives' Choice*, 294, 298, 369; *Kentucky Minstrels, The*, 259, 292, 294; *Martins and the Coys, The* (ballad opera), 307; *Music Hall*, 259; *Music While You Work*, 288-9, 293, 303fn; *Pop Go the Beatles*, 324, 337fn; *Saturday Club*, 324, 337fn; *Sincerely Yours, Vera Lynn*, 287; *Variety Bandbox*, 288; *Workers' Playtime*, 288
BBC Television programmes: *Billy Cotton Band Show*, 227, 295, 298; *Good Old Days, The*,227; *Juke Box Jury*, 298; *Old Grey Whistle Test*, 367, *Six-Five Special*, 308; *Top of the Pops*, 298, 369
British Lion, short films, 262
British Movement, The, 378
British Pathé, 222, 237
Broadside ballads, Chapter 5 (Sport, sex and drink) and

Chapter 6 (Crime, punishment and socio-economic comment); 59-61, 65fn,
Broonzy, Big Bill, 307, 333fn, 343, 344, 355fn
Brown, James, 351, 352, 353, 368
Brown, Ruth, 252, 350
Brown Sugar, 371
Bruce, Jack, 346
Bruneau, Ruby and the Hawaiian Islanders, 262
Burning Spear, 368, 369
Burton, Jess, 192,
Burtonwood, America base, 322
Bygraves, Max, 231fn, 233, 304fn
Bryant, Marie, 361
Bryden, Beryl, 308

C

Calypso, Chapter 21; 305, 307, 308, 323, 360-2, 363, 377, 379fn, 380fn; Belafonte, Harry, 360, 362, 380fn; Cribbins, Bernard, 362; Duke of Iron, 362, 380fn; Duncan, Johnny, 308, 380fn; Percival, Lance, 362, 380fn; Lord Invader, 379fn; Lord Kitchener, 361; Lord Woodbine, 323; Mighty Dictator, 362; Mighty Sparrow, 379fn; Mighty Terror. 362
Cantor, Eddie, 271
Carney, Kate, 152, 153, 154
Carroll Troupe, The, 202, 212fn
Casey, Pat, 150
Casinos, 130, 138fn, 139fn
Caruso, Enrico, 253, 275
Casani, Santos, 237
Castle, Irene and Vernon, 261
Champion, Harry, 134, 160fn, 202, 207, 220, 221, 222, 226, 228, 231fn, 251, 266fn
Chant, Mrs Ormiston, 111, 134
Chapbooks, 57-61, 66fn
Chaplin, Charlie, 46, 132, 268fn
Charleston, The, see Dances
Chas 'n' Dave, 215, 228
Chevalier, Albert, 115, 154, 164, 166, 171, 181fn

Chevalier, Maurice, 253
Chirgwin, G H, 'The White-Eyed Musical Kaffir,' 202-3, 209, 212fn, 213fn, 220; Chirgwin Family, The, 202
Churchill, Randolph, 187
Cinema, 216, 220, 222, 223, 227, 230fn, 235, 244, 245, 299, 303fn, 308, 311, 312, 319fn; Cinematograph Film Act, 1927, 262; and see also Film musicals
Civil Rights, America, 350, 351, 352, 368, 380fn, 382fn
Clan Johnstone Troupe133, 191, 195fn
Clapton, Eric, 346, 348, 351, 353, 355fn, 368
Clare, John, 15fn, 19, 27, 29fn, 33, 35, 37-9, 40, 43, 44. 50fn, 54, 57, 60, 64fn, 78, 333; *The Village Minstrel*, 30; *The Shepherd's Calendar,*38; *The Parish*, 29fn, 102fn, 103fn
Clark, Dave, 327
Clark, Henry, 188
Clash, The, 372, 374
Cleethorpes, 109
Cliff, Jimmy, 360, 363, 366, 367, 373, 381fn
Clifton, 'Handsome' Harry, 144, 173, 179fn
Coal Hole Companion, The, 143
Coburn, Charles, 147, 160fn, 185, 188, 266fn
Cochrane, Eddie, 310, 313, 349
Cockneys on Their Travels, (Alf George and Nelly Glover), 110
Coffee bars, 299, 300, 306, 308, 334, 349
Cogan, Alma, 296, 301, 304fn
Cole, Nat 'King,'317
Collette, Charles, 185
Colley, Linda, 191
Collins, José, 219; *The Maid of the Mountains*, 229fn
Collins, Lottie, 154
Colyer, Ken, 307, 309, 342
Commercial television, 226, 227,

297, 298, 332, 344; Programmes: *Blues and Gospel Train*, 344, 345; *Cool For Cats*, 298; *I Hear the Blues*, 244; *Oh Boy!* 298; *Ready Steady Go*, 298; *Sunday Night at the London Palladium*, 226, 227, 298
Commercialisation, 3, 8, 14fn, 17, 27, 47, 61, 94, 106, 211fn, 301, 310
Community singings, 270, 277-9; and see National songs
Como, Perry, 295, 300
Concertinas, 2, 107, 135fn, 154, 208, 213fn, 336; concertina bands, 11, 107, 128
Conway, Russ, 295
Cooke, Sam, 348, 350
Copper Family, The, 19, 54
Corri, Pat, 131, 133
Corvan, Ned, 'Cat-Gut Jim,' 115, 154, 174
Costello, Tom, 189
Cotton, Billy, see BBC and Dance bandleaders
Country music, see Country and western
Country and western, 301, 314, 321, 322, 325, 350; Autrey, Gene, 322; Carter Family, The, 307; Charles, Ray, 320fn, 349, 350, 353; Guthrie, Woody, 307; Ives, Burl, 307; Rodgers, Jimmy, 307, 322; Williams, Hank, 307, 314, 320fn, 322, 356
Courtneidge, Cicely, 223, 263, 264
Coventry, 109, 160fn, 284fn, 313, 356
Coward, Henry, 225
Cowell, Sam, 12, 123fn, 143; *Comic Song Book*, 143, 158fn
Coyne, Fred, 184
Crawdaddy Club, 345, 347, 348
Crazy Gang, The, 222, 263
Cream, 346, 349
Crickets, The, 313, 323, 356fn and see Holly, Buddy
Crumit, Frank, 252

Cunliffe, Walt, 169, 217, 219
Customary calendar, 17-20, 28fn, 29fn; catterners, 17, 28fn; clemmers, 17, 28fn; harvest home, 19, 94; mummers, 8, 17, 18, 107, 385; pace-egging, 17, 18, 19, 28fn; plough-bullocks, 17, 19, 28fn, 29fn; sheep-shearing supper, 19, 72; St Blaise, feast, 19; St Crispin's day, 19; St Clement's day, 19; wassailers, 17, 28fn, 72

D

Dance and dancing: Chapter 3, Chapter 8 and Chapter 14; 2, 9, 11, 12, 13, 21, 28fn, 29fn, 78, 148, 152, 159fn, 193, 197, 199, 200, 201, 202, 205, 208, 212fn, 216, 220, 221, 224, 225, 250, 251, 255, 257, -60, 261, 273, 284fn, 286, 290, 291, 292, 295, 298-9, 306, 349, 353, 359, 364, 366, 372, 374, 377, 385, 390, 391, 393
Dance bands, 237, 238, 253, 262, 289, 305, 306, 312, 317, 349
Dance bandleaders: Ambrose, 237, 253, 262, 264, 267fn, 273, 275; Cotton, Billy, 235, 260, 269, 295, 298, 308, 312; Geraldo, 262, 288, 295; Gibbons, Carroll, 237, 264; Gonella, Nat, 222, 240, 264; Hylton, Jack, 238, 240, 253, 260, 262, 264, 267fn; Loss, Joe, 262, 288, 289; Savoy Orpheans, 257, 267fn; Payne, Jack, 237, 253, 257, 267fn, 288, 296; Roy, Harry, 264, 275, 288; Silvester, Victor, 237, 288, 289, 295; Troise, Pasquele, 222, 289, 303fn
Dance halls, Chapter 14; 6, 137, 225, 226, 234-5, 238, 241, 242-4, 245, 246fn, 248fn, 255, 261, 286, 290, 299, 360, 371, 372
Dance tunes, published collections, 35, 37; Aird's, *Collection of Scotch, English and Foreign Airs*, 35, 37;

Fraser's *Airs and Melodies Peculiar to the Highlands of Scotland*, 44; Preston's *Twenty Four Country Dances for the Year 1793*, 38; Thompson, C & S, *Compleat Collection of 200 Favourite Country Dances*, 36, 40, 45; Wilson, T, *Complete System of English Country Dancing*, 48fn; Walsh's *Collection of Lancashire Jiggs, Hornpipes, Joaks etc*, 44

Dances: Big Apple, 291; Black Bottom, 239; The Boston, 234; Bunny Hop, 220; Cakewalk, 234; Charleston, 6, 224, 236, 239, 245, 273, 291; cha-cha-cha, 305; clog-dance, 42, 46, 52fn, 131-2, 139fn, 204; conga, 291; cotillion, 35, 36, 239; country dances and dancing, 33, 34, 36, 38, 40, 41, 42, 44, 48fn, 212fn, 259; foxtrot, 220, 225, 233, 234, 237, 239, 247fn, 261, 273, 288, 290; Grizzly Bear, 220; Handsome Territorial, 240; Hokey Cokey, 291; hornpipe, 36, 37, 38, 40, 41-7, 55fn, 56fn, 131, 133, 134, 201, 210, 395; jitterbug, 286, 291-2, 312; jive, 292, 299, 312; Kangaroo Dip, 220; Knees Up Mother Brown, 240, 291; Lambeth Walk, 224, 230fn, 240, 244, 245; Lindy Hop, 291; mambo, 305; Mashed Potato, 299; quadrille, 41, 44, 51fn, 128, 132, 210, 214fn, 290, 361; Old Time, 245, 295, 299; Park Parade, 240, 245; quickstep, 40, 41, 42, 43, 47, 51fn, 142, 237, 247fn, 290; Sand dancing, 131, 221, 230fn; sequence dances and dancing, 234, 235, 240, 244, 299; Stomp, 299; tango, 220, 225, 234, 237, 239, 247fn, 261, 262, 272, 288, 301; Turkey Trot, 220; Twist, 299; Under the Spreading Chestnut Tree, 240; waltz, 38, 39, 40, 41, 42, 43, 47, 51fn, 125, 128, 130, 142, 214fn, 223, 236, 237, 239, 247fn, 252, 273, 288, 290, 301, 379fn

Dancing booths, 2, 21, 23, 24, 31fn, 136, 387
Dancing masters, 42, 44, 45, 209
Dancing saloons, Chapter 8; 2, 126-30, 137fn, 138fn, 233, 388, 391
Dancing Times, The, 236
Darin, Bobby, 317
Davies, Cyril, 325, 345, 346, 353
Davis, Thomas, 149, 160fn, 284fn,
Dawson, Nancy, 26, 35, 36, 45, 143
Dawson, Peter, 269, 281
Day, Doris, 16fn, 300
Dean, Ella, 116
Dekker, Desmond, 363, 366, 372, 381fn
Dempsey, W P, 174
Denmark Street, 305
Dibdin, Charles, 36, 59, 60, 97, 99, 211fn
Dickens, Charles, 21, 30fn, 100fn, 101, 158fn, 241
Dilke, Charles, 185
Disraeli, Lord Beaconsfield, 134, 184, 185, 186, 187, 188, 193fn, 275
Dixon, Willie, 347, 348
Donegan, Lonnie, 227, 306, 307, 308, 309, 315, 316, 317, 319fn, 323, 345
Doo Wop, 323, 350
Doonican, Val, 336
D'Orma, Aileen, 229fn
Dormer, Daisy, 165, 166, 219
Drifters, The, 350
Dryden, Len, 'The Kipling of the Halls,' 189
Dupree, 'Champion' Jack, 343
D'Urfey, Thomas, *Wit and Mirth: Or, Pills to Purge Melancholy*, 35, 48fn, 57, 58, 66fn, 76, 81fn, 82fn
Dusty Road Ramblers, 362
Dwight, Reg, 346

E

Earl Van Dyke Six, The, 350
Eastbourne, 109
Eckstein, Billy, 336
Eddy, Nelson, 255
Elen, Gus, 16fn, 115, 122fn, 139fn, 153, 154, 155, 165, 168, 173, 191, 202, 209, 221, 222, 262
Emmett, Dan, 200, 214fn
Ennis, Seamus, 343
Etting, Ruth, 252
Everly Brothers, 310, 316, 323, 325, 337fn

F

Fairs, 20-4
Falkner, Keith, 264
Fame, Georgie, 349, 353, 355fn, 363, 372, 378
Farnell, Nelly, 184
'Fats' Domino, 314, 320fn
Feenan, Paddy, 131
Feeney, Pat, 131, 150, 191
Femininity, 4, 5, 103fn, 176-7, 219, 243, 244, 256, 272 and see Gender, Masculinity and New Woman
Ferrier, Kathleen, 295
Field, 'Happy' Fanny, 176
Fields, Gracie, 221, 222, 223, 228, 251, 253, 286, 317, 336
Film musicals, 2, 233, 262, 265, 317, 336, 338fn; *42nd Street*, 223, 264; *Blossom Time*, 263; *Blue Danube*, 263; *Broadway Melody*, 252; *Calling All Stars*, 223, 263; *Carefree*, 223; *Carmen*, 263; *Carousel*, 317, 327; *Chu Chin Chow*, 223, 263; *Elstree Calling*, 222, 263; *Footlight Parade*, 264; *Girl from Maxim's, The*, 263; *Gold Diggers of Broadway*, 223, 268fn; *Good Companions*, 263; *Goodnight Vienna*, 263; *Happy Ever After*, 263; *Kathleen Mavourneen*, 263, 264; *King and I, The*, 317; *Lambeth Walk*, 224; *Maid of the Mountain, The*, 229fn, 263; *Me an My Girl*, 224, 241; *Minstrel Boy, The*, 263; *Mountains of Mourne, The*, 263; *Music Hall*, 263; *Music Hall Parade*, 263; *Musical Beauty Shop*, 262; *My Fair Lady*, 317; *My Irish Molly*, 263; *Okay For Sound*, 263; *Oklahoma!* 317; *Pagliacci*, 263; *Prince of Arcadia*, 263; *Rose of Tralee, The*, 263; *Shall We Dance*, 223, 265; *She Shall Have Music*, 264; *Sing As You Swing*, 263; *Song of Soho, The*, 263; *Sound of Music, The*, 336; *South Pacific*, 317; *Southern Maid, The*, 263; *Stars on Parade*, 223; *Stepping Stones*, 263; *Swing Time*, 264, 268fn, *Top Hat*, 223, 264; *West Side Story*, 317; *You'd Be Surprised*, 262
Findlater, Piper George, 191, 192, 195fn
Fitzgerald, Ella, 295
Flamingo Club, 345, 349, 363, 378
Flanagan, Bud, and Allen, Chesney, 285, 295, 389
Fleetwood Mac, 346, 349
Folk revival, 305, 307, 309, 342, 343
Folkes Brothers, The, 362
Forde, Florrie, 134, 180fn, 216, 251
Forde, Walter, 262
Foresta, Franco, 264
Formby, George, 221, 223, 228, 253, 260, 264, 274, 282, 292, 317, 337fn, 375
Foster, Stephen, 200, 201, 209, 224
Franklin, Aretha, 347, 351, 352, 353, 368, 382fn
Freddie and the Dreamers, 326
Free and easies, 46, 108, 112, 118, 122fn
Freece, Walter de, 111
Freed, Alan, 297
French, Percy, 149, 252
Fury, Billy, 322, 349

G

Gaiety Girl, A. musical comedy, 190

Garlands, 58, and see Chapbooks
Gender, differences and roles, 4, 5, 6, 7, 10, 164, 175, 198, 199, 235, 237, 244, 245, 271, 322, 334, 344, 364, 371, 391 and see Femininity, Masculinity and New Woman
General Strike, 6, 278
Gerry and the Pacemakers, 327
Gitane, Gertie, 216, 219
Gladiators, The, 368
Gladstone, W E, 184, 185, 187, 188, 193fn, 194fn
Glasgow, *Brown's Royal Music Hall*, 110
Godfrey, Sir Dan, 224
Gramophones, 249, 250, 254, 258, 290, 308
Grant, Cy, 343
Great Depression, 6
Great Northern Troupe of Characteristic Male and Female Dancers, 133, 139fn, 191
Green, Pat, 262
Green, Peter, 346
Gunsky, Maurice, 252

H

Haley, Bill, 305, 310, 311-2, 314, 317, 319fn
Halifax, 107, 108, 109, 119, 121fn, 122fn, 126, 138fn, 289, 304fn, 354fn
Handley, Tommy, 223, 263
Harcourt, G B, 189
Hardy, Thomas, 19, 29fn, 41, 49fn, 50fn, 51fn, 64fn
Harrison, Denham, 180fn
Hartley John, 'The Yorkshire Burns,' 115
Harty, Herbert Hamilton, 225
Heimann, Carl, 240, 245
Helm, Brigitte, *Maria's Dance, (Metropolis)* 261
Hill, Jenny, 'The Vital Spark,' 131, 153, 156, 161fn, 166, 172, 175, 176
Hitchcock, Alfred, 222

Hoggart, Richard, 283fn, 302, 304fn, 308
Holland, Jules and His Rhythm and Blues Orchestra, 16fn, 349
Holliday, Michael , 301
Holly, Buddy, and the Crickets, 310, 311, 312, 313, 314, 315, 316, 317, 323, 325, 331, 347, 349, 356fn
Hone, William, 21
Hooker, John Lee, 343, 345, 355fn
Home Rule, 150, 151, 152, 184, 185, 192
Hopkin, Mary, 336
Howlin' Wolf, 348
Hudd, Roy, 226
Huddersfield, 21, 107, 108, 109, 110, 119, 121fn, 122fn, 124fn, 128, 138fn, 139fn, 158fn, 190, 201, 212fn, 231fn, 360, 372
Hulbert, Jack, 223, 263, 264
Hull, 23, 31fn, 81fn, 127, 128, 144, 158fn, 184, 190, 213fn, 225
Hunt, G W, 142, 188
Hunter, G W, 173
Hunter, Harry, 203, 204, 213fn
Hurley, Alec, 154, 169, 220

I

Identity, 2, 4, 5, 7, 9, 17, 18, 19, 97, 126, 148, 153, 158fn, 191, 198, 203, 226, 284fn, 350, 352, 362, 370, 389, 390
Ifield, Frank, 336
Immigration, post-1945, 7, 8, 336,
Imperial Society of Teachers of Dancing, 221, 236
Imperialism, 5, 133, 135, 136, 189, 190, 192, 195fn, 199, 210, 216, 276, 352
International Novelty Orchestra, 252
Ireland, 6, 9, 15fn, 43, 47, 91, 93, 151, 153, 159fn, 160fn, 189, 212fn, 229fn, 231fn, 253, 263, 280, 281, 322, 341, 357fn
Irish music, 9, 43, 52fn, 62, 67fn, 87, 89, 98, 131, 133, 139fn, 148-53, 154, 156, 158fn, 159fn,

160fn, 189, 191, 192, 199, 200, 202, 204, 210, 213fn, 224, 225, 246fn, 253, 254, 264, 270, 277-8, 280-1, 283fn, 297, 307, 323, 336, 341, 357fn, 359, 376, 388, 390 and see Song and tune Index
Isaacs, Gregory, 382fn
Island record label, 367
Isle of Man, 129, 137, 230fn

J

Jam, The, 349
Jamaica, 274, 360, 362, 364, 366, 367, 375, 377, 380fn
Jazz, 11, 216, 224-5, 226, 231fn, 235, 237, 244, 246fn, 276, 277, 295, 305, 306, 307, 309, 318fn, 322, 328, 337fn, 341, 342, 343, 345, 350, 353, 355fn; Duke Ellington, 257; Louis Armstrong, 257, 355fn trad jazz revival, 307, 309, 322, 328, 342
Jefferson, Blind Lemon, 355fn
Jewel, Jimmy, 222
Jiggerum Juggerum bands, 11, 107, 306
Jingoism, 187-91, 192
Johnson, Amy, 275
Johnson, Blind Willie, 345
Johnson, Lonnie, 307, 343, 344, 355fn
Johnson, Robert, 346
Johnson, Winifred, 211fn, 230fn and see sand dancing
Jolson, Al, 252, 271, 309
Jones, Paul, 348, 349
Jones, Tom, 298
Jubilee Singers, 350
Judge Dread, 228, 375, 391
Juke boxes, 299, 300, 304fn, 308, 311, 319fn, 349

K

Kay, Janet, 371
Kay, Kathie, 296
Kelly, Gene, 227
Kettering, North Park Club, 351
Kidd, Johnny, 314, 325
Kidderminster, 110

Kiepura, Jan, 264
King, B B, 345
King, Jonathan, 375
King Tubby, 368
Kinks, The, 8, 228, 231fn, 304fn, 322, 326, 330-5, 338fn, 373
Kool Cats, 309
Korner, Alexis, 309, 345
Kramer, Billy J, 337fn

L

Laine, Frankie, 300, 301
Lane, Lupino, 224, 240
Lashwood, George, 178, 274
Lauder, Harry, 216, 228fn, 251, 264
Lawrence, Katie, 166
Lead Belly, 307, 344, 354fn, 355fn
Leeds, 46, 108, 109, 110, 112, 113, 114, 115, 118, 119, 122fn, 127, 128, 130, 132, 138fn, 139fn, 158fn, 241, 360, 371
Lennard, Arthur, 165
Leno, Dan, 46, 131, 132, 202
Leonard, Georgina, 166
Leslie, Roy, 272
Lewis, Jerry Lee, 310, 311, 312, 315
Leybourne, George, 144, 145, 146, 147, 148
Lincoln, 37, 110
Liskard the Musical Clown, 110
Little Richard, 310, 311, 312, 314, 315, 319fn
Little Walter, 346, 348
Liverpool, 81fn, 90, 109, 110, 112, 114, 117, 118, 124fn, 126, 127, 128, 129, 130, 137fn, 138fn, 148, 150, 151, 153, 188, 200, 201, 220, 241, 307, 322-3, 326-7, 336, 343, 353, 357fn; as 'Nashville of the north,' 307, 322
Livingstone, Dandy, 365
Lloyd, Arthur, 131, 144, 145, 148, 165, 166, 186, 189
Lloyd, Marie, 13, 115, 131, 153, 154, 169, 216, 230fn, 375
Lomax, Alan, 307, 308, 318fn, 343

London, 19, 20, 24, 25, 31fn, 39, 42, 43, 44, 58, 59, 78, 87, 89, 91, 98, 100, 101fn, 105, 108, 109, 110, 111, 114, 115, 116, 121fn, 122fn, 124fn, 125, 127, 128, 130, 132, 134, 135, 136, 139fn, 140fn, 148, 151, 152, 156, 171, 176, 177, 181fn, 184, 186, 188, 190, 192, 194fn, 195fn, 199, 200, 202, 203, 204, 205, 208, 211fn, 212fn, 214fn, 217, 221, 225, 230fn, 231fn, 234, 239, 243, 259, 260, 267fn, 274, 283fn, 303fn, 311, 321, 327, 328, 329, 330, 331, 336, 338fn, 343, 345, 347, 349, 350, 353, 355fn, 360, 361, 363, 364, 368, 369, 370, 371, 374, 383fn, 390
Longstaffe, Ernest, 275
Lorraine, Violet, 219
Lover, Samuel, 149, 158fn
Lovers' Rock, 370-2, 382fn
Luton, 241, 336
Lynn, Vera, 222, 286-7, 293, 295, 301, 389
Lyttleton, Humphrey, 343

M

McCormack, John, 150, 159fn, 252, 253, 267fn, 269, 281
MacDonald, Jeanette, 253
MacDermott, The Great, 13, 185, 186, 187, 188, 194fn
MacNaughten, Frank, 111
Macka B, 379, 384fn
Mackintosh, Ken, 289
Madness, 228, 360, 364, 372, 378, 382fn, 385, 393
Magic Sam, 348
Manchester, 109, 110, 112, 114, 117, 118, 124fn, 127, 128, 129, 139, 148, 151, 159fn, 190, 200, 212fn, 228fn, 241, 248fn, 295, 337fn, 343, 346, 349, 353, 354fn, 360, 367, 368
Manfred Mann, 348, 355fn and see Jones, Paul
Manuscript collections, dance tunes and songs, 35-7, 38, 44, 48fn, 49fn, 50fn, 51fn, 214fn; Atkinson, Henry, 35; Buttrey, John, 37, 49fn; Calvert, William, 36; Clare, John, 27, 35, 37-9, 50fn; Jackson, Joshua, 36, 37, 48fn, 49fn; Turner, Michael, 49fn; Vickers, William, 49fn; Winder, John, 49fn; Winter, William, 39-40
Margate, 110, 122fn, 129, 202, 204, 241, 332
Mark, Louise, 371
Marley, Bob, 360, 367, 368, 371, 375, 379, 381fn, 383fn, 388
Marquee Club, 345, 346, 347
Martha and the Vandellas, 350
Martin, Dean, 301, 336
Martino, Al, 301
Masculinity, 5, 70, 71, 80, 98, 144, 244, 272, 276, 334 and see Femininity and Gender
Mass Observation, 226, 235, 276, 293, 303fn
Matthew, Jessie, 223, 263, 264
Matumbi, 369
Mayall, John and the Bluesbreakers, 346, 353
Mayhew, Henry, 20, 42, 47, 55, 78, 83fn, 128, 172, 208, 209
Mayne, Clarice, 229fn
Mayne, Ernie, 217
Mayne, Richard Sir, 126
Mayo, Sam, 154, 274
McDevitt Chas, 306, 308, 310, 319fn
McGhee, 'Brownie,' 307, 343
McGlennon, Felix, 142
Mecca ballrooms, 235, 240, 241, 245, 351
Menageries, 20, 24, 25, 29fn; Wombwell's 12, 25, 31fn
Memphis Slim, 343, 346, 355fn
Middlesbrough, 9, 109, 110, 123fn, 127, 148, 158fn
Middleton, Richard, 3, 15fn
Mighty Diamonds, 376
Migil 5, 363

Miller, Glen, 290, 291
Miller, Mandy, 301
Miller, Max, 13, 221, 338fn, 375
Mills, Jock, 176
Milly (Small), 363
Misty in Roots, 369, 372, 374
Mitchell, Guy, 301
Mods, 7, 8, 9, 306, 329, 338fn
Montez, Chris, 299, 324
Moody Blues, The, 348
Moore, Thomas. 40, 149, 281, 283fn
Moore, Annabelle, *Butterfly Dance*, 261
'Moral economy,' 4, 94
More, Hannah, *Cheap Repository Tracts*, 60, 77
Morecombe, 108, 128
Morgan, Jane, 317
Morris dancing, 8, 18, 19, 27, 28fn, 29fn
Morris, Lily, 180fn
Morton, Charles, 108, 116
Moss, Edward, 110, 221, 228fn, 234, 307
Motown, 324, 325, 328, 348, 350, 351, 357fn, 371, 372; 1965 Tamla Motown tour, 350
Muddy Waters, 307, 341, 344, 345, 347, 348, 388
Mummers, 8, 17, 18, 107, 385
Murphy, Matt, 344
Murray, Ruby, 295, 317
Murray, Pete, 297
Music hall, Chapter 7, Chapter 9, Chapter 10, Chapter 11, Chapter 13; 4, 9, 11, 12, 13, 21, 27, 56, 105, 106, 107, 108-20, 120fn, 121fn, 122fn, 124fn, 125, 131-6, 137, 141, 200-8, 209, 212fn, 249, 251, 257, 259, 262, 263, 264, 266fn, 270, 272, 273, 274, 279, 282, 293, 294, 296, 298, 315, 325, 330, 338fn, 373, 375, 376, 380fn, 385, 386, 387, 392; audiences: 116-8; comic songs, 154-6; and dance, 131-6, 149; everyday life, 154-6; Great War, 216-9; love and marriage, 164-70; and minstrelsy, 200-8; party politics, 184-7; patriotism and jingoism, 187-92; the police; 177-8; post-1945, 226-7; social problems, 170-7; stage Cockneys, 153-4; stage Irish, 148-53; swells, 144-8
Musical Youth, 376, 383fn

N

Nancy Dawson's Cabinet of Choice Songs, 143
Nash, 'Jolly' John, 144, 148, 187, 189, 274
National Front, 365, 374, 378
National songs, 123fn, 277, 279, 280
National Jazz and Blues Festival, 345
National Vigilance Society, 111, 242
Nazamova, Alla, *Salomé*, 261
Nelson, Ricky, 315
Nesbit, Max and Harry, 222
New Cockalorum Songster, 143
New Woman, The, 135. 164, 179fn and see Femininity and Gender
Newcastle, 24, 42, 58, 59, 66fn, 82fn, 115, 123fn, 126, 154, 171, 197fn, 337fn, 354fn
Nielson, Asta, *Afgrunden (The Abyss)*, 261
Noble, Denis, 222
Northampton, 29fn, 31fn, 109, 138, 351
Northern Soul, 13, 351
Northumbrian pipes, 24, 33, 48fn, 52fn, 61fn, 388
Notting Hill Carnival, 362, 380fn
Notting Hill, riots, 1958, 8, 352, 362; 1976, 374
Nottingham, 20, 21, 29fn, 82fn, 90, 110, 114, 127, 190; Goose Fair, 20, 21

O

Obernkirchen Children's Choir, 301

O'Hara, Maureen, 263
Oi bands, 383fn
Oliver, Paul, 309, 342, 352, 353
Operettas, 11, 223, 259, 261, 263
Orbison, Roy, 324, 336

P
Pacer-egging, 17, 18, 19, 28fn, 81fn
Pantomime, 24, 119, 130, 133, 177, 178, 227
Parnes, Larry, 314
Pavlova, Anna, *Dumb Girl of Portici, The*, 261
Penny gaffs, 2, 78, 127
Penrose, Charles, 274
Perkins, Carl, 325
Pickering, Michael, 197, 211fn
Pickles, Wilfred, 222, 304fn
Piglets, The, 375
Pioneers, The, 372
Playford, 27, 34, 35, 39, 41; *Dancing Master, The*, 34, 39, 44, 45, 48fn
Pleasant, Jack, 167
Pleasure gardens, 25-6, 59, 119
Plough bullocks, 17, 19, 28fn
Police, 24, 70, 92-3, 95, 100, 113, 114, 122, 123, 126, 144, 164, 177-8, 181fn, 214fn, 246fn, 274-5, 365, 369, 370, 374, 375, 391
Police, The, 376
Poole, Brian, 325
Poor Soldier, The, 1783 comic opera, 26
Portsmouth, 23, 24, 30fn, 110, 115, 127, 209
Powell, Clive, 349
Powell, Enoch, 353
Power, Nellie, 146
Presley, Elvis, 295, 312, 313, 314
Preston, 73, 110, 115, 128
Pride, Dickie, 349
Priestley, J B, 236
Prince Buster, 16fn, 363, 364, 372, 375
Punk, 79, 374, 375, 378, 384fn

Q
Quarrymen, The, 309, 323 and see The Beatles

R
Race, 8, 10, 13, 14, 131, 151, 189, 197, 198, 203, 205, 206, 207, 210, 224, 225, 235, 237, 244, 291, 309, 337fn, 341, 342, 351, 352, 357fn, 361, 362, 364, 365, 369, 374, 377, 380fn, 384fn
Radio, 2, 6, 7, 216, 222, 223, 227, 237, 240, 249, 250, 254-61, 264, 265, 273, 276, 281, 286-8, 289, 294-5, 300, 301, 308, 310, 325, 337fn, 386, 387; Poste Parisien, 260, 267fn; Radio Birmingham, 368; Radio Caroline, 297; Radio London, 368; Radio Luxembourg, 259, 260, 267fn, 286, 292, 296-7, 310, 354fn; Radio Normandie, 259, 260, 267fn, 292, 296; and see BBC Radio
Rafferty, Pat, 149, 150, 189, 192
Ragtime, 11, 205, 210, 216, 219, 224, 226, 228fn, 230fn, 234, 235, 341, 342, 353
Ranking Roger, 364, 365
Rastafarianism, 7, 362, 369, 370, 371, 376, 377, 378, 381fn
Ray, Johnny, 301
Redcar, 109
Records and record industry, 2, 249, 250-4, 260, 276, 281, 286, 297, 299, 300-1, 308, 310, 311, 314, 317, 330, 342, 343, 360, 364, 366, 375
Redding, Otis, 347
Reeves, Jim, 301, 336
Reggae, Chapter 21; 357fn, 360, 362, 363, 364, 366-70, 371, 372-9, 381fn, 383fn, 388, 389; British reggae, 368-70; white reggae, 372-5
Reith, Sir John, 256, 304fn
Revues, 220, 222, 227, 228fn, 252; *Bric à Brac*, 218; *Blackbirds of 1928*, 252; *Shell Out*, 218; *Swing It*, 222, *Three Cheers*, 228fn

Rhythm and blues, Chapter 20; 323, 324, 325, 328, 330, 337fn, 342, 345-9, 350, 351-4, 361
Ricardo Family, The, 110
Richard, Cliff, 226, 228, 231fn, 298, 314, 315, 316, 317, 320fn, 353
Rickard, Harry, 186, 187
Roadrunners, The, 323
Roaring Twenties Club, 363, 378
Roberts, Robert, 165, 234
Robeson, Paul, 252, 264, 269
Robey, George, 139fn, 219, 221, 264
Robinson, Smokey, and the Miracles, 350
Rock 'n' roll, Chapter 18; 13, 227, 297, 298, 302, 305, 306, 310-6, 317, 319fn, 321, 323, 325, 335, 336, 337fn, 345, 349, 353
Rock Against Racism, 365, 374
Rock Steady, 362, 364, 366, 367, 371, 372, 377
Rockers, 8, 9, 306, 314
Romeo, Max, 366
Roe, Tommy, 324
Rolling Stones, The, 13, 231fn, 327, 346, 347, 348, 355fn
Rooney, Pat, 159fn
Ross, Diana, 382fn
Ross, W G, 143, 152fn
Rowley, J W 'Over,' 109, 115, 116, 131, 202
Royal Command Performance, 133, 215, 327
Rude Boys, 363, 364, 378
Rumsey, Henry St John, *Ballroom Dancing*, 238, 247fn
Russell, Dave, 1, 121fn, 279
Ruts, The, 372, 374

S

Salford, 212fn, 241, 247fn, 248fn
Salisbury, Lord, 187, 188
Santley, Maud, 178
Scarborough, 109, 129, 138fn, 190, 209
Scott, Clement, 12

Screaming Lord Sutch and the Savages, 346
Seaside resorts, 107, 109, 122fn, 129, 190, 209, 214fn, 227, 230fn, 259, 289
Secombe, Harry, 231fn
Seeger, Pete, 307
Selecter, The, 364, 365, 372, 381fn
Settle, 115
Seymour, Syd, and His Mad Hatters, 222
Shapiro, Helen, 234
Sharp, Cecil, 65, 76, 212fn, 226, 277; *British Songs for Home and School*, 277
Sheffield, 103fn, 114, 117, 130, 137fn, 138fn, 190, 212fn, 220, 231fn, 354fn
Shelton, Anne, 288, 295, 301, 303fn, 317
Silvester, Victor, 237, 238, 288, 289, 295
Simone, Nina, 348, 350, 351
Sinatra, Frank, 301, 317
Ska, Chapter 21; 228, 354, 360, 362-4, 365, 366, 368, 372, 373, 375, 376, 377, 378, 379 and see Two Tone
Skatalites, The, 363, 365, 366
Skiffle, Chapter 18; 227, 302, 305, 306-10, 314, 315, 316, 317, 319fn, 321, 322, 323, 328, 330, 342, 345, 346, 349
Skinheads, 7, 9
Small Faces, The, 328, 348, 351
Smethwick, 352
Smiley Culture, 370, 378
Smith, Betty, 308
Smith, 'Whispering' Jack, 270
Song-and supper clubs, 78, 143, 158
Songsters, 26, 54, 59-63
Soul, Chapter 20; 13, 325, 346, 349-51, 353, 354, 366, 368, 371, 372, 378, 382fn, 383fn
Sousa, J P, marches, 201, 251
Sound systems, 360, 362, 363, 366, 370, 371, 372, 380fn

Southall, 374
Southend, 109, 129
Specials, The, 16fn, 359, 360, 364, 365, 372, 381fn
Spencer Davis Group, The, 348, 351
Spivey, Victoria, 344, 354fn
Springfield, Dusty, 351
Squeeze, 349
St Clair, F V, 65fn
St Helens, 109
Stanford, C V, 277, 278, 280, 283fn; *New National Song Book*, 277
Steel Pulse, 360, 369
Steele, Tommy, 237, 228, 314, 316, 317
Stewart, Rod, 309
Stockton-on-Tees, 110, 123fn, 316
Stockwell, Walter, 115
Stoll, Oswald, 110, 186, 192
Style Council, 349
Sunderland, 127, 158fn, 190, 314, 354fn
Suppé, F von, 251
Supremes, The, 16fn, 350
'Swinging London,' 321, 329, 330, 331, 336
Symarip, 378

T
Tabrar, Joseph, 142
Tagg, Philip, 2, 3, 11, 15fn, 318fn
Tauber, Richard, 263
Taylor, Eddie, 348
Teddy boys, 7, 9, 306
Temple Church, The, 251
Terry, Sonny, 307, 343
Tharpe, Sister Rosetta, 344
Them, 348
Tiller, John, 132; John Tiller dancers, 132, 134, 139fn
Thompson, Flora, 19, 29fn, 119
Thornton, Richard, 108, 110, 111
Thurnhill and Fothergill, 110
Tilley, Vesta, 169, 178, 185, 186, 188, 193fn, 216, 218
Tin Pan Alley, 210, 230fn, 270, 281, 305, 307

Tippa Irie, 370
Toots and the Maytals, 365, 366, 372, 381fn
Townsley, William, Lancashire dialect poet, 115
Travelling theatres, 24-5
Trinidad, 307, 360-2. 377, 380fn, 390
Trojan record label, 367, 375
Two Rascals, 220
Two Tone, 13, 364-6. 370, 372, 378, 381fn
Two Tykes, The (Silly Billy Elliot and Soft Tony Benson); 116

U
UB40, 360, 364, 372, 373, 379, 388
Urbanisation, 3, 4, 27, 95, 106, 152, 278

V
Valentino, Rudolph, 261, 275; *Four Horsemen of the Apocalypse*, 261
Vance, The Great, 110, 119, 144, 148, 178, 193fn, 202, 213fn
Variety Theatre, see Music Hall
Vaughan, Sarah, 336
Vee, Bobby, 336, 353
Veterans of Variety, films, 230fn, 262
Viceroys, The, 378
Victor, Ethel, 179fn
Victoria, Vesta. 167, 264, 266fn
Vincent, Gene, 310, 311, 313, 349
Vipers, The, 306, 308, 310; Whyton Wally, 308

W
Wakes, 18, 21, 22
Waller, 'Fats,' 225, 231fn
Walsall, 110
War, 26, 97, 98, 136, 183, 187-8, 189, 219, 224, 229fn, 235, 265, 275, 278, 279, 300, 389; American War of Independence, 26; Boer War, 136, 189, 190, 191, 277; Crimean War, 103fn, 187; Great War (World War 1), 6, 215, 216-9, 224, 229fn, 234, 243, 246fn,

267fn, 270, 274, 276, 279, 303fn; Revolutionary and Napoleonic Wars, 8, 60, 86, 389; Seven Years' War, 98; War of Jenkin's Ear, 98; World War II, 6, 226, 240, 265, 275, 285-93, 294, 295, 300-1, 307, 312, 316, 322, 352
Warrington, 109
Washington, Geno, and the Ram Jam Band, 346
Wedgewood, Josiah, 22
Weedon, Bert, *Play in a Day*, 315, 317
Weller, Paul, 349
Whinham, Robert, 42, 209
White, Josh, 343
Whitman, Slim, 301
Whitfield, David, 301
Who, The, 321, 322, 326, 328-30, 331, 334, 335
Wigan, 316, 349, 351
Wilde, Marty, 316; Marty Wilde Big Beat Show, 349
Williams, Andy, 336
Williamson, Sonny Boy, 343, 348
Wilson, Joe, 123fn, 154, 164, 170, 174
Winter, Mark, 336
Wonder, Stevie, 350, 368
Wolverhampton, 148, 360, 384fn
Woods, Ronnie, 309
Wooley, Sheb, 317
Woolworths, 251, 317
Working Men's Clubs, 119, 131, 227, 238, 389
Wycherley, Ronnie, 322

X

Y

Yardbirds, The, 348, 353, 355fn
Yarmouth, 26, 109, 115, 138fn, 209
York, 276, 367; S Rowntree, *Poverty and Progress*, 276
Yorkshire Dales, dances and 'minstrels,' 41, 43, 51fn
Young, Jimmy, 295, 301, 317
Youth clubs, 308, 322

Youth culture, 242, 306, 316, 327, 329

Z

Song and Tune Index

5-4-3-2-1, 349

A
Abdulla Bulbul Ameer, 158fn
Abide with Me, 107, 267fn, 279, 292
Acute Schizophrenia Blues, 333
Admiral Rodney's Delight, 36
Adolph Sinkins, 146, 147
Adventures in Astrilly, 180
Adventures of a Policeman, The, 93
After the Ball, 102, 252
Afton Waters, 283fn
A-hunting We Will Go, 283fn
Aim Not Too Low, aka Fortune My Foe, 57, 65fn
Ain't That A Shame, 314, 323
Ain't We Got Fun, 276
Al Capone, 364
Alcohol, 333. 334
Alewives' Invitation to Married-men and Bachelors, The, 74
Alice Gray, 55
All Coons Look Alike to Me, 205
All My Loving, 324
All Shook Up, 313
All Through the Night, 40, 278, 279, 280, 283fn
All Traitors, 91
All You Fascists Bound to Lose, 307
American Beef, 179
American Patrol, 290
Amy, Wonderful Amy, 275
And I Love Her, 325
Angelina Was Fond of the Soldiers, 161
Annie Laurie, 254, 283fn
Another Girl, 326
Another Little Drink, 160fn
Any Old Iron, 215, 226, 279, 302
Any Time's Kissing Time, 229
Are You from Dixie? 220
'Arf a Pint of Ale, 154, 252, 279
Armaggideon Time, 374
Around the Corner and Under the Tree, 272
Arthur, 330, 332
As I Love You, 317
As Oyster Nan Stood by her Tub, 58, 76
Ash Grove, The, 283fn
Ashley's Hornpipe, 51fn
Astrilly, or the Pitman's Farewell, 174
Astrilly's Goold Fields, 180fn
At Finnegan's Ball, 281
Au Fond du Temple Saint, 295
Auf Wiedersehen Sweet Heart, 301, 302
Auld Lang Syne, 59, 278
Auld Hoose, The, 278
Away with Melancholy, 40
Away Ye Brave Foxhunting Race, 81fn

B

Baby Boy Has Passed Away, 207
Baby Love, 356fn
Baby Please Don't Go, 350
Babylon Makes the Rules, 369
Back to Africa, 369
Bad Boy, 316
Baggy Trousers, 373
Bailiff's Daughter of Islington, The, 278, 285fn
Baked Sheep's Heart Stuffed with Sage and Onion, 229fn
Ballad Singer, The, 53
Banana Boat Song, The, 362
Band that Jack Built, The, 265
Bang Her Well Peter, 74
Barbara Allen, 56, 59
Barley Mow, The, 56, 72, 81
Barley Stack, The, 43
Barnacle Bill the Sailor, 266fn
Bachelor Boy, 315
Battle of the Nile, The, 36
Battle of Prague, The, 39, 50fn
Bay of Biscay, The, 280, 283
Because I Love You, 251
Because You're Mine, 301
Bedelia, 283fn
Begone Dull Care, 283fn
Believe Me If All Those Endearing Young Charms, 40
Bell Boy, The, 329
Belle Jeanette, La, 40
Bésame Mucho, 337fn
Best Things in Life Are Free, The, 273
Big Black Smoke, 334
Big Five, 375
Big Seven, 375
Big Six, 375
Black Ey'd Susan, 39
Black Joak, The, 44
Black Philosopher, The, 207
Black Power, 361, 380fn
Black Ram, The, 72
Blackbird, The, 283
Blacksmith, The, 54
Bless 'Em All, 293
Blighty, the Soldier's Home, Sweet Home, 217
Blind Boy, The, 203-4, 279
Blood on the Streets, 384fn
Bloody-minded Husband, The, 65fn
Bloom is on the Rye, The, 201
Blue Skies Just Around the Corner, 273
Blue Suede Shoes, 278
Bluebell's of Scotland, The, 278
Bob the Policeman and Charming Bet, 92
Bobbies of the Queen, The, 178
Bobbing Joan, 38
Boers Have Got My Daddy, The, 189
Boiled Beef and Carrots, 154, 217
Bold Robert Emmett, 6, 150
Bonaparte's March, 42
Bonnie Dundee, 158fn, 283fn
Bonny Grey, The, aka Cockfight, The, 81fn
Boogie Woogie Bugle Boy, The, 293
Boom, Boom, 348
Boomps A Daisy, 273
Bother the Men, 175, 180fn
Bower that Stands in Thigh Lane, The, 157fn
Boy in the Gallery, The, 175
Boys of the Old Brigade, The, 190, 192
Boys of Wexford, The, 159
Bravo, Dublin Fusiliers! 189
Bright Lights, Big City, 348
Brighton Camp, aka Girl I Left Behind Me, The, 36, 38, 40, 43, 158fn, 283fn, 395, Appendix 400
Bring It on Home, 348
Bring Us in Good Ale, 72
Bristol Hornpipe, The, 201
Bristol 'Prentice Boy, The, 90
British Grenadiers, The, 278, 283fn
Britons, Strike Home, 98, 99, 389
Broomfield Hill, 56
Buffalo Soldier, 367
Burden of Shame, 373

By the Light of the Silvery Moon, 206
Bye, Bye Johnny, 347
Bye, Bye Love, 316

C

Cackle, Cackle, Cock-a-doodle-doo, 113
Call Out the Boys of the Old Brigade, 190
Caller Herrin', 283fn
Campbells Are Coming, The, 103fn, 278, 283fn
Camptown Races, The, 201, 206
Can Can, 373
Capt Reeds or 2d of Gards March, 36
Captain White's Dance, 41
Career Opportunities, 374
Carol, 347
Carolina Moon, 252
Carry Me Back to Old Virginny, 206
Casey Jones, 307
Cathy's Clown, 325
Cats in Our Backyard, The, 204
Caught You in a Lie, 371
Caveat for Cutpurses, A, 30fn
Caveat for Young Men, A, 65fn
Chains, 324
Cherry Oh Baby, 373, 390
Chalk Farm to Camberwell, 218
Chalk It Up to Gladstone, 185
Champagne Charlie, 107, 144, 147
Chapter of Cheats, A, 95
Chapter of Kings, The, 37
Charleston, The, 273
Charlie Is My Darling, 278, 283fn
Charms of a Good Little Wife, The, 80
Chartists Are Coming, The, 103fn
Chattanooga Choo Choo, 290
Che Gelida Manina, 269
Cheshire Rolling Hornpipe, The, 45, 395, Appendix 406 (2 versions)
Chevy Chase, 56, 57
Chickaleary Cove, The, 153, 155

Children Get Ready, 378
Chillingowullabadorie, 161fn
Chinese Children Call Me Daddy, 362
Cholera's Coming, The, 103fn
City Cheat Discovered, The, 65fn
City Toff, The, 146
City Waif, The, 172, 180fn
Clarenet (Handel), 36
Class War, 384fn
Cliquot, Cliquot, 144
Close the Shutters, Willy's Dead, 207
Clouds Will Soon Roll By, The, 273
Cock and Hen, The, 37
Cock Linnet song, aka My Old Man (Said Follow the Van), 141, 170, 179, 217
Cock of the North, The, 133, 191, 195fn
Cockfight, The, see Bonny Grey
Cockles and Mussels, 280
Cockney Coon, The, 203
Cockney Translation, 370
College Hornpipe, The , 36, 41
Collier's Death, The, see Perils of the Mine, The
Come All You Gallant Britons Bold, 72
Come into the Garden Maud, 16fn, 107, 375
Come Jolly Bacchus God of Wine, 26
Come Landlord Fill the Flowing Bowl, 72, 81fn
Come Lasses and Lads, 33, 34, 48fn, 278, 280, 283fn, 392
Come On, 347
Come Outside, 375
Come Where the Booze is Cheaper, 160
Come Write Me Down, 56
Coming in on a Wing and a Prayer, 288, 292
Complain Neighbour, 370
Concrete Jungle, 365
Convict Maid, The, 90

Coon Ambassador, The, 207
Copper Stick, The, 157fn
Cork Leg, The, 112, 123fn
Coster Muvver, 165
Cotton Lords of Preston, The, 13, 95
Countryman's Visit to St Bartholomew's Fair, The, 21
Cousin Kevin, 328
Cow's Courant or, Galop and Shite, The, 36
Crib and Molineaux, 72
Cricket, Lovely Cricket, 361
Croppies Lie Down, 37, 50fn, 91
Croppy Boy, The, 91, 150, 159fn, 253
Cruel Mother, The, 56
Cry, 301
Crying, Waiting, Hoping, 337
Cucaracha, La, 282fn
Cumberland Gap, 306, 307
Cunning Little Coon, The, 207
Cut My Hair, 329

D
Daddy Has A Sweetheart (Mummy Is her Name), 272
Daisy Bell, aka Bicycle Made for Two, A, 279
Dance of the Fire Brigade Girls, The, 218
Dancing in the Streets, 356fn
Dancing on the Ceiling, 223
Dancing with My Shadow, 271
Dandy Coloured Coon, The, 205, 211fn
Danny Boy, 12, 264, 269, 390
Dansomanic, La, 39
Darby Kelly, 40
Dardenella, 252
Darkies' Jubilee, The, 201
Dashing White Sergeant, The, 44
Daughters of Britain, Work with a Will, 218,
David of the White Rock, 278, 283fn
Dawning of the Day, The, 54

Day That the Rains Came Down, The, 317
Days of Queen Elizabeth, The, 54
Dead End Street, 330, 331
Dear Little Shamrock, The, 280, 281
Death of Sayers, The, 72
Dedicated Follower of Fashion, 330, 331
Deep in a Dream, 271
Deep in the Heart of Texas, 289
Demolition, 333
Dialogue and Song on the Starvation Poor Law Bill, A, 96
Did Tosti Raise His Bowler Hat? 273
Did You Ever See a Dream Walking? 296
Dido, Bendigo, aka Noble Foxhunting, 71, 81fn
Dimples, 348
Dingle Regatta, 52fn
Dirty Jobs, 329
Do Not Nurse Your Anger, 213fn
Do Not Speak the Angry Word, 213fn
Do the Reggay, 366, 381fn
Do Wacha Doo, 282fn
Do Wah Diddy Diddy, 349
D'Ye Ken John Peel? 279, 280, 283fn
Do You Want to Know a Secret? 324
Dobbs in Paris. 161fn
Doctor Says I'm Not to be Worried, The, 200
Does Your Chewing Gum Lose Its Favour (On the Bedpost Over Night)? 315
Don't Be Cruel, 313
Don't Let Me Be Misunderstood, 348, 356fn
Don't Let Me Die an Old Maid, 56
Don't Like Police, 370
Don't Say a Word to the Wife, 170
Don't Sit Under the Apple Tree, 293

Don't Touch Me Nylons, 361, 379fn
Dorsetshire Hornpipe, The, 51fn
Double Barrel, 367
Double Crossing Time, 346
Dove Will Fight for Freedom, The, 151
Down at the Old Bull and Bush, 141, 154
Down in the Village, 54
Down with the French, 36
Downfall of Paris, The, 39, 42, Appendix 403
Dreadlocks Love Affair, 382fn
Dream Lover, 253, 267
Drop of Good Beer, A, 69
Drunkard Reformed, The, 73
Drunkard's Dream, The, 74
Drunken Wife, The, 74
Duchess's Slipper, The, 36
Duke of Reichstadt's Waltz, The, 40
Duke of York's Troops, The, 40
Durang's Hornpipe, 46
Durham Gaol, 92
Dusty Miller, The, 38

E
'E Dunno Where 'E Are, 175
Early One Morning, 283fn
Easy Snappin', 362
Eightsome Reel, The, 44, 51fn
Eileen Aroon, 253
Eleanor Rigby, 326
English Civil War, 374
Enjoy Yourself, 1, 14, 293, 293fn
Eton Boat Song, The, 304fn
Every Time We Say Goodbye, 295
Everybody's Trying to Be My Baby, 325
Execution of Fish the Murderer, 88
Exodus, 67

F
Faint Heart Never Won Fair Lady, 65fn
Falling in Love Again, 337fn
False Bride, The, 56

Farewell to You Judges and Jurries aka Transports, The, 90
Fascinating Rhythm, 282fn
Father, Dear Father, the Brokers Are In, 170
Father's Got the Sack from the Waterworks, 219
Favourite Quickstep, 41
Ferdinand the Bull, 274
Ferret and the Coney, The, 30fn
Ferry Across the Mersey, 327
Fiddle About, 328
Fig for Men, A, 175
Fighting the System, 384fn
Fille Sauvage, La, 40
Fings Ain't What They Used to Be, 233
Finnegan's Ball, 281
Finnegan's Wake, 149
First Love – Last Love – Best Love, 219
Fisher's Hornpipe, 43
Floral Dance, The, 269
Flowers of Edinburgh, The, 36, Appendix 400
Flyme Clarke's Wild Lament, 92
Follow My Lover, 41
Follow the Swallow, 273
Fool on the Hill, The, 325
Fools Like Me, 320fn
Fool's Paradise, 316
For the Benefit of Mr Kite 338fn
Freight Train, 306
Friendly Visit, The, 47, Appendix 408
Frog He Would A-wooing Go, A, 50fn, 143
Froggie Went A-courting, 59
Frolicksome Farmer, The, 46
From Me to You, 324

G
Gabio, The, 37
Gamblin' Man, 307
Garden Where the Praties Grow, The, 281
Garry Owen, 51fn
Gay Gordons, The, 51fn
Gee Ho, Dobbin, 76

General's Fast Asleep, The, 274
General Ludd's Triumph, 103fn
Gentle Maiden, The, 280, 281
Gentleman Soldier, The, 78, 272
Gentlemen! The King, 275
Gentle Jenny Gray, 201
Gently on My Mind, 336
German Band, The, 161fn, 169
Gertie, the Girl with the Gong, 275
Get a Job, 365,
Get Up, Stand Up, 367
Ghetto of the City, 369
Ghost Town, 359, 365, 381fn
Giddy Up a Ding Dong, 319fn
Gilly, Gilly, Ossenfeffer, Katzeneller, Bogen, By the Sea, 304fn
Girl, 325
Girl I Left Behind Me, The, see Brighton Camp
Girl of My Dreams, 252
Give Me a Ticket to Heaven, 180fn
Give Us Once a Drink, 56
Give What You Can to those in Distress, 173
Glad All Over, 327
Glad to See You Back, 218
Glorious Beer, 160fn
Go Down Moses, 350
God Save Ireland, 150, 159fn, 228fn, 253, 281
God Save the King, 62, 99, 103fn, 159fn, 228fn, 278
Going Ober De Mountain, 208
Golden Slumbers, 283fn
Golden Vanity, The, 283fn
Good Advice to Bachelors How to Court and Obtain a Young Lass, 65fn
Good Ale, 72, 74
Good Blow-out for Fourpence, A, 160fn
Good Day Sunshine, 325
Good Little Wife, 167
Good Luck, Little French Soldier Man, 216

Good Man is Hard to Find, A, 272
Good Old London Town Girl, A, 203
Good Old Yorkshire Pudden', 160fn, 229fn
Good Ship Lollipop, The, 274
Goodbye, 336
Goodbye Dolly Gray, 189, 194fn
Gorgonzola Cheese, 160fn, 229fn
Gossip Calypso, 362
Got My Mojo Working, I've, 341, 346, 347, 349
Got to Get You into My Life, 325
Gown of Green, The, 54
Grandad' Flannelette Nightshirt, 228, 375
Great Balls of Fire, 312
Great Big Saw Came Nearer and Nearer (to Poor Little Vera), The, 272, 280
Great Pretender, The, 319fn
Green Door, 381fn
Greenback Dollar, 306
Greensleeves, 18, 35, 294
Greenwich Pensioner, The, 59, 97
Grow Some Taters, 217

H
Hail Smiling Morn, 55
Hands Off, Germany, 216
Hands Off, She's Mine, 381fn
Handels Gavot, 39
Handsworth Revolution, 369, 370
Happy Am De Boys Down Here, 213fn
Happy Days Are Here Again, 273
Happy Little Sam, 213fn
Happy Wanderer, The, 301
Hard Day's Night, 326
Hare Hunting Song, The, 81fn
Harp that Once Through Tara's Halls, The, 133, 278, 283fn
Harry Was a Champion, 215
Haste to the Wedding, 40, 41, 51fn, Appendix 404
Have Another Drink, 333
Have a Drop of Gin, Joe, 160fn

SONG AND TUNE INDEX

He Played His Ukulele as the Ship Went Down, 238
He Wad Be a Noodle, 154
Hear My Prayer, 251
Heartbreak Hotel, 313, 317
Hearts of Oak, 39, 40, 97
Heaving of the Lead, The, 37
Helpless Dancer, The, 329
Here Come the People in Grey, 339fn
Here in My Heart, 301
He's a Bloke as I'd Like to Walk Out Wiv', 194fn
He's a Pal of Mine, 119
Here 'Tis, 348, 356fn
Hiawatha, 315
Highland Lassie, The, 81fn
Highway to Dublin, The, 36
Hindustan, 272
Hippy, Hippy Shake, 337fn
His Majesty the Baby, 282fn
Hi-tiddey-hi-ti, 229fn
Hold Your Hand Out, You Naughty Boy, 170, 302
Hole to Put Poor Robin In, A, 76, 82fn
Holiday, 333
Holmfirth Anthem, The, aka Pratty Flowers, 81fn
Homing Waltz, The, 301
Honey Don't, 325
Hoochie Coochie Man, 348, 356fn
Hot Meat Pies, Saveloys and Trotters, 160fn, 229fn
House in the Country, 331
House of the Rising Song, The, 348, 356fn
How Do You Do It? 326
How Long Jah, 369
How Much Is that Doggie in the Window? 302, 304
Hullo, Hullo! It's a Different Girl Again, 219
Hundred Pipers, The, 283fn

I

I Can't Be Satisfied, 347
I Can't Explain, 328
I Can't Find Brummagen, 95, 102fn
I Can't Get No Satisfaction, 347
I Can't Give You Anything but Love, Baby, 252
I Can't Stop Loving You, 356fn
I Did What I Could with my Gas Mask, 292
I Do Like Yer Cocky (Now You've Got Your Khaki On), 216
I Dreamt that I Dwelled in Marble Halls, 107
I Got to Find My Baby, 325
I Just Want to Make Love to You, 347, 355fn
I Like It, 326
I Miss My Swiss, 273
I Saw Her Standing There, 324
I Shot the Sherriff, 367, 368
I Want a Girl, Just Like the Girl that Married Dear Old Dad, 166, 272
I Want to Hold Your Hand, 324
I Want Loving, 218
I Want to Tell You, 325
Idler, The, 207
If It Wasn't for the 'Ouses In-between, 12, 155
If the Girlies Could be Soldiers, 218
If You Hadn't Gone Away, 271
If You Want to Know the Time (Ask a Policeman), 178
If You Were the Only Girl in the World, 219
If You're Brown, 361
If You're Not White, You're Black, 361, 379fn, 380fn
I Lift Up My Finger (And I Say Tweet Tweet), 280
I Like Bananas (Because They Have No Bones), 269
I Live in Hopes, 169
I'll Be Home, 295
I'll Be Loving You – Always, 271
I'll Be Seeing You, 293
I'll Cry Instead, 325
I'll Keep You Satisfied, 337fn

I'll Make a Man of You, 216
I'll Meet You Love Along the Line, 175
I'll See You in My Dreams, 271
I'll Take You Home Again Kathleen, 149
I'll Walk Beside You, 287, 288
I'm a Pink Toothbrush (You're a Blue Toothbrush), 304fn
I'm Determined No Longer to Stand It, 167, 175
I'm Falling in Love, 253
I'm the Father of a Little Black Coon, 207
I'm Forever Blowing Bubbles, 252, 273
I'm Going to Charleston Back to Charleston, 273
I'm in Love with a Dreadlocks, 371, 382fn
I'm One, 329
Imagine Me on the Maginot Line, 292
Immenseikoff (The Shoreditch Toff), 145-6
In the Days I Went Drinking a Long Time Ago, 73
In Eleven More Months and Ten More Days (I'll Be Out of the Calaboose), 296
In Grandma's Day They Never Did the Foxtrot, 220
In Memory of the Hartley Catastrophe, 115, 174
In the Mood, 290
In My Life, 326
Independence Ska, 363
Indian Love Call, 253, 267fn
Inner City Violence, 373
Ireland, Mother Ireland, 254
Ireland Will Once More Arise from the Dust, 150
Irish Are Always at the Front, The, 189
Irish Washerwoman, The, 37, 39, 139fn, 320fn, Appendix 401
Is He Guilty? 183
Is This Love? 367
Island in the Sun, 362
Isle of Beauty, 55
Israelites, The, 366, 381fn
It Ain't Alright, 346
It Ain't Gonna Rain No Mo', 280
It Mek, 366, 381fn
It Takes a Worried Man, 306
It's a Bit of a Ruin that Cromwell Knocked about a Bit, 169
It's a Great Big Shame, 168, 262
It's a Lovely Day Tomorrow, 287
It's Love Again, 223
It's Lovely to be in Love, 229fn
It's Not Our Wish (That We Should Fight), 369
It's Part of a Policeman's Lot, 178
It's Up to You, 365
I've Been a Good Woman to You, 167
I've Got the Ooperzootic, 213fn
I've Had Enough, 329
I've Never Wronged an Onion, 273
I've Never Seen a Straight Banana, 282
I Will Always Speak of Old Ireland with Pride, 150

J
Jack Chance, 86
Jack Hall, 86, 89, 100, 152fn
Jack O'Donahue, 89
Jack Swing, 95, 103fn
Jack with his Broom, 54
Jah Wah, 374
Jailhouse Rock, 313, 349
Jamaica Farewell, 362
Jean and Dinah, aka Yankees Gone, 379fn
Jeanie With the Light Brown Hair, 201
Jeerusalem's Dead, 171
Jessie, the Flower of Dunblane, 37
Jim Crow, 40
Jim Crow from Kentucky, 59
Jim Crow's Visit to Newcastle, 59
Jingo Song, The, 183, 187, 194fn, 216, 389

Joan's Ale, 58, 81fn
John Anderson, My Jo, 35, 59, 80, 144
John Appleby, 74, 75
John Barleycorn, 56
John Bull's Letter Bag, 189
John Bull's Little Khaki Coon, 216
John Green, 86
John of the Greeny Cheshire Way (hornpipe), 45, Appendix 405
Johnny B Goode, 537fn
Johnny I Hardly Knew You, 103fn
Johnny Reggae, 375, 383fn
Jolly Dogs Galop, The, 144
Jone of Grinfilt Junior, 102
Jone of Grinfilt's Ramble, 94
Jump Jim Crow, 155, 197, 200, 206, 208, 211fn
Just to Show Who Was Boss in the House, 167

K

K-K-K Katy, 229fn
Kathleen Mavourneen, 149, 253
Keel Row, The, 35, 283fn
Keep the Home Fires Burning, 217, 303fn
Keep Right on to the End of the Road, 229fn
Keep Your Feet Still Geordie Hinny, 170
Keep Your Hand Upon Your Little Ball of Yarn, 79
Keep Your Sunny Side Up, 276
Keeper, The, 76
Kentucky Babe, 207
Kerry Dance, The, 281
Kerry Recruit, The, 103fn
Killarney, 253, 281
Kimberley March, The, 194fn
King Charles of Sweden, 26, Appendix 396
King Creole, 313
King of the Cannibal Islands, The, 115
King Ska Fa, 373
Kiss Me Goodnight, Sergeant Major, 292

Knees Up Mother Brown, 240, 291
Knight and the Shepherd's Daughter, The, 57
Knocked 'Em in the Old Kent Road, 175
Ku Klux Klan, 369

L

La Donna e Mobile, 253
Laddies Who Fought and Won, The, 228-9fn
Lady Mackintosh's Reel, 36
Lady Nairn's, 278
Ladysmith March, The, 194fn
Lambeth Walk, The (Alex Hurley), 154
Lambeth Walk, The (Lupino Lane), 224, 230fn, 240, 244, 245, 265
Lamentation of Thomas Henry Hocker, The, 101fn
Land of My Fathers, The, 278
Lass of Richmond Hill, The, 39, 59, 283fn
Lasses Pisses Brandy, 36
Last Melody of Pestal, The, 40
Last Rose of Summer, The, 59, 133, 158fn, 283fn
Last of the Steam Powered Trains, The, 332
Last Time, The, 347
Last Train to San Fernando, The, 307, 362
Laugh, Clown, Laugh, 271
Laughing Darkie, The, 213fn
Laughing Policeman, The, 274
Lay Down Your Arms (And Surrender to Mine), 295, 301, 317
Lay My Head Beneath a Rose, 252, 266fn
Lazy Coon's Dream, The, 207
Lead Kindly Light, 107
Leaning on a Lamppost, 274
Let Me Call You Sweetheart, 252
Let's All Go to the Music Hall, 105
Let's All Sing Like the Birdies Sing, 274

Let's Have a Basin of Soup, 160fn
Let's Over the Hills, My Brave Boys, to the Chase, 81
Life Let Us Cherish (Freut Euch des Lebens), 37
Life is Like a Game of Seesaw, 173
Lillibulero, 57, 65fn
Lili Marlene, 287, 293
Lily of Laguna, 107, 197, 205, 302
Lincolnshire Poacher, The, 283fn
Lines on the Great Fight between Tom Sayers, Champion of England, and Bob Brettle of Birmingham, 71
Lion and the Bear, The, 188
Little Alabama Coon, The, 207
Little Brown Jug, The, 74
Little by Little, 373
Little Dolly Daydream, 205
Little House Under the Hill, 26, 43
Little Man You've Had a Busy Day, 259
Little Miss Lancashire, 218
Little Miss Queen of Darkness, 334
Little of What You Fancy Does You Good, A, 154
Little White Bull, The, 315
Liverpool's An Altered Town, 102fn
Lloyd George Knew My Father, 275
Lock Lomond, 280, 283fn, 320fn
Lola, 334
London Adulteration, 95
London, I Love, The, 287
London 'Prentice Boy, The, 87, 90
London's Misnomers, 143
Long Shot Kick De Bucket, 366, 381fn
Long Tall Sally, 325, 330
Look for the Silver Lining, 273
Looking Glass for a Christian Family, A, 65fn
Lord Cathcart, 39
Lord Nelson (hornpipe), 51
Lords of the Air, 275
Lost Chord, The, 107, 292

Lost John, 308
Love Me Do, 324, 336
Love Me Tender, 313
Love Will Find a Way, 219
Love's Old Sweet Song, 259, 287
Lovesick Blues, 336
Lovesick Coon, The, 207
Lovesick Nigger, The, 207
Low-backed Car, The, 158fn
Lucille, 325
Lunardies Trip in the Air Balloon, 36

M
Ma, He's Making Eyes at Me, 272
Mack the Knife, 317
MacPherson's Lament, 62
McNamara's Band, 6
Madam Medusa, 373
Mafeking March, The, 194fn
Maidstone Gaol, 91
Mairzy Doats and Dozy Doats, 293
Major Malley's Reel, 51fn
Makin' Whoopee, 272
Man a Reason, 371
Man Who Broke the Bank at Monte Carlo, The, 147, 156, 175, 223
Manchester's An Altered Town, 102fn
Man's Yard of Stuff, 157fn
Many Rivers to Cross, 373
March in Scipio, 39
March to Pretoria, The, 194fn
Marching Thro' Georgia, 280
Married Man's Advice to the Bachelor, The, 74
Married to a Mermaid, 161fn
Martin Said to his Man, 56
Mary Blane, 40
Master Race, 384fn
Matilda, 362
Matilda Baker, 146
Matrimonial Bliss, 80
Matrimonial Handicap, The, 169
Me and the Old Folks at Home, 282fn

Meeting of the Waters, The, 278, 283fn
Memphis Tennessee, 325, 337fn
Men Cry Too, 371
Men of Harlech, The, 278, 280, 283fn
Mermaid, The, 283fn
Message in a Bottle, 376
Message to You, Rudy, A, 365, 375, 383fn
Michelle, 325
Midnight Special, 306
Milking Pail, The, 54
Miller of Dee, The, 139fn
Miner's Dream of Home, The, 189
Minstrel Boy, The, 144, 153, 158fn, 278, 280, 281, 283fn
Mirror in the Bathroom, 381fn
Miseries of the Framework Knitters, The, 93
Miss Baker's Hornpipe, 46
Miss Macleod of Ayr, 51fn
Missing Words, 381fn
Mississippi Goddam, 351, 357fn
Missouri Waltz, 273
Mistletoe Bough, The, 55
Mitchel's Address, 102fn
Mockin' Bird Hill, 363
Molly Bawn, 158fn
Money, 324
Monkey Man, 365
Monkey Murder, 365
Moonlight and Roses, 254
Moonshine is Better than Sunshine, 253
More Work for the Undertaker, 171
Morgan Rattler, 76, 82fn
Morning is Fair, The, 71
Morning Star, The, 229
Most Lamented Lines on the Prison Torture of Mr William O'Brien, 102fn
Mother and Me, 219
Mother Macree, 253
Mother's Advice, 165
Motto for Every Man, A, 173
Mountains of Mourne, The, 158
Move It, 315
Move Over Darling, 375
Mozart Waltz, 39
Mrs 'Enery Hawkins, 107
Mrs McGrath, 103fn
Mrs Mitchell's Lament for Her Husband, 102fn
Mrs Smith O'Brien's Lamentation, 102fn
Murder (Mirfield, 1847), 87
Muswell Hillbilly, 333
My Blue Heaven, 251
My Bonnie, 324
My Boy Lollipop, 363, 380fn
My Dear Old Cabin Home, 213
My Fiddle is My Sweetheart, 203, 204
My Generation, 321, 328
My Girl Lollipop, 373
My Heart Belongs to Daddy, 296
My Jealous Heart Would Break, Should We Have One Day Asunder, 62
My Little Octroon, 205
My Lodging is in the Cold, Cold Ground, 40
My Meatless Day, 217
My Old Dutch, 107, 166, 179, 302
My Old Man, 166
My Old Man (Dan Leno), 169
My Old Man (Said Follow the Van), see Cock Linnet Song
My Old Man's a Dustman, 315
My Ragtime Missus, 220

N
Nairobi, 315
Nancy Dawson, 35, 36, Appendix 399
Nation Once Again, A, 12, 149, 253, 281
Naughty Lord & the Gay Young Lady, Damages, £10,000, 76
Ne Wark, 174
Neebors Daan Belaw, The, 170
Negro Drinking Song, The, 62, 211
Negro Know Thyself, 362, 380fn

Nellie the Elephant, 301
Never Do a Tango with an Eskimo, 301
New Bailey Treadmill, The, 92
New Police, The, 93
New Police Act, The, 178
New Policeman, The, 93, 178
New Song on O'Brien's Arrest, 102fn
New Song of the Times, A, 94
Newcastle Champion, The, 71
New-Rigged Ship, The, 41
Nice Fine Day, aka Postman's Holiday, The, 262
Night Before Larry Was Stretched, The, 89
Night Has a Thousand Eyes, The, 336
Night Train, 350
Nightingale Sang in Berkley Square, A, 287
No More Looking Back, 333-4
No! No! A Thousand Times No, 272, 276, 282fn
No Woman, No Cry, 367
No Wretched Captive of His Prison Speaks Unless with Pain, 62
Noble Fox Hunting, see Dido, Bendigo
Nobody's Child, 308
Nora, 361
Norah, My Village Queen, 149
Not Fade Away, 347, 356fn
Not For Joseph, 160fn
Not Like Everybody Else, 330
Now That the Lights Are Low, 217
Nowhere Man, 325
Nut Brown Joak, The, 44
Nymphs and Shepherds, 295

O
O Carolina, 262, 390
O Charming Cunning Man, 26
O Katharina, 282fn
O Sole Mio, 253
Ob-Le-Di Ob-La-Da, 375

Off She Goes, 37, 39, 42, 51fn, 57, Appendix 402
Off to Philadelphia in the Morning, 281
Ogo Pogo, The (The Funny Foxtrot), 233, 273
Oh Arranmore, 281
Oh Boy, 313
Oh, Dem Golden Slippers, 197, 206
Oh, My Papa, 302
Oh Susannah, 40, 206
Oh, What a Wicked Young Man You Are, 179fn
Oi Against Racism and Political Extremism but Still Against the System, 384fn
Oklahoma USA, 333
Old Oak Tree, The, 112
Old Dan Tucker, 201, 214fn
Old Dun Cow, The, 231fn
Old Folks at Home, 206, 209, 214fn, 280
Old Red Lion, The, 160fn
Old Snowball, 71, 81fn
Old Woman Tossed Up, 18
Olga Pulloffski, the Beautiful Spy, 280
On My Radio, 381fn
Once Upon a Time, 229fn
One of the Deathless Army, 191
One Love, 367, 381fn
One of the Sights of London, 172
One Step Beyond, 372
Only a Working Man, 180
Only You, 319fn
Opossum Up a Gum Tree, 62
Our Brave Colonials, 216
Our House, 373
Our Threepenny Hop, 154
Over the Hills and Far Away, 35
Over My Shoulder, 223, 230fn

P
Pace-egging song, 17
Pacifick Fleet, The, 97
Packington's Pound, 34, Appendix 398

SONG AND TUNE INDEX

Paddle Your Own Canoe, 173
Paddlin' Madeleine Home, 272
Paddy McGinty's Goat, 281
Paddy Whack, 157fn
Pal of My Cradle Days, 273
Parchman Farm, 350
Parker P.C., 274
Parson and the Cook, The, 169
Pass the Dutchie, 376, 383fn
Pass the Koutchie, 376, 383fn
Passing Strangers, 336
Patricia Gone with Millicent, 362
Patty Proudly Packs for Privates Prepaid Paper Parcels, 219
Pawnshop Bleezin', The, 171
P.C. 49, 274
Peacock Followed the Hen, The, 37
People Get Ready, 367, 382fn
Pease Upon a Trencher, 26, 35, Appendix 396
Penny Lane, 326
Peggy Sue, 313
Peggy Sue Got Married, 316
Pennsylvania Six Five Thousand, 290
Perils of the Mine, The, or the Collier's Death, 115
Peter Potts the Peeler, 178
Phil the Fluter's Ball, 158fn
Piccadilly Trot, The, 230fn
Pick a Bale of Cotton, 306
Pick Yourself Up, 273
Picture Book, 332
Pinball Wizard, 328, 336
Planxty John O'Connor, 26, Appendix 397
Play to Me Gypsy, 272, 296
Please, Please Me, 324, 336
Police and Thieves, 374
Police Officer, 370
Policeman Who Boned the Mutton, The, 92
Policemen on Drill, The, 92
Polly Cockatoo, 204
Polly Wolly Doodle, 207
Poor Mary Ann, 40
Poor Frozen Out Gardeners, 93

Poor Joe the Miller, 74
Poor Old Joe, 207
Poor Unhappy Transported Felon, The, 102fn
Pop Goes the Weasel, 155, 324
Postman, The, 161
Postman's Holiday, The, 262
Praise the Lord and Pass the Ammunition, 292
Pratty Flowers, see Holmfirth Anthem, The
Pretty Maid to the Miller Would Go, A, 76
Pretty Polly Perkins of Paddington Green, 144, 174
Prince, The, 372
Private Tommy Atkins, 190
Purple People Eater, The, 317, 320
Put a Bit of Treacle on My Puddin,' Mary Ann, 160fn
Put It Down to Gladstone, 185
Puttin' on the Style, 308

Q
Quartermaster's Stores, The, 292
Quayside Shaver, The, 59
Queenie of the Dials, 154

R
Ragtime Coon, 220
Ragtime Cowboy Joe, 219-20
Ragtime Navvy, 220
Ragtime Suffragette, 220
Rakes of Mallow, The, 37, Appendix 401
Ramblin' on My Mind, 346
Ramona, 252
Ratcatcher's Daughter, The, 143
Red Cross Knight, The, 55
Red, Red Robin, The, 274
Red, Red Wine, 373
Red Sails in the Sunset, 337fn
Redemption Song, 367
Reel of Tullack, The, 36
Reggae in Your Jeggae, 381fn
Relief of Mafeking, The, 194fn
Respect, 351, 357fn
Returned Convict, The, or the Horrors of Transportation, 90

Revolution, 367
Riding in the Ammunition Van, 191
Rise in Baccy, the, 115
Roast Beef of Old England, The, 39, 278, 283fn
Robin Adair, 283fn
Rock Around the Clock, 305, 319fn
Rock with the Caveman, 314
Rock Island Line, The, 306, 307, 308, 317, 343, 354fn
Rock and Roll Music, 325
Rocky Road to Dublin, The, 144, 149
Rogue's March, The, 98
Roguery of Every Trade, The, 95
Roisin the Beau, 73
Roll Along Prairie Moon, 271
Roll Out the Barrel, 293
Roll Over Beethoven, 323, 324
Rollicking Irishman, The, 47, Appendix 409
Roots Reality, 370
Rory O'More, 43, 281
Rose and the Thistle and the Shamrock Too, The, 191
Rose of Tralee, The, 254, 280
Roses of Picardy, The, 267fn
Route 66, 347, 348
Row Dow Dow, 51fn
Row on the Stairs, The, 170
Roxanne, 376
Rude Boy, 381fn
Rule Britannia, 36, 39, 62, 97, 99, 103fn, 278, 280
Rum and Coca Cola, 379fn
Run, Rabbit, Run, 275
Runaway Train, The, 301

S
Sad News from Salisbury, Dreadful Frost and Snow, 65fn
Saddle the Pony, 52fn
Safe in My Heart, 287
Sailing Along on a Carpet of Clouds, 265
Sailor's Journal, The, 39

Sailor's Hornpipe, The, 45
Salisbury and Gladstone, 187
Sally in Our Alley, 59
Sally Wheatley, 164
Sam Hall, 143, 157fn
Samuel Fellows, 86, 88
Sandman Joe, 77, 83fn
Santa Claus Is Bringing You Home for Christmas, 303fn
Sarah's Gone and Left Me, 164
Saxona's Hornpipe, 37
Say It Loud, 351, 357fn
Sayer's and Heenan's Great Fight, 71
Sayer's and Heenan's Struggle for the Championship and £400, 72
Scots Wha Hae, The, 283fn
Sea is England's Glory, The, 112
Scrapheap City, 331, 333
See the Conquering Hero Come, 35, 36
See See Rider, 348
See You Later, Alligator, 319fn
Seek to Do the Right Thing, 213fn
Sellenger's Round, 34, Appendix 398
Send for A Policeman, 178, 274
Seven Years with the Wrong Woman, 272
Sha La La, 349, 356fn
Shadows on the Blind, 166
Shall England Give In? 188
Shan Van Vocht, 150
She Loves You, 324
She Sells Sea Shells, 154
She Was Only A Postmaster's Daughter, 272
She's A Woman, 326
She's Leaving Home, 326
She's a Thoroughbred, 207
Shells of the Ocean, The, 43
Shenandoah, 280
Shepherd Kept Sheep on a Hill so High, A, 57
Shepherd's Hey, 18, 210, Appendix 396
Shining Light of England, The, 186

Shop Around, 350
Silly Games, 371
Silver Threads Among the Gold, 166, 254, 302
Simmer Down, 381fn
Since My Wife Joined the WAAC, 219
Sing, Gypsy, Sing, 259
Sing Mighty Marlborough's Story, 58
Sing as We Go, 223, 280
Sir Roger de Coverley, 34, 37, Appendix 397
Sister Susie's Sewing Shirts for Soldiers, 219
Skinhead Moonstomp, 378, 384fn
Skylark, Skylark, 165, 213fn
Slap Bang, Here We Are Again, 144, 145
Slum Kids, 333
Smile, Darn Ya, Smile, 296
Smokestack Lightening, 348, 356fn
Snowy Breasted Pearl, The, 253
Softly, Softly, 317
Soldier of Love, 325
Soldier's Delight, The, 91
Soldier's Joy, The, 35, 45, 50fn, 51fn, Appendix 399
Soldiers of the Queen, The, 189
Sonny Boy, 252, 254
Sons of Criminals, 369, 382fn
Sons of the Sea, 190
South American Joe, 272
South of the Border, 272
Spanish Eyes, 301
Spare the Old Mud Cabin, 149
Speed the Plough, 37, 39, 40
St George that O! Did Break the Dragon's Heart, 30fn
St Patrick's Day, 43
Stage-struck Keelman, The, 154
Stand to Your Guns, 188
Stand Down Margaret, 365
Starvation, 363
Staten Island, 37
Steady and True, 187
Steal Away to Jesus, 350
Stein Song, 253

Steppin' Out, 346
Still I Love Him, 83fn
Stockholmsläten, 52
Stranger in Paradise, 317
Strawberry Fields Forever, 326
String of Pearls, The, 290
Such a Mash, 146
Suffolk Miracle, The, 57
Suffragee, The, 176
Suffragette, The, 176, 181fn
Summer Holiday, 315
Sunny Havana, 272
Sunny Side of the Street, The, 273
Sweating System, The, 174
Sweet Georgia Brown, 282fn
Sweet Little Sixteen, 323
Sweet Sensation, 373
Sweetest Song in All the World, The, 323
Sword Dancer's Lament, The, 115

T

Tablet of England, The, 186
Take A Pair of Sparkling Eyes, 107
Take These Chains from My Heart (And Set Me Free), 356fn
Ta-Ra-Ra-Boom-De-Ay, 119, 120, 193fn, 223
Tartar Drum, The, 55
Taste of Honey, A, 337fn
Teach You to Rock, 319fn
Tears of a Clown, 381fn
Teddy Bear, 313
Teddy Blink and Bandy Jack, 86
Teddy Boy Calypso (Bring Back the Cat O' Nine), 361, 384fn
Tell My Daddy to Come Home Again, 217
Tequila, 373
That Old Fashioned Mother of Mine, 273
That's Alright (Mama), 313, 325
That'll Be the Day, 313, 316
The 22nd Regiment's Quick-step, 36
There Is A Place, 326
There'll Always Be an England, 275

There's a New Star in Heaven
   Tonight, 275
There's Silver in Your Hair, Dear
   (But Gold in Your Heart), 219
There Was an Old Woman Lived
   under a Hill, 58
Thereby Hangs a Tale, 172, 179
These Hard Times, 217
They Needed a Songbird in
   Heaven, 275
They Sang "God Save the King",
   216
This Is the Army Mr Jones, 292
Thor's Comfort in a Smoke, 154
Three Babylon, 369, 382fn
Three Blind Mice, 56
Three Minute Hero, 381fn
Tiger Rag, 282fn
This is the Rhythm for Me, 262
Ticket of Leave Man, The, 146,
   153
Tiddly Fol Lol, 146
Time Hard, 365
Tink-a-Tink, 37, 201, 212fn
Tipperary, 267fn, 279
Tom Bowling, 97, 139fn, 144,
   283fn
Tom Tackle, 39
Tom Tinker, 76
Tommy Carr's Adventures in
   Astrilly, 180fn
Tommy is as Good a Man as Any
   Knight of Old, 216
Tommy Make Way for Your Uncle,
   155
Too Nice to Talk To, 381fn
Toon Improvement Bill, The, 59,
   115
Tough Times, 363
Toy Drum Major, The, 274
Toy Town, 218
Transports, The, 90
Transport's Lamentation, The, 89fn
Transvaal March, The, 194fn
Travelling Tinker, The, 76
Tripping Upstairs, 47, Appendix
   409
Triumph, The, 51fn

Truly, Truly Fair, 301
Trumpet Hornpipe, The, 45,
   Appendix 407
Turks March, 39
Twentieth Century Man, 333
Two Lovely Black Eyes, 147, 223
Two Sisters, 334

U
Unchained Melody, 317
Uncle Ned, 206, 207
Unhappy Transport, The, 102fn
Up, Up! My Brave Boys to the
   Chase, 81fn

V
Van Diemen's Land, aka Gallant
   Poachers, The, 85, 90
Venus in Blue Jeans, 336
Vesti La Giubba, 253
Victoria, 332
Village Green Preservation Society,
   The, 332
Vilikins and his Dinah, 153
Violette, 229

W
Wabash Cannonball, The, 308
Wait Till the Work Comes Round,
   13, 173
Waiting for the Robert E Lee, 219
Wake Up Little Susie, 316
Wakefield Gaol, 92
Walking on the Moon, 376
Walking in the Zoo, 146
Walter, Walter (Lead Me to the
   Altar), 223
Walworth Murder Discovered, 86
Wanderer's Warning, The, 252
Wanna Be Your Man, 324, 347
War Song, The, see Jingo Song
Warning to Drunkards, A, 73
Wash, Wash, 364, 380fn
Watching the Detectives, 376
Water Parted from the Sea, 36
Water Piece (Handel), 36
Wayward Wind, 336
We All Go to Work but Father, 165

We Didn't Want a European War, 216
We Won't Go Home Till Morning, 57, 158
Wearing of the Green, The, 150, 151, 159fn, 281
Weaver and the Factory Maid, The, 96
Wedding of the Painted Doll, The, 252
Weep Not, I Pray, 278
Well Respected Man, 330, 331
We'll Have a Holiday in the Summertime, 217
We'll Meet Again, 287, 303fn
We're Going to Hang Out the Washing on the Siegfried Line, 275, 285
West's Awake, The, 149, 281
Wet Dream, 366
What Cheer, Ria, 163
What Do You Think of the Irish Now? 189
What Happened to the Manx Cat's Tail? 154
What Is Life to Me Without Thee? 295
What Shall We Do with Our Heroes? 192
What Should We Do Without Parnell? 185
What Should We Do Without Them (War Girls)? 218
What Would You Like to See? 187
What's the Matter with P.C. Brown? 275
What's New Pussycat? 381fn
When Father Laid the Carpet on the Stairs, 165
When Father Papered the Parlour, 165
When I Get Home, 326,
When I Leave the World Behind, 219
When I'm Sixty-Four, 325
When I Prove False to Thee, 166
When I'm Cleaning Windows, 274
When It's Springtime in the Rockies, 253
When Pershing's Men Go Marching into Picardy, 267fn
When They Sound the Last All Clear, 287
When This Old Hat Was New, 94
When You and I Were Seventeen, 253
When You Walk in the Room, 326
Where Are the Girls of the Old Brigade? 218
Where Did You Get That Hat? 279
Where Do Flies Go in Winter? 274
Where Have All the Good Times Gone? 331
Where Will the Dimple Be? 304fn
Which Switch is the Switch, Miss, for Ipswich? 219, 229fn
Whistling Coon, The, 197, 204, 205
Whistlin' Yellow Gal, The, 205
White Cliffs of Dover, The, 293
White Cockade, The, 39, 40, 42, 157fn, Appendix 402
White Joak, The, 44
White Riot, 374
Who is Sylvia? 62, 254
Who Takes Care of the Caretaker's Daughter? 273
Who'd Be a Mother? 167
Whole Hog or None, 200
Whole Lotta Shakin' Going On, 312
Whole World's Shaking, The, 350, 356fn
Wholesome Advice to Drunkards, 73
Why Did She Fall for the Leader of the Band? 265
Why Do I Always Remember? 252
Why Don't They Give Us Home Rule? 185
Wife's Lamentation, The, 74
Wild Raccoon Track, The, 214fn
Wild Rover, The, 390

Wilkinson and His Thirteens, 95
Will the Angels Play Their Harps for Me? 252, 266fn
Will You Love Me When I'm Mutton? 223
Willafjord, 52fn
Windmill Blown Down by the Witch's Fart, The, 30fn
Wings Over the Navy, 275
Wish Me Luck as You Wave Me Goodbye, 275
Wishin' and Hopin', 337fn
With Her Head Tucked Underneath Her Arm (She Haunts the Bloody Tower), 296
Within a Furlong, 26
Within You Without You, 325
Woe Is Me (Shame and Scandal in the Family), 362
Woe is the Mother who owns Eleven, 167
Wolf, The, 55
Woman's the Pride of the Land, A, 80
Woman's Work is Never Done, A, 167
Women of the Homeland (God Bless You Every One!), 219
Women Who Wait, The, 218
Wonderful World, Beautiful People, 367, 381fn
Won't Get Fooled Again, 335
Woodman Spare that Tree, 40
Words of Love, 325
Work and Be Contented, 174
Work Boys, Work and Be Contented, 173
Work It, 378, 383fn
Working in the Factory, 334
World Is Round, The, 350
Wreck of the Old 97, The, 307

X

Y

Y Viva Suspenders, 375
Yankees Gone, see Jean and Dinah
Ye Banks and Braes (of Bonny Doon), 283fn
Yes Sir, That's My Baby, 271
Yes, We Have No Bananas, 274, 302
Yonder Comes a Courteous Knight, 58
Yorkshire Lasses, 47, Appendix 409
You Are My Sunshine, 293
You Can't Call Them Traitors Now, 189
You'd Better Think Twice, 272
You Forgot to Remember, 271
You'll Never Walk Alone, 327
You Made Us Fight You, We Didn't Want to Do It, 228fn
You Really Got Me, 330, 338fn
You're a Thing of the Past, Old Dear, 169
You're Wondering Now, 365
You Win Again, 320fn
You Won't See Me, 325
Young Gifted and Black, 351, 367, 382fn
Young Man's Repentance, A, 65fn
Your Cheatin' Heart, 356fn
Your Mother Should Know, 325
Your King and Your Country Want You, 217
You've Got to Hide Your Love Away, 325
You've Really Got a Hold on Me, 324, 325

Z

Zedekiah the Jew, 67fn
Zekiel Homespun's Trip to Town, 67fn
Zing Went the String of My Heart, 271
Zip Coon, 115, 210